D1349576

RUDRA CHAUDHURI

Forged in Crisis

India and the United States since 1947

HURST & COMPANY, LONDON

First published in the United Kingdom in 2014 by
C. Hurst & Co. (Publishers) Ltd.,
41 Great Russell Street, London, WC1B 3PL
© Rudra Chaudhuri, 2014
All rights reserved.
Printed in India

The right of Rudra Chaudhuri to be identified as the author
of this publication is asserted by him in accordance with the
Copyright, Designs and Patents Act, 1988.

A Cataloguing-in-Publication data record for this book
is available from the British Library.

ISBN: 978-1849043045

www.hurstpublishers.com

This book is printed using paper from registered sustainable
and managed sources.

For my mother, Leena

CONTENTS

ACKNOWLEDGEMENTS

This book is a result of eight years of research and re-authorship. It would not have been possible without the firm support of mentors and colleagues at King's College London. Moreover, as a young lecturer at the War Studies Department, I learnt to look beyond purely academic questions to those more to do with matters of historical intuition. I appreciated the need to study and understand the emotions and motivations of those who helped shape India's approach to the world over the last six and a half decades.

A War Studies Research Fellowship, a Teaching Fellowship at the Defence Studies Department, King's College London, an Overseas Research Studentship awarded by the British Government, and numerous other research awards and bursaries gave me the opportunity and luxury to work on a script free from the usual anxieties internalised by writers. I would like to thank Matt Uttley at the Defence Studies Department for offering to renew several teaching contracts—allowing a smooth and less-worrisome transition to professional academe. Mervyn Frost at War Studies provided me with the comfort and space to continue to work on this project as a member of staff. Mervyn's delicate approach cannot be overstated.

In their own very unique ways, Theo Farrell, Satish Jayarajan and Srinath Raghavan gave me what might be considered unexpected but crucial 'breaks': it is almost absurd thanking them. Satish first prompted me to think about politics whilst frequently refining the way I do so. Theo introduced me to scholarship and helped shape this book from even before its beginning—lightly but obviously pressing me to challenge myself. Srinath made me believe in the importance and relevance

ACKNOWLEDGEMENTS

of history, but not without losing sight of the imperatives of change and the present. The incalculable number of hours spent in his casual but poignant tutorship opened a range of possibilities. In short, without them this book would not have been written. Mostly, I remain ever-grateful for their kindness and friendship.

Sunil Khilnani pushed me to think beyond the obvious. He unfailingly supported this project from its infancy. Having offered me a Visiting Fellowship at the School of Advanced International Studies (SAIS) at the Johns Hopkins University, Sunil openly and graciously introduced me to key personalities who helped define the present state of Indian-American diplomatic relations. His move to King's allowed me to remain absorbed in his easy and exclusive reading of Nehru and history more broadly. I could not have asked for a more compassionate friend and colleague than Anatol Lieven. He has consistently challenged the premise of my argument but not without providing me alternatives to consider. I also thank Anatol for willingly offering to take my lectures and tutorials when panic absorbed this project.

A crucial section of this book relies on interviews and conversations with those who helped inform India's relationship with the United States and her approach to international affairs more generally. Their time and willingness to engage with me brought a sense of life and reality to the story at hand. Further, many colleagues and friends helped in making the task of writing a book less daunting. They often read drafts, discussed ideas as they emerged, or allowed me to remain enthused. In particular, I would like to thank: John Mackinlay, Peter Busch, Michael Goodman, M. J. Akbar, Shyam Saran, Stephen Tankel, Kanti Bajpai, Tanvi Madan, Gurmeet Kanwal, Christopher Coker, Jahnavi Phalkey, Joe Maiolo, Christopher Dandekar, Christophe Jaffrelot, Disha Mullick, Yashas Chandra, Varun Khanna, Payal Wadhwa, Sahil Khanna, Aditya Yadav, Aprajita Dhundia, Ashley Lait and Swapna Nayudu. I had the benefit of a patient editor and publisher—Michael Dwyer. He and his team at Hurst dealt with the manuscript carefully. I also thank Oxford University Press (New York) and Harper Collins (New Delhi) for co-publishing this title.

Most of all, I thank my family in Bangalore. My mother allowed me the freedom to pursue interests closer to my heart. She has unswervingly encouraged me to shape my life accordingly. This book is dedicated to her.

ABBREVIATIONS

AEC	Atomic Energy Commission
AICC	All India Congress Committee
BJP	Bharatiya Janata Party
CCS	Cabinet Committee on Security
CIA	Central Intelligence Agency
CPI	Communist Party of India
CPI (M)	Communist Party of India (Marxist)
CRO	Commonwealth Relations Office
CTBT	Comprehensive Test Ban Treaty
DOD	Department of Defence
FATA	Federally Administered Tribal Areas
FCO	Foreign and Commonwealth Office
FMCT	Fissile Material Cut-Off Treaty
IB	Intelligence Bureau
INC	Indian National Congress
IAEA	International Atomic Energy Agency
LOC	Line of Control
MEA	Ministry of External Affairs
MEDO	Middle East Defense Organization
MoD	Ministry of Defence
MTCR	Missile Technology Control Regime
MFN	Most Favoured Nation
NA	National Archives
NEFA	North East Frontier Agency
NDA	National Democratic Alliance
NMML	Nehru Memorial Museum and Library

ABBREVIATIONS

NPMS	Nixon Presidential Material Staff
NPT	Nuclear Non-Proliferation Treaty
NSAB	National Security Advisory Board
NSC	National Security Council
NSG	Nuclear Suppliers Group
PLA	People's Liberation Army
PNE	Peaceful Nuclear Explosion
PRC	People's Republic of China
RSP	Revolutionary Socialist Party
RSS	Rashtriya Swayamsevak Sangh
SOS	Secretary of State
UPA	United Progressive Alliance
USAF	United States Air Force

INTRODUCTION

In early 1950 Chester Bowles volunteered to represent the United States in India. He was to become the third ambassador to independent India. A businessman turned politician—he won the governorship of Connecticut in 1948—Bowles was an atypical official. Born into a family of Republican voters, this New Dealer was a passionate advocate of change and reform, and as a leading light in the Democratic Party he was considered the 'eminently eligible' successor to President Harry S. Truman. Hence his choice of India over the Soviet Union, Japan and West Germany, all crucial posts in the early construction of Cold War politics, was baffling. Why India? This, after all, was a country Truman associated with 'people sitting on hot coals and bathing in the Ganges'— it was hardly 'important'.[1]

Yet, for Bowles, India, and its first prime minister, Jawaharlal Nehru, represented the future. Nehru's 'radicalism'—or communism, as Truman narrowly understood it—was the very reason why the United States needed to know India better. In his last conversation with the president before leaving for New Delhi in the spring of 1951, the ambassador-designate made plain that this was the 'new world' and that 'only those who think in fresh, radical terms can be effective'—it was vital that the United States embrace this 'new world' and not 'fear change'.[2]

But this was easier said than done. Rather quickly, and despite Bowles' best intentions, the popular perception of India in the American press and within elite debate came to be framed in a less than flattering light. India's foreign policy of non-alignment, which sought to craft a distinct persona for a newly independent nation, was anachronistic in the prevailing architecture of Cold War politics and the division of the world

1

into rival ideological blocs. The idea, as Nehru explained in his first broadcast as vice president of the interim government, was, 'as far as possible, to keep away from the power politics of groups, aligned against one another, which have led in the past to world wars and which may again lead to disasters on an even wider scale'.[3] The central objective of this cerebral approach to international affairs was to assert India's autonomous place, in both thought and action, on the pressing issues of world politics. Nonetheless, as Sarvepalli Gopal writes in his estimable biography of Nehru, in the beginning 'there was little precision and definiteness about this objective'.[4] The resultant ambiguity surrounding this uniquely Indian approach led analysts to dub it a 'social disease'. The cause: 'intimacy in some form with communism; its symptoms: mental confusion and moral dereliction; its cure: unknown'.[5] To an extent, academic scrutiny was inspired by official opinion—Loy Henderson, Bowles' predecessor, believed that the government of India was inherently 'inclined to regard the United States with suspicion and dislike'.[6]

While Nehru set about building Indian foreign policy 'brick by brick',[7] soon replacing vague prescriptions with quantifiable decisions, the misgivings underlying the very construct of non-alignment generally remained firm. Successive Indian envoys tried hard to dislodge America's presuppositions. In this regard, G.L. Mehta, the third Indian ambassador to the United States, after Asif Ali (1947–8) and Nehru's sister Vijayalakshmi Pandit (1949–52), was perhaps the most active. Encouraged by the likes of Albert Einstein to 'give even to rigid American minds',[8] Mehta understood his role as that of an educator. Popularly dubbed the 'teacher in our midst', Mehta's message to the United States was simple: relationships between free nations were not defined by 'conformity and acquiescence but comprehension, patience, and tolerance'.[9]

This message, as straightforward as it might have seemed, took elites, institutions and publics in both India and the United States some fifty years to absorb. Finally, following the end of the Cold War, the intellectual and bureaucratic rigidity that Einstein had once spoken of gradually softened. The collapse of the Soviet Union no doubt played its part in redefining the US approach to India, but the fresh terms of exchange were equally laid down by changes in political energy within the country itself. In February 1998, the Bharatiya Janata Party (BJP), successor organisation to what was the Bharatiya Jan Sangh (BJS), led a thirteen-party coalition—called the National Democratic Alliance (NDA)—to power in

New Delhi.[10] A month later, Jaswant Singh, an Indian Army officer-turned-politician (a rarity in India's political life) and senior BJP leader, informed visiting US envoys that he was authorised to initiate a back-channel dialogue with the United States.[11] 'Nothing like this had been proposed by the Indian government before', one of those American envoys later recalled. For the Clinton White House, 'it was clear that the BJP wanted to engage the US in a way none of its predecessors wanted to'.[12] This was in keeping with the BJP's chief foreign policy aim of 'engaging with all major powers',[13] and most importantly, the United States.

The offer of a clandestine dialogue was seen as an opportunity to do away with what President Bill Clinton saw as the past practice of 'clumsy diplomacy' that had 'kept India and the United States apart for too long'.[14] What followed was nothing less than a 'transformation' of US–India strategic relations.[15] Despite the change of Indian government in 2004, the new Congress-led alliance made it apparent that the idea of engagement with the US had 'cut across party lines'.[16]

India under Nehru had once considered the sale of US military hardware to Pakistan a form of 'intervention' that had brought the Cold War to South Asia;[17] yet now, soon after the 1998 opening, India became a signatory to a ten-year bilateral defence pact with the US.[18] In September 2008, the US Congress authorised President George W. Bush to sign into law a bill that permitted the American administration to enter into nuclear-related trade with India. Described as the 'deal of the century', the so-called US–India Nuclear Deal for the first time opened the way for the US to engage in nuclear commerce with a country that refused to sign the Nuclear Non-Proliferation Treaty (NPT).[19] India's policy of strategic engagement appeared to have paid off.

Indeed, although a critic of the deal, George W. Bush's successor, President Barack Obama, made sure to visit India early on in his presidency. Addressing a joint session of the Indian Parliament, Obama argued emphatically that the relationship between the US and India would serve as 'one of the defining partnerships of the 21st century'.[20] This need to engage with India, recognised by both Republican and Democrat American leaders, is rooted in the spreading realisation that India's growing economic, political and military might will increasingly shape international relations in an ever more connected world.[21] For most Western governments, therefore, building positive relations with India is considered a priority.

This book focuses on key turning points in Indian diplomacy and its approach to the US. It seeks to both uncover and recover India's calculated motivations, and thereby to identify the faint yet distinctive edifice of an Indian approach to foreign affairs. It maps periods of crises which have either been under-researched or overlooked, but which reveal the complex and distinctive manner in which India has simultaneously sought to pursue both material objectives and ideational values.

The book argues that Indian behaviour in the arena of foreign affairs, and specifically in its relations with the US, is best explained by the interaction between embedded ideas about *who we are* and material interests. This is, of course, not a novel argument.[22] That nations and their leaders are influenced both by ideas and interests is widely accepted. Nevertheless, what is less clear is *how* such interactions actually take place. The existing literature pays scant attention to what might be considered the finer questions of detail, or what historian Paul Schroeder calls the 'pure particular'.[23]

* * *

In the case of the US–India relationship, and despite its purported transformation, the qualms that Mehta and Bowles had tried so hard to dislodge in the 1950s continue to plague present-day elites. Even Atal Bihari Vajpayee, the leader of the most pro-engagement party since Indian independence, remained cautious of America's enthusiasm for a closer partnership. This sense of guardedness was evident in both official rhetoric and behaviour. Take for instance a speech delivered by the prime minister in New York in 1998—while Vajpayee spoke of the US and India as 'natural allies', a bold gesture unthinkable in the 1950s and 1970s, he also insisted that India was prepared to place its relationship with the US 'on an equal footing' based on the 'mutuality of interests' between the two countries. These caveats were significant because they spoke of India's nuanced approach to international politics, where both ideational and material assertiveness made it imperative for Indian leaders to guard against any indication of subservience.

That India would prove to be a tough negotiator was soon recognised to be a colossal understatement. US officials negotiating the nuclear deal understood this all too well. Words such as 'sovereignty', 'autonomy' and 'independence' were translated into politicised ideas that mattered more to India than they did to almost any other state. Hence negotiating with

India became a matter of negotiating with a nation convinced of the exceptionality of its own imperatives. This became clear to policymakers like Condoleezza Rice, the former US secretary of state and national security advisor. As Rice recollects in her highly detailed memoir, many of the Indian bureaucrats and pundits continued to 'value their country's non-aligned status'. She adds that the difficulties confronting Prime Minister Manmohan Singh's government stemmed from 'the Indian national security elite's almost existential attachment to the "independence" of its nuclear programme'.[24]

To some extent, the observation that India's approach to international politics is informed by the miasmic legacy of non-alignment is an obvious one. After all, India is widely seen as a post-colonial nation struggling with the history of its own past, where the need to remain independent or non-aligned is said to be rooted in its long years under colonial rule. In keeping with this tradition, scholars point to India's 'post imperial ideology' to explain the stance taken by New Delhi during bilateral negotiations.[25] Others caricature contemporary elites as blindly 'cling[ing] to the conceptual and intellectual framework' of non-alignment as articulated in the 1940s and 1950s.[26]

To a certain extent this is hardly surprising, given that, for much of independent India's history, advances and gains in the country's external affairs were explained away as either the lingering and institutionalised by-product of India's anti-colonial struggle, or as the consequence of Prime Minister Jawaharlal Nehru's Machiavellian schemes to fashion a less than evident alliance with one of two Cold War superpowers. Broadly, two schools of thought prevail. First, Nehru is popularly charged with a 'messianic utopianism'[27] that paid little if any attention to what commentators have called national interests—though they have rarely defined what these might be.[28] Accordingly, the prime minister is alleged to have adopted an 'Olympian disdain' for 'power politics'.[29] Such critics have suggested that Prime Minister Nehru was simply incapable of drawing the link between foreign policy and national security.

Second, as stressed by both American and Indian writers, Nehru was said to hide behind the veil of unaligned rhetoric, while in reality pursuing an alliance-like relationship with either the West or the East.[30] In the early years following independence, for example, non-alignment was widely considered as nothing more than a masked attempt to move India 'inexorably towards the west'.[31] Yet a few years later, and following

Nehru's visit to Russia in 1955, followed in turn by the visit to India of Soviet leaders Nikita Khrushchev and Nikolai Bulganin, India was said to side with Moscow. In either case, the central aim was seen as securing military supplies and economic assistance.

In more recent times, advocates interpret Indian calculations as increasingly shaped by the need to pursue material interests in a domain of international politics that has been structurally transformed since the collapse of the Soviet Union. Accordingly, India is expected to embrace 'alliance formation' and 'balancing'. As these were 'tools in the kits of all great powers', they are 'likely to be in India's as well'.[32] Those at the extreme end of this argument suggest that 'Washington's decision to trade nuclear-recognition quid for a strategic-partnership quo was a reasonable move', one that could ultimately provide US forces with 'over the horizon bases' for contingency operations in the Middle East.[33] Senior policymakers in the Bush administration spent much of their time debating India's apparent and new-found desire to move away from 'idealism' while taking to 'great power competition'.[34] In short, the first school highlights Indian leaders' crippling attachment to non-alignment, an ideational construct that purportedly eclipsed the relative need to invest in material heft. The second, and diametrically opposite argument, emphasises the imperatives of realpolitik and the ruthless pursuit of material—that is, economic and military—power.

Curiously though, the very scholars who make a case for an interest-led approach to foreign affairs, where the need for trade or military hardware is said to drive policy, also recognise that material interests are often trumped by ideational reservations. As one notable scholar argues, 'the traditional Indian resistance to change appeared to hold back a total rejection of non-alignment'.[35] The question then arises: Why? What explains this resistance to change?

Some writers have recognised the strains embedded within India's international policies and negotiation styles as it seeks to move forward from ideas cemented in the era of bipolarity, but few unpack these pressures in a systematic manner. In fact, allowing for some variation of approach as noted above, most scholars and commentators argue that Indian behaviour is driven either by material needs or is ideational. Committed to one or the other of these exclusive perspectives, very few focus on the interrelationship between material interests and ideational commitments. The result is a burgeoning literature on India's approach to foreign affairs which remains trapped in simplistic dichotomies, and which advances largely prescriptive theses that are weakly grounded in empirical analysis. This is especially true of the historical material on Nehru, non-alignment and Indian foreign policy more generally.

* * * *

One consequence of the simplistic dichotomies discussed above, which have become the standard lens through which to view the US–India relationship, is a serious misreading of the history of this relationship. For instance, Strobe Talbott, former deputy secretary of state under President Clinton, and a diplomat whose discussions with Jaswant Singh in the late 1990s did more for the US–India relationship than any other initiative, dubbed the first fifty years following Indian independence as the 'lost half century'.[36] Dennis Kux's masterful history of the US–India relationship, by far the most widely read and best written in the field, characterised the relationship as one between 'estranged democracies'. Of course, for Kux, diverging views on international security rather than a natural misalliance led to 'estrangement'[37]—a term that Washington insiders came to use to describe just about anything with regard to India prior to the mid-1990s. Possessed by non-alignment, India was squarely identified as a Soviet well-wisher with limited interest in free markets and a less-than-objective approach to the West. In India too, a particular disdain for the US grew out of a combination of structural factors—perhaps above all the close US relationship with Pakistan—as well as institutionalised ideas about a hegemonic leviathan that sought to absorb and circumscribe the very foundations of India's new-found freedom.

Notwithstanding the widely accepted views and interpretations highlighted above, a re-reading of this relationship suggests that in fact the US relationship was by far the most comprehensive and significant association as far as Indian elites were concerned. Whether it was Nehru or his daughter, Prime Minister Indira Gandhi, for India's leaders maintaining a considered and sometimes fractious association with American counterparts outweighed the bureaucratic scepticism inherent in individual accounts. This was undoubtedly a relationship forged in crisis. The transformation witnessed more recently—since 2000—is in many ways precisely the result of the resilience built up during the so-called 'lost half century'. In fact, those five decades could well be termed the 'essential half century'—a necessary and sometimes prolonged epoch in which a degree of mutually inclusive self-belief was forged between two of the world's largest, and highly disparate, democracies.

* * * *

Revisiting key chapters in India's dealings with the US affords the opportunity to query some commonly held assumptions about India's rise. For instance, Western leaders appear convinced that forging a 'special relationship' with India is essential to meet shared challenges in what is widely considered a 'new era of international affairs'.[38] President George W. Bush made clear that the nuclear deal not only 'signaled the country's [India's] new role on the world stage' but, as importantly, would potentially allow it to be 'one of America's closest partners'.[39]

Yet despite the popular rhetoric of a 'rising India', an accepted argument among scholars and policymakers is that India 'lacks an instinct for power'.[40] For a variety of reasons, Indian elites are alleged to be 'devoid of big ideas backed by political conviction'. Pushing this case, some have argued that 'ad hocism' is said to be India's preferred guiding star on matters related to foreign policy.[41] How do these diagnoses tally with the popular assumption that India will play a key role in international affairs? The fact is that little is known of what drivers shape Indian behaviour: in particular, what influences and tensions underlie major strategic decisions? Indeed, as India's political leadership aspires to so-called great power status, it remains unclear exactly what it is that they believe themselves to be pursuing.

In providing a reinterpretation of India's relations with the US, this book aims to show, through the theatre and drama of moments of crises, what the motivations that pushed Indian leaders to make key decisions were, and how those motivations changed over the course of more than sixty years. More explicitly than ever before, this book demonstrates how tensions between ideas and interests actually played out in terms of India's dealings with the US between 1947 and 2011.

The book makes three contributions to scholarship and policy. First, it re-tells an important part of the US–India story while challenging present accounts authored by both American and Indian writers. Second, it insists that the conventional binary construct of ideas *or* interests as driving foreign policy is less than interesting and potentially misleading. Rather, the interrelationship between ideas and interests is a far more illuminating approach to uncovering motivations, and it also helps to answer a rather basic question: exactly what factors shaped, and continue to shape, India's relationship with the United States? Third, this book exposes a prevalent myth of malaise in India's foreign policy bureaucracy. An analysis and assessment of successive crises outlines how and why elites are perhaps far more proactive and even creative than informed outsiders wish to recognise or are willing to accept. The latter point is particularly important—it contests the somewhat generalist reading of India's foreign policy bureaucracy and elite leadership that is widely—but wrongly—accepted in conventional analysis. This is not to say that the criticism, at least in part, may not be merited, but rather that the trend of choosing censure over fact has often done little more than twist the tale to suit the teller.

Sources and Structure

Two sets of sources are analysed in this study. The first deals with the historical narrative on India–US strategic relations (Chapters 1–6). The second set of sources informed the study in more contemporary times (Chapters 7 and 8). On history, primary source material was surveyed in three countries. The book looks carefully at documents and declassified papers in archives in India, the US and the UK, and it makes extensive use of official publications.[42] The book also engages in wide analysis of daily newspaper articles in the *Times of India* and *The Hindu*, as well as secondary source material, including memoirs and published diaries.

The second part of the book widely references secondary source material and published memoirs and diaries. Primary source material was derived from detailed interviews conducted with politicians, Cabinet ministers, retired foreign service and military personnel, former intelligence officials, journalists, think tank analysts and scholars. As Paul Kapur points out in his excellent work on nuclear deterrence in South Asia, the use of interviews can be problematic. 'Policymakers may have significant incentives to mislead authors and readers.' However, as he also realised during his study, accurate secondary information on South Asia is scarce, especially when engaging in contemporary analysis. Hence, as he himself concluded, 'If researchers are to offer a reasonably complete account … they must speak with the officials involved.'[43]

In order to assess how self-serving some of these interviews might be, I engaged in conversations with personnel and policymakers both in the

US and India with the hope of triangulating a 'complete account'. I also closely surveyed daily newspaper reports and editorials in the periods of study (2003 and 2007–8) in four Indian national dailies: *The Times of India*, *The Hindu*, *The Asian Age* and *The Indian Express*.

The book is divided into three parts: negotiating non-alignment, negotiating change and negotiating engagement. Part I looks at the early foundations of non-alignment as well as its practice by a recently decolonised nation. It is made-up of three chapters. Chapter 1 establishes the historical background to US–India relations through an analysis of US attitudes towards India prior to independence, before elucidating the key strands of non-alignment as conceived by Nehru. Chapter 2 examines India's early dealings with the Truman White House, analysing how it chose to negotiate the tricky issues of military assistance and economic aid. Chapter 3 looks closely at India's response to the Korean War.

Part II analyses the very conception and practice of change in Indian foreign policy and its relations with the US. It consists of three chapters which elucidate the early contours of strategic transformation in the minds and actions of Indian leaders—that is, they demonstrate how and why India's approach to the United States changed. Chapter 4 examines the 1962 border war between India and the People's Republic of China (PRC) and demonstrates how military defeat sowed the seeds of change. However, as Chapter 5 shows, despite President John F. Kennedy's attempts to pressurise Indian leaders, and Nehru in particular, to solve the Kashmir dispute with Pakistan in exchange for long-term military assistance, India remained undeterred. Chapter 6 looks at the process of further change under new leadership in India, that of Nehru's daughter, Indira Gandhi.

Part III considers the foundations of what might be called the strategy of engagement as understood and practised by both the BJP- and Congress-led governments. It looks specifically at two altogether separate forms of crises. Chapter 7 examines an under-researched and almost forgotten episode in the story of India–US strategic relations: India's response to the US request to send troops to Iraq in 2003. Chapter 8 analyses the negotiations for and the ultimate ratification of the India–US Civil Nuclear Cooperation Agreement (2007–8). The conclusion revisits the thesis set out in this book and outlines the wider policy implications that stem from it.

PART I

NEGOTIATING NON-ALIGNMENT

1

'NEW INDIA'

Pre-1947

In November 1946, as the Indian delegation to the UN jostled for membership to a variety of recently fashioned councils and committees, Nehru encouraged India's early envoys—led by his sister—to be nothing less than 'tough' with those who chose to be 'tough' with India. It was, according to Nehru, then the vice president of the interim Cabinet, 'about time' that the world understood they were dealing with a 'new India'. This soon-to-be independent nation would do everything possible to resist 'old practices' of control. It would 'play for high stakes', even if this meant 'losing the first round or two'.[1] Notably, India was elected a non-permanent member of the Security Council in 1950. In 1953, Vijayalakshmi Pandit became the first female president of the General Assembly. India was not only playing for high stakes—it was also working hard to be a high-stakes player.

India's very role as a 'player' would be determined and shaped by India alone. Its approach to foreign affairs and the US more generally came to be rooted in directives situated between ideas and interests. It was, as Nehru put it, about 'expediency' as much as what India considered the 'right course'.[2] In time, this idea found a brand name in 'non-alignment'—a term first used in 1953 by V.K. Krishna Menon, then the head delegate of the Indian mission to the UN. In some respects, the fact that Menon introduced the terminology of 'non-alignment' itself

13

emboldened both American and British officials. After all, this Kerala-born, LSE-trained, former Indian high commissioner to the UK was once described—by MI5—as a 'dishonest', 'immoral' 'opportunist' with deep sympathies for communism.[3] What is more, he was 'Nehru's evil genius'[4]—someone the prime minister trusted, but at times found intolerable. As Nehru once queried aloud, 'What can one do with him?'[5]

While the following two chapters look carefully at India's dealings with Truman, and later Eisenhower, this chapter can be considered a scene-setter. It starts with a short note on India and the United States prior to Indian independence, before going on to introduce non-alignment as constructed and interpreted in the late 1940s.

The United States and Indian Independence

In contrast to his eventual successor, Harry S. Truman, President Franklin D. Roosevelt was a staunch proponent of better relations with India. Roosevelt's enthusiasm was partially rooted in the belief that if India fell apart, or worse, if it 'should start a movement against Britain', the Axis powers would 'surely reap benefit'.[6] After all, India served as the bulwark against Japanese aggression, as well as a staging ground for the War in the East. Following the fall of Rangoon, eastern India had provided a base for the campaign in Malaya and the re-conquest of Singapore.[7] Further, as early as May 1941, US assistant secretary of state for economic affairs, Adam A. Berle, advocated India's case because of the potential economic advantages that greater volumes of trade would bring to the US.[8] India, as the newly founded Central Intelligence Agency (CIA) revealed, was an important producer of strategic materials such as cotton, mica, manganese, monazite (a source for thorium) and beryl. Engaging India was thus a matter of common sense.

Yet apart from the strictly strategic value of India, Roosevelt's interest was equally motivated by his conviction that those fighting against fascist regimes ought to be free themselves. This Democrat was a 'thoroughgoing anti-imperialist'.[9] As Harold Macmillan, who was a junior minister for the colonies in the early 1940s, put it, the very notion of empire was a 'bugbear' to Roosevelt. Its 'liquidation' remained one of his aims.[10] The idea, for this New Dealer, was to bolster nationalism.[11]

In keeping with this reputation, Roosevelt determinedly argued that India would cooperate better during the war if it were guaranteed freedom at the end of it.[12] This was a matter of some debate between him and the British prime minister, Winston Churchill. In fact, as Arthur Herman, author of perhaps the only account of Gandhi *and* Churchill, puts it, among the few 'shaky moments' between the two wartime leaders, 'almost all of them came over India'.[13] Pressed by his American counterpart, Churchill often insisted that India was Britain's dilemma, and should necessarily remain so. America, the prime minister stressed, should 'lend no countenance to putting pressure upon His Majesty's Government'.[14]

This notwithstanding, US officials were keen on opening a channel of discussion with Indian leaders. In some cases this led to direct confrontation with British authorities. For instance, in the midst of the Second World War, American officials posted in India were asked by the British government to return to the United States because they were found to be too close to Mahatma Gandhi.[15] In other instances, the Americans found a way around Britain's reluctance to permit any expansion of US engagement with India. For example, in the mid-1940s, when Gandhi asked Vijayalakshmi Pandit to visit the US in order to alert the American people to India's plight, she was allowed to do so despite her passport being confiscated by the British government. Pandit travelled on an aircraft arranged by US General George E. Stratemeyer, the chief of Allied Air Command in the Eastern theatre.[16]

The evident incongruity in Anglo-American outlooks finally came to a head in August 1942, when the Commonwealth Relations Office (CRO) and the US administration worked on the wording of the Atlantic Charter. In its broadcasts, the US Office of War Information stressed that charter signatories should agree to the principle of 'self-determination of all people'.[17] Roosevelt tried to include all free nations, potentially also India, in the charter.[18] This no doubt irked Churchill and his Gorakhpur-born secretary of state for India, Leo Amery. Churchill argued that the wording could lead to 'great embarrassment' with regard to the 'defence of India'. He wanted the Office of War Information to stop making statements without Britain's 'mature consideration'.[19] What did not help in this were newspaper headlines that made a case for the 'Dark Races.'[20] Placed under considerable pressure, Roosevelt was made to bow to London's demands. 'Strictly speaking,' he stated, it was 'none of my business.'[21] As Kux surmises, while India was undoubtedly important, 'winning the war was the top order of business'. In this respect, nothing was worth upsetting the Anglo-American alliance.[22]

While unable to convince Churchill to consider independence,[23] Roosevelt appointed Louis Johnson—later to become Truman's secretary of defence—as the head of the new economic mission to India and the US commissioner to Delhi. Soon, Johnson was named Roosevelt's personal representative to the government of India.[24] A few years down the line, in his role as the top man in the Pentagon, Johnson would order the first 'comprehensive' National Security Council (NSC) plan to better understand Asia, and India.[25] The document, circulated on 23 December 1949, made a case for using 'cultural and philanthropic contacts' in Asia to 'exert counter-influence against the Kremlin'.[26] Notably, as personal representative, he was joined by Grady, a former assistant secretary of state. Grady would later argue that his deputation to the Johnson mission allowed him to acquire 'a genuine interest in the Indian people'. Crucially, he wrote, 'I understood the economy … quite well.' These qualities were to be tested when he returned to India as ambassador in the latter part of June 1947.[27]

The US might not have been, as J.N. Dixit suggests, the 'principal Western power which was instrumental in facilitating India's freedom',[28] but under Roosevelt's leadership there was a concerted effort to recognise India as an independent nation-state.[29] Following Roosevelt's sudden demise in April 1945, Truman was left with the highly complex task of advancing the game-changing initiatives—such as the Potsdam Conference—that had been kick-started by his predecessor.[30] India quickly ceased to occupy the attention of the White House. Focused on Europe and to a lesser extent the Middle East, Asia soon came to be understood as Truman's 'weak point'.[31] His limited interest in India was evident too.

In the spring of 1945, the Truman administration got a taste of nationalist India at the San Francisco Conference. Pandit, who headed a delegation of Nehru's choosing, opposed to the delegation sent by Viceroy Lord Wavell, addressed the gathering.[32] Her fervent and articulate plea to recognise Indian independence with the aim of heralding 'the dawn of a new and a better day for an all but crucified humanity' was not entirely lost on the new administration.[33] Truman invited Nehru's sister to the White House but, unlike Roosevelt, he refused to push India's case any further.

However, as Anita Inder Singh makes clear, within a year of San Francisco, the 'independence of thought and action, when it asserted itself against the US, came as a disagreeable shock to American officials'.[34] The interim government, which convened on 2 September 1946, while struggling to come to terms with the new-found responsibilities of governance, outlined non-alignment—although not as yet in these terms—as its chosen approach to international politics.[35] Vague though the concept might have been, it clearly signalled a distinctive Indian approach to international affairs. It was not formally defined by the government, nor was it officially endorsed. As K. Shankar Bajpai—who joined the Indian Foreign Service in the early 1950s—notes, 'It was an attitude, a way of approach, a basis for developing policies.'[36] Yet such an approach ran counter to the prevailing logic of Cold War politics. In time, as Dean Acheson recounted, it would prove both 'irritating and pretentious', giving the former secretary of state 'the creeps'.[37] Acheson's reading of non-alignment was, of course, highly selective. For India, Nehru and the early captains of an emerging Indian Foreign Service, it was something quite different. It surfaced from the essential belief that 'we [Indians] must think for ourselves'. It was an altogether 'simple' principle,[38] which, as Bajpai maintains, was extraordinarily difficult to 'grasp'.[39]

Non-Alignment: Between Ideas and Interests

In the foreword to Nehru's *Selected Works*—contained in all of the forty-three volumes published to date—Indira Gandhi, in her capacity as the chairperson of the Jawaharlal Nehru Memorial Fund, surmised that Nehru's significance lay in adjusting the 'seeming contradictions' in 'his struggles, both within himself and with the outside world'.[40] In many ways, the emotional *and* intellectual strains in the mind of one man gave shape to the policy of non-alignment. This is not to say that non-alignment belonged to Nehru, or that its intellectual framework was owned by him alone, but rather that the thought-provoking nub of Indian foreign policy was very much a product of this man's struggles.

Nehru underestimated his own agency in, as Sunil Khilnani argues, 'his determination to secure India's sovereignty'.[41] For Nehru, non-alignment was the natural by-product of the 'traditions, urges, [and] objectives' of India's 'recent past'.[42] There is little doubt that the forceful syntax underlying the language of what came to be called non-alignment was informed by the history and collective memory of colonial rule. After all, Indians were, according to India's first prime minister, 'conditioned' by their 'own experiences'.[43] As M.J. Akbar notes, Nehru's own experience through years of resistance 'influenced his self-taught knowledge of the past'.[44] During short visits to England in November 1935 and January 1936, his commitment to post-colonial ideals became a well-known fact. As *The Tribune* put it, Nehru was 'in an immeasurable degree much more than a politician'.[45] He was a transporter of ideas. Yet, and equally, he was not spellbound by history. The 'key to Nehru's greatness', as Gopal recounts, was 'his ability to leave past conflicts behind him as he enters new situations'.[46] Though he was often guided by history, he also remained alive to the challenges of the present. In fact, his own writings and actions, as explicitly demonstrated by Srinath Raghavan, suggest that 'non-alignment embodied pragmatism as much as principle'.[47]

Yet, in practice, the connection between India's past and non-alignment as a product of history could hardly be taken for granted. It required a norm entrepreneur like Nehru to 'call attention' to issues.[48] Much like Ben-Gurion in Israel and Eamon de Valera in Ireland, Nehru provided expression, although in a less than structured way, to matters of historical intuition. He was, at least in part and in the years before and immediately after independence, the glue between India and those further away from it.

Discovering Non-Alignment

Inspired by the likes of Mahatma Gandhi, Rabindranath Tagore and Bertrand Russell,[49] Nehru was convinced that India's nationalism was 'based on the most intense internationalism'.[50] He well understood that, in the fight for freedom, it might appear a 'foolish waste of time' to talk about international relations. But as he made clear in his first major note on foreign policy, the lack of thought given to international affairs would leave India rudderless when free. The 'cost of principles,' he argued, could only lead to 'disruption at the moment of crisis'.[51] The idea was to 'understand world movements and politics', all the while keeping in mind what was to India's 'advantage'.[52] In this vein, and from 'purely a point of view of opportunism', 'an independent policy,' according to Nehru, was the 'best' course for India.[53]

This, it would seem, has missed most authors and commentators. Instead, it has become somewhat fashionable to pigeonhole Nehru as a statesman taken more to 'idealism' than 'the imperatives of power'.[54] Due to their preoccupation with the public rhetoric around non-alignment, scholars and policymakers alike have mistaken the demands of democratic politics for what was actually a far more thought-out and practical approach to world problems. It was imperative, as Nehru argued, not to 'propose to be subservient to anybody' or accept 'any kind of patronage',[55] but at the same time, and given India's relative material weakness, it was important to craft a policy that spoke to needs.[56] In part, Nehru's inner struggle was habituated by a combination of both prudent and ideational factors. He was a judicious rationalist, guided by his own understanding of reason. Apart from the general force of history, Nehru's approach can be traced to his travels in both the East and the West.

Enthused by the prospect of connecting with like-minded actors from across the world, Nehru stumbled upon the League Against Colonial Oppression while in Berlin. They were soon to organise an International Congress against Colonial Oppression and Imperialism in Brussels. Appointed as the Indian National Congress' representative, the meeting in Brussels proved a 'turning point in Jawaharlal's mental development'.[57] Indeed, it seeded the idea of an Afro-Asian conference held almost three decades later in Bandung. At thirty-eight years of age, Nehru met with representatives from Egypt, Syria, China, Korea, Morocco, the United States, Mexico and Latin America. He was most impressed by the Kuomintang's delegates. The 'outcome in China', he pressed leaders back home, mattered to India more than a second world war did.[58] His discussions led him to argue that nationalism trumped the more generalist political philosophy underpinning communism. Many years later, he would maintain that 'each country has its own particular problems'.[59] Indeed, according to Nehru, the very conception of the 'East and West' was a misguided approach that took away from the uniqueness of its various components or nations. These thoughts would play a key role in the articulation of non-alignment.[60]

His time in Europe, coupled with his intense excitement for contemporary history, convinced Nehru that India must not 'cut off from the rest of the world'. When merited, it would take part in 'international joint action'.[61] With a view 'to profit by the good things of other countries,' India would 'cooperate with the progressive forces of the world'.[62] The key was to shun 'narrow nationalism', and instead favour 'real internationalism'.[63] This would prove immensely difficult. As he complained to Tagore, 'unfortunately,' 'most' Indian politicians were 'engrossed in their domestic problems,' paying 'little attention to world events'.[64] He wrote about the need to remain forward-looking, which inherently meant thinking about India's place in the world. Imperial domination, according to Nehru, risked stagnating 'creative work' and innovative thought, thereby limiting the focus of nationalists to the more restricted issue of independence. It was imperative to 'develop' a sense of 'internationalism' within India[65] in order to avoid what Tagore called 'hungry nationalism'.[66] In the last decade prior to independence, Nehru set out to do just this.

The field of international relations was soon to be widely considered 'Nehru's special preserve.'[67] He served as the principal spokesperson on foreign policy, and this was 'generally regarded as his domain'.[68] Moreover, he was sure that the pursuit of foreign affairs was not a 'game at which only free nations can play'. This was a 'half-truth'. Free·India would 'make her weight felt in world affairs',[69] and hence it was essential to start thinking about the same.

Generating Power in Non-Alignment

In order to matter, India would need to strengthen its defence forces. Nehru was absolutely clear that 'the strength of the country in defence is always relative to the strength of other countries and to the world situation'.[70] He was not oblivious to the conceptual underpinnings of the numerous theories of balances of powers. Here he differed from Gandhi, who very much hoped that India would not 'join the race for the increase of armaments'.[71] Nehru saw in the US and Russia 'first rate military powers capable of resisting aggression'.[72] Unlike Gandhi, Nehru was hardly blind-sided to the idea of generating material power.

Indeed, in understanding power, Nehru was more guided by history than by individuals. Yet, in using power, he was influenced by a combination of factors, including mentors like Gandhi as well as current trends in world politics. After all, 'foreign affairs', as he put it, was an 'utterly realistic' business.[73] The contest in Europe persuaded him that 'power' is what 'coerces the opposite party'. Material growth was not only essential for the defence of the country, but also because it 'compels opponents to change their ways'. While travelling around China in the late 1930s, which was then contending with Japanese aggression, he learnt that 'national power must precede national freedom'.[74] In 1942, following the Japanese conquest of Singapore, Nehru told Louis Johnson that the Indian Congress was 'ready to hitch "India's wagon to America's star"'. As a leader, Nehru was not shy of using force, as long as it served Indian interests. He was a product of Gandhi's inspiration, but he was equally moved by his own convictions. Notably, Gandhi 'saw no good in American troops entering India'.[75]

Nehru stressed that 'fitness comes only with the exercise of power'.[76] India would need to keep-up, and not 'submit to the humiliation of depending on foreigners for defence'.[77] It was imperative to remain as independent as possible. This would inevitably take time, as Nehru told Indians in Malaya, necessitating 'political as well as economic treaties with Britain',[78] cooperation with Russia 'where it [is] manifestly to our advantage'[79] and developing relations 'with our neighbours as we may desire'.[80] He even spoke of 'defence arrangements' in the Middle East.[81] Hence alliances and treaties were not to be spurned automatically, but would need to be negotiated according to Indian interests. The first recorded public statement on the early manifestations of non-alignment spoke exactly to this need to be free but friendly with the principal powers—Britain, the Soviet Union and the United States. However, and as he made clear to journalists, 'India would not like to entangle itself with other people's feuds and imperialistic rivalries.' 'Every country,' he argued, 'puts its own interests first when it reviews an international situation.' India too would do the same.[82]

Guidelines

Accordingly, the central tenets of non-alignment, as outlined by Nehru, were necessarily to retain the capacity to judge every international issue on its own merits, irrespective of the views of either bloc in the Cold War. Put simply, the policy of non-alignment came to mean 'the exercise of one's independence in the field of foreign relations'.[83] The objective, as Nehru argued, was to 'lead ourselves'[84] rather than to lead on behalf of others or because of others. It was an approach to foreign affairs that was designed to shield India from Cold War politics without losing sight of Cold War realities.[85] As Nehru told the Constituent Assembly of India:

Whatever policy you may lay down, the main feature of the foreign policy of any country has to be to find out what is most advantageous to her. We may talk about international goodwill and may mean what we talk. We may talk about peace and freedom and earnestly mean what we say. But in the ultimate analysis a government functions for the good of the country it governs and no government can do anything which in the short or long run is manifestly to the disadvantage of that country.

Non-alignment did not imply that India would interact with certain countries while avoiding others,[86] or that India would never adjust its positions 'in order to gain something worthwhile'.[87] As Nehru explained, 'when I say that we should not align ourselves with any power blocs, obviously it does not mean that we should not be closer in our relations with some countries than with others'.[88] Again, in a fortnightly letter to his chief ministers, Nehru wrote: 'the policy [non-alignment] does not mean that India cannot have more reactions with one country compared to another—but what it does mean is that these arrangements have not been allowed to influence our major policy'.[89]

Non-alignment was not 'psychologically rooted in isolationism', as some scholars have argued.[90] It was not designed to detach India from world politics or as a means for India to remain neutral.[91] To the contrary, Nehru himself stated that non-alignment had 'nothing to do with neutrality … or passivity'.[92] Rather, it meant the freedom to decide independently 'which is to our [India's] interest when the choices come to it'.[93] This was a 'positive and dynamic approach to world problems' and not an indication that India suffered from what at the time was argued to be a 'passivity of mind, lack of conviction, a listless desire for non-involvement'.[94] Of course, while non-alignment meant acting 'according to one's own judgement', Nehru was clear that 'such a judgment is not to be given in a vacuum. It is obviously to be related to the objectives and purposes of the countries concerned.'[95] Thus, non-alignment was far from being akin to an ideology rooted in predetermined directives. Rather, it was an approach to foreign policy informed by the idea of non-dependence that had been institutionalised during and after colonial rule, and which sought to allow India the freedom to strike bargains to its liking: forced by none. The key was to communicate and maintain contact with all.

The idea of fostering contact without discrimination—in order to avert violence and war—was little understood by US officials. In recollecting her experience in the US, Pandit wrote, 'it seemed the betrayal of freedom … the very word non-alignment became synonymous in

America with sitting on the fence'. This made it very difficult to get Indian views across on a number of issues.[96] As Vincent Shean made clear in the early 1950s, in America 'a difference of opinion from abroad is repelled as if it were an attack'.[97]

What of course did not help was the fact that 'Nehru started with the premise that Russia was not an enemy of India.'[98] In American popular imagination, and as Edward Luce, owner of *Life, Time* and *Fortune* magazines, told Pandit, resistance to joining the Western camp or following the rules of the game, as perceived at the time, obviously meant that India had decided to side with the Soviet Union.[99] Although Luce was known to use his publications, including those on art and architecture, to 'spread his anti-communist gospel',[100] in the case of Nehru, media coverage was mirrored in official reportage. Early reporting in the American NSC had Nehru down as anti-West.[101]

Dealing with the US in the early years following independence would require an enormous effort on the part of Nehru's envoys to dispel this potent label of being anti-West. In many respects, the prospect of dealing with Nehru himself was a demanding experience that excited all but disappointed many, including American officials and three successive presidents, from and including Truman. At times, the success of US discussions with Nehru depended solely on his demeanour; for the most part, however, it simply required interacting with difference. Journalists, too, were conflicted. Some immediately found him 'brilliant and sensitive'.[102] Others saw him 'no more obviously brilliant than the average English headmaster'. He was, for many, 'an old-fashioned Fabian agnostic' or a 'brown Englishman',[103] with his schooling at Harrow and Cambridge no doubt serving to inform these labels, at least in part. Following his death on 27 May 1964, he was described as an 'over-idolized' statesman who placed 'a higher value on principle than on expediency'.[104] This is the way the more common history of our times remembers both him and the intellectual fog around non-alignment: as an idealistic and unachievable aspiration. The following two chapters revise these sometimes uninspired, and at others, overly inspired, interpretations. Rather than looking to Nehru's manner or sometimes clumsy rhetoric, they focus on actions, deeds and outcomes in times of crisis to unpack the lesser-visited story of India's approach to the United States during Jawaharlal Nehru's lifetime.

2

'MAXIMUM HARDSHIP POST'

1947–9

For the Truman administration, the prospect of a newly independent India was neither exciting nor important. That British rule came to an end, leaving India, the most populous nation in the subcontinent, with the task of realising its 'tryst with destiny', was more a matter of popular curiosity[1] than political import. In the summer of 1947, American bureaucratic energy was mostly focused on the Mediterranean, where Britain was soon to withdraw its military and financial support. The burden of assistance to both Greece and Turkey was now squarely placed on American shoulders, pushing Truman and his secretary of state, George C. Marshall, to consider the early foundations of what came to be called the strategy of 'containment'.[2] In the long list of countries the State Department found it 'necessary and desirable' to engage and assist, India did not figure.[3] These were early days in the edifice of the Cold War, and Truman, the 'first cold warrior',[4] was less concerned with the happenings of a far-off nation where Britain was expected to remain in the 'shop window'.[5] Further, in Asia, the 'sinking fortunes' of Chiang-Kai-shek,[6] the Chinese nationalist leader, exercised American diplomats much more than the promise of India.[7]

In the following two years, American attitudes gradually changed. Truman, Marshall and Dean Acheson, Marshall's successor, all grew increasingly irritated with this newborn nation. Their bureaucracies and

25

representatives realised that the momentous changes underway in India were potentially significant, but it would be a while before the Truman White House was to accept this. India was significant for checking Soviet expansion. Moreover, India was quite simply the 'more valuable diplomatic prize' in South Asia.[8] Intelligence reports suggested that India could serve as a 'friendly' bastion and even a staging ground for operations in the Middle East. Nehru might not have been 'pro-American', but, as Loy Henderson, America's second ambassador to India, argued, what was crucial was that he had 'tremendous influence through-out much of non-Soviet Asia'. Nehru was, in Henderson's opinion, 'one of the great world figures', and 'ruler' of 'one of the great countries of the globe'.[9] It was hence considered prudent to get on his better side.

In turn, India's approach to the United States was ambivalent at best. Its first ambassador, Asif Ali, played a somewhat low-key role. Appointed on 6 December 1946, well before India became independent, Ali 'worked' Washington without a clear understanding of what he was meant to achieve. Nehru pressed his first envoy to be 'exceedingly friendly', but to remain 'tough if necessity arises' in both political and economic matters.[10] Yet translating these guidelines to the everyday function of diplomacy would prove harder to realise.

The early years of the Cold War coincided with the premature manifestations of the policy of non-alignment, an approach to world politics that still required 'the place of rigorous thought'. It was, as Gopal recounts, 'a technique to be tested by results'. It was not a predetermined concept; nor was it easy to understand.[11] It remained all that more nebulous to an American audience. The Truman administration, for instance, had little time for subtle intellectual paradigms. After all, as the president often remarked, the Cold War had begun to 'overshadow' American lives—there was not a day in office that was not 'dominated' by the 'all embracing struggle' between good and evil.[12]

In sum, there was no cerebral space whatsoever to consider what Nehru saw as a method that was to 'fashion a nation's destiny' away from the perils of conflict and potentially another world war.[13] This intellectual divide coupled with the fact that India remained outside the politically charged map of the Cold War in Europe made it 'a maximum hardship post' that only a few found enticing.[14] In the early years, it attracted those who were either considered staunch critics of Truman and his State Department—such as Henry F. Grady, the first ambassador to India—or those who were virtually banished from Washington, such as Henderson, who disagreed with Truman's decision to recognise Israel. In either case, India was a safe distance away from all that mattered to American politics and enterprise. This was the prevailing consensus among Washington insiders, at least until the end of 1949.

As discussed earlier, the existing literature on the early period of Indian foreign policy and the relationship with the US remains trapped in the simple dichotomy of ideas and interests. One school of thought makes a strong case for the 'high ideals of non-alignment' that was supposedly 'tilt[ed] towards the Soviet Union'. Accordingly, the 'fear' of the 'return of colonial dependence' pushed India to the Soviet corner.[15] Further, India was said to view the world, and especially America, 'through a newly-forged prism of anti-imperialism'. In short, this was considered an age of idealism, where the spirit of anti-colonialism was said to shun all that was Western.[16]

The somewhat more convincing counter-argument—by those advocating the primacy of material interests—suggests that while Nehru's rhetoric was in keeping with the contours of the policy of non-alignment, in reality he was interested in forging closer military and political ties with the US. The Truman White House, however, paid little attention to Indian advances. As Dennis Merrill puts it, 'while high-ranking U.S. officials showed little interest in India, Indian leaders, non-alignment notwithstanding, considered close relation to the United States to be of paramount importance'. Merrill examines the role played by key Indian officials, including Sir Girija Shankar Bajpai, the secretary general of the Indian Ministry of External Affairs (MEA). Bajpai, according to Merrill, had made it clear to the United States that, in the fight against communism, India would support US policy.[17]

Robert McMahon, in his exceptional book on US foreign policy in South Asia, states that 'despite his public pose of non-alignment, Nehru's disillusionment with the Soviet Union and the need for American aid were moving him inexorably towards the West'.[18] To support his claim, McMahon also cites exchanges between US and Indian officials in Washington.[19] M.S. Venkataramani claims that the need for military aid pushed India to seek out a de facto alliance with the US. Similarly, A.G. Noorani argues that Nehru was willing to ally with the United States if President Truman was prepared to support India's position on

Kashmir, following the first India–Pakistan War in 1947–8.[20] For Bharat Karnad, the bottom line was that Nehru's 'ostensibly Third World-non-alignment weighted foreign policy ... was something of a smoke-screen behind which he practiced ... his mainly First World-oriented politics'. Nehru, in Karnad's view, had 'virtually integrated' India 'into the Western strategic defence system'.[21]

Indian and British sources present a very different picture of US–India relations in the formative years after Indian independence. In these accounts, Nehru was not mesmerised by the history of the past; nor were Indian elites oblivious to the pressing needs of the hour. In fact, Indian policy towards the US was informed both by material necessity and ideational concerns.[22] The tension between the idea and need to remain as independent as possible—informed by the institutionalised memory of colonial rule—and the desperate requirement for military and economic assistance pushed Nehru and other Indian elites to follow a measured path that few in America found enticing.

This was indeed a newborn state recently released from the shackles of empire, but whose prime minister well understood that 'in this world of wars and impending wars' it was crucial to have 'proper arms and equipment as well as industrial backing for them'. The fact was that 'modern arms could only be obtained from abroad'. The key, as Nehru put it, lay in forging 'some kind of association' that might help India 'go ahead fast and yet leave us completely free'. These were not easy choices, and as he made clear to his colleagues, there would be 'no easy living' for those engaged in the business of delicate diplomacy.[23] When it came to the United States, this could partially be considered a period of exploration, but overall it was about avoiding dependence at times of military and economic crisis.

A Military Alliance

In 1949, prior to Nehru's first ever visit to the US in October of that year, the CRO in Britain compiled and distributed a dossier on India. It was titled: 'Economic Aid to India as Part of [a] Counter Attack Against Communism.'[24] As far as palpable titles go, this one did well to articulate the underlying and plain thinking within both the British and American administrations. The bottom line, as Sir Archibald Nye, the British high commissioner to India, put it, was that the 'oft proclaimed policy of neutrality and independence' had 'irritated' American colleagues, whose support was essential if the subcontinent was to be turned into an 'effective bastion against communism in Asia'.[25] 'Building up healthy' economic conditions, the dossier stressed, was an urgent task.[26] In this context, every interaction, meeting or even casual engagement with Indian officials—whether in Delhi, London or Washington—was closely monitored, analysed and discussed. The Truman administration might have been less enthusiastic about India, but this did not stop the State Department from maintaining meticulous records of conversations with their Indian counterparts. Much of this analysis has been used to construct the 'smokescreen' thesis mentioned above.

On 20 March 1948, Grady met with H.V.R. Iengar, the officiating Indian secretary general for external affairs.[27] According to Grady, Iengar had been asked by Nehru to tell him that India would not support the Soviet Union in the event of war. Iengar said, 'it was unthinkable that India should be on Russia's side in event of conflict between Russia and [the] US. American principles of democracy and those of India were identical.' According to Iengar, Nehru wished to 'maintain officially for his government a neutral position', but Nehru's public speeches, Iengar argued, were not to be misunderstood[28]—the prime minister would ultimately side with the West.

A few days later, in Washington, Bajpai told US officials that 'should the world once again become involved in conflict, India could only associate itself with those nations holding the same ideals of freedom and democracy'. Bajpai stated that the only reason that the Indian government is 'not able to make an open declaration of its position' is because it could not 'withstand the aggression from Russia or the internal difficulties which might ensue'. He told Henderson—then the director of Near Eastern Affairs in the State Department—that a firmer commitment from the United States would go some way in reassuring India that the Truman administration was on India's side.[29]

Bajpai also met with the acting US Secretary of State Robert Lovett and once again made his position known. He said that India would not gain any effective economic or military assistance from Russia. According to Lovett, Bajpai had made it very clear that he was echoing Nehru's thoughts in making these remarks. As far as the Indian secretary general was concerned, 'the US is the only country which is in a position to aid India', and that there was no question of joining the Soviet camp.

Lovett, obviously impressed by Bajpai's statements, writes, 'I told Sir Girija that we were very grateful to receive his assurances of the friendly disposition of his government.'[30]

Bajpai also told Raymond Hare, the chief of the Division of South Asian Affairs in the State Department, that India wanted military aid from the United States. Bajpai stated that the current Indian defence budget—of roughly $3 billion[31]—was not sufficient to sustain its army of over 360,000 men. The US State Department even filed these conversations under the title: 'Indian request for financial and military aid.' Indeed, Colonel B.M. Kaul, the former Indian military attaché in Washington, had previously made a request for a squadron of B-25 bombers from the United States Air Force (USAF), which US officials did not even entertain.[32] Bajpai's plea was also turned down.

Bajpai's approach was adopted by other Indian officials as well. On 10 May 1948, in a conversation between I.S. Chopra, the first secretary in the Indian embassy in Washington, and Joseph Sparks, of the Division of South Asian Affairs in the US State Department, Chopra reiterated Bajpai's sentiments. According to the memorandum drawn up by Sparks, Chopra states that 'there is no doubt at all as to which side India would take should there be a third World War—the United States could count absolutely on having India at its side in such a conflict'.[33] Chopra later made it clear that India needed 12,000,000 rounds of ammunition for training purposes. In making this request, he seemed to have suggested that US acceptance of India's needs might lead to an 'era of good feeling and friendly, full understanding'.[34] Subsequently, Chopra's request was also rejected.[35] Much like American impressions of Indian bureaucrats, State Department officials were equally endeared by Brigadier D. Chaudhuri, the Indian military attaché in Washington. Chaudhuri, according to American officials, 'clung tenaciously to his basic sympathy for the United States', and operated 'consistently from such a basis'.[36]

At first glance, it is not difficult to see why these conversations would lead authors to conclude that India was indeed looking to forge a military alliance with the US. Yet declassified and published American sources only reveal one part of a much larger story. By triangulating these with available Indian and British sources it becomes clear that non-alignment was not a mere rhetorical 'smokescreen' behind which an alliance was being considered—nor should the words and wisdom of Indian officials be taken literally. Here, two points are worth bearing in mind. First, it is essential to query the reasons why Indian officials chose to adopt language suggesting that, at the very least, India was open to the idea of a closer relationship with the US. Second, ultimately, in the arena of foreign policy, officials had limited agency in pushing policy imperatives.

Assuming Cold War Rhetoric

From the very dawn of independence, Indian representatives were careful to condition their language. The Indian government was looking to acquire military hardware and apply for much-needed economic assistance. Hence government officials often chose to temper Nehru's forceful rhetoric as regards non-alignment, adding for good measure statements that promised to encourage US officials to give India's demands serious consideration. Their choice of rhetoric was, at least in their minds, calibrated to ensure the most promising outcome, as they saw it, for a recently independent and desperate nation.

Take for instance the case of Asif Ali, the first Indian ambassador to Washington and a senior Congress leader who had previously worked on defence-related matters.[37] A fortnight after Ali was appointed ambassador, Nehru wrote to his new envoy: it was important, the prime minister argued, to make sure that India was not seen to be 'subservient to anyone' or 'welcome any kind of patronage'.[38] The United States was no doubt a 'great power', but, as Nehru went on to state, it was crucial to remember that India had 'plenty of good cards'. There was no need to 'appear as suppliants before any country'.[39] Yet when Ali presented his credentials to Marshall in February 1947, he appeared, as Kux puts it, 'to have forgotten Nehru's advice'.[40] Much like Bajpai and Chopra, the ambassador made a case for American investments in India's economic and political future. He suggested that India 'would be a bastion for the world against the great northern neighbor [presumably Russia]'. Further, Ali went on to state that India could even serve as a 'strong centre between weaker neighbours [Pakistan to the east and China in the west]'.[41] The discrepancy between Nehru's guidance and the tone underlying official dealings was evident.

In the case of Bajpai, and especially in the late 1940s, this inconsistency might even have been expected. The secretary general previously held the post of an agent general in the US (1941–6) on behalf of the British Indian government. Nehru himself told Bajpai that he had 'not agreed with much' of Bajpai's past, but the fact remained that Bajpai was a 'capable' officer, one of few in an emerging Indian Administrative and Foreign Service.[42] According to Bajpai's own calculations, the Indian services needed at least 1,200 officers. In the middle of 1947, it only had 410.[43]

These were trying and uncertain times. Despite repeated statements around non-alignment, there was little clarity with regard to what this meant in terms of diplomatic engagement. Nehru appeared to have understood this himself. A few weeks before his trip to Washington, he stressed—in a letter to his sister—the need to 'adapt' to the 'new environment'. He knew that the press and officials would 'weigh every word' he spoke. This would prove to be challenging and 'difficult'. He was not used to such 'inhibitions'. He even asked Vijayalakshmi Pandit, then the ambassador to the United States, to temper rhetoric around 'our [Indian] high ideals,' which could well 'lay ourselves open to a courteous retort'.[44] Equally, Nehru spent considerable time thinking about his approach to the US. He pondered about alliances,[45] his own British schooling[46] and the tact he would require once in America. These were only some of Nehru's concerns for a trip that was to last less than a month. Considering these matters on an everyday basis was surely harder for India's envoy, allowing for a degree of elasticity in their approach to the United States.

Official views were further shaped by the pressing political context of the time. During the first Indo-Pakistan War of 1947–8, fought over the fate of Kashmir, Marshall cancelled the export of arms and ammunition to India and Pakistan. This was not a formal embargo, but a no-armaments policy was very much in effect.[47] This was done with the aim of halting the fighting and arriving at a peaceful settlement on the ensuing dispute over Kashmir.[48] But it was almost certainly a major source of concern for the Indian government—it was, after all, partly outfitted with US equipment that had been supplied under the Lend-Lease Agreement during the Second World War between the US government and the British Indian government.[49] As a sovereign nation-state, India needed to work out an agreement on a bilateral basis, and this was becoming difficult. Importantly, India—much like Pakistan at the time—was barred from applying for export licences to purchase military material. It no longer had access to information or training modules, which, prior to 1947, were made available through the US Joint Chiefs of Staff.[50]

The need for suppliers and equipment exercised the defence minister, Baldev Singh, even prior to independence.[51] Immediately after, the Indian government was additionally fretful as it learnt of a Pakistani request to the US for military aid. In October 1947, Pakistan had asked for $170 million from the United States for strengthening an army of over 100,000 soldiers. Pakistan wanted US assistance in creating one armoured division, five infantry divisions and a small cavalry establishment. For the air force, the Pakistanis wanted $75 million for twelve fighter squadrons, three bomber squadrons of fifty aircrafts, four transport squadrons and 400 training wings of 200 aeroplanes.[52] Although Pakistan's enormous shopping list was not immediately approved by the US, the prospect of an improved and well-equipped Pakistani military was without doubt a matter of concern for Indian envoys. This was noted both by American officials and their British counterparts.[53]

As the India–Pakistan War came to an official end—with a ceasefire in effect from New Year's Day 1949[54]—General K.M. Cariappa, the first Indian commander-in-chief of the Indian Army,[55] made clear that the war placed India in an unenviable position,[56] where it desperately needed defence equipment from abroad. It was against this backdrop that Indian envoys sought to purchase military equipment from the US. Hence their language during potentially significant meetings and conversations was deliberately attuned in order to arrive at an outcome that would ameliorate the situation India found itself in, and can hardly be taken at face value. Moreover, the fact remained that, in the end, what mattered was not the position taken by Indian government officials, but those adopted by Prime Minister Nehru, who also held the Foreign Ministry portfolio.

The Buck Stops with Nehru

Nehru was well aware of India's military needs and was open to receiving foreign military equipment as long as it was procured rather than given as aid. He was even willing to assuage US fears that 'there was not the least chance of India lining up with the Soviet Union in war or peace'.[57] During Grady and Henderson's initial call on the prime minister soon after the ambassadors had arrived in Delhi—in June 1947 and November 1948 respectively—Nehru said that he very much 'hoped India would receive expert assistance from [the] USA'.[58] Henderson wrote that Nehru wanted something much more than an association; he wanted a relationship 'based on principles of high order'.[59] To Grady, he even complained that Pandit's posting in Moscow—where she was ambassador before taking up the post in Washington—was proving to be a 'difficult one'.[60] There was no doubt that the Indian prime minister was reaching out to the US. He made no secret of the fact that Washington was the 'most important' diplomatic mission of the time. Equally, he argued, it would require finesse to take 'full advantage' of the United States while keeping 'perfectly clear from any entanglement'.[61]

Maintaining this fine line was better understood by British diplomats based in London and Delhi.[62] They appreciated that there was no chance of India supporting the United States in the event of war, as had been suggested by Bajpai and others. They also understood that Nehru's pitch to US envoys was no doubt partially informed by the ensuing war in Kashmir, which, as the prime minister suggested, had 'brought the problem of defence very much to the fore'. 'A country today,' he argued, 'is completely helpless if it has not got proper defence forces as well as the machinery to produce the necessary equipment.' Nehru pointed out that the only two countries able to provide India with this equipment were Britain and the United States. However, he noted that whatever the case, 'I am anxious to avoid any dependence on the USA. I do not like the way they are going and they have a method of trying to get their pound's flesh in the shape of vested interests and the like.'[63]

In fact, shortly after the interim government was constituted, Nehru, along with Baldev Singh, made clear that the 'defence of the country from the possibility of external aggression' was a 'paramount duty of the government'.[64] Singh often reminded the prime minister that the heritage of the British Indian army was such that independent India's approach to the very 'science of war' was 'completely mixed up with Britain' and the West more generally—it needed the import of goods.[65] Nehru agreed—India would not 'rule out treaties of alliance', as long as it was to 'our advantage'.[66]

This need for equipment was forcefully articulated by Sardar Vallabhbhai Patel, the 'determinedly inward-looking' deputy prime minister, who held the portfolios for both the Home Ministry and the States.[67] Patel urged Nehru to consider 'outside sympathy and support'.[68] Patel and Singh were engrossed in the everyday and gruelling events associated with running a war, an endeavour that necessarily required seeking urgent assistance and developing reactionary policies to support the men at arms. Nehru, in contrast, was able to take a bird's-eye view on issues that could well have sucked India into an unobvious but nevertheless dependent relationship with both Britain and the United States. For the prime minister, defence was not something to be considered in isolation. It was only one arm of a much larger construct of national development.[69] The idea, as he himself explained, was to keep a 'free hand' while 'ultimately get[ting] more from them [the US] and at the same time get the friendship and cooperation of other countries also'.[70]

This carefully calibrated approach was founded, as he argued, 'on materialistic, idealistic, and even opportunistic grounds', where maintaining 'an attitude of dignified, friendly aloofness' had greater potential to serve India's long-term interests.[71] According to Stephen Cohen, Nehru was hardly someone who had developed 'a strong distaste for armed forces and things military';[72] nor did he succumb to the temptations of being trapped in the immediate history of colonialism. Rather, his approach was informed as much by a lingering suspicion of alignment as it was by the needs of the army.

Either way, alignment with the United States was out of the question. The State Department itself realised this. On 16 October 1948, Marshall met with Nehru and Pandit in Paris. This was the first meeting between the Indian premier and a high-ranking US official. At Nehru's request the meeting was kept quiet to avoid unnecessary speculation among the Indian press.[73] Having met with Nehru, Marshall writes that there was no indication of Nehru taking a position either with the Soviets or the US. According to Marshall, the 'tone of the meeting was friendly, even cordial, but on Nehru's side, at times guarded and occasionally defensive'.[74] If what the Indian officials said in Washington really did echo Nehru's thinking, it would seem unlikely for Nehru not to have given Marshall any reason to believe that India would side with the West in the event of war.

Nehru was crafting a unique international persona for India. For the prime minister, non-alignment was an unwritten strategy designed to avoid entanglement in issues that did not directly concern India. He understood that non-alignment had brought India 'sharply against the ugly forces of power politics'.[75] This was not a prime minister determined to forge an alliance even at a time of military crisis, no matter what his officials had related to their American counterparts.

Nehru's misgivings about his own officials as well as the high-minded policy pursued by him are evident in a letter to George Bernard Shaw, where he argues that the few 'answers' that did exist to the big 'questions' of the time could not be 'implemented because of the human beings that should implement them'.[76] The somewhat ambiguous idea of detachment was almost destined to be twisted, manipulated and even reinterpreted by those who were yet to realise the very opportunity of India. This would take time for a newborn nation. Indeed, Nehru's attempts to maintain a degree of measure in times of crisis were that much more obvious in negotiating economic assistance.

Economic Aid and Alliance

On 10 November 1947, some four months after Grady first arrived in India, he authored what might well be considered the most important cable during his sixteen-month posting. To Marshall, he determinedly argued, 'I am convinced it is fundamental for [the] US government to support Nehru in every way possible. If he should fall, disintegration in India could easily follow.'[77] In no other instance did Grady make such an urgent plea to his own nation.[78] He had recently and separately met with Bajpai, Nehru and officials from the Agricultural Ministry.[79] On top of the mounting crisis around partition and the emerging troubles in Kashmir, where Pakistan had informally learnt about Maharaja Hari Singh's decision to accede to India,[80] maintaining 'controlled hunger' was a top priority.[81] The food crisis, more than anything else, agonised the ambassador.

An economist by training, Grady grew increasingly wary of what he saw as British attempts to undermine India's potential for growth. He was irritated by the likes of Lord Louis Mountbatten, the last viceroy of British India and the first constitutional governor general of independent India, who pressed Nehru and C. Rajagopalachari, who succeeded Mountbatten as governor general,[82] to stay clear of 'dollar imperialism'.[83] Grady genuinely believed that economic assistance, which India desperately needed, could only be guaranteed if Nehru and the top leadership played to Truman's Achilles heel. This meant evoking the 'Russia card' when and if the opportunity arose. For his part, he made clear to Marshall that 'Russia would in my opinion rather control India than several Greece's.'[84] Much like the language during the discussions on military assistance, Indian officials, in Grady's opinion, would at the very least need to exercise Cold War rhetoric. This was, after all, a crisis of enormous proportions.

In the post-independence period, 85 per cent of 350 million Indians lived with inadequate irrigation facilities. To policymakers in New Delhi, 'India's economic woes underlined the paramount importance of cordial relations with the US.' If India was to survive famine, the import of wheat was essential. In July 1947, Nehru told Grady that America was the only country that could give India the economic aid and produce to avoid famine.[85] There was no likelihood of grain imports from the Middle East and Australia. The position adopted by the Argentinean government—a major grain-producing nation—remained uncertain.[86] Importantly, there was no indication of Russia stepping-up to the plate. A request for food grains prior to independence evoked no reply.[87] Shortly after independence, the Soviet Foreign Ministry informed the Indian chargé d'affaires in Moscow—Rajeshwar Dayal—that it would not be possible to provide surplus grain.[88] In fact, by early 1948 Nehru was convinced that Joseph Stalin saw India as little more than a 'stooge of the Anglo-American block'.[89] As late as 1949, when India's economic position was nothing short of desperate, Russian attitudes and potential for assistance were ambiguous at best.[90]

The calamitous food situation was made worse by India's early fiscal imbalance. Henderson estimated the deficit to be as high as $135,000,000.[91] The Economic Department in the CRO stressed that 'India will not be able to raise locally more than a quarter of the cost of internal expenditure on development.' In the next five to seven years, a cable underlined, India would need nothing less than foreign investments amounting to £700 million. It was hence essential, according to the CRO, to convince Washington to support India.[92] This was not going to be easy.

In the late 1940s, American officials adopted stringent guidelines for providing underdeveloped countries with economic assistance. Newborn nations like India were not to be handed a free ride, especially when it adopted political stances that did not directly and publicly express support to the Western bloc of nations in relation to the Cold War. The cautious economic policies were clearly articulated by Willard Thorp, the American representative to the UN Economic and Social Council. Thorp argued that Washington wished to see greater local investments in developmental projects. He claimed that underdeveloped countries should invest 80 per cent, leaving the remaining 20 per cent to be covered by the United States.[93]

Further, the International Bank for Reconstruction and Development (IBRD) made clear that it could not authorise loans of more than $150 million to India, which barely covered 25 per cent of what India needed from them.[94] The Export–Import Bank resisted giving India additional loans to meet the deficit in food grains. Even the International Monetary Fund (IMF), according to British officials in Delhi, had 'shown no desire to continue to permit India to purchase dollar[s] for rupees'.[95] Moreover, given India's protectionist policies, private US investors found little reason to either aid India or to lobby the US Congress to do the same.[96]

In these fraught times, it would thus make sense either to forge an alliance with the United States—as has been suggested in existing works—or at the very least to consider a closer relationship with a country India desperately needed. Instead, India's approach, as will be demonstrated below, continued to be informed by the objective of balance. While the shadow of anti-imperialism, as Grady understood it, played some part in steering policy objectives, the scheme, as Nehru argued, was to maintain distance from adopting reactionary policies that would have long-term consequences. 'The safest policy,' he noted, was to be 'friendly to America, to give them fair terms, to invite their help on such terms, and at the same time not to tie ourselves up too much with their world or their economic policies.'[97] He pursued these goals in negotiating American proposals and during his trip to the US.

Dealing with American Overtures

In January 1948, Grady approached the Indian Commerce Ministry—and later Nehru himself—with the idea of considering a 'Special Treaty for Friendship, Navigation and Commerce' to foster closer economic and cultural relations between the United States and India.[98] This was, in Grady's view, a sensible technique by which India and the US could be institutionally bound. It was by no means a proposal for an alliance, but rather a nominal overture that would go some way in convincing US lawmakers of India's potential importance. At the time, it was brushed off. Nehru and the interim Cabinet had other pressing matters to deal with.

Importantly, the case of Kashmir in the UN exercised Indian officials. Noel Baker, the Commonwealth secretary and the lead British negotiator at the UN, had ignored India's complaints—made on 31 December 1947—with regard to Pakistani interference in Kashmir, and instead pushed for a plebiscite, a position in line with Pakistani demands.[99] As far as Nehru was concerned, the UK, 'the chief actor behind the scenes', along with the US, 'played a dirty role'.[100] According to the prime minister they had clearly 'taken up an attitude in favour of Pakistan'.[101] Only much later, between the summer of 1948 and the winter of 1949,[102] did India consider the full significance of the proposed treaty.

A thirty-four-page document with twenty-nine articles of discussion, the treaty stated that Indian and American businesses would be given a fillip by the proposed mutually beneficial arrangements.[103] In essence, this was akin to what is commonly called a Most Favoured Nation (MFN) agreement. This was hardly unusual even in the 1940s; Pakistan was negotiating a similar agreement with the US at the time.[104] The central tenet, as described in Article IV of the treaty, was that both nations would enjoy rights 'to organize, control and manage companies for engaging in commercial, manufacturing, financial, processing, construction, mining, publishing, educational, philanthropic, religious, and scientific activities'. Importantly, and for good measure, the State Department added a clause—Article 28 (4)—stating that 'political activities' or advocacy remained outside the scope of the agreement.[105]

Yet, and notwithstanding American attempts to make it easier for India to accept the language of the treaty, Nehru remained wary, and for a number of good reasons. In a note to K.P.S. Menon, India's first foreign secretary, he argued that the ministry would need to tread carefully. On the one hand, there was no doubt whatsoever that the treaty would help India. Indeed, it was not the 'question of economic domination' that 'frighten[ed]' the prime minister, rather, it was both the immediate and long-term repercussions of entering into an agreement with one of the two superpowers.

First, while this was an economic agreement, there was every potential for India's political position on non-alignment to become sidelined. Second, it could well reinforce Stalin's view that India was nothing more than an Anglo-American outpost in Asia. Third, and most importantly, an agreement such as this could incrementally, and without obvious intent, draw India into the Cold War, doing little, if anything, for its own development.[106] To John Mathai, the finance minister, Nehru made clear that the 'larger picture' needed to be kept in mind. Economic want, he added, no matter how desperate, should in no way have 'political implications' that may 'come in our way later'.[107]

For Loy Henderson (who replaced Grady) and his team in Delhi, Indian attitudes were baffling at best. Here was a country that needed assistance. Its envoys, including Pandit, made a strong case for 'closer friendly relations' that were yet to be 'cemented by action'. In turn, Russia, as Henderson argued, had shunned Indian advances. The ambassador simply could not understand what he described as a 'vague' approach.[108] What Henderson failed to recognise was that he and his chancery were dealing with a country and a prime minister that foresaw the potential menace of entanglement. Indian elites intently understood that non-dependence would ultimately allow the advantage of options in a world transforming into a complex net of alliances and counter-alliances. Finally, on 12 September 1949, Mathai informed Henderson that the treaty could not be accepted at this point.[109] Pushed instead by Mathai, Desai and eventually Patel to reflect on 'practical considerations',[110] Nehru prepared to depart for the United States.

Much like their Indian counterparts, British officials were also engaged in intense discussion about the importance of this trip for India's economic development. In a series of meetings between Bajpai and Nye, it was made clear to the Indians that although Britain was doing a lot to strengthen the Indian economy, 'additional support must come mainly from the US'. Writing back to Whitehall, Nye stated that 'while I knew that Pandit Nehru's visit to Washington next month [October] was primarily a goodwill mission, I hoped that one of its results might be an increasing readiness on the part of America to co-operate in strengthening India's economy and of India to welcome and encourage such cooperation'.[111] Bajpai, Nye asserted, was fully aware of India's predicament, and that 'he [Bajpai] felt that our own [UK–US] energies should be directed to preventing Nehru from saying or doing unwise things in Washington, and if possible to making use of his visit to interest the US in giving economic aid to India'.[112]

Days before Nehru's visit, Henderson, for his part, tried hard to sell India's want of economic aid to the US Congress, but with little success. Robert Lovett, who dealt with Asian affairs, claimed that there was no reason why the US should support India and its 'overt neutrality'.[113]

After all, Nehru's speeches on non-alignment and his cautious, almost suspicious, attitude towards the US had found little favour among America's political officials and intelligentsia. Turning down the Special Treaty only reinforced these accepted viewpoints.

This state visit could potentially have served to unpick India's financial woes. If, as scholars contend, India's early disposition was to cement a closer relationship with the US, surely this visit would have allowed for India to do this. Yet the twenty-four days Nehru spent between the United States and Canada, while important in themselves, did little for the prospects of a treaty. Significantly, while Nehru returned from North America with enthusiasm for a nation he came to admire, Truman and Acheson could not have grown more sceptical of what they saw as the dipping fortunes of a country led by a 'difficult' and 'irresponsible' prime minister.[114] Needless to add, Nehru's firm stance on a dependence-free approach to international affairs failed to move his American counterparts.

Nehru's Visit to America

For Henderson, an envoy who grew increasingly irritated by the State Department's limited attention to Nehru's visit, this was the opportunity to turn the prime minister. He was not 'pro-American' at the 'present time', but could potentially be lured by 'brass bands'. Writing to Truman's military aide, he argued that it was vital to 'find ways of tickling his [Nehru's] vanity'. In short, Henderson argued, the administration must offer him the 'works'.[115]

In Washington, Henderson's plea carried limited weight. Sir Oliver Franks, the British ambassador to the United States, who was in constant touch with Nye and the Foreign Office, made clear that 'no one in Washington had apparently been considering Nehru's visit as anything but one of courtesy'. Moreover, Nehru's public utterances with regard to non-alignment dampened 'the attitude of Congress and the public'. The 'only interest', as far as US legislators were concerned, was to see India publicly side with the West against communism.[116]

Frank's counsel notwithstanding, the public were warmer than anticipated. The liberal press 'lauded Nehru as the hope of Asia'.[117] *Time* magazine—the owner of which, Edward Luce, had previously criticised the prime minister for not falling in line with the West—now placed him on the cover with the byline, 'A hard climb, a harder climb ahead.'[118] In short, and as Guha put it, 'non-official America took him to its heart'.[119] There was little doubt that there was something enigmatic about Nehru that both bemused and intrigued a public too used to the less balanced rhetoric around anti-communism.

Contrary to academic speculation, as far as official meetings were concerned, the visit went far better for Nehru than was commonly understood. The prime minister, as Kux underlines, might have found Truman and Acheson 'condescending', but this in itself did not perturb him.[120] Indeed, Nehru and his interlocutors might have 'often talked past each other', as McMahon rightly contends, but this did not mean that the trip was one of the 'least successful state visits in recent history'.[121] True, the visit achieved almost nothing in terms of quantifiable returns; there was no agreement reached on any issue of importance and even the much-discussed topic of food assistance was not concluded.

However, in the immediate term, it altered the prime minister's analysis of America. In the longer term, and in so far as US officials were concerned, it engrained a sense of definiteness around Indian foreign policy. It was soon clear even to Acheson that this was no fair-weather approach to the world and its problems. These were still early days in a relationship that insiders could only vaguely grasp. Despite Henderson and Nye's obsession with leveraging the visit for food grains, Nehru appeared to have understood from the start that this was at best a visit designed to forge a better understanding of American views. It was about sensing a pulse of a nation he soon came to admire, but at the same time, to disagree with. This was, as he put it, more about learning than it was about teaching. It was about 'seeing their good points' while not being 'swept away by them [Americans]'.[122]

On 12 October, Nehru met with Acheson. He highlighted two issues: the need for 1 million tons of wheat and India's views on the recently formed People's Republic of China (PRC). With regard to the former, it soon became apparent that the State Department had given little thought to the issue of economic assistance. Henderson's pleas and Nye's recommendations—made through Oliver Franks—had little impact on the administration. On the latter, while Nehru made clear that his government sought to recognise the PRC, which India did on 30 December 1949, Acheson clearly differed. For the secretary of state, no 'advantage could be gained' by 'according early recognition'.[123] While the issue of

China was discussed in subsequent meetings with Acheson and Truman—it would render a rift in US and Indian relations with the outbreak of the Korean War—the request for wheat was seldom highlighted by Nehru.

From the outset, and as McMahon records, it could be surmised that 'the prime minister kept silent about India's broader economic needs for fear that Americans might insist on a quid pro quo'. McMahon quotes letters written by Nehru to a whole host of close friends and colleagues, where, essentially, he makes clear that 'it is better to starve than to beg'.[124] Asking for assistance, it would seem, was beneath Nehru. At the time, State Department officials, Henderson included, were brought to believe that Nehru's wariness had much to do with India's anti-colonial struggle. The mere thought of attachments or international obligations, it was assumed, would offend Indian sensibilities. This thinking was partially informed by Henderson's own observations, and more so by interactions with Pandit and Bajpai.[125]

Interestingly, when surveying American, British and Indian sources, it becomes abundantly clear that Nehru's position was fundamentally misunderstood. There is no doubt that the prime minister was reticent. He often spoke about the 'ending of imperialism and colonialism',[126] and the 'immaturity' of America's approach to politics, where subtlety and detail were often subsumed by single-minded determinedness.[127] Yet Nehru took the issue of food assistance seriously. The problem, it would appear, lay in the manner in which issues were approached in the first place. Nehru tried to explain this to Henderson. In a note, he stressed that the 'variety of psychological make-up of various people is tremendous'. The 'lack of understanding, or rather of emotionally appreciating a different psychology', was what, according to Nehru, led 'so frequently to misunderstanding and conflict'.[128] India remained guarded, but this did not mean that it would refuse to entertain American offers if and when they came. Further, as he admitted to his sister, public pronouncements made by him could, at times, be 'rather superficial'.[129] Rhetoric could not be taken at face value.

In fact, months prior to his visit, Nehru encouraged Pandit, the Indian ambassador to the United States, to develop 'informal ways' to approach the State Department to discuss pressing matters 'fairly fully'.[130] While aware of America's apparent interest to 'tie' India to her foreign policy goals,[131] he encouraged his Foreign Service officers to 'take advantage' of the modest openings made to India.[132] Keeping with this line of thought, it was Nehru who pushed Pandit to take up the matter of India's formal request to the IMF in June 1949, and with the US Treasury Department.[133] He instructed Mathai, his finance minister, not to 'lay stress on the helplessness of India', but at the same time to accept a 'free gift' of wheat as long as the offer was made by the Americans.[134] This was hardly a man who was steadfast in what Henderson and others wrongly believed to be a doctrinaire position regarding the acceptance of help. Given the 'far reaching consequences' of devaluation in India, which led to an acute shortage in its dollar reserves, Nehru even queried the possibility of wheat supplies from the US on a deferred payment scheme.[135]

In an address aptly titled 'a voyage of discovery' to the US House of Representatives, he stressed that 'India may speak in a voice' that America may not 'immediately recognise', but India too realised that 'self-help is the first condition of success'. He welcomed the prospects of 'aid and cooperation', as long as it was mutually beneficial. The last paragraph of his speech was perhaps most telling; Nehru stressed that India was 'neither blind to reality' nor did it 'propose to acquiesce in any challenge to man's freedom'.[136] This was one of the first occasions on which the prime minister read from a 'carefully prepared speech'. According to Nye, it was written to 'please an American audience' and 'illustrates the very gradual development of responsible thinking' on the matter of asking for assistance.[137] Importantly, the speech did not once mention communism or Russia. In private, Nehru told officials that he had 'lost all faith in Russia'.[138] Clearly, much like many officials before him, he too conditioned his language and demeanour to gain what India needed most: food grains from abroad. The only caveat was that this should be given without any prospect of entanglement.

In the subsequent two weeks Nehru travelled extensively around America. In New York, he told Indian residents that while 'India will stand on her own feet', he would accept a deal 'based on terms of mutual advantage'.[139] In almost all his public utterances, he made sure to balance the need for assistance with the basic demand of a policy based on the idea of non-alignment. Whether it was at a press club in New York, the UN Trusteeship Committee, the universities of Wisconsin and California or to journalists in Washington, the message was unwavering. This was duly noted by Oliver Franks and Nye, who watched every move of Nehru's much more closely than their American counterparts.[140]

Indeed, the prime minister himself recounted the extra effort he had made to 'create a favourable atmosphere' so that at the very least it may 'produce a great feeling of interest' and a 'desire' among Americans to 'cooperate' with India.[141]

For too long, scholars and practitioners have harped on petty matters to reach the conclusion that 'Nehru was not inclined to see the American light' or that America's corporate culture, and relaxed nature with regard to talking about money, irritated him and dealt a blow to the entire visit.[142] Take for instance the oft-mentioned case of Nehru's luncheon with a group of bankers in New York. As Pandit, who actually accompanied Nehru, put it, his 'embarrassment and annoyance were acute'.[143] This might well have been so, but to assume that the whole arch of Nehru's approach was coloured by this one luncheon is close to absurd. What is more, Henderson also actually believed that incidents like this displeased Nehru and informed his less than flattering impressions of America. Alarmingly, Henderson's false belief was kept bottled up for a year. It was only in November 1950 that he brought it up with Nehru. As the prime minister told Henderson at the time, and made equally clear to his close coterie of advisors during the state visit, America enticed him in a way he could not have imagined.[144] It was bizarre to think that this 'extraordinary experience' would be distorted by a luncheon or any other single event during the trip.[145]

His return to India, which coincided with his sixtieth birthday on 14 November, led both American and British officials to report that the visit had made a 'deep impression on his mind'. The prime minister, unlike before, suggested that the 'prospects of American investments in Indian industries were bright'. These were the kind of statements Henderson had banked on industrialists like G.D. Birla to make[146] when they visited the US, rather than a prime minister who was seen as evasive and confused.[147]

Most importantly, quite unlike the recent past, he was reported to have openly discussed 'the extraordinary idealism and sentimentality, which was no less characteristic of the American people than their materialism'.[148] Indian Foreign Ministry officials, Bajpai included, were pleasantly surprised by Nehru's frankness. He even wrote to his chief ministers:

I felt how foolish it was for us here in India or elsewhere to sit down in our little corner and criticise others for their failings, calling them materialistic and worshippers of the almighty dollar and no more. That was true enough to some extent. But it was a very partial truth and it was a cheap way of describing a country.[149]

The difficulties in actually attaining aid at this time had little to do with Nehru's cautious or reserved negotiating style, but the fact that the Truman administration was simply not prepared to make an offer. As McMahon himself argues, 'for all the talk in Washington of India's centrality … the administration had made no hard decisions before Nehru's arrival'. The ensuing discussions between officials and Nehru 'make it clear that the administration had not yet decided what to do about India—or in some respects even what to think about India'.[150] Truman found Nehru's views on China and non-alignment 'unacceptable', and Acheson saw the prime minister as one of the most 'difficult men' he had to deal with,[151] an 'excruciating hurdle against US strategies meant for structuring of the post-Second World War international order'.[152] It would appear that the quest for engagement without entanglement, as attempted by Nehru, was simply not within the conceptual comprehension of official America. Acheson would later grumble about how Nehru spoke to him 'as Queen Victoria said of Mr. Gladstone, as though I were a public meeting'. Yet, perhaps dealing with an equal was something an otherwise 'quick', 'gregarious', 'outspoken' and 'often impatient' secretary of state was simply unwilling to accept.[153] He was, as James Chace put it, someone who 'created the American world', one in which India had a limited if not altogether invisible role.

In short, in 1949, it made little sense for the United States to engage on equal terms with a nation that did nothing to declare its support for the West. Following Nehru's departure from America, a proposal for a $500 million economic aid package made by Henderson prior to Nehru's visit was rejected by US lawmakers. The million ton request for wheat was turned down too. A year down the line, Nehru admitted to Henderson that, for one reason or another, all existing proposals simply 'fell through'.[154]

Conclusion

The first two years following independence were largely spent negotiating what was often—and rightly—considered an obscure and easily misread conception that in time would bear the title non-alignment. It took time for Indian and American officials to even vaguely grasp what such an approach was all about. In many ways, this was a strategy devised by Nehru and best understood by him alone. It was an approach that necessarily lacked the clarity of a written policy. Little doubt, then, that scholars and practitioners read the early script around non-alignment as either some sort of masked scheme to align with the United States or something 'enthusiastically anti-colonial'.[155] That the import of food grains from America would prove tougher to negotiate had as much to do with the emotional, political and strategic need for non-dependence as the Truman administration's opposition to something bold and original.

In a detailed note to Dorothy Norman, the photographer, writer and social activist, Nehru lays out the difficulties in dealing with the US. He stressed that 'there was a grave misunderstanding' between the US and India. While this was partially due to the misplaced views held by practitioners, it also had something to do with historical circumstances. For instance, there was a widespread belief in the State Department that Nehru would not accept free grain, when in fact he 'had no objection' to this whatsoever. In practice, American officials presupposed what they believed to be the prime minister's approach; a great deal was simply lost in translation.

It was undoubtedly difficult to understand India. Its prime minister functioned on the basis of his 'lifetime way of looking at things'.[156] History mattered, but, as demonstrated above in the negotiations over military and economic assistance, this did not mean that India was disconnected from interest-based realities. It meant that the push-and-pull tension between ideas and interests often got in the way of easier relations. What was needed, as Nehru put it, was a deeper consideration for 'difference'; it was about shaping 'understanding' without the need for 'agreement about everything'.[157] This would take time to realise. The early articulation of an approach underpinned by the mantra and rhetoric of non-dependence, which was equally rooted in the still-burning memory of oppression as well as the need to tread cautiously around the much easier option of alliance formation, was clearly understood by few.

In the following few years, the so-far evident and respectively fractured interpretations of international politics were filled, to a degree, with a greater measure of perception. Although the Korean War and its aftermath—discussed in the next chapter—partly strengthened existing American assumptions, it also served, at least partially, to confirm the strategic import of non-alignment, even for the United States.

3

'FUNNY PEOPLE'

1950–1954

Despite the growing interest and contact between Indian and American principals in the latter half of the 1940s, Henderson and his team of diplomats found themselves working out of 'crowded and hot' facilities housed in 'unconnected old rented buildings' in New Delhi. This was hardly the kind of infrastructure that was going to impress Indian elites and, as importantly, visiting envoys from Washington. After all, buildings are widely considered 'markers' that 'signify purpose' and 'symbolise presence'. What Henderson wanted was an embassy that would be a 'credit to us [America] and a credit to India'.[1] With this in mind, he found 13 acres of prime property in the capital's diplomatic enclave on Shantipath. The new embassy was finally inaugurated on 3 January 1959 by Ellsworth Bunker, the sixth US ambassador to India. Widely considered an architectural tour de force, *The New York Times* reported that it was 'probably the most elegant in the world'. Nehru was 'enchanted' and quite obviously impressed by the construction, which, according to him, combined 'typically Indian motifs with [the] latest modern technology'.[2] As architectural historian Jane Loefler writes, it unambiguously demonstrated 'Indian importance to the United States in the 1950s.'[3]

Yet apart from symbolic signals such as this, capturing the importance of Indian–US relations was excruciatingly difficult. The outbreak of the

Korean War in 1950 and, after November 1952, the Eisenhower administration's fixation with military alliances, did anything but convince Nehru of American earnestness when it came to India. Eisenhower himself was hardly captivated by India. Indians, according to the president, were 'funny people'. Moreover, they were led by 'a personality of unusual contradictions',[4] something that unnerved this former chief of Army Staff. It certainly did not entice John Foster Dulles, his 'stubbornly inflexible' secretary of state.[5] The historiography of this period also suggests that it 'diminished India's relative significance to the United States'.[6] According to Gopal, the Korean crisis, in particular, exasperated Indian and American differences.[7] This was especially true when it came to the newly established PRC, which India had recognised as early as December 1949, but which both Truman and Eisenhower refused to recognise or admit to the UN Security Council. Key officials like Pandit also argued that 'Korea marked one of the worst phases in Indo-American relations.'[8] However, existing accounts lose sight of the fact that this period of crisis instilled a much greater and even farther-reaching sense of confidence among actors in India and the US, who came to work intimately together during the first hot conflict of the Cold War. This was the 'first real international test' both for India's foreign policy and for its approach to the United States.[9]

Rather than driving India and the US further apart, the following narrative shows how Indian policy, in fact, led to mutually exclusive outcomes. At one level, or what might be considered that of everyday diplomacy, it led to a much closer understanding of each other's standpoints. Even Dulles, who once described 'neutrality'—as he understood non-alignment—as an 'increasingly obsolete conception',[10] was forced to admit that India's approach to the Korean War was advantageous in at least some ways. In the end, India was the only acceptable choice for the West, the PRC and the USSR to head what came to be called the Neutral Nations Repatriation Commission led by General K.S. Thimayya, who later became the Indian chief of Army Staff.

Adversely, and at another level, India's method of diplomacy grated the Eisenhower White House. India's approach to the PRC, its curious (in American reading) voting pattern in the Security Council, where India served as a non-permanent member, and its opposition to regional defence treaties authored by Dulles did little more than confirm Eisenhower's 'funny people' thesis. He could never quite understand or 'actually trust' India.[11] In America, this was a period of 'rampant materialism' and 'reactionary cant'; neutralism was seen as a threat to national security.[12] Nehru's instructions to his envoys to maintain 'poise' and the 'equilibrium of mind' was hardly the kind of advice the likes of Dulles found inviting,[13] even though it was exactly this determination for balance that served the interests of India, the US and the UN at large. Crucially, Indian choices during the Korean crisis show how and why non-alignment came to be seen and understood as a practical and novel approach to world politics. Such an approach was designed keeping Indian interests in mind while seeking innovative ways to reach a peace settlement in the Korean Peninsula.

This chapter is divided into two parts. The first part examines India's immediate response to the Korean War. It traces how Indian envoys sought to guard against the counter-Chinese positions adopted by Truman and Acheson, while working towards the cause of mediation. In the second part, the chapter shows how India and the United States came to work closely together in the UN through a process of forceful argumentation that eventually led to the end of hostilities. Further, it demonstrates how India chose to do so while refusing to heed to US Congressional pressure with regard to the tricky and hugely political issue of food assistance.

India, China and the Outbreak of War

On 25 June 1950, the UN Security Council briefly discussed North Korea's 'unprovoked attacks' along the so-called 38th parallel, the circle of latitude and border line, concluded in 1945, that divided North and South Korea. At around 18.00 hours, an American-backed resolution was tabled and passed by nine out of the eleven members of the Security Council. It called for the immediate cessation of hostilities and the withdrawal of all North Korean forces from Southern territories.[14] The pro-Soviet state of Yugoslavia abstained, while the USSR was absent. It had temporarily left the Council to protest the PRC's non-admittance. In fact, and bizarrely, the Chinese seat continued to be held by the Kuomintang, despite their exile from the Chinese mainland.[15]

Sir Benegal Narsing Rau, an eminent jurist, served as the Indian ambassador to the UN as well as being the president of the Security Council. Without consulting Nehru, Rau voted in favour of the American resolution. He hardly had time to telegram or telephone New Delhi.[16] As president of the Council, Rau was familiar with the legal issues around Korea. India was also a key member of the United Nations Temporary Commission on Korea (UNTCOK)—established in 1948 to oversee free and fair elections—where K.P.S. Menon served as the unanimously elected chairman. Also, as recounted in Shiv Dayal's excellent book on the crisis—by far the most detailed from an Indian perspective—unknown to Nehru, Rau was in contact with an Indian delegate to the Commission based in Seoul, who provided an eyewitness account of the North's aggression, helping the ambassador make his quick decision.[17] Either way, and as the prime minister later told his envoy, he had made the right call.[18] Nehru was absolutely certain that 'the North Korean Government had committed aggression on a large scale on South Korea'.[19] However, from here on, he urged Rau not to commit India 'further in any way without reference' [to New Delhi].'[20]

Two primary conditions exercised Nehru and informed India's approach throughout much of the crisis. First, Nehru fully understood that the North's aggression, the US-led response and Truman's unwillingness to recognise the PRC could draw the latter to war on the side of North Korea. So far, the North had served as a necessary buffer between the Western-supported regime in Seoul and the PRC. Limiting the scope of the war, according to the prime minister, could be achieved by admitting the PRC to the UN as a permanent member. He said so to both Stalin and Acheson soon after the outbreak of hostilities.[21] As a member of the UN, the PRC, at least according to Nehru, would be given a voice, and consequently, encouraged to take a less hostile position.[22]

Second, the idea was to push the cause of reconciliation. As he told his friend Thakin Nu, also known as Un Nu, Burma's first prime minister, there was always a 'slight chance' for 'mediation'.[23] To journalists, he openly declared that 'India can offer her good offices for mediation', but 'only if requested to do so.'[24] By this token, India would also serve as a messenger between Communist China and the US. To maintain measure and play its part as an interlocutor, it was imperative not to 'fall in line' with the US.[25] Further, it was essential that India did not get 'hustled' into what could very easily turn into a US-led war in the Far East.[26] The aim was to judge events 'as objectively as possible', and not be 'swept away by passion'. This would be hard. It was, as Nehru well understood, 'a frightfully difficult matter to try to balance oneself on the edge of a sword'.[27]

The Second Resolution

On 27 June, another US-backed resolution was passed in the Security Council. It called on member states to 'furnish such assistance' to the Republic of Korea as required to 'repel the armed attack'.[28] India abstained. Rau was again unable to telephone New Delhi in time to discuss the text, although, even if he had, Nehru's advice, as the prime minister later wrote, would have been to practise caution, and so to abstain.[29] While Nehru did not have much of a problem with the text of the second resolution, he took issue with the context in which it had been tabled by the Americans. In a statement, Truman had connected the attack upon Korea to 'Communism's' apparent determination to occupy Formosa. He even ordered the US Seventh Fleet to prepare for such an attack, increased military assistance to the government in the Philippines and stressed the need for a peace settlement with Japan.[30] As far as Nehru was concerned, this was an 'exceedingly maladroit' approach that had every potential to drag India into a US-led war against China, its neighbour.[31] What is more, Nehru was aware that on 19 June the US Senate Foreign Relations Committee had passed an Appropriations Bill authorising the use of funds to contain the PRC. There was little doubt that Formosa was very much on the minds of the American executive as well as the legislature.[32]

Still, Nehru did not want to isolate the United States. On 29 June, following consultations with the prime minister—who in turn discussed this in the Cabinet—Rau accepted the 27 June resolution. However, in his statement, he made clear that the government of India 'earnestly hope[d]' for mediation, opposed the use of force in the first instance to resolve the conflict and, most importantly, highlighted that there was to be no 'modification' of India's foreign policy. Notwithstanding India's votes in the Security Council, it would remain 'friendly' with all countries.[33] The statement, as Nehru told Pandit, was designed to 'satisfy' the US and the UK while maintaining 'balance' to 'act as we chose'.[34] Accordingly, India refused to contribute military forces to what came to be called the 'Unified Command' under General MacArthur's charge. Instead, it offered a field ambulance unit consisting of around 300 officers and soldiers.[35]

For Raymond Hare, the US assistant secretary of state for Near Eastern and South Asian affairs, this was all good news. Hare read India's statement as the 'manifestation' of a 'more positive foreign policy', or one more closely aligned with US interests. In a note to Acheson, he asked the secretary of state not to be perturbed by the statement that accompanied India's acceptance of the second resolution. Hare was operating under the assumption that the US should not 'worry about public statements' but should focus 'only on actions'. This is what Bajpai had told American officials. Accordingly, Hare suggested that India was on the US side, even reporting that during a visit to Burma and South East Asia Nehru had launched an all-out attack against communism in Indonesia and warned against the threat of forcing socialism in Burma—in this respect, the prime minister was thought to have served American 'interests admirably'.[36] Henderson, however, did not quite see it this way. On 28 June, the ambassador visited Nehru to explain the US positions on both resolutions. The prime minister forcefully argued that Truman's statement greatly complicated matters. India would not support issues linked to Formosa, which it believed could drive China to war.[37]

At this time, and as far as Acheson was concerned, neither Hare nor Henderson's views on India were particularly significant.[38] India's support in the UN was important to mobilise Asia's vote of confidence,[39] but the thought of dealing with Nehru on a one-on-one basis or as a potential mediator was not yet considered. Indeed, while Nehru pushed Acheson to allow the PRC 'to take their seat in the Council',[40] the latter had little time for what he read as naïve and ill-considered suggestions by a statesman he found irksome. Indeed, Truman's statement of 27 June, while discussed in advance with Attlee, was not once considered worth sharing with Rau.[41] The suggestion of using India as a courier to reach out to China emerged only towards the end of July.[42]

The China Question

Nehru's views on China were shaped as early as the 1920s, but they had little to do with communism. At the time, Nehru was much more taken by the nationalist fervour of Chiang Kai-shek, who had taken charge of the Kuomintang following Sun Yat-sen's demise in 1925. Nehru was convinced that India and China had 'much in common'.[43] He was massively impressed by the strong Chinese representation at the International Congress against Colonialism in Brussels in 1927. They had 'energy' and 'driving force', and could serve with India as the 'battle fronts against imperialism'.[44] Mao Zedong's triumph and the establishment of the People's Republic on 1 October 1949 did not once shake Nehru.[45] The fact was that China had 'huge mass with strength in it', and by virtue of this alone was 'destined to making a difference to Asia'.[46] Nehru predicted that if the 'UN endures', China will 'come in'. Hence it was in India's interest to take 'advantage of a suitable opening'.[47] Apart from Burma, India was the first non-communist country to recognise the PRC.[48]

Unlike Truman, Nehru was certain that communism did not in itself tie the PRC to Russia. As he often confessed in anguish to his sister, it was a 'complete misunderstanding of the Chinese situation' to think of the PRC as a 'satellite state of Russia'.[49] This was a fallacy weakly grounded in historical reality. Chinese nationalism was distinct from its communist philosophy, a point that became far clearer to the rest of the world in the early 1960s, when Mao branded Soviet communism as revisionist. Indeed, during Mao's first visit to Moscow in December 1949, Stalin barely acknowledged his presence.[50] For his part, and as Arne Westad puts it, Stalin doubted 'the authenticity of Chinese Communist leaders'.[51] Nehru understood this. These philosophical guidelines shaped Nehru's approach as war broke in the Korean Peninsula. In this, he was supported by Clement Atlee's government, which also recognised China, but in turn was rebuffed by the PRC because of Britain's recognition of Formosa. In fact, regular and fortnightly reports drafted on behalf of Krishna Menon, the Indian high commissioner to the UK, made clear that Attlee would work closely with Nehru to push Truman away from issues linked to Formosa.[52] India, according to Menon, could leverage the 'calm attitude' in Britain that promised to serve as a 'stabilising influence'. Also, Attlee's government simply could not afford the economic danger posed by another world war.[53] In many ways, the following story is about India as mediator, with Britain as its supporter, and China and America as the sharply divided protagonists.

In August 1950, the Soviet Union returned to the UN. The Soviet representative—Yakov Alexandrovich Malik—assumed the presidency of the Security Council. Almost immediately, Malik, supported by India, tabled a resolution against the presence of nationalist China in the Security Council. It was summarily defeated.[54] Apart from the fact that the American delegation was not going to budge on the question of the PRC's admittance, both Rau and Nehru quickly realised that the Korean issue was bound to become embroiled in superpower contest. With a view to creating the space for middle ground, Rau suggested setting-up an informal committee that could engage all parties—including North Korea and the PRC—without the risk of official reprimand. While a noteworthy idea, it did not evoke much support from Warren Austin, the US ambassador to the UN. This, for Nehru, was a deal-breaker. American support, according to the prime minister, was critical—if this was not forthcoming, 'no practical benefit' could be realised.[55] Nye records the same: the high commissioner told Ernest Bevin, the British foreign secretary, that Indian actions made clear that India supports the fundamental idea underlying the UN—that of reconciliation—but this meant working with the US. However, he also warned that India's position should not be taken for granted. It was 'restive', and a lot would depend on the way the UN and the US chose to deal with the PRC. In this, 'Nehru's line is perfectly clear.'[56]

Interestingly, Nehru's approach had much less to do with what scholars often misunderstand to be his apparent anti-Western outlook and much more to do with the adoption of prudent strategies. There was no doubt in his mind that the 'matter' of the PRC 'ha[d] to be kept in the forefront',[57] but the reality was that only the Americans could admit Communist China into the UN. He understood this all too well. Accordingly, at every given opportunity, Pandit engaged American officials, including Dulles, Dean Rusk and George McGhee. Undeterred by their belief that non-alignment was an 'unrealistic' approach,[58] she doggedly presented the case for admitting China while outlining the potential role India could play in this process.[59] These conversations went some way in convincing State Department officials that India's policy in the UN had little to do with Russia, ideology or anti-Americanism. The vote on Malik's resolution might have led to critical reporting in the American press, which it did, but overall India's stance was seen as one designed to limit the conflict. As McGhee put it, greater consultation was of paramount importance, and 'should be a two-way street'.[60]

The 38th Parallel

By the third week of September, the merits and demerits of consultation were tested. On 21 September, K.M. Panikkar, historian, former diwan of Bikaner and the Indian ambassador to Beijing, met with General

Nieh Jung-Chen, the Chinese chief of Army Staff. In a telegram to Bajpai, the ambassador stated that, according to Chen, 'China could no longer remain patient.' In a second telegram, also sent on the 21st, Panikkar reported a conversation with Zhou Enlai, the PRC's first premier and foreign minister. Zhou argued that since the 'United Nations claims to have no obligation towards us [PRC] we also have none to them.' Both these telegrams were shown by Bajpai to Nye, who sent them to the CRO to forward on to Acheson. There was little doubt, as Nye argued, that China had decided on a 'more aggressive policy'.[61] In Delhi, Nye, and later Bajpai, shared the contents with Henderson.[62] For the most part, American officials were in a state of disbelief. They could not accept that the PRC might actually intervene. Despite Zhou's forewarning, there was no attempt to reach out to India.[63] Further, advances on the battlefield and within the UN gave American officials little reason to force the issue with India.

By September UN forces had largely routed the North Korean invaders. A decision needed to be taken whether or not UN forces could cross the 38th parallel and hence take the war to the North. Two draft resolutions were discussed in the First Committee of the General Assembly. The first, the so-called eight-power resolution—mooted by the UK—suggested setting-up a Peace Observation Council to consider elections in a unified Korea, making provisos for holding an emergency session of the Assembly, and called on member states to contribute armed units.[64] Known as the 'Uniting for Peace' resolution, it was adopted in the Assembly on 3 November.[65] The second, which came to be called the five-power resolution, was co-sponsored by the Soviet Union. It called for the cessation of hostilities, withdrawal of all foreign forces and for elections to be held under the auspices of the UN.[66] It did not pass; Rau rejected both resolutions.

Despite explanations provided by Bevin and Nye, who were in turn asked by Rusk to discuss the draft with India, Bajpai made clear that the UK-sponsored resolution invariably made allowances for crossing the 38th parallel, and hence could not be supported.[67] For Nehru, this was a 'misconceived' move.[68] Austin and his team at the UN also understood that 'Indian reluctance' was rooted in the belief that China may well intervene if UN forces crossed the 38th parallel,[69] but they themselves refused to take this threat seriously. As for the five-power resolution, Nehru and Rau were uneasy about the suggestion of withdrawing all foreign forces, which would no doubt serve the interests of North Korea, leaving them to return to the South if the opportunity arose. Also, Nehru suspected that despite his public stance, Stalin did not at this time want the PRC to enter the UN.[70] Instead, and in an effort to break the deadlock between the two parties, Rau suggested creating a sub-committee to work through the wording of both resolutions to find common ground. Seen simply as a means to delay the decision to cross the 38th parallel, the Indian draft was soon discarded.[71] It was defeated by a margin of thirty-two to twenty-four, primarily because of 'US lobbying against the resolution.'[72]

Unmoved by American scepticism with regard to Zhou's message, Nehru pressed the Chinese premier to 'exercise patience and restraint'. He made clear that America's approach had been 'wrong', but also argued that at least the UK had 'definitely come around'.[73] To Bevin, Nehru made a strong plea to consider Panikkar's messages. 'Any attempt,' the prime minister wrote, to 'cross the 38th parallel will convince them [China] that such invasion is imminent and they will react accordingly.'[74] The correspondence with Bevin, along with Nye's approach to the CRO in support of Nehru's cautionary notes, appeared to have had some effect on the US.[75] At the end of September, Acheson asked Bevin in turn to request Nehru to reach out to Zhou. The Chinese had protested the American-led bombing of parts of Manchuria, and Acheson was keen to make sure that China understood this to be an accident and offered to make informal arrangements for an investigation.[76] For the first time, India's position as a mediator was taken seriously, even though all of the mediation and correspondence was to be conducted through 'British channels'.[77] America could hardly be seen by its frenzied public to have directly approached the Communists. As William Head put it, Truman and Acheson understood the 'futility' of non-recognition but were restricted by domestic circumstances.[78]

Both British and American officials were highly suspicious of Panikkar.[79] Truman himself argued that Panikkar's warning was nothing more than 'the relay of communist propaganda'. It was a 'bold attempt' by Zhou to 'blackmail the UN'.[80] British officials in Washington argued that caution needed to be observed as there was no way of cross-checking Panikkar's reporting.[81] Nye himself urged Bevin to keep in mind that the 'somewhat alarmist reports' by Panikkar were what had informed 'Nehru's policy'.[82] During a meeting between Y.D. Gundevia, the Indian ambassador to Switzerland, and Nye, the latter even said: 'I have just returned from London, and I am told that your man Panikkar in Beijing is trying to panic the world but our reliable information is that there is nothing in it.'[83] Nehru himself readily accepted that Panikkar, although 'a man of extraordinarily acute intelligence', was given to 'overshoot the mark.'[84] He insinuated to Nye that Panikkar was perhaps a bit too sensitive for his own good,[85] but the fact remained that even if 25 per cent of what the ambassador in Beijing said was true, then that should be considered a matter of urgent concern.[86] After all, if China was to clash with UN forces, it would 'become impossible to localise the conflict'.[87] On 30 September, paying little heed to India's counsel, Austin argued in favour of crossing the 38th parallel. He stated that the UN should remove the 'opportunities of new acts of aggression' by denying to 'aggressor forces' any 'refuge behind an imaginary line'.[88] On the same day, the 3rd Division of the South Korean Army made their way across the 38th parallel.[89]

On 3 October, and alarmed by Austin's arguments, Zhou once again told Panikkar that 'if the American army crosses [the] 38th parallel China will be forced to take immediate steps'. This would mean the 'enlargement of the war'.[90] Doing its part to localise the conflict, India made clear that it would not support any diplomatic move that even hinted at crossing the 38th parallel.[91] On 7 October, India voted against a resolution to unify Korea.[92] On 10 October, India voted against another resolution that asked UN member states to reserve some forces for contribution to the Korean affair.[93] Finally, the External Affairs Ministry put out a statement underlining the need to give peace a second chance. It asked concerned parties to invite North Korea to cease hostilities and offer the hand of cooperation.[94] These initiatives, it would appear, had no bearing on events whatsoever. US Secretary of Defence George C. Marshall authorised MacArthur to 'feel unhampered' to 'proceed north'.[95] Accordingly, on 7 October, the US First Cavalry Division joined their South Korean allies.

In response, Mao, in his capacity as chairman of the Chinese People's Revolutionary Military Commission, ordered the North East Border Defence Army to be turned into the Chinese People's Volunteers (CPV). They were to 'move immediately into the territory of Korea' to 'repel the invasion launched by the American imperialists and their running dogs'.[96] A day later, Zhou flew to Moscow to secure Soviet assistance.

On 19 October, CPV troops made their way across the Yalu River. Within a fortnight, South Korean troops were evicted from areas near the Yalu and 15,000 were killed.[97] As expected by Nehru, in the beginning of November, Chinese troops were found engaging UN forces. Indeed, as one American National Intelligence Estimate (NIE) put it, the fighting had been accompanied by the 'marked stiffening of North Korean resistance'. There was no doubt that the 'immediate occasion' of the PRC's entry had to do with the 'crossing of the 38th parallel by US forces'.[98] By 10 November, the CIA reported that some 30,000–40,000 Chinese troops were stationed south of the Korean–Manchuria border.[99] Within a fortnight, by 24 November, this number had increased to 300,000. As McArthur was forced to point out, the US-led UN forces now faced 'an entirely new war'.[100]

Paradoxically, as Kux argues, 'being right about the Chinese intervention won Nehru no friends in the US press or in the American leadership'.[101] The fact, according to Chester Bowles, was that 'no one took him [Nehru] seriously'.[102] Moreover, India's vote against the eight-power resolution, combined with Nehru's refusal to look upon China as aggressor, turned American opinion sharply against both India and the prime minister. As McMahon argues, none of this did anything for the US–India relationship.[103] *The New York Times* stated that Nehru had been 'obstructive'; he had followed a policy of 'appeasement' and he represented the 'voice of abnegation'.[104] *The Sunday Times* in Britain stated that Nehru's approach was designed to 'placate Russia'. He was 'bargain[ing] with the devil', and this in turn had lost him the 'good will of the United States'.[105] Nehru was called a 'hypersensitive egoist', branded a 'socialist' with 'deep-rooted suspicions of our [American] capitalist economy and its intentions in Asia'.[106] Truman allegedly even told a congressman that 'Nehru has sold us [the US] down the Hudson. His attitude has been responsible for our losing the war in Korea.'[107]

Much of this anger was understandable. As McGhee pointed out, 'America liked to be liked' and was not 'used to open criticism from friendly countries'.[108] Yet, apart from McGhee and the more vocal State Department officials, American insiders themselves began to recognise the advantages of working with India. Those on the China desk had previously argued that the 'Indian position [on China] should be taken into consideration'.[109] It was 'evident', according to these officials, that India wanted a 'viable solution'. Rather than distancing the delegation in the UN, it would help to give it more 'responsibility for working on the problem'. During the debate on the 38th parallel, they even suggested adhering to Nehru's advice and sending across only South Korean forces, which Zhou would find less threatening than MacArthur's army.[110] In time, India also reached out. In the third week of October, B.V. Keskar, the Indian deputy foreign minister, met with American officials to explain exactly why India had chosen not to support the eight-power resolution.[111] Bajpai anguished over Nehru's critical utterances against the US, but urged Henderson to look at India's actions rather than focus on words.[112] For his own part, Nehru asked Rau not to be 'affected' by the 'spate of hysterical' attacks against him and India. What mattered was working for cooperation in the UN, which meant dealing with the US at close quarters. It was imperative that Indian officials were not influenced even in the 'slightest by this exhibition of immature mentality'.[113] Pushed by Pandit, who in turn was pressed by McGhee, Nehru even agreed to meet with Henderson more often.[114]

Nehru's approach up to this point thus disproves the casual analysis of Indian strategic behaviour during this period as one informed by its so-called imperial hangover, where anything American is said to have been considered immediately suspect.[115] Indeed, the Indian response to the outbreak of the Korean War was action-based, and not a case of 'fence-sitting', an all-too convenient charge that has little or no basis in reality.[116] In turn, and as should be clear, Indian manoeuvres—as suggested by some—had nothing to do with forging an alliance-like relationship with the Truman White House. In part, India's cautious but thoughtful approach was shaped by the consistently clear idea that siding with the United States would ultimately mean opposition to the PRC, India's immediate neighbour.

Indian decisions were motivated by Indian interests. This was difficult for American officials to grasp. As *The Daily Telegraph* put it, it was 'not always so easy to sympathise' with Nehru's attitude 'in practice'. Refusal to take sides, but instead to invest in and develop India's own position on the merits of the case was an approach that was out of step with the realities of the time. For most Western observers, the only explanation lay in considering this as a sort of 'naïve lack of realism'.[117] It would seem that present-day commentators also accept this popular but weakly grounded analysis. Yet India developed its own agency and reasoning, something that at first irked American officials, but which, as the follow-

61

ing section shows, they soon came to grasp, albeit reluctantly. In some ways, and as Ramakrishna Reddy points out, 'there was more realism than idealism' when it came to India's positions in the UN.[118]

Working the UN

At the end of November, a Chinese delegation set forth for New York. It was the first time the PRC was to be directly heard in the UN. Lester Pearson, the Canadian foreign minister, reached out to Nehru. He urged the prime minister to call publicly for a ceasefire. Nehru, according to Pearson, had 'consistently' pushed the case for peace,[119] and was perhaps the only public figure that could influence the Americans as well as the Chinese. The prime minister, following consultations with the newly formed Foreign Affairs Committee of the Cabinet, declined. Quiet diplomacy, according to Indian officials, had a better chance of giving substance to a potential ceasefire proposal.[120] Accordingly, Nehru's first move was to contact Bevin. A ceasefire would be that much more acceptable to the Chinese, the prime minister thought, if it came with the promise of entry to the UN.[121] Also, he was well aware of India's limitations. Attlee's support would be essential to 'make a difference' if Acheson and his coterie were to be moved.[122]

Second, he wrote to Bajpai—it was essential to get both the US and the UK delegations on board before any proposal could be taken to the Chinese.[123] This would not be easy. Just as Rau was mandated to make a case for an acceptable ceasefire proposal, the US and the UK sought to adopt their own resolution branding China an aggressor. If this proposal were introduced, Nehru made clear to Rau that India should vote against it,[124] but in the meantime, it was important to be as in touch with American officials as possible.[125] Indeed, it was far easier for Rau to be in contact with Austin than with Wu Hsiu-Chuan, the PRC's lead negotiator at the UN. Despite previously made appointments on 28 and 30 November, Wu reneged on meeting Rau. The Indian ambassador was convinced that Russia had much to do with this.[126]

On 1 December, Rau finally met with Wu and alerted him about the Indian initiative. Wu, according to British officials, was encouraged. To make sure that nothing was lost in communication, Nehru requested Panikkar to explain India's plan to Zhou in Beijing,[127] while he kept Henderson informed in Delhi.[128] At the General Assembly, Rau lobbied member states to support what came to be called the thirteen-power resolution. At the centre of this resolution was the suggestion of a cease-fire committee made up of three representatives to advise the United Nations Command in Korea. Both Truman and Attlee were on board. In fact, Truman told congressmen that the US and India were exchanging information on a regular basis; he was seemingly enthralled by India's active role. There was even some evidence of positive reporting in the press.[129]

Further, Rau introduced another draft resolution, supported by twelve member states, in the First Committee of the General Assembly to discuss 'the peaceful settlement of existing issues', which meant issues to do with Formosa, a key Chinese demand.[130] By introducing two resolutions, Rau had done what he thought was necessary to keep both sides of the divide satisfied. Indeed, Rau made sure to maintain equal contact with both the Chinese and the American delegates. On the American side, he often met with Ambassador Ernest Gross, the US deputy representative to the UN. From within the Chinese team, and apart from Wu, Rau kept in touch with Chiao Kuan-hua, a member of Wu's delegation, and someone who would play a key role in the armistice talks a few months down the line. At every stage, the Americans were kept informed of Indian manoeuvres. Details of the ceasefire proposal were discussed at every given opportunity, and finally led Gross to 'favour immediate consideration'. Rau achieved one of Nehru's central aims, to get America on side. Similarly, questions posed by Chiao with regard to the proposal were carried by Rau. The Americans, aware that India was doing all it could to influence the US delegation to consider discussing Formosa with the PRC, clearly acknowledged the value of India's role as mediator.[131]

In turn, even faint accolades for India from the American administration could well have discouraged Chinese support. To make sure that the Chinese were not put off by Indian cooperation with the US, Rau told Wu that India would either abstain from any American-backed resolution condemning China or push for amendments. These would include working towards an agreeable framework to discuss Formosa, a key Russian and Chinese demand,[132] which had been rejected by the US and the UK.[133] At the same time, Nehru understood that Wu's demand for a 'complete withdrawal' of foreign forces from both Korea and Formosa was a deal-breaker for Acheson and Bevin.[134] Indeed, Nehru also disagreed with such a hasty withdrawal policy. He sketched out these arguments in what was perhaps the most detailed message to Panikkar to date. These were to be treated as guidelines for the ambassador's upcoming discussions with Zhou.[135]

On 11 December, Panikkar met with the Chinese premier. For Zhou, the most important aspect of the Indian proposal had to do with Formosa. Yet while he was seemingly appreciative of Indian advances, he plainly argued that nothing could be achieved without American support. Zhou repeated this 'three times'. Also, suggesting a slight softening in the PRC's stance, he said that China has its 'door open' for 'direct negotiations'. This was a significant development,[136] and was immediately intimated to Rau in New York.[137]

For the time being, and despite the lack of American support for any debate on Formosa, it looked as though India's well-positioned and delicate approach was paying dividends. Zhou had for the first time indicated a willingness to negotiate, while the promise of a ceasefire was at least considered by all sides. On 12 December, both the Indian and the US-backed resolutions—the latter condemning China—were tabled in the General Assembly. While the US resolution was adopted only in early 1951, the former was accepted forty-eight hours later. On 14 December, the Iranian president of the Assembly, N. Entezam, announced that a three-member committee would be constituted 'to determine the basis on which a satisfactory ceasefire' could be arranged. It was to be staffed by himself, Pearson and Rau. Yet this diplomatic victory was quickly blunted by its condemnation from the Communist quarter. Malik, the head Soviet delegate, argued that the Indian-sponsored resolution would provide a much-needed 'breathing spell' for MacArthur's bleeding forces.[138] On 22 December, Zhou even branded the thirteen-power resolution as 'illegal', undermining any hope for an immediate ceasefire.

On one level, it would appear that not much was achieved by India's politicking at the UN. Frustrated by the British-supported effort to condemn China and the American refusal to discuss Formosa, Nehru stated to Attlee that there was an 'utter lack of understanding, especially in the United States, of present conditions'. Chinese non-admission to the UN only antagonised China rather than 'weakened' her.[139] However, in hindsight, India's efforts were in fact useful in at least three ways. First, Panikkar's meetings made clear that Zhou was open to negotiation, something the Americans would not have been able to grasp as quickly as they did if it had not been for the line of communication opened by India. Second, ideas around a ceasefire were, at the very least, beginning to be considered, again something that would not have happened given the American determination to brand China as an aggressor.[140] Rau's efforts had provided forceful counter-offers in favour of conciliation to the largely condemnatory nature of discussions at the UN. These efforts in fact pushed Acheson to outline the parameters of a future ceasefire and demilitarisation proposal.[141] Lastly, despite Communist criticism of Rau and the thirteen-power resolution, it positioned India as a significant player in a complicated and gradual process towards an eventual truce. Indeed, India maintained its poise despite considerable pressure from the Truman White House, which, although impressed by India's efforts, remained embittered by Nehru's stance on recognising China. This was fully revealed in the concluding stages of negotiations for a food assistance bill advocated by Henderson. The following section shows how India dealt with an issue of national need while following its own approach—undeterred by American interests and demands—in foreign affairs.

Negotiating for Food

On 11 June 1951, the US Congress passed the Emergency Food Act Bill authorising the government to extend a loan of $1.9 million for the purchase of 2 million tonnes of American grain. Four days later, the bill was signed into law by Truman.[142] Nehru welcomed this 'generous gesture' and argued that it was initiatives like this that would 'bring the two people nearer'.[143] Yet, despite the offer of relief, which began to reach India as early as August, negotiating the bill aggravated both US and Indian officials. For Nehru, two chief considerations needed to be borne in mind: first, that the food negotiations were treated as a process completely separate from India's position with regards to Korea; and second, to make sure that the American legislation would in no way interfere with India's domestic affairs. In this, India achieved both her objectives.

In the summer of 1950, just as the Korean War broke, the requirement for food became all that more potent. Floods in Northern Bihar, heavy rains in West Bengal, an earthquake in Assam, drought in Orissa and the failure of monsoons in the south left India with a deficit of around 4 million tonnes of grain.[144] On 16 December, Pandit made a formal request to the State Department for food assistance. For his part, McGhee placed his weight behind the request. He pushed Truman to think of it as a fight for democracy—in India—to withstand 'communist domination'.[145] On 15 February, the bill was introduced in the House and the Senate. From the outset, Pandit made it clear that 'the hymn of hate against India' continued at a 'high pitch'. A large portion of the American press and legislators remained cognisant of India's positioning in the UN. They were 'devoted to arguments in support of rejecting' India's request.[146]

In the House, the Foreign Relations Committee did not see how its assistance would safeguard America's 'defence or general welfare'. Republican representatives made it clear that the US 'cannot do charity'.[147] Democratic senators too showed little consideration, holding the Indian government responsible for the 'man made' crisis.[148] Former officials pushed India to 'shed illusions against the US' and instead enter into defence pacts with it.[149] In addition, officials in charge of economic cooperation stated that 'aid should be given in fullest measure to those who are demonstrably on our [American] side [in the Korean War] and willing to fight for it'.[150] Correspondence between Henderson and Acheson indicates that the release of aid to India was directly connected to its stance on the ongoing war.[151] Henderson made sure that Bajpai understood this.[152]

Yet, rather than buckling under pressure, India's posture in the UN grew increasingly taxing for Acheson and Austin. In February, India voted against the British-backed proposal to brand China an aggressor nation.[153] It also abstained in a vote to impose an arms embargo against the PRC and North Korea.[154] Moreover, Nehru maintained that China should be brought 'into the picture'.[155] Disappointed and anguished, Henderson reported that Nehru did not 'express any hopes on the subject [of food aid] or any appreciation of the efforts on India's behalf of the United States'.[156] Nehru remained unmoved by what might be considered the politics of leverage.

In May, the State Department released a large amount of emergency supplies at discounted rates, including the use of thirteen ships which were diverted from travelling to Italy.[157] To Henderson's annoyance (although he had expected such a move),[158] India was also offered 100,000 metric tonnes of rice from the PRC, which ultimately could not be transported.[159] Grating American sensitivities, and following slow and tiresome negotiations, India accepted 50,000 tonnes of wheat-on-cash basis from Russia. It also concluded an agreement by which India would barter jute and tea for an additional 100,000 tonnes of Russian wheat.[160] While Nehru publicly thanked the US for urgent supplies, he openly indicated that India would investigate all avenues for assistance. Notwithstanding the relatively small amount of combined grain sold by the two Communist countries, the message was clear: India would not be hemmed-in.

Further, Congressional pressure to attach conditions to the bill steadily grew. In March, the House of Representatives Rules Committee placed a hold on a vote to consider these conditions.[161] In April, Republican senators stressed that the distribution of grain should be supervised by US officials. They also stressed that part-repayment was to be made in exchange for strategic materials, while a part of the loan was to be put aside for development projects within India. For Nehru, these drafts came as a 'shock'.[162] To some extent, he was taken aback by what he considered America's somewhat ham-fisted policies, but equally, he was annoyed with his sister in Washington. He could not understand why the embassy had not acted quicker to stop conditions from being attached. These would, in Nehru's perhaps exaggerated opinion, lead India to be treated as a 'semi-colonial country' or 'at least a satellite' of the US.[163] Even relatively minor conditions, such as affording diplomatic status to US observers, were to be removed. After all, this could limit Indian 'sovereignty'.[164]

In Washington, McGhee, Pandit's principal contact during much of this time, highlighted that most of the conditions were standard affixations to Congressional bills.[165] For India, this did not fly. This was a nation persuaded by the uniqueness of its own imperatives. While Nehru was convinced that McGhee and his team were doing everything possible to assist India, and that both they and the Congress did not necessarily mean to rebuff Indian advances, it was important to make sure that even the mere possibility of any binding conditions did not apply to India. In the end, Nehru did not want to 'embarrass' the Truman administration further with what even he considered far-reaching and highly unusual Indian attitudes. He simply asked Acheson to provide a letter underlining that nothing in the bill would 'interfere' or 'influence' India's foreign or domestic policy. He agreed to the provision regarding US observers, but only in exchange for grain provided by the US. He also agreed to the setting up of a Special Fund for Development, but only on the condition that this was to be overseen and utilised according to India's demands.[166] On their part, US officials accepted Nehru's revised demands. In an exchange with Bajpai, McGhee wrote that the 'language of the agreement need not go beyond the provisions of the legislation'. He made sure to add that the 'United States assistance did not constitute an attempt to dictate India's foreign and domestic policy.'[167] Interestingly, much of this had been scripted in advance by Rajagopalachari, who played a key role in ironing out the differences on this potent issue.[168]

American records suggest that Nehru's approach had much to do with protecting Indian sovereignty from America's supposed economic and imperialistic hubris. This was, according to both officials and historians, a direct result of the recently fought anti-colonial struggle. To a large extent this is of course true. India's grating and almost pedantic approach was connected to the pervasive memory of economic domination. Giving credence to this line of argument, Nehru often spoke of maintaining India's 'self-respect' and 'freedom of action'.[169] He repeatedly told C. Deshmukh (the finance minister and someone who pushed for US aid)[170] and Pandit that India would not accept a deal with 'political strings'.[171] In Parliament, he made a strong, even emotional, case to 'avoid dependence'.[172] Officials argued that India's 'chief enemy' was 'not communism but Western imperialism'.[173] Newspaper editorials likewise highlighted the need to shield India's 'freedom'.[174] This was a matter of charged debate. For the most part, it was authored in what might be considered the popular language of a vividly post-colonial script.

Nonetheless, what commentators and officials fail to report is that this was not about blanket anti-Americanism, or unqualified impracticality. It was about disaggregating the Korean matter from that of domestic need. Following the passage of the bill in June, Nehru recalled how it was perhaps 'unnecessary' to force issues on a clause-by-clause basis with the State Department, but at the same time, this was 'no easy matter' for India.[175] It was the first of many such agreements that India would need to negotiate. At a time when jingoistic talk of alliances against communism consumed America, it was crucial to distinguish India's approach publicly, and even unfeelingly, in foreign affairs from the mere possibility of attachment. This of course also worked in America's favour, as India evolved dispassionate initiatives at the

UN. Indeed, in early 1951, an NSC directive—98/1—too recognised the importance of India. It made clear that 'the loss of India to the Communist orbit would mean that for all practical purposes all of Asia will have been lost'.[176] Although brief, this was clearly a powerful argument for working closely with India.

Changing Faces and an Indian Resolution

On 1 November 1951, Chester Bowles presented his credentials to President Rajendra Prasad. Soon after, he met with Nehru. Much to the new ambassador's regret, he 'saw that the Prime Minister was falling asleep'. The meeting lasted all of fifteen minutes. His second meeting, however, was alive to the issues that tickled Bowles' imagination. Nehru argued that 'sooner or later, the Chinese would break loose' from Russia.[177] Unlike Henderson, Bowles was not only receptive, but in fact advocated similar lines of argumentation in Washington.[178] He quietly accepted that the prime minister was 'right' about Korea and Zhou's warning not to cross the Yalu River.[179] No wonder, then, that Acheson soon saw his envoy as a 'pest' and a 'pro-Indian enthusiast'.[180] Nehru acknowledged the latter, and was convinced that Bowles was 'desirous of good relations between China and America'.[181]

Within India, this was a period marked by the confirmation of continuity. The first General Assembly elections took place between October 1951 and March 1952. As was expected, the Congress won 364 out of 489 parliamentary seats in the Lok Sabha, or the Lower House. With 173 million voters and around seventy registered political parties, the Congress' return was, as Gopal recounts, a 'personal referendum in Nehru's favour'.[182]

On the ground in Korea, a stalemate had taken root. Frustrated by Washington's inability to find a political solution, MacArthur openly threatened the PRC and repeatedly hinted at again crossing the 38th parallel. Such statements, as Truman himself put it, were 'unauthorised and unexpected'. The differences between the ageing general and his political masters were acute. Finally, on 11 April 1951, Truman dismissed MacArthur. Lieutenant General Ridgway, a paratrooper, took charge.[183] For Nehru, this decision, while a welcome move, was better dealt with from the backseat. At this point, China, in his opinion, had little appetite for anything new.[184] Indeed, India lay low for more than a year,[185] refusing to commit troops or military assistance to the UN Command unless an armistice agreement was reached.[186] Formal negotiations between the competing sides only began on 8 July 1951, and ended on 27 July 1953, when a truce was finally agreed upon.

In the spring of 1952, Zhou reached out to Panikkar. The PRC made official complaints about the United States' supposed use of bacteriological material in Allied operations. The Chinese premier invited India, along with Burma and Indonesia, to investigate the charges. Nehru refused. Seen to be siding with the PRC would, in his view, 'entangle' India.[187] Unbeknown to Nehru, this was a prudent step. Despite India's earlier initiatives to reconcile East–West differences, American diplomats in South Asia maintained that India had 'shut its eyes to communism.'[188] Further, and well understood by Nehru, a new opening with America appeared possible. The idea was to capitalise on the post-MacArthur era, and not be branded pro-Chinese even before the armistice talks gained ground. Nehru also enjoyed the confidence of Bowles and now a 67-year-old Eleanor Roosevelt—who spent thirty days in India in March. Widely known as the First Lady of the World, Mrs Roosevelt was an important ally to lobby American opinion in the UN.[189] She understood at once that India would make 'its own way and on its own strength', and would not be jostled.[190]

In May, the prime minister found a low-key and unofficial way to connect with Zhou. Pandit was in China heading an Indian cultural mission. Anthony Eden, foreign secretary to the new Conservative government in London, told Nehru that the 'crucial question' in negotiations had to do with the exchange of the prisoners of war (POWs). This was 'the sole stumbling block for peace'. The UN Command pushed for 'voluntary repatriations', while the Chinese were clear they wanted 'full repatriation'. The latter position, according to Nehru, had to do with the 15,000-plus Chinese POWs who did not want to repatriate.[191] This was out of 83,000 soldiers, according to Chinese accounts, held by UN forces.[192] Pandit was to interview both Mao and Zhou.[193] Moreover, she was to carry a letter by an unnamed source in America for the premier. It was authored by Acheson. The central message was straightforward: it read, 'The United States has no territorial designs against any other nation.' Acheson's anonymous communiqué appeared to have some effect. Following three meetings with Zhou, and a forty-minute talk with Mao, the latter asked Pandit to convince the US and the UK to reach a final settlement. Peace was on the cards.[194] Seizing the moment, Nehru asked Panikkar to investigate if the Chinese were amenable to a repatriation body run by neutral nations.[195] Encouraged by Mao's positive exchange with Pandit, for the first time, Nehru even pushed Panikkar to seek out suggestions from Zhou on India's behalf. Rather than the role of an interlocutor, the prime minister advocated a lead position in the tricky and potentially explosive issue of the POWs.[196] Equally, he kept in close touch with Bowles.

In July, and before he was able to get a reply from Zhou, Panikkar left his post for one in Egypt. In the autumn of 1952, Sir Narayanan Raghavan Pillai was appointed the new ambassador. Pandit too had moved from Washington to New York, where she headed the Indian delegation to the UN. In September, G.L. Mehta, the Gujarat-born LSE-graduate and former member of the Planning Commission, moved into the Indian ambassador's Georgian residence at 2700, Macomb Street. Purchased by Bajpai during the Second World War, it remains the official residence of the Indian ambassador to Washington.[197]

In Delhi, Bajpai reluctantly accepted the governorship of Bombay. Most importantly, having outstayed his welcome in London, Krishna Menon was given charge of Indian deliberations on Korea at the UN, leaving the high commission in London to B.G. Kher. This was a compromise formula. Menon declined a Cabinet post and the ambassadorship to Moscow. He refused to serve as Pandit's deputy, and was hence given the Korean portfolio by Nehru. As far as US officials were concerned, this was by far the most disheartening change of posts. They had not only lost a close ally in Bajpai, but would need to work intimately with a man widely considered as 'very anti-American'.[198] With all these changes, ripples in approach might have been expected, and there is no doubt that professional one-upmanship ultimately got the better of coordinated policy formulation. However, and despite Menon's new position, India and the US appeared to have reached a modicum of mutual appreciation, faint though this might have been.

In September, General W.K. Harrison, the blunt and bull-headed lead American delegate at the UN-sponsored armistice talks,[199] suggested a solution to the impasse between him and his Communist interlocutors. Rather than forcing the matter of repatriation, Harrison suggested asking neutral representatives to interview those who did not want to be immediately repatriated. As far as Nehru was concerned, this demonstrated a 'definite advance on the part of America'. He was not only convinced that there was a real desire for peace in Washington, but that India should do everything possible to convey this change of position to Zhou, which it did.[200] On 18 October, the Chinese premier met with the new Indian ambassador. Zhou presented Raghavan with an eight-page statement. Unmoved by Nehru's plea and Harrison's offer, he maintained that the PRC would like the repatriation of 'all' prisoners. However, interestingly, he suggested that the procedure for repatriation was up for discussion.[201] A 'limited compromise' was possible.[202] Yet, in the third week of October, the UK and the US floated what came to be called the 21-power draft resolution, stressing the need for voluntary repatriation. Soon after, an eleven-power draft backed by Russia made a case for unification under Soviet supervision.[203] These were, according to Menon, extreme stands that warranted a middle path.[204]

An Indian proposal, Nehru thought, if it was to convince both the US and the PRC, required the force of international law. Hence the prime minister referred to the clauses relating to repatriation in the 1949 draft of the Geneva Convention. Accordingly, he sketched-out guidelines for what would soon become an Indian resolution. Essentially, it made provisions for a 'protecting power' or a Neutral Powers Committee (Articles 8 and 13), internment of POWs who were still to decide on repatriation and a role for an 'umpire'—a term directly lifted from the Geneva text—or chief of Committee (Article 132). He asked Raghavan to discuss these guidelines with Zhou.[205] The ambassador made the case, but did not receive a reply. For Nehru, 'silence' did not automatically mean 'rejection'; it could have simply meant the inability to accept agreeable terms publicly.[206] Finally, Menon introduced the draft in the Political Committee on 19 November.[207]

The resolution was widely seen as a 'constructive move' to 'reconcile the two ideas' on repatriation forced by America and Russia. According to Pearson, then the president of the Assembly, India, and more specifically Menon, worked hard to produce a text 'perfectly acceptable to practically all delegations at the assembly'. Twenty-one parties to the earlier US proposal supported the Indian resolution. Despite Acheson's strong objections to the Indian formula for internment and the referral of uncommitted POWs to a committee,[208] America too supported India. Moreover, the resolution received the support of fifty-four other nations. Every Asian, Latin American and African state supported India. The resolution was endorsed by a majority of the members of the Assembly on 3 December. Much to Nehru's chagrin, Russia voted against it, while China abstained.[209] In Beijing, Raghavan was notified that the PRC could not accept even partial repatriation.[210] For Andrey Vyshinsky, the Soviet foreign minister, the Indian resolution was seen as having been 'artificially fabricated' to mask American language on repatriation.[211] In an official protest note, Zhou argued that India had in fact thrown its weight behind the US. The resolution's use of the term 'no forcible repatriation', according to Zhou, essentially meant 'voluntary repatriation', which had been rejected by the PRC. It deemed it an 'illegal resolution'.[212]

In the end, while the American delegation praised Indian efforts,[213] Russia and China branded India as pro-American. American elites may not have liked Menon, but in this case he had delivered. His efforts, while they peeved Pandit, who had little or no access to him during this time, and also Mehta, who was mostly kept in the dark, provided new ground for discussion having reconciled the erstwhile and sharply opposed points of view in the Assembly. British officials, aware of 'the kind of person he [Menon] is', made clear that he proved 'very useful' in New York.[214] As the following and final section of this chapter shows, India's dogged and tireless efforts came together in the final leg of negotiations. Importantly, it convinced the incoming Eisenhower administration that options were available in dealing with the thorny issue of repatriation.

Repatriation: The Final Leg

Following Vyshinsky's pointed criticism of the Indian resolution, Nehru understood that India was being 'driven to supporting' the US at the cost of its relationship with Russia and China.[215] Yet he refused to back down, or withdraw the Indian resolution.[216] This could, according to the prime minister, only reinforce the earlier impasse. He was not the only one thinking along these lines. On 7 May, China introduced its own eight-point proposal. The 'salient points', according to Zhou, were taken from the Indian resolution.[217] Further, T.N. Kaul, the Indian counsellor in Beijing, and Raghavan, were convinced that China's earlier abstention was due to Russian pressure. The PRC, it would appear, was keen to end the fighting,[218] but communicating this would not be easy.

Zhou was dealing with a new administration in Washington. Eisenhower not only won the elections, but carried thirty-nine states. His 'implacable', ever-powerful and now 65-year-old secretary of state,[219]

Dulles, something of a 'tree trunk of a man',[220] was known for his 'unbridled hatred of communism'.[221] This did not bode well for peace in Korea and the stalling armistice talks. Indeed, a fortnight after his inauguration, Eisenhower stated that the US could no longer guarantee the protection of mainland China from threats emanating in Taiwan. Republican officials even hinted at expanding military operations in Korea. Dulles made this point on several occasions to his British colleagues. Yet, and just as it looked as though peace was an objective buried in a new-found chauvinism in America, Zhou told Pearson that the PRC was ready to begin the repatriation process immediately after the cessation of hostilities. Unwilling POWs would be handed to a 'neutral state'.[222] This was, in many ways, the Indian prescription drafted by Nehru and Menon. Already, on India's initiation, both sides considered exchanging sick and wounded prisoners as a means to generate good will. Once again, Zhou used India's good offices to convey his agreeability to the US.[223] There was no doubt that India's past efforts were beginning to pay dividends.

Further, Ambassador Henry Cabot Lodge, the new head of the US delegation at the UN, made it a point to meet with Pandit as early as February. Revealingly, he made clear that Eisenhower's announcement about not being able to guarantee Taiwanese restraint was because of the 'many election promises' made by the president. He argued that the new administration did not want to do anything to 'further aggravate a delicate and dangerous situation'. Lodge highlighted that 'the key to peace in the East was in India's hands'.[224] British officials in Washington were convinced that the new administration was closely studying the Indian resolution. After all, the Chinese plan introduced in the General Assembly was much like the one floated by India, a point recognised by the new officials in the State Department.[225]

In the first week of May, Zhou told Raghavan that he had nominated India to head the Repatriation Committee. On 7 May, the MEA sent cables to all important Indian diplomatic posts indicating that it was ready to participate in this process.[226] On 26 May, Nehru made a public statement to the effect that the Chinese proposal was indeed akin to India's, and that the government was in touch with Beijing.[227] American negotiators made some noise about nominating Pakistan, but this turned out to be a ploy on General Harrison's part. Although he did nominate Pakistan, this was rejected by the PRC, as the US had anticipated.[228] As far as Nehru was concerned, both China and the US had finally come around.

Later in the month, Dulles visited India and met with Nehru. Despite disagreements about the so-called threat of communism, the prime minister appeared convinced that Eisenhower was determined to sign a truce. Unlike before, he agreed to provide Indian troops to man the repatriation camps and take charge of the Commission as a whole.[229] In the following months, and despite India having being excluded from a political conference on Korea, on the behest of President Syngman Rhee of South Korea, India made sure to maintain a sense for neutrality.

Finally, on 8 June 1953, the US and China signed a prisoner of war agreement. On 27 July, the 38th parallel was reset as the boundary between the North and the South. The irony was not lost on Bowles. He recalled how, two and a half years after the PRC intervened, America 'negotiated a peace on the very line that we [US] had three years earlier'.[230] India might not have been, as Krishna Menon argued, a central player in the road to peace,[231] but it was certainly an important and unique actor that the Eisenhower administration came to rely on.

A Neutral Nations Repatriation Commission was formally established on 10 September 1953 led by Lieutenant General K.S. Thimayya. It was supported by Sweden, Switzerland, Poland and Czechoslovakia. Notably, India was the only country—acceptable to both the US and the PRC—to provide a Custodial Force. By 24 September, the Indian Force took charge of 22,604 POWs from the UN Command, and 359 POWs from the CPV and the Korean People's Army Command. According to its terms of reference, the Commission was dissolved ninety days after its establishment at its 79th meeting on 21 February 1954.[232]

Conclusion

In 1950, the 13 acres of land identified by Henderson for a new American embassy was second in the choices offered by Indian officials. Britain had first refusal for embassy property in an international enclave developed in what was then a 21-year-old city. Unwilling to invest in a less important part of the world, the State Department under Acheson had initially refused Henderson's plans. Indian officials held the 'parcel' of land. It was finally purchased in 1951, just as Henderson left for his next diplomatic posting in Tehran. By the end of 1953, New Delhi was placed at the 'top of the list of construction priorities'. In these interceding years, the American mission was greatly expanded. Bowles not only won the confidence of the prime minister, but backed his zeal for India with concrete and visible steps towards technical cooperation and development.[233] He brought 115 technocrats to New Delhi, and, as Eleanor Roosevelt puts it, introduced a 'new idea of American officialdom' to Indian elites.[234]

The White House's view had also changed. Until the end of Truman's tenure, policy language on South Asia and India authored by the NSC staff—located in the Executive Office of the president—spoke about 'contain[ing] Communism',[235] 'counter-influencing [sic] against the Kremlin',[236] developing India's 'military power' as a bulwark against the East[237] and exploiting strategic materials.[238] In sum, 'neutralism' was seen to be 'favourable to the Soviet Union'.[239] By 1954, and following the experience of the Korean negotiations, it made clear that the 'present' Indian policy of 'non-involvement would continue'. It suggested making use of India's role as a 'mediator'.[240] There was little doubt that the value of 'non-involvement', even though it grated Dulles' strategic sensitivities, had been understood. It deepened what might be called operational-level understanding beyond the sabre-rattling in the US Congress as also in popular discourse. Contrary to the accounts of the crisis inked by the likes of Gopal and even Pandit, the Korean episode did not lead to a virtual break in India–US relations. If anything, it introduced American officials to the reality and importance of non-alignment. They may not have liked the display of such independence in crucial matters of international politics, but as suggested above, they welcomed its significance at a time when partisanship and the Cold War practice of blanket opposition failed to produce an acceptable outcome.

To an extent, and as was clear during the negotiations for food assistance, this approach was rooted in what Mrs Roosevelt quickly recognised as the determination 'not to fall under the influence of any other'.[241] Equally, and as was constantly highlighted by Nehru, it was about safeguarding India's regional interests. This meant encouraging reconciliation with the newly born People's Republic of China. The PRC inside the UN system, Nehru thought, would eventually soften its elites' antipathy towards the West. In turn, and perhaps in a less obvious way, it would encourage Zhou and Mao to approach India on its own terms, divorced from the assumed polarities of the Cold War. That

Nehru's approach was eventually caught-out in the autumn of 1962, as discussed in the next chapter, should not take away from the empirically tested fact that Indian foreign policy during the early years of the Republic was not about idealism, but rather the sometimes nebulous interrelationship between ideas and interests.

PART II

NEGOTIATING CHANGE

4

'SHAKEN'

1962

At precisely 5.53 p.m. on 26 October 1962, Brij Kumar Nehru, the Indian ambassador to the United States and the prime minister's cousin, entered the Oval Office. Educated at both the LSE and Oxford, the younger Nehru had a critical message for President John. F. Kennedy. The ambassador carried a copy of a letter from Nehru, the first of fifteen that the prime minister would exchange with his 44-year-old counterpart.[1] As a State Department memo put it, this particular note had the 'appearance of circular communication to friendly heads of state'.[2] In the operative last paragraph, Nehru wrote, 'I am asking for your sympathy and support.'[3]

The People's Liberation Army (PLA) had stormed Indian territory only six days earlier. To survive this, India required external assistance. It needed the US like never before, and perhaps like it never has since. These were extraordinary times. As B.K. Nehru put it to Kennedy, 'there is obviously a great deal of rethinking' in India, a 'reappraisal' of sorts.[4] After all, a prouder Nehru often warned against 'relying on others'. 'If India is to survive', he once stated in public, 'India will survive by her own strength, self-help and self-confidence.'[5] This was no longer to be the case.

On 19 November, betraying every political fibre in the then 73-year-old prime minister's body, Nehru unambiguously asked Kennedy to order the US military to intervene on India's behalf. The situation, according to the prime minister, was 'really desperate'. 'Unless something is done immediately to stem the tide,' he made plain, 'the whole of Assam, Tripura, Manipur, and Nagaland would also pass into Chinese hands.'[6] Two days later, and in a decision that was vaguely connected to what has been called India's 'darkest hour',[7] when this fateful letter was written, the PRC announced a unilateral ceasefire, leaving India, its elite and its public dazed and changed.

Nehru was alive to the rapid changes forced upon his nation. He freely admitted that India had been 'living in an artificial atmosphere' of its 'own creation'. It was now 'shaken out of it'[8]—1,383 Indian soldiers were killed in fighting and another 5,600 or so were either taken prisoners or were missing in action.[9] Fought on two fronts, the short and—as the Indian MoD's official historians put it—'puny' affair, in terms of actual divisions deployed in the fighting, led not only to the loss of Indian territory,[10] but notably, as Guha suggests, 'represented a massive defeat in the Indian imagination'.[11] India would not be the same again.

For those directly involved in the conflict, the appeal for assistance could be read in no other way than the complete dismantlement of the so-called policy of non-alignment. India could hardly claim to be non-aligned as American planes dropped hundreds of thousands of rounds of ammunition, as well as machine guns and mortar over Calcutta's Dum Dum airport. Among the early works on the 1962 War, Neville Maxwell is a notable contributor to the thesis that India had forsaken non-alignment.[12] A journalist for *The Times* in the 1960s, and author of the controversial book *India's China War*, Maxwell argued that the 'whole arch' of Nehru's policies had been brought down by the China War.[13] In more recent scholarship, an entire cast of actors engaged in the messy business of defeat forcefully argue that, in effect, India threw its lot in entirety with the US. The chief proponents of the alliance thesis include B.K. Nehru, Brigadier (later Major General) D.K. Palit, the Director of Military Operations (DMO) during the war, and Dennis Kux, a diplomat turned scholar.

According to Ambassador Nehru, in the post-war period 'we [India] continued to talk in terms of non-alignment but we had become in fact the allies of the United States in their confrontation at least with China'.[14] Palit notes that asking the US to intervene 'could be seen in no other light than that of entering into a form of military alliance'.[15] Kux wrote that, following the war, 'India's non-alignment seemed to be a thing of the past.'[16] These recent works, authored nearly thirty years after the war, reinforce the widely accepted argument that India had abandoned non-alignment.[17] The Pulitzer Prize-winning journalist-scholar Walter Lippmann even went so far as to claim that 'India can no longer afford to be non-aligned.' There can be no doubt, as J.N. Dixit, the former foreign secretary and national security advisor, put it, that Nehru was subsequently required to adjust to 'more realistic moorings' and deal with 'the pressures born out of these trends on India'.[18]

Yet while the familiar historiography of this period treats this shift in Indian policy as a move away from its so-called 'idealistic' phase to the hard-nosed reality of power politics—where generating material strength is said to have mattered more than woollier ideas[19]—the empirical evidence of this change is highly questionable. First, the treatment of non-alignment as a product of idealism, as discussed in previous chapters, is in itself dubious. Second, with the benefit of hindsight and the triangulation of existing works, commentary and selected archival source material, negotiating change in this period of emergency appears less black-and-white than practitioners and commentators accept.

The following narrative shows how and why the very conception of change in Indian foreign policy needs revision. The prime minister, his coterie of advisors and military elites did grow closer to Kennedy and his envoys, but their efforts to improve US–Indian relations were still characterised by a high degree of caution. Rather than a complete break from the past, the diplomatic initiatives developed in the face of defeat were hardly those of a nation desperate to join a mix of alliances. It speaks instead of a defeated nation that was shocked into negotiating change, an involved and layered process that sought to safeguard Indian interests as far as circumstance warranted. This chapter in Indian strategic history, as outlined below, makes clear that India's deep and complex approach to international politics withstood the temptation of alliances despite the tragedy of defeat.

The efficacy of ideas—rooted in the history of pre-independence India—coupled with the need to acquire arms for free led to a policy that was curiously Indian. In the face of defeat and even invasion, Indian bureaucrats, ministers and the prime minister refused to enter into an alliance or alliance-like relationship with the US. Instead, as will be demonstrated below, in these testing times Indian representatives carefully negotiated their need for arms while avoiding even a mere suggestion of any entanglement in an alliance with the US. While India was fortunate to have found a cooperative partner in Kennedy, Nehru and his team stayed clear from a course of action that could well have mortgaged Indian interests to those of America. The apprehension regarding receiving arms and assistance from abroad was no longer a sacrosanct element in Indian policy, but this hardly meant that non-alignment was abandoned. At best, the 1962 crisis altered the basis of how non-alignment was to be read and practised by Indian leaders.

The chapter is divided into five parts. The first provides a very brief background to the dispute over the border. The second introduces a new cast of actors who played a central role in this period of change. The third and fourth parts go on to provide a detailed analysis of the two stages of the conflict: the first, the early stage between 8 September and 11 October, and the second between 11 October and 21 November. The main objective of the latter two sections is to show what exactly motivated Indian elites in these trying hours of crisis. The concluding part of the chapter takes stock of Indian predicaments following military defeat and how and why Pakistan came to occupy a central part in India's effort to secure long-term military assistance.

The Border

Girija Shankar Bajpai once remarked that the McMahon Line, discarded by the PRC, but which the Indian government recognised and continues to recognise as the international border between India and China, was one of the 'scars left by Britain in the course of her aggression against China'. The latter, he argued, 'may seek to heal or erase this scar on the basis of frontier rectifications that may not be either to our [India's] liking or our interest'.[20] The origins of these 'scars' could be traced to the late seventeenth century, but more pertinently to 1914, when Britain, Tibet and China negotiated a treaty that was accepted as the legal boundary between India and China—the so-called McMahon Line, named after the British Indian Foreign Secretary Henry McMahon. The treaty was signed at a convention in Simla in 1914.[21] However, as Pannikar noted, the Chinese government did not ratify the treaty. In 1951, the PRC occupied Tibet, leaving some 20,000 troops garrisoned close to the Indian border.[22] Dealing with Chinese aggression was going to prove tricky.

The idea, according to the prime minister, was to seek 'some kind of understanding with China'[23] while not losing sight of the need to gain control over swathes of territory that lay outside the administrative reach of British India. Accordingly, India took control of Tawang in 1951, an administrative post close to the border and on the Indian side of the McMahon Line.[24] As R.K. Nehru, who became foreign secretary in July 1952, argues, the prime minister was deeply concerned 'over the possibility of the Chinese revolution going astray', but the fact was that securing 'the difficult terrain' in the border areas would prove near impossible. The diplomatic route was the best and perhaps only option for a nation with a much smaller, nascent administrative system.[25]

To foster closer relations, in 1954 Nehru and Zhou introduced the 'Five Principles of Peaceful Coexistence' or *Panchsheel*. India even officially accepted Chinese sovereignty over Tibet.[26] In April 1955, at the first Afro-Asian Conference, also known as the Bandung Conference, Nehru and Zhou stood on the same podium denouncing colonialism. The five principles of *Panchsheel* served as the ideational basis of the Non-Aligned Movement (NAM), which had been tacitly recognised at Bandung. African and Asian nations declared that they would not join either of the Cold War camps. For Nehru, Bandung was a success both for NAM and for closer Sino-Indian relations.[27]

However, by the late 1950s, the underlying basis of *Panchsheel* had been overturned. In December 1958, Nehru wrote the first of many letters to Zhou about the misrepresentation of the border in official Chinese maps.[28] Complicating these delicate initiatives, and following a revolt in the Tibetan capital of Lhasa in 1959, the Dalai Lama fled to India. Nehru, who had so far recognised Tibet as a region of China, was now viewed with suspicion by the Communist regime for hosting the Dalai Lama.[29] Further, the Chinese Communist Party (CCP) grew suspicious of Indian collusion in a CIA-backed effort to support Tibetan guerrillas.[30] For Nehru, the entire matter of Tibetan independence needed to be kept in balance. He had previously told the Dalai Lama that India 'cannot help'.[31] It was imperative not to risk a deadlock with China. Following the Lhasa revolt in March 1959, and with the Dalai Lama at India's doorstep, the prime minister had little choice but to grant him and his follower's refugee status. Between 1959 and 1962, relations between the two sides rapidly deteriorated. The Chinese, as K.P.S. Menon put it, 'began to nibble here and there'. They started building a road through Aksai Chin that India regarded as part of its territory.[32] Skirmishes and short exchanges of fire along the border followed shortly thereafter, eventually leading to the outbreak of war.

The war was fought on two fronts: in the Western sector and the Eastern sector.[33] In the Western sector, the territorial dispute was primarily over the Aksai Chin, the high wastelands located in the extreme north-east of Kashmir.[34] The Eastern sector, which India claims to have been demarcated by the McMahon Line, is some 700 miles long. In the East, the area in which the war was actually fought, lay between the McMahon Line and the Chinese line, and was referred to as the North East Frontier Agency or NEFA.[35]

Team India

On 8 April 1961, John Kenneth Galbraith arrived in New Delhi as the new US ambassador to India. The 6-foot, 8-inch-tall professor of economics replaced Ellsworth Bunker, a sugar tsar-turned-diplomat. Galbraith was in charge of an embassy much larger than anything Henderson or Bowles had to contend with, where 300 Americans and 726 Indians made up the staff in a new embassy building.[36] There was little doubt that the US had infiltrated New Delhi's diplomatic landscape. Galbraith's British counterpart, Paul Gore-Booth, who arrived a year earlier, worked with far slimmer human resources. Soon, Booth and Galbraith would seek to craft a coordinated diplomatic initiative to deepen ties with India. Unlike Grady, who was often irritated with his British counterparts, Galbraith found it easy to engage officials in the British High Commission. As Booth writes, during the China War, this form of 'constant and intimate' cooperation was particularly vital.[37] His residence, 2 King George's Avenue (renamed Rajaji Avenue in 2004 after C. Rajagopalachari) became a familiar address for Indian and American officials alike.

As was also evident, the US, and not Britain, would prove to be the more important diplomatic actor as the crises developed. The Kennedy administration, which entered office in January 1961, took a very different view to India and the non-aligned states more generally. Kennedy, according to McGeorge Bundy, the special assistant for national security affairs, 'rejected the state rhetoric of the Cold War'. As he highlighted in his oft-quoted inaugural address, Kennedy asked nations to 'begin anew the quest for peace'.[38] The idea, as Robert Dallek put it, was to 'develop non-military techniques of resistance that would not create suspicions of new-imperialism'.[39] The president was hugely impressed by India's democratic constitutional system. And although he once found Nehru—during a visit to Asia in the mid-1950s—'arrogant and offensive',[40] he was open to the idea of engaging with difference.[41] India was important, and Kennedy understood this. Indeed, this was reflected in his choice of staff.

Apart from Galbraith, who considered the post to India as his 'prime aspiration',[42] Kennedy chose Dean Rusk as his secretary of state. An internationalist by instinct, Rusk had served Truman in the early days of the Korean War. His experience of Nehru's correspondence with Truman made him aware of the prime minister's forceful manner when it came to non-alignment.[43] Additionally, Rusk favoured extending economic assistance to India, but he was equally mindful that this would not mean winning over India in the Cold War.[44] In some respects, Rusk adopted a non-idealistic approach to India. He was someone, as Chester Bowles once remarked, who felt the 'frustrations' of dealing with India 'even more strongly than others', but all the same he was encouragingly modest about Nehru's India.[45] As was highlighted in the introduction to the first State Department guidelines for 'policy and operations' with regard to India, the administration understood well that the key lay in 'quiet, personal diplomacy'.[46] Much as architecture had mattered for Henderson as a symbol of commitment, Rusk's department invested in people.

Bundy, for instance, was very much absorbed by the potential of India. He befriended Bajpai in the late 1940s, and, much like Kennedy, he appreciated that democracies like India and the US would need to 'agree to disagree' without necessarily 'destroying' a 'new found friendship'.[47] In this vein, Bundy was supported by an old South Asia hand, Philips Talbot, who later became the head of the Asia Society. Chosen personally by Bowles, then the undersecretary of state and later the president's special advisor, Talbot occupied the assistant secretary's post for the Near Eastern–South Asian Bureau.[48] This was, in many respects, Team India.

Some new faces also dotted the bureaucratic landscape on the Indian side. M.J. Desai became foreign secretary in 1961. A Gujarati Hindu, Desai would often meet with Galbraith in an effort to strengthen Indian and American relations. In the early part of 1962, when Pakistan referred the matter of Kashmir to the Security Council, Desai was convinced that Galbraith was 'extremely anxious to keep Kashmir out' of the same,[49] a position equally favoured by the Indian government. Desai's slightly more open and less awkward—than most—approach to the US was shared by his envoy in Washington, B.K. Nehru. Nehru had a casual manner of engagement, and found it easier than most to converse with Kennedy and his coterie of advisors. Indeed, as he himself notes, his 'appointment was much welcomed in Washington'. A headline in the *Washington Post* perhaps put it best: 'Local Boy Makes Good!'[50] He would, as the narrative below shows, serve as an interlocutor, often explaining why particular American decisions may invite a backlash in New Delhi. In this, he was irreplaceable.[51]

The third key figure was Y.D. Gundevia. A 'heretical Parsi'—as he described himself[52]—Gundevia served in Moscow in aid of President Radhakrishnan. He was a former acting high commissioner in London, a former ambassador to Switzerland and became Commonwealth secretary in December 1960. Only Krishna Menon stood out. As defence minister, and someone who was blind to the Chinese threat, he found himself at odds with an otherwise engaged group of 'top ranking civil servants'.[53] These were not men afraid to speak their minds, at least for the most part. Although not all of them got along—Gundevia and Desai for instance disagreed on policy issues—they introduced a degree of enthusiasm into bureaucratic parley. As will be demonstrated in Chapter 6, this team would hold fort as their leader, the prime minister, came to terms with a newer verve in India's political and international life.

'Flames of War'

8 September 1962–11 October 1962

On the night of 20/21 September, the *People's Daily* reported that Indian troops had attacked a Chinese border post. An editorial stated that India had now been 'warned'. The 'flames of war' could break anytime.[54] In fact, the first significant contact had taken place on 8 September at a forward post set up by the Indian Army in June 1962 in what is known as the Dhola area—located at the tri-junction where Bhutan, Tibet and India meet—of the Kameng sector of the NEFA. This, as D.R. Mankekar argues, was the 'spark that ignited the tinder'.[55] After all, the PLA had taken Thagla Ridge, the disputed watershed that separated India from

China. Nehru was at a Commonwealth conference in London. On 10 or perhaps 11 September, Krishna Menon, on behalf of the prime minister, ordered the Indian Army to expel the PLA from the southern basin of the Thagla Ridge,[56] which the government believed to be Indian territory. The eviction order was codenamed Operation Leghorn.[57]

However, Lieutenant General Umrao Singh, 33 Corps Commander, and Major General Niranjan Prasad, 4 Division Commander,[58] argued that it was beyond the capability of the Indian Army in the NEFA to challenge a superior Chinese force. Prasad made clear that the 'inadequate build-up of supplies and equipment and deficient fire support' made this an impossible task.[59] Singh, on the other hand, suggested withdrawing to the south of Thagla, without having to take the ridge. Between 9 September and the first week of October, despite the government's insistence on evicting the Chinese, Singh and Prasad maintained that this was a task that simply could not be fulfilled.[60] On 14 September, General P.N. Thapar, the army chief, warned the government of the many deficiencies suffered by the Indian Army posted in the NEFA.[61] At an intelligence briefing three days later, Thapar argued that the army was unprepared for an all-out conflict in the Frontier.[62] Lieutenant General Daulat Singh, General Officer Commanding in Chief (GOC-in-C) of Western Command, also warned Krishna Menon that the Indian Army in the NEFA risked annihilation if they attacked the Chinese.[63]

On 22 September, Thapar cautioned that the Chinese reaction to India's attempt at engaging them in the Dhola area could result in retaliation elsewhere in the NEFA and even in Ladakh, in the Western sector. Yet for Foreign Secretary M.J. Desai, eviction operations were informed by political considerations. Desai pushed the army to follow orders, even if it meant retaliation in Ladakh.[64] A written order—probably authored by H.C. Sarin, a joint secretary in the MoD—was passed to Thapar and the Eastern Command. K. Raghuramaiah, the deputy minister for defence, impressed upon Thapar the political rationale for immediately executing the eviction.[65] This was, as Nehru later stated, a matter of regaining public confidence. It left Thapar with little choice but to act on political decisions, yet Umrao Singh refused to budge. He maintained that a numerically superior Chinese army would eliminate an opposing Indian force. Eventually, Thapar, Menon and Lieutenant General L.P. Sen, the GOC-in-C Eastern Command, replaced Singh.[66] B.M. Kaul, commander of the newly created 4 Corps, was given the task of evicting the Chinese from the NEFA.[67] Trusted by Nehru, Kaul was said to have been brought in to 'save' the situation.[68] Contrary to military convention, he was given direct access to the prime minister.[69] Indeed, he was appointed as the chief of General Staff a year earlier by Menon because Nehru liked him.[70] Kaul was often, at least according to him, invited to Teen Murti Bhavan, Nehru's residence, for after dinner conversations with the prime minister.[71] Yet, as Gopal recounts, Kaul had 'no sharp intellect', and more importantly, he was 'inexperienced in battle'.[72] What he did have was some experience of China, which he visited in December 1953. He was then 'impressed to see' the 'great speed' at which roads and buildings were constructed.[73] Nothing could have prepared him for dealing with the lightning speed of a Chinese attack.

Interestingly, and notwithstanding the warnings issued by the army high command, there was no chatter whatsoever about reaching out for military assistance, not even a newspaper report.[74] Instead, in the third week of September, Krishna Menon left for New York for a General Assembly meeting at the UN. He hardly believed that a full-scale war was possible. For reasons that remain mysterious, he told Gundevia and B.N. Mullick, the director of the Intelligence Bureau (IB), that there were 'heavy Pakistani movements' in the western border. These were largely unsubstantiated. Even Rajeshwar Dayal, the Indian high commissioner to Pakistan, was befuddled.[75] Nehru was still in London, and Morarji Desai, the Indian finance minister, was in Washington. En route to Canada, the somewhat puritanical Desai, who had once been the 'moving spirit' behind prohibition in Bombay, the Indian film city[76]—stressed that 'there was no question' of India 'veering from the path of non-alignment'.[77] In some respects, although the political class was absent from the theatre near the action, they were, at least, away on government work. Kaul was holidaying in Srinagar. He returned only on 2 October.[78] It was almost as though the Chinese did not exist. Indeed, as Galbraith records in his diary, 'if the Chinese decide[d] to take Delhi,' they would have found 'few important captives'.[79] Of all the biographies written by the principal actors, only Mullick surmised that the army had what it took to drive out the Chinese.[80] Were these over-optimistic accounts by India's most senior intelligence figure or merely overzealous assessments by someone also caught-out by the scale of the Chinese offensive a few weeks down the line?

Beaten Back

General Kaul arrived in Tezpur, Assam, on 4 October. Following a survey of Indian positions in key locations such as the Namka-Chu Valley below Thagla, Kaul understood the difficulties his men had endured and which Prasad and Singh highlighted. Men were attired in summer clothing at 16,000 feet and had only fifty rounds of ammunition each. Supplies were hard to come by—only a fraction of air-dropped goods were actually retrieved—and according to Palit, the DMO, this would at best stock the men for maybe an hour-long battle. Nonetheless, having been given command of the 4 Corps and to prove his mantle, Kaul 'could not bring himself to recommend the slightest retraction from the government's belligerent stance'. He would describe at length 'the futility of the situation', he was 'sensitive to helplessness and vulnerability of our [Indian] troops',[81] but at the same time his telegrams to New Delhi were 'extremely optimistic'.[82] It was almost as though Kaul recognised the impossible task of ousting the Chinese while, at the same time, he was clearly unwilling to disappoint Nehru, and in fact the Indian people. The general, something of a thespian—he apparently liked acting[83]— had mentioned in passing that, if he failed, the government would fall.[84] Kaul's predisposition only lasted until 10 October.

This was the date chosen by Brigadier John Dalvi, commander of the 7 Infantry Brigade in the NEFA, who would write a book aptly titled the *Himalayan Blunder* seven years later, for the commencement of operations to evict the PLA.[85] Indian troops would have to travel across an area known as Tseng-Jong to reach Yamtso La, positioned west of the Thag La Ridge, behind Chinese lines.[86] On 8 October, a Company belonging to the 9 Punjab Infantry Brigade left for Tseng-Jong and established a bridgehead on the north bank of the Namka-Chu River (which flows below the Thag-La ridge).[87] The Chinese did not react. The following day, 9 Punjab occupied Tseng-Jong.[88]

On 10 October, the strength of China's forces was proven in battle. While the Indian Army made its way to cross the Namka-Chu River into Yamtso La, a full battalion of the PLA prepared for an attack on Tseng-Jong. At 9.20 in the morning,[89] the Chinese opened fire, and, as Kaul recalled, 'this was the first time that China had engaged herself in a battle with us in the real sense'.[90] The Chinese onslaught, which in objective terms was hardly a military disaster,[91] had a strong impact on

Kaul. Mullick remembers a 'frightfully alarming' telegram sent by Kaul to the army headquarters. Nehru's trusted general stated that the Chinese had superior numbers, artillery and mortars. He thought they had the capability to occupy Towang and Bomdila, two major Indian-administered posts in the NEFA, as well as the plains of Assam.[91] Within a few hours, Tseng-Jong had been lost and the Chinese were said to be 'pouring out of Thag-La like ants'.[93] Kaul later said, 'frankly speaking, I had now fully understood all the implications of our predicament'. 'I thought we should consider the whole of our position in this theatre.'[94] On 11 October, Kaul hurried back to New Delhi, where a meeting was to be held in the prime minister's house. Before leaving he suspended the eviction order and even told Brigadier Dalvi that orders to expel the enemy were simply impractical.[95]

Military Assistance: A Suggestion

The meeting took place at 10.30 p.m. on 11 October. It was attended by everyone in a position of authority, both military and civilian, who had something to do with India's defence and the war with China. This of course included Nehru, Thapar, Menon, Cabinet secretaries, secretaries for external affairs and defence and the General Staff officers, including Lieutenant General L.P. Sen, who was in charge of the entire Eastern Command.[96] It is important to note that although there are mixed accounts of the eventual decisions made in the meeting, one thing is certain—Kaul had clearly and without ambiguity told Nehru and the rest of his advisors that the Chinese threat was real and that the Indian Army was not capable of evicting the Chinese from Indian territories. Mullick, an attendee in this meeting, states that for 'nearly half-an-hour, he [Kaul] argued with great strength and conviction that not only was it impossible to drive the Chinese across the Thag La ridge, but it would be impossible to hold the Namka-Chu river front'.[97] Kaul himself states that 'if we attacked the Chinese, as things stood then, we were bound to have a reverse'. 'The Chinese were in a better position to build up a superior force due to good communications behind the forward position, an advantage we [the Indian Army] did not enjoy.'[98] Kaul told Palit that 'the PM had seemed to accept his assessment without demur'.[99]

Interestingly, Maxwell, having conducted a number of interviews in the post-war period, including those with Kaul, states that Kaul proposed during the meeting that 'India should seek speedy and copious military assistance from the United States.' His suggestion, however, 'was dismissed, apparently with some irritation, by Nehru'.[100] While Maxwell is the only author to provide this particular piece of information, there is little reason to doubt his account. Early in 1961, Kaul advocated asking the US for military equipment, in terms of aid if need be.[101] Accounts of conversations between B.K. Nehru and Kaul often highlighted the fact that the Indian Army was in desperate need of advanced weaponry.[102] This led the ambassador to speak with George McGhee, the US undersecretary for political affairs, in the first few months of 1961 with regard to military aid.[103] Given Kaul's earlier position with regard to military assistance, it is hardly surprising that in October 1962, after having actually witnessed China's military superiority and admitted to the weaknesses of the Indian Army's position in the NEFA, Kaul suggested asking the US for assistance. Indeed, Desai himself met Galbraith on multiple occasions to discuss the possibilities of purchasing American F-104 fighter bombers and C-130 transport planes. Defence procurement was very much on the minds of Indian elites.[104] At the end of the meeting at the prime minister's house on 11 October, it had been decided that the Indian Army would no longer launch offensive operations against the Chinese. Rather, they would defend the positions they currently held.[105]

Curiously, even after having been told about the difficulties faced in the NEFA, neither Nehru nor his political advisors considered approaching the US or the West more generally for military assistance. At first glance this is puzzling. The army informed Nehru of China's apparent superiority. Nehru had seemed to accept this; after all, why else would the Indian leadership suspend eviction orders? Clearly, the all-too-real tension between the idea of remaining completely autonomous and the hard-to-digest strategic reality of the time was not easily reconciled. Equally, and given the potential for diplomatic defencelessness at a time of urgency, the leadership appeared to follow a well-measured and even prudent design. Nehru, for one, understood that a dramatic change in Indian policy in this moment of crisis would have far-reaching implications for a nation that, so far, and prior to the Chinese attack, had done well to safeguard its interests. The next steps, as will be seen below, spoke of elites tied between interests and ideas, without losing sight of either. In fact, and contrary to the alliance thesis pushed by those at the centre of action in 1962, Nehru's, and India's approach more generally, did well to follow the general contours of a policy based on the idea of non-alignment.

'Invasion'

October to 21 November 1962

On 12 October, Nehru left for Colombo. At Delhi airport he told journalists, 'Our instructions are to free our territory,' he continued, 'I cannot fix a date, that is entirely for the army.' The declaration was widely read as an attempt to aggravate the Chinese and, according to Thapar, pressure the Indian army, it would give the 'impression that a decisive action plan was planned'.[106] However, it was, as Gopal states, 'a wholly unobjectionable statement'. The prime minister was merely reiterating fact.[107] Either way, the PLA had aggressive plans of its own. On 20 October, the Chinese offensive began in full strength.[108] On 21 October, Nehru told his chief ministers that 'Chinese forces had attacked us all along the frontier in the NEFA and Ladakh in great numbers and have dislodged positions that our forces had taken up at various places.' He admitted that the Chinese had 'overwhelming strength and firepower', and added that 'all the consequences of this conflict will be borne by us'.[109]

The offensive was to be divided into two parts. The first lasted for a week between 20 and 27 October, followed by a lull, and then continued between 14 and 21 November, when the PRC announced a unilateral ceasefire. In the first part of the offensive, India lost all important administrative posts in the frontier regions.[110] In fact, on the first day of battle, the army's position in Khinzemane, Dhola and Tsangdhar, all crucial defensive posts, had been silenced. The 7 Infantry Brigade, which had been ordered to hold their position south of the Namka-Chu River, virtually ceased to exist.[111] Towards the end of October, some twenty-one army posts were either overrun by the Chinese or abandoned by a retreating Indian Army.[112] Thapar told Palit that the government was under the impression that the 'invasion' would press down to the plains. In these extremely difficult circumstances, the army chief asked for six new divisions to be raised, and if needed, for arms to be procured from abroad.[113] He stressed that India should approach 'whichever source is available to us', even on the basis of 'rupee payment'.[114] The latter point is important. The suggestion of rupee purchases—in lieu of dollar payments—indicated an openness to accept a degree of aid or at least some form of subsidy. The 'consequences' that Nehru once spoke of would not, in fact, be 'borne by us [India]' alone.

This notwithstanding, there was as yet no public evidence of Indian elites asking for military assistance. *The Guardian* in Britain reported that there was a concerted effort not to ask for help, as this could 'widen the conflict and hamper bilateral relations' between India and China, once thought to have shared a closer relationship.[115] In fact, between 8 September and 15 October, the Indian government made successive requests to the UK and the US for spare parts and equipment, but on a procurement basis. On 2 October, Desai approached his friend Galbraith to hurry spare parts for a C-119 transport aircraft. On the following day, the American embassy was asked to furnish licences to permit the purchase of 250 ANGRC-9 radios. A day later, the MoD made a request for two Caribou transport planes.[116] Robert McNamara, the US defence secretary, approved this immediately. The planes were to reach India by the end of the month.[117] This made headline news in both the *New York Times* and the *Washington Post*,[118] but was carefully treated as an appeal for quick procurement and nothing else. An Indian admiral asked Booth for 2,000 FN rifles 'with bayonets'—indicative of the need to engage in hand-to-hand combat—and 3 million rounds of ammunition. They too were to be ordered 'on payment'.[119]

For their part, both Galbraith and Booth refused to call this anything but procurement. As Booth relayed to his Foreign Office, the government in India would not 'welcome a sudden public offer of all possible aid'. It should not look as though Britain was using the 'situation for Cold War purposes'.[120] This, of course, they did later on, when Booth and Prime Minister Harold Macmillan understood the extent of the help that India would need. For the moment, Galbraith, too, took to expressing 'quiet sympathy'.[121] Like Booth, he told the State Department, and Rusk specifically, that the embassy would be 'restrained' in its expression of support 'so as to give the Chinese no pretext for alleging American involvement'. The ambassador was acutely aware of Nehru's predisposition and the fact that any suggestion—even if made in the spirit of support—to consider alignment could only backfire.[122] Indeed, just as Indian envoys made their enquiries, Nehru stated on All India Radio (AIR) that 'India would stick to her policy of non-alignment and would not give up her basic principles because of the present difficulty.'[123] Clearly, the need for balance, or at least, the need to demon-strate balance publicly, was uppermost on the prime minister's mind. Behind closed doors, Nehru was grudgingly convinced that there was no way to survive the onslaught without Western assistance. The question was how this could be sought without mortgaging Indian interests to those of so-called 'friendly nations'.

Roll Back

On 23 October, Menon and Nehru visited Kaul. The 4 Corps Com-mander was back in Delhi. He was suffering from 'exhaustion', having toured troops situated at some 12,000 feet in the Dhola area.[124] Kaul made three suggestions. First, and most importantly, that India 'seek military aid from some foreign powers or power'; second, that India reorganise the command and control of the Indian Army; and lastly, that Indian force levels should be raised. Even at this time of crisis, Kaul mentions that both Nehru and Menon were not 'enamoured' by the suggestion of foreign aid, although they agreed to the immediate expan-sion of the Indian Army.[125] According to other accounts, however, Kaul had a lot more to say. Palit notes that the ailing commander advocated forging a military alliance with the US and Taiwan 'to create a joint front against Communist China'. Kaul allegedly also told Nehru that India ought to seek US army or air force intervention in case of further Chinese attacks.[126]

The prime minister, according to Palit, 'found no difficulty in reject-ing Bijji's [Kaul's] somewhat naïve suggestion'.[127] India would not join an alliance but, given the rapidly changing ground situation, he hesi-tantly agreed to seek military aid. Accordingly, S.S. Khera, the Cabinet secretary, was sent to jot down a list of items that Kaul thought were needed.[128] In a letter, which remained unsigned, Kaul's tenor was one of a 'defeated army Commander'. He had clearly given up the fight. He instructed Khera to 'persuade' not only the Taiwanese, but also the South Koreans and the US in the West Pacific seaboard to 'invade Chinese mainland'.[129] In short, and as John Lall, a joint secretary in the MoD, put it, 'Kaul confided that he had advised his government to abandon non-alignment and seek American assistance.'[130]

In this time of crisis, and as muddled and rushed as things seemed to have been, a strategy was quickly crafted. First, envoys were to make sure that a call for aid and assistance would not altogether invite the West—the USSR remained neutral at this time, it could hardly risk intervention in the backdrop of the Cuban missile crisis—to exercise some sort of control over Indian decisions and actions in the present or the future. Second, having secured such assurances in as definite a way as possible, given the circumstances, Nehru would make a formal appeal. This was hardly a well-crafted or well thought-out plan. It was simply a means by which the idea of non-alignment was to be sustained despite the desperate requirement for material assistance.

Accordingly, both M.J. Desai and Morarji Desai met with Galbraith. They told the American ambassador that the government would very soon have to turn to the US for 'substantial assistance'.[131] At the same time, the foreign secretary and the finance minister 'hoped' that this would not 'force' India 'into an alliance' or even 'impose security inspection procedures for the arms they receive which would be inconsistent with their sovereignty'. Galbraith reassured both the Desais that this would not happen.[132] The ambassador also made clear to both Kennedy and Rusk that when Nehru did make a formal appeal, it should be treated carefully. It was important to avoid saying anything that might serve to irk Nehru and his coterie.[133] On the British end, Menon sought similar assurances from Booth.[134] Nehru wrote to Macmillan making clear that Chinese aggression had imposed a 'very heavy burden on' India. This was, in one sense, an attempt to prepare the ground prior to an appeal for direct assistance and aid.[135] In London, R.K. Nehru, now secretary general for external affairs, met with British MPs to see if they could reach out to Pakistan. Aid to India was bound to invite protest, and possibly push Islamabad closer to Beijing.[136] After all, as Galbraith recollects, Pakistan had been making 'pro-Chinese noises'.[137] While the question of Pakistan would eventually devastate relations between India and the US and the UK, for the moment, Macmillan made clear to Ayub Khan—the Hindko-speaking Pathan and president of Pakistan[138]—that the UK would be 'ready to meet' India's needs.[139] With these assurances in hand, on 26 October Nehru authored the first of three crucial letters with regard to military assistance.

A thirteen-page document, the letter was handed by B.K. Nehru to Carl Kaysen—an economist by training and a key member of Kennedy's NSC staff and Bundy's deputy—at around 6 or 7 p.m. on 25 October in Washington, or 5.30 a.m. or so on the 26th in Delhi. Soon after,

Kaysen asked to see Kennedy. It was after-hours in the White House, and Kaysen managed to see the president only at 9 p.m. He was sitting next to Jackie Kennedy, who, of course, had come to know Nehru during her visit to India and was rather fond of him. Reading the letter along with the president, Jackie said: 'My, I always thought he was the peaceable sort.' Kennedy immediately called Sir Ormsby-Gore, the British ambassador to Washington and the 'President's pal.' He kept repeating: 'This is mad. This is mad!' Clearly, Nehru's call for arms and assistance was so out of character that it had the First Couple in the United States utterly stumped.[140]

As mentioned earlier, on the following evening, 26 October, B.K. Nehru handed a copy of the letter personally to Kennedy. The ambassador, wary that his uncle, the prime minister, had found himself in an impossible situation, urged Kennedy to avoid the terms *military alliance* and *military aid* in any response. The approach would be to offer support without 'spelling it out'.[141] These nuances, which had once baffled the likes of Eisenhower and Truman, albeit never in a situation such as this, were immediately absorbed by John Kennedy. Importantly, and, as Theodore Sorenson points out, the threat to his own 'hemisphere' and the potential for conflict over missiles in Cuba aside, Kennedy was not distracted for a second in dealing with India's envoy in Washington.[142] He was found studying a large map of India as the ambassador entered the room.[143] The president understood that his administration would have to do everything possible to help, while not making it look as though the US was 'coming in'. In the end, Galbraith was asked to figure out how best 'sympathy' and 'support' were to be 'implement[ed]' given the caveats underlined by B.K. Nehru.[144]

Within forty-eight hours, the contents of the letter had been leaked.[145] *The Hindu* reported that although there was no mention of aid in Nehru's appeal, Kennedy was expected to 'assure the Indian premier that the US would be willing to provide anything that India required by way of assistance'.[146] The *New York Times* went to the extent of stating that American 'air transport loaded with guns and ammunition' would soon arrive. This would result, as the article put it, in 'an emotional and political turning point in India'.[147] Writing in the *Washington Post*, Henry Bradsher was a little less reserved. He made clear that Nehru was 'no longer worried about compromising his long-cherished non-alignment policy'.[148] To an extent, press reports were not far off the mark. Kennedy's reply was indeed carefully crafted. The president made no mention of arms or aid.[149] The letter, received in Delhi on 28 October, simply read, 'this is a practical matter'. Studiously avoiding the word 'assistance', it stated that American 'support' would be made available in a way that was 'practically most useful'.[150] Clearly, those engaged in the business of assistance—both in India and Washington—found themselves walking on egg shells. An editorial in the *Economic Weekly*—somewhat unsurprisingly—stressed that buying arms from abroad did not 'strip us [India]'. Non-alignment, according to the article, would 'withstand this acid test'. In fact, the prime minister, the man whose sensitivities were apparently so damaged, was alive to the needs of the hour. The reality was that India's approach was being adapted. The opinion of the *Economic Weekly* aside, India had been shocked into change.

On 29 October, in a meeting with Galbraith, 'Nehru made a definite request for US military assistance.'[151] The sometimes loftier language with regard to non-alignment was rolled back. Indeed, only a few weeks earlier, the prime minister had stated that seeking the provision of foreign military aid would amount to India becoming part of 'someone else's block'. He highlighted that 'taking military help is basically and fundamentally opposed to a non-alignment policy, [it] means practically becoming aligned to that country'.[152] This was no longer the case. Nehru quickly, and less reluctantly than otherwise assumed, made procurement a priority. However, he only did so after having received the assurances he needed. Much like his envoys before him, in the 29 October meeting with Galbraith, Nehru tested the American ambassador. He 'hoped that this would not mean a military alliance between the United States and India'. Galbraith immediately shot back: 'we insist[ed] on no such thing'.[153] Pushing this line of enquiry, T.N. Kaul, the new Indian ambassador to Moscow, pointedly asked Galbraith if the US was out to unpick non-alignment.[154] Clearly, and not without hesitation, the parameters of assistance were being carefully guarded by Indian elites. On Galbraith's advice, Talbot in Washington underlined to the press that the US was 'helping a friend in need', and 'not seeking to gain a military ally'.[155] In India, the MEA's reply to the offer of American assistance avoided the term 'aid'. Officially, bureaucrats were instructed to treat assistance as nothing more than 'procurement'. It was, at least in letter, to be paid for in rupees. The fortified approach found little resonance in the American press. A.M. Rosenthal, the

Pulitzer Prize-winning columnist for the *New York Times*, put the MEA's response in context for his American readers:

A spokesman however, still avoided saying what has been printed in every newspaper in India, and known throughout the world—that Mr. Nehru himself asked the United States for help. Americans here do not attach enormous importance to Mr. Nehru's obvious reluctance to state flatly that he had to abandon his long standing policy of not requesting military aid.[156]

The Indian press was slightly more guarded. *The Hindu* called this a 'commercial transaction'.[157] Further, and demonstrative of the self-moved controls placed on the appeal for aid, Nehru refused to sign any agreement for the supply of arms. Assistance was sought on an ad hoc basis, and necessarily so. A formal agreement could potentially limit Indian choices in the future. The idea was to avoid knee-jerk responses until the facts had been better understood. Officials like Kaysen, who would play a vital role in dealing with Nehru's more desperate call for intervention a few weeks later, were no doubt irritated. Arms assistance needed to be 'regularised'. He was finally convinced by Sir Ormsby-Gore to let it go. Nehru was, as Gore put it, 'very sensitive' about the 'supply of arms'.[158]

Removing the Symbol of 'Anti-Americanism'

On 26 October, President Sarvepalli Radhakrishnan, the philosopher, former ambassador to Moscow and the second president of India after Rajendra Prasad, declared a state of emergency. It was ratified by the Indian Parliament when it reconvened on 8 November 1962.[159] The war, the military's unpreparedness and the approach to the West were a matter of considerable political contestation in the halls of power. Earlier in 1962, the third Indian General Assembly elections, which saw the Congress return to power with a sweeping majority of 361 seats in the Lok Sabha, had also witnessed the slow but steady growth of dissent. Much like the elections in 1952, the CPI occupied the largest number of seats in the opposition, but unlike the early 1950s, the political centre-right—represented by the newly constituted Swatantra Party—won eighteen seats.[160] The party was formed only a few days prior to the elections and was led by C. Rajagopalachari, the former Congress leader. Almost immediately, Rajaji became the 'principal' behind 'public attacks on Menon', as one British official put it.[161] For his part, C.R or Rajaji, as Rajagopalachari was popularly known, called for a 'more dynamic military policy'. C.R was clear that India 'must build friendship and alliances with western powers'. Menon had to go.[162]

The defence minister was seen as the principal hindrance underlying the effort both to oust the Chinese and equally to equip the armed forces. Seen by some—mostly those on the left—as a 'scapegoat' and a 'perfect target' for those who 'dared not question the Prime Minister',[163] Menon was removed from his post on 30–31 October. Rather than ousting him completely, he was made minister for defence production, a less prominent portfolio, and later dropped from the Cabinet altogether.[164] As far as Galbraith was concerned, the 'symbol of anti-Americanism' had been removed.[165] Kennedy, too, was relieved. Menon, the president once remarked, was nothing less than a 'disaster'.[166] Even Indira Gandhi, the prime minister's daughter and someone for whom Menon was something of a 'father figure' and a 'friend',[167] found his 'anti-Americanism a nuisance'.[168] Invested in the war effort, helping the government exchange gold for arms,[169] she too called for his resignation. Indeed, a sharper-tongued Indira bluntly confessed to a friend: 'if people do not function, they must go'. In a way, and as Katherine Frank suggests, her attitude was demonstrative of a personality and approach to politics 'less bound by emotional ties',[170] qualities that India's future prime minister would come to be defined by in matters of both domestic politics and international affairs.

As for Menon, he somewhat ludicrously argued that one of the reasons behind the Chinese attack was for the anti-rapprochement lobby in Beijing to 'get him thrown out'.[171] To his credit, which is seldom given to a man most found scheming and haughty, until his death in October 1974 he never sought to make his case or defend decisions that he had taken as defence minister. He only once maintained that rather than 'tearing a hole in non-alignment', and depending purely on the West for help, the government should have 'gone all out to both sides'.[172] Yet, and as facts would have it, there was only one side India could have turned to: the West, especially the US, and in a more limited sense, the UK.

Russia

Khrushchev had adopted a neutral position ever since the outbreak of hostilities. Citing the Cuban missile crisis and wary not to break with

Communist China, Moscow did not even provide rhetorical support for India. Instead, and as the Soviet mouthpiece *Pravda* put it, the blame lay with 'the imperialist powers' for having drawn the McMahon Line in the first place.[173] Negotiations, Khrushchev publicly stated, were the way forward. However, he provided little by way of how these might materialise.[174] Indeed, Khrushchev's less-than-veiled attacks against China were evident only in December.[175] In short, and for the moment, Moscow went neutral. Interestingly, while India, at least initially, was left in the cold, Beijing too believed that Khrushchev was unhelpful.[176]

Following the dispatch of Nehru's first letter for assistance on 26 October, and in a meeting with the Indian chargé d'affaires, Khrushchev 'avoided taking any definite line'.[177] Indeed, T.N. Kaul believed that in case of a 'showdown', the Soviets would support the Chinese.[178] A fortnight after the first letter was dispatched, Kaul was convinced that the Soviet Union could not be expected to 'take a pro-Indian and an anti-Chinese attitude at this juncture'.[179] As far as British diplomats were concerned, the Russians were 'embarrassed by the Chinese resort to force', but at the same time 'limited their reactions' under 'strong Chinese pressure by bloc solidarity' in what was a 'difficult moment for themselves'.[180] In fact, Kennedy was well aware of this.[181] He was wary that while the US would end up doing all the heavy lifting, Khrushchev and Russia would 'emerge … in a rather beneficial light'.[182] Menon certainly saw it this way. However, on the ground, and as was factually evident, America's heavy lifting was soon obvious.

American Arms

Within four days of making a request for arms, American C-130s loaded with infantry weapons and light artillery arrived in Calcutta.[183] By 11 November, the first set of orders had been furnished. Forty-one sorties carrying a total of 41,000 tonnes of equipment reached Dum Dum airport.[184] For his part, Galbraith well understood that the mere fact of American equipment being supplied to India placed Nehru in a less enviable position. The ambassador knew better than most that the US was dealing not only with a 'very tired leader', but one whose principles and ideas had been 'badly shattered'.[185] He wrote to Kennedy: 'nothing is so important to him [Nehru], more personally than politically, than to maintain the semblance of this independence'. Yet the ambassador was also alive to the fact that the American bureaucratic machinery and the US Congress would have limited tolerance for recalcitrance on India's part. After all, America, according to Galbraith, was supplying India's war efforts. In the ultimate analysis, Galbraith made clear to Kennedy, 'We [the US] cannot decently help someone who is afraid to be seen in our company.'[186]

Philips Talbot insisted on having something in writing. On 14 November, the assistant secretary of state and B.K. Nehru exchanged notes that in effect amounted to a defence agreement between the US and India. However, and ever conscious of the fact that pushing India too hard in these trying times could undermine the good will generated by the assistance provided, the agreement was largely free of conditions. It only asked that the Indian government provide some limited facilities to American representatives involved in reviewing and auditing military equipment, and that India return defence material that was 'no longer needed for the purposes for which originally made'.[187] Given the circumstances, these were hardly objectionable clauses.

In Parliament, MPs were absorbed by the kind of fervour expected by elites of a nation at war. One member of the opposition went as far as to state that he and his party—The Praja Socialists—were ready to 'surrender' themselves 'to the government for the sake of the nation'. Military aid was 'welcome' from any country.[188] Another argued:

There should be a strategic or rather a national re-orientation of our policy of non-alignment. We should remove our bias against the Western democracies as agents of imperialism. We should weigh their every action and should support them in their hour of need.[189]

There was never a better moment for Anglo-American goodwill generated and augmented inside the 530-metre circumference of what was then a 35-year-old Parliament building. Even the Communists, although wary of Swatantra's call for allying with the US and dropping the 'dream' of non-alignment—a proposal made several times by its founding member N.G. Ranga[190]—accepted and argued that arms from the West could be worked into an 'honourable framework of non-alignment'.[191] No doubt, especially for most Congress and Communist Party members, asking for military assistance was scripted into what might be considered an elastic interpretation of non-alignment. Stripped down to its bare bones, non-alignment, according to Nehru, was still a plausible idea because the 'help' given was 'unconditional and without any strings'. Doggedly chary about American cargo planes landing and taking off from Indian airfields, in his opening speech to the emergency session of Parliament the prime minister did not mention the US or Britain even once. He simply thanked 'friendly nations' for their assistance and argued that Indians would have to face the 'burden' of aggression 'ourselves'.[192] Clearly, and notwithstanding the fact that the government and its envoys had ensured that assistance from abroad would not risk India tumbling into an alliance with US, change was underway. There was no getting around the harsh reality that the very idea and notion underlying autonomy was under negotiation.

'Total Silence', 17 to 19 November

On 17 November, Kaul sent a signal to Thapar, the army chief, of the hazardous position the 4 Corps found itself in. He stated:

It is my duty to urge that the enemy threat is now so great and his overall strength is so superior that you should ask the highest authorities to get such foreign armed forces to come to our aid as are willing, without which, as I have said before and I reiterate, it seems beyond the capacity of our armed forces to stem the tide of the superior Chinese forces which he has and continue to concentrate against us to our disadvantage.[193]

On reading the signal, Thapar was shocked. He allegedly said that Bijji (Kaul) had 'finally lost his mind'.[194] However, this time, Kaul was not far off the mark. His appeal to the army chief was genuine and urgent. Indeed, Kaul later wrote that the suggestion of foreign intervention was not 'a counsel of fear', but rather the fact that the army and more generally the country was 'facing a stark reality', that of Chinese dominance.[195] Indeed, this was hardly a matter of exaggeration or insanity. In fact, a day earlier, T.T. Krishnamachari or TTK, the new minister for defence coordination and supply, had been worried about Calcutta being bombed and had asked Galbraith for interceptor aircraft and half a billion dollars in loan. Whether this appeal was approved by Nehru remains unclear. For the moment, TTK was rebuffed.[196] Also on 17 November, M.J. Desai pushed Galbraith to provide transport planes to move Indian troops from the border in Punjab to the NEFA, but Washington, for its part, was 'psychologically unprepared' to adhere to hasty requests and have America embroiled in a war not of its choosing.[197] These requests, it would appear, were founded on the basis of reaction to the debilitating and demoralising state of affairs in the border. They did not, as yet, enjoy the backing of the prime minister, at least not directly.

By the evening of the 17th, the PLA overran the majority of the army's posts in the Eastern sector. Poshing La and Nuranang, important army and administrative posts in the Kameng division, had been captured. The PLA also established two road blocks between Bomdila and Dirang Dzong that effectively cut off the Indian Army's supply chain into the NEFA.[198]

At 19.30 hours, Kaul, based at the 4 Corps headquarters in Tezpur, was joined by Thapar, Sen and Palit. The gravity of the situation was such that it demanded the army chief, the Eastern Corps commander and the DMO to be present. Between the evening of the 17th and the early hours of the 18th, the Indian Army in the NEFA all but collapsed. At 06.45 hours on 18 November, the 4 Division, under the command of Major General Anant Pathania, which was supposed to have served as the last line of defence in the NEFA, closed its headquarters at Dirang Dzong. Pathania called for withdrawal. Why exactly he chose to do so remains a mystery.[199] Soon after, Se La, Dirang Dzong and Bomdila fell.[200] Palit notes, 'Total silence had reigned within the wireless and telecommunications network of 4 infantry division. There could be no doubt that everybody was on the run. 4 infantry division had ceased to exist.'[201] Sen recommended to Thapar that the army should ask for a ceasefire and surrender.[202]

Sen's anxiety was wholly understandable. Booth noted that in the NEFA there was virtually nothing 'between them [PRC] and the military and economic centre of Tezpur on the Brahmaputra River'.[203] All civilian flights were stopped.[204] It was clear to those like Gundevia that the Chinese 'successfully penetrated southwards at every point'.[205] In the NEFA, reports began to come in that the army was fleeing, 'artillery and stores left where they stood. Among these were the American automatic rifles' dropped off at Dum Dum only a few days earlier.[206] Some 1,800 soldiers made their way across the border into friendly Bhutan, which had signed a Treaty of Friendship with India in August 1947. Others pulled back to the north bank of Assam and then near Tezpur. The city itself was a 'ghost town', all but eleven journalists left, of which only two were Indians. For the most part, information on and from the front was being heard on Peking Radio.[207]

In Delhi, there was widespread belief that 500 Chinese paratroopers were about to be airdropped into the capital. Some argued that the PLA was already outside Tezpur. Others speculated that Kaul had been taken prisoner, a rumour that President Radhkrishnan dismissed as 'unfortunately, untrue'.[208] Absorbed by both conjecture and alarm, Lal Bahadur Shastri, the union home minister, even argued that the Chinese plan was to invade Asia.[209] On a plane back to Delhi, and following the two-day stint in Tezpur, Thapar mused whether he should resign.[210] On the 19th he offered his resignation, and following some hesitation on Nehru's part, the prime minister finally accepted the same. J.N. Chaudhuri was asked to officiate as the acting chief of Army Staff.[211]

On 19 November, when Walong—in the Eastern Luhit Valley—fell and the Chinese steamed past the Se La Pass, New Delhi panicked and thought that Calcutta too would soon be taken. As Kux underlines, 'the loss of the province of Assam and perhaps all of Eastern India was dreaded'.[212] Indira Gandhi, who happened to turn forty-five that day, flew immediately to Tezpur. She took with her some Indian Red Cross supplies, but could do little more than serve as a source of inspiration to those in the NEFA who faced migration.[213] Bereft of an army chief, and given the hopelessness of the situation at the border, Nehru shot-off the first of two letters to Kennedy that at least in part informs the accepted and popular narrative according to which 'non-alignment lay in shambles'.[214]

A 'Dignified' Appeal, 19 November

On the afternoon of the 19th, M.J. Desai informed Galbraith that Washington should expect two letters from the prime minister.[215] The second was 'highly confidential' and was to be transmitted through the Indian embassy in Washington by the prime minister's trusted cousin. The Indian government wanted the American air force to 'back them [India] up so that they [India] [could] employ theirs tactically without leaving their cities unprotected'. The request, according to Galbraith, made 'non-alignment far out of date'.[216] This followed comments the ambassador had made two days earlier, when he told Dean Rusk that Indian vulnerabilities placed the US 'on the edge of great opportunity'. In exchange for assistance, the Americans could expect 'reconciliation between India and Pakistan, security for the whole subcontinent', and a 'decisive reverse for communism in its area of its greatest opportunity'.[217] Yet, and despite Galbraith's scheming machinations, for the moment Rusk appeared unmoved. Peace with Pakistan was important, but the potential invasion of eastern India far more so.

A copy of the first letter—from Nehru to Kennedy—was handed by Desai to Galbraith on the 19th and relayed at 4.47 p.m. (IST) to the White House[218]—before Bomdila fell. A hardcopy had been delivered by B.K. Nehru a little earlier at 4 p.m. (IST).[219] The telegram, according to the Indian ambassador, 'went counter to our policy of non-alignment', but was 'nevertheless couched in terms, which, given all the circumstances, continued to be dignified'.[220] The short, two-and-a-half-page letter started with the prime minister thanking Kennedy for the 'speed with which the urgently needed small arms and ammunition were rushed to India' in early November. He then explained the impossible situation India found itself in. Bomdila, the headquarters of the NEFA Command, he wrote, 'had been surrounded and the equivalent of two divisions engaged in the operations' were 'fighting difficult rear-guard actions'. The Chinese, Nehru made certain to convey, were 'in possession of the greater portion' of the NEFA and were 'poised to over-run Chushul in Ladakh', in the Western sector.[221] What Nehru did not state was that the PLA were thought to penetrate the Middle sector too, potentially reaching Punjab, Himachal Pradesh and Uttar Pradesh.[223] The prime minister officially endorsed TTK and Desai's previous appeal to Galbraith, 'the need for air transport and jet fighters'. India was facing a 'grim situation', and 'a lot more effort' from India and her friends was needed to 'roll back' an 'unscrupulous and powerful aggressor'.[224]

The letter's intent was clear, but it perhaps did not as yet communicate the sort of panic that had gripped Indian elites in these hard-pressed times. The letter, as B.K. Nehru suggested, was still respectable. Indeed, Nehru also wrote to Prime Minister Macmillan as well as to friends he trusted. On the 18th, he asked Field Marshall Bernard Montgomery, the first viscount Montgomery of Alamein, for help. Montgomery knew Zhou and Nehru, and pressured Alexander Douglas-Home, the British foreign secretary, to use his services.[225] In London, M.C. Chagla, the Indian high commissioner, pushed Duncan Sandy, the British Commonwealth secretary, to consider providing two Royal Air Force (RAF) planes to fly further supplies to India.[226] Clearly, the Indian prime minister and his team were exploring all of the options they could possibly think of. For Nehru, the very act of asking for this sort of assistance was alien to both his demeanour and conscience. Yet, and the popular charge of a broken prime minister aside, Nehru responded to the needs of the hour.

'Fight for Survival', 19 November

In Delhi, once M.J. Desai left Galbraith, the American ambassador again messaged Rusk and the State Department. As mentioned above, he had just learnt from Desai that a second letter was in the making. Galbraith stressed this was 'in reaction to new disasters and further large Chinese advances today'. The Indians, Galbraith continued, were to ask Kennedy to authorise the United States Air Force (USAF) to help provide 'joint air defence' for India. The 'Indian mood,' Galbraith underlined, was 'desperate'. He also mentioned how 'senior ministers' in Delhi were not informed of this request. The American embassy staff were also kept in the dark. Importantly, and given the seriousness of the issue at hand, he asked that Rusk and the president 'protect [the] fact of my [Galbraith's] knowledge and this warning now and indefinitely'.[227]

Authored on Nehru's behalf, potentially by M.J. Desai, the 'main advisor on the move',[228] the letter was seen by H.C. Sarin and John Lall, joint secretaries in the MoD, Palit,[229] S. Soundararajan deputy secretary in the MoD, Vincent Coelho, joint secretary in the MEA, K. Subrahmanyam, who then shared an office with Soundararajan and only heard of the letter,[230] and of course, B.K. Nehru. Indeed, it was marked 'personal' and was not circulated in the Indian chancery in Washington, where it was telegrammed.[231] No copies were given directly to Galbraith or sent officially to the US State Department, which would otherwise have been the protocol as it had been for the letter that arrived earlier that day. Not even Krishna Menon, who remained Nehru's close friend,[232] or Mullick, the IB director, had known of the existence of the letter.[233] In an interview with Michael Brecher six years later, Menon maintained that 'Panditji did not make this request.' So disbelieving were the contents to Nehru's dear friend that he forcefully argued that the prime minister 'would not do a thing of that kind'.[234] Gundevia too was kept in the dark. As late as in 1984, he commented, 'Yes, we did ask for arms and ammunition, but we did not ask and did not expect the West to step in and fight the battle for us on our soil.'[235] The note to Kennedy was undoubtedly both far-reaching and almost world-shattering given India's watchful approach to military assistance and the United States thus far. In the White House, it was kept a closely guarded secret. Nothing was even shared with British officials like Gore or Prime Minister Macmillan.

The letter was probably written soon after Bomdila fell, and finally sent to the chancery in Washington between 9 and 10 p.m. (IST).[236] B.K. Nehru delivered it by hand to Carl Kaysen to be handed over to the president. After having read the letter, and somewhat uncannily, Kaysen apparently said: 'so your spirit couldn't stand even a minor attack for two weeks'.[237] This sense of condescension was, however, Kaysen's alone. Kennedy's response, at least for the moment, overcame any hint of superciliousness. Indeed, the urgency and sheer alarm, as explained by the prime minister, was absolute.

Nehru underscored that 'with the advance of the Chinese in massive strength, the entire Brahmaputra Valley is seriously threatened'. He now also highlighted the threat to the Middle sector. He acknowledged that India hitherto had not asked for 'comprehensive assistance particularly air assistance because of the wider implications of such assistance in the global context'. Further, and indicative of Nehru's continuing hesitation in reaching out, he mentioned that India had not wanted to 'embarrass' her 'friends'. The present crisis, however, was 'really desperate'. Nehru made clear:

We have to have more comprehensive assistance if the Chinese are to be prevented from taking over the whole of Eastern India. Any delay in this assistance reaching us will result in nothing short of a catastrophe for our country.

To survive the onslaught, India had hoped to deploy its 'air arm in support' of its forces, but could not do so because of the poor state of radar and air defences in the event of 'retaliatory action by the Chinese'. Hence the prime minister made the astonishing and much-needed—at least as Indian elites saw it—request for 'a minimum of 12 squadrons of supersonic all weather fighters' and radar installations. Importantly, USAF personnel would have to 'man these fighters and installations'. Indeed, there was no doubt whatsoever that the intent of the letter was to invite the USAF to fight India's war with and on behalf of India. The letter stated:

US fighters and transport planes manned by US personnel will be used for the present to protect our cities and installations from Chinese air attacks and to maintain our communications. We should if this is possible also like US planes manned by US personnel to assist the Indian Air Force in air battles with the Chinese air force over Indian areas where air action by the IAF against Chinese communication lines, supplies and troop concentration may lead to counter air action by the Chinese.

Further, the prime minister asked for two B-47-type bombers to 'neutralize' Chinese 'bases and air fields'. The only caveat that conditioned the use of American planes and fire power was that 'air action' beyond the limits of India—such as in Tibet—would be taken by the IAF alone. Also, assuaging Kennedy's potential concern about Pakistan and Ayub Khan's reaction, Nehru stressed that 'all the assistance or equipment given to us to meet our dire need will be used entirely for resistance against the Chinese'. The four-and-a-half-page letter ended on a forceful note akin to words that could be expected from the likes of Eisenhower or even George H.W. Bush. It said:

We are confident that your great country will in this hour of our trial help us in our fight for survival and for the *survival of freedom and independence in this sub-continent as well as the rest of Asia.*[238]

Summoned immediately to the White House, Rusk met with Kennedy. Having received the first letter on 19 November, the secretary of state had recommended sending a high-level team of military and civilian experts to India as soon as possible. He also suggested dispatching twelve or more C-130 transport planes for 'any necessary movement of forces and equipment to Assam area or to Ladakh'. This was finally approved on 20 November.[239] However, when it came to the second letter, Rusk immediately took to reservation. He wrote to Galbraith that 'this message' amounted to a 'request for an active and, practically speaking, unlimited military partnership between the United States and India to take on Chinese invasion of India'. Somewhat astutely, while Rusk understood that this would mean taking a call on 'far reaching political and strategic issues' that could potentially land the United States in a direct fight against the PRC for the second time in a decade, he also appreciated that Nehru's call had more to do with panic than forethought. Indeed, he was 'not at all convinced' that the Indians were 'prepared to face the situation in the same terms'.

In short, Rusk was not in the least convinced that Nehru and his advisors were themselves fully aware of what they were asking for. After all, this sort of assistance would mean 'not only a military alliance between India and the United States but complete commitment by us [the US] to a fighting war'. It could no longer be 'reconciled with any further pretence of non-alignment'. Clearly, authorising small arms, light artillery and even C-130s was one thing, but actually fighting a war on India's behalf was completely different. 'If this is what Nehru has in mind,' Rusk continued, 'he should be completely clear about it before we even consider our own decision.' Further, he made clear to Galbraith, this sort of assistance would need the support of the UN, the Commonwealth more generally and peace in Kashmir. Astonishingly, and having received the most desperate call for help by a prime minister who genuinely believed that he was about to lose the eastern quarter of his country, Rusk made plain that the 'United States cannot give maximum military support to India while most of India's forces are engaged against Pakistan.'[240] Before Galbraith would have a chance to raise these questions with M.J. Desai and Nehru, the war ended.

On 20 November, an editorial in the *People's Daily* asked India to 'come back to the conference table'.[241] A day earlier, the British Foreign Office received a fifteen-page note signed by Zhou. It stated that the PRC favoured 'reopening of peaceful negotiations to settle the boundary dispute', and called for a '20 kilometre withdrawal by the armed forces of each side from the line of actual control'.[242] At 00.00 hours on 22 November, Chinese Frontier Guards would ceasefire along the entire border. On 1 December, they would move 20 kilometres behind the line as it existed on 7 November 1959.[243] However, in the Western sector, the Chinese occupied territory claimed by them in 1960. In Delhi, the Chinese note was received on 20 November.[244] In effect, the PRC did not gain any territory in the NEFA, but instead safeguarded their strategic advantage in the Aksai Chin area in the Western sector.[245] In a meeting with Galbraith on 22 November, the prime minister was 'inclined to think that the Chinese offer of ceasefire and withdrawal was real'. One of the reasons shaping Chinese motivations, according to Galbraith's exchange with Nehru, was the 'speed of the American response'.[246]

Conclusion

Following the ceasefire, an editorial in the *Economic Weekly* argued that India was poised to 'develop western leanings' due to the help it had received.[247] Writing in the *New York Times*, A.M. Rosenthal stated that India's 'emotional balance' had 'swung westward'.[248] A CIA brief noted that India was undergoing 'metamorphosis', opening up 'new opportunities for the west'. Most of all, India would be 'more susceptible than ever before to influence by the US and the UK'.[249] Kux, too, argued that Nehru 'reversed policy 180 degrees to seek military assistance'.[250] To an extent, these assessments are certainly justified.

After all, the prime minister had once boasted how seeking arms aid amounted to becoming a part of 'someone else's bloc'. He forcefully argued that 'taking military help' means 'practically becoming aligned to that country'.[251] In Parliament, Nehru made clear that 'the act' of asking for 'protection and seeking aid disables us and makes us weak and feeble and dependent on others'.[252] There was no doubt in anyone's mind that the war changed India and its prime minister. Writing in *Foreign Affairs* in 1963, in an article aptly titled 'Changing India', Nehru himself admitted that there was a need to 'adjust our relations with friendly countries in the light of the changing actualities of the international situation, and, above all, to preserve and consolidate national unity'.[253] The Chinese, 'devious and deceptive' as they had proved to be, required that India pay 'considerably more attention to strengthening' her armed forces. This task, Nehru added, would inevitably need 'external aid in adequate measure'.[254] The tone underlying his message was in stark contrast to the last time the prime minister had written in the same journal in 1937. He then asserted that if India was able to dislodge British imperialism, it would seem 'to follow that she will also be strong enough to resist fresh aggression'.[255]

The shock of war, and more importantly, the shock of defeat, made Indian decision-makers open to the idea of 'perceptual change'.[256] According to one defence economist, the war 'aroused a new defence consciousness in the country'. By 1965, the MoD had set up a Planning Cell to look into long-term defence needs. On its part, the US contributed transport aircraft and helped establish production factories for the Indian Army.[257]

Yet the assertion that India entered into an alliance or that 1962 transformed India's relations with the US—with India as a junior and vulnerable partner—remains empirically untested. Whether or not the second letter on the 19th was really India's 'darkest hour' is arguable at best. Any prime minister in his right mind could—and perhaps should—be expected to do the same in the interest of the nation. Further, as Gopal writes, whether or not the request would have pushed India into an alliance remains a 'hypothetical' proposition.[258] What was more noticeable and perhaps imperative was the fresh tension between a repertoire of older habits and styles and the harsher realities of the time. In a way, this tension informed strategies of action during the war—such as getting assurances for non-alignment from Galbraith before asking for aid and in the face of military defeat.

At one level, the war cemented the idea of America in the hearts and minds of Indian elites and the public. No one, not even the Communists, could deny that America had come to India's aid. It also strengthened bonds of friendship between bureaucrats like M.J. Desai and Galbraith, or B.K. Nehru and the likes of Kaysen. However, at another level, it introduced, more forcefully than ever before, the United States' unassailable need to balance its relations with both India and Pakistan, an act that no American incumbent can claim to have mastered to date. Kennedy came to Nehru's assistance swiftly and without argument in the early part of November 1962, but, as detailed above, when it came to the matter of actually fighting alongside the Indian Air Force, the president and his advisors stalled. They, immediately and without forgiveness, considered what was felt to be a matter of equal concern: assuaging Pakistani concerns, even though it was India that faced possible peril.

In practice, and as will be made clear in the following chapter, the manner in which the United States chose to deal with the matter of balance in the aftermath of Indian defeat introduced a sense of realism to a relationship that was no longer grasping unfamiliar terrain. Bizarrely, it forged the idea of mutual need that turned into an uneasy partnership, between India and America. Here on, the relationship was shaped by a much-needed and even necessary sagacity. Kennedy and the American Foreign Service bureaucracy learnt of the extent to which India had embraced the tension of change, while Nehru, henceforth his successor daughter, and Indian diplomats more generally accepted that Pakistan would play a vital part in Washington's approach to India.

5

'SWUNG BACK'

1962–3

On 28 March 1963, Sudhir Ghosh, a less-recognised figure in Indian history, met with Kennedy. A serving Congress MP in the Upper House of the Indian Parliament and a social worker once close to Gandhi,[1] Ghosh was considered something of a busybody. Yet, his notes, particularly on the conflict with China and American assistance, were carefully read by Nehru.[2] Over the years, Ghosh developed an 'unusual' rapport with American legislators and officials.[3] Galbraith even referred to him as the 'strongest pro-American Congressman' he knew.[4] Bundy was sold on the idea of Ghosh, and arranged the meeting with the president. Predictably, the issues discussed most were military assistance and Kashmir.

Following the ceasefire, American officials set out to 'persuade' and 'encourage' Nehru to find a solution to the conflict in Kashmir.[5] In fact, American diplomacy—egged-on by Britain—was akin to coercion, using the desperately needed prize of dollars as bait to pressurise India into talks. The deal, according to Kennedy and his co-conspirator, British Prime Minister Harold Macmillan, was relatively straightforward: the US, the UK and the Commonwealth were prepared to provide India with military assistance to deter the 2.6 million-strong PLA in exchange for peace with Pakistan. In turn, the latter was pushed to 'take advantage of [the] opportunity of the moment'.[6] Needless to add, the plan failed—the dispute remains unresolved to this day. Nehru and

Indian bureaucrats more generally proved harder to crack than either the State Department or the CRO were first prepared to accept. In his meeting with Ghosh, Kennedy grudgingly accepted that Kashmir 'was perhaps more complicated than Americans realised'. The president confessed that Galbraith, a key protagonist in the cash-for-Kashmir script, 'was wrong in putting pressure on the Indian government immediately after the Chinese invasion'.[7] Indeed, a fortnight before he left his post in July 1963, Galbraith himself wrote that 'there is no hope of a settlement of the Kashmir issue in the foreseeable future'.[8]

The cheering expressions of optimism—both for survival in the war and for friendship with the US—underlined by American assistance in the earlier part of November 1962, were diluted by an increasing sense of suspicion and frustration in the trying months following the war. In fact, Jammu and Kashmir—on the Indian side of the border, as it exists today—could have looked very different had it not been for a determined prime minister and a more than a remarkable team of bureaucrats and ministers. These included the likes of M.J. Desai, Y.D. Gundevia, Y.B. Chavan (the new defence minister and former chief minister of Maharashtra) and Swaran Singh (the railways minister who later became the first Indian foreign minister after Nehru).

Far too often and for far too long, commentators, insiders and writers have led themselves and much of their readership into thinking that the war left Nehru a 'broken man'.[9] There is no doubt, as Katherine Frank puts it, that the prime minister found himself 'politically vulnerable' and 'psychologically depressed'.[10] After all, the most acute consequence of the war was its impact on foreign policy, which was being remade in front of Nehru's eyes. Greater military-to-military contacts with the West and later the Soviet Union were deemed essential. The language used to define and inform foreign policy also changed. Words such as 'survival', 'self-help' and 'freedom' were used less often after 1962. The shock of military defeat led to an approach, which, as Gopal recounts, was 'unthinkable but a few months before'.[11] Yet, Nehru's stewardship and doggedness, albeit with strong guidance from his advisors, saw India through a crisis that is less understood and written about in existing works.[12] For the better part of six months, between December 1962 and May 1963, Indian representatives were left to wrestle with and figure out how best to get military assistance while remaining firm on Kashmir.

This chapter details how Nehru and his team sought to negotiate the future of Kashmir, the desperate need for long-term military assistance and what turned out to be a demanding and initially rigid Washington bureaucracy. In some ways, this can be considered a central chapter in the larger scheme of the book in that it establishes how strategic change is a process rather than a revolution. The prime minister might have deviated from what would be considered the normal course in Indian foreign policy, but, as Kennedy observed, Nehru and other elites soon 'swung back' to their 'original position with regards to the United States'.[13] As the US president put it, the 'conversion', most apparent in the request for B-47 squadrons, 'lasted only a few days'.[14] The call for arms did not, as B.K. Nehru asserted, alter the 'very fundamentals' of India's relations with the United States.[15] At best, it introduced a tension that was most palpable in the manner in which post-war India approached the question and destiny of Kashmir. In the end, it partially received the assistance it needed, leaving Indian positions along the border with Pakistan as they were on 31 December 1948, when a cease-fire in Kashmir was first announced.[16]

The chapter is divided into five parts. It begins with a very short background to the Kashmir dispute, before going on to outline why Pakistan was seen by Eisenhower, Kennedy and their respective administrations as a central pillar in America's wider fight against communism. The third section—entitled 'preparing for talks'—aims to determine exactly the kind of pressures India faced towards the end of 1962 by delineating a set of conditions that made the US indispensable to Indian strategic interests. Crucially, and as the following part shows, despite the unique position held by the US, Indian elites were not spell-bound by American overtures and they refused to bend to American demands. The pressure for change might have forced representatives to negotiate with Pakistan, but this did not mean that they were going to give away even an inch of Kashmir. The conclusion highlights how misgivings on India's part were manageably organised into a relationship further forged in crisis.

Kashmir: A Primer

By August 1947, around 560 princely states had been absorbed into the independent dominion of India. Not one acceded to Pakistan. The Punjabi-speaking state of Bahawalpur would be the first, and did so only in October 1948.[17] In India, the *nawabs* of Junagarh and Hyderabad and Maharaja Hari Singh, the Hindu *Dogra* ruler of Jammu and Kashmir, were yet to make up their minds. While the *nawabs* were soon pushed into signing what was called the 'instrument of accession', the legal apparatus through which states joined either dominion, the case of Kashmir would eventually lead to the outbreak of war. Following an invasion of tribal hoards, or 'raiders', from the Frontier regions of Pakistan, Hari Singh acceded to India.[18]

Almost immediately, rickety Dakotas packed with Indian troops departed for Srinagar, the summer capital of Jammu and Kashmir. By December, the Pakistani Army actively supported the tribal effort, and by the spring of 1948, Pakistani regulars joined the fight for Kashmir.[19] What ensued was the first Kashmir War, which lasted until 31 December 1948, ending with a ceasefire announced under the auspices of the UN. Accordingly, Azad (free) Kashmir (hereafter AJK), a third of the former princely state, including the northern areas of Gilgit–Baltistan (GB), came to be administered by Pakistan. The remaining two-thirds, or the Indian state of Jammu–Kashmir (hereafter J–K), including the mountainous terrain of Ladakh, Hindu-majority Jammu and the Muslim-majority Kashmir Valley, were administered by India.

Both India and Pakistan soon accepted the ceasefire line (CFL). In time, the entire state was to be demilitarised, as per UN resolutions, followed by a free and impartial plebiscite. In reality, demilitarisation proved impractical. Neither side was willing to draw-down their forces. Importantly, Pakistan refused to discontinue the training of militias in Azad Kashmir,[20] making it impossible for India, which agreed to demilitarisation, to follow suit.[21] The trust deficit instituted a virtual gridlock. In sum, Pakistan assumed the character of a revisionist actor, demanding the end of Indian 'occupation' of Jammu and Kashmir. As far as Pakistani elites were concerned, Hari Singh had little or no authority to accede to India because of a popular revolt in the princely state that led him to flee Srinagar.[22]

India, on the other hand, came to be considered the status quo actor. The key demand hinged on converting the CFL into an international border. The seeds of dissatisfaction were undoubtedly sown with respect to these differing positions. As M.C. Chagla, the Indian high commissioner to the UK at the time of the China War and later the Indian representative to the UN, noted, Kashmir was 'an integral part of India'. There was absolutely no question of changing or even tweaking the CFL.[23] This is, of course, the public line that continues to be maintained by Indian ministers and bureaucrats. Interestingly, and as will be demonstrated below, behind closed doors, some minimal give-and-take was in fact considered in the more testing months following defeat. The importance of Pakistan to both American and British elites made it almost incumbent upon India to accept negotiations. The rationale underlying this fixation with Pakistan is discussed below.

'God Shall Protect Pakistan'

Reportedly, these were the last words of Liaquat Ali Khan,[24] the Pakistani prime minister who was assassinated on 16 October 1951 during a meeting in Rawalpindi. The following few years saw some half a dozen prime ministers come and go. Finally, in October 1958, Muhammad Ayub Khan, a non-Pashto-speaking Pashtun became the first of Pakistan's military dictators. As chief of Army Staff during the tumultuous period prior to the 1958 coup, Ayub had fought hard for Washington to ally with Pakistan. Often circumventing American bureaucrats and policy advisors who were wary of the amount of military assistance demanded by Pakistan, the chief would go straight to Capitol Hill. Ayub's appeal, as far as US congressmen and representatives were concerned, rested on the strong anti-Communist sentiments that he frequently aired.

Pakistani prime ministers also made loud claims about how 'any country that is overrun by communism may be lost forever'.[25] Unlike Nehru and India more generally, Pakistani elites had little trouble in using anti-communist discourse to win over the Eisenhower administration. As Kux concludes, Pakistan 'remained committed' to such posturing 'as the best means of improving its security against India'. It is exactly this approach that led to the first mutual defence agreement between Karachi—the Pakistani capital city until 1958—and Washington, institutionalising a highly transactional relationship that, in some form and shape, has survived up to the present day. Clearly, Pakistani leaders looked to America to help save Pakistan from its own domestic problems, and much more importantly, from the military threat that in their reading was posed by India to the very existence of the Islamic Republic.

A Defence Pact with Pakistan

On 24 February 1954, George Allen, Henderson's successor and the former US ambassador to Iran and Yugoslavia, delivered a note authored by Eisenhower to Nehru.[26] The letter informed the prime minister that the Republican administration had decided to supply Pakistan with military equipment under what was known as the US Mutual Defence Assistance Programme. In fact, an official request was made by Pakistani Prime Minister Mohammad Ali two days earlier.[27] On 25 February, Eisenhower went public. He forcefully argued that 'no nation can stand alone today'. 'Regional groupings,' according to the president, were the 'most effective means to assure survival and progress.' Pakistan was thought to serve as a buffer against Soviet expansion in the East, an especially potent position given Eisenhower's disquiet 'over the weakness of defensive capabilities in the Middle East'.[28]

Arab nations, according to both Eisenhower and Dulles, could hardly be relied upon to stem communism. Indeed, during a trip to Pakistan and the Middle East soon after coming to office, Dulles was left unimpressed by Arab leaders and most taken by Pakistan. Ayub Khan, according to the secretary of state, had what it took to do the West's bidding.[29] Notably, Dulles was received in India by some 4,000 demonstrators chanting: 'Go Back Dulles.'[30] This was, of course, reminiscent of the popular 'Go Back Simon' slogan in the late 1920s, when an all-white commission had been appointed by the British government to review the Indian constitution. Nehru later called such hostile greetings 'foolish and misguided', but the deed was done.[31] The stark contrast between Ayub's wooing and India's less receptive approach to Dulles and America more generally highlighted what later turned out to be the false promise of Pakistan.

The pact was finally signed in May. Pakistan, according to Ayub, became 'America's most-allied ally in Asia.'[32] In October, the US Congress authorised 171 million dollars of military aid to be spread over three and half years. Above and beyond the financial pledge, Pakistan was to be given a whole range of big ticket items tilting the military balance in South Asia. This included 730 million dollars of offensive equipment, M 47/48 Patton Tanks—used against India in the 1965 War—and another billion dollars in logistics and communication equipment.[33] Clearly, Ayub's lobbying on the Hill had paid off.

With a view to assuage Indian anxieties, Eisenhower wrote that this arrangement was 'not directed in any way against India'. If the equipment were to be 'misused' or 'directed against another in aggression,' the president told Nehru, he would take 'appropriate action both within and without the UN to thwart such aggression'.[34] The idea of using Pakistan as a staging ground both for intelligence operations against Russia and for ground operations in the Middle East was intently discussed during Truman's term in office. The trouble lay in reaching an agreed approach with Britain, which was hardly keen to provide one of two recently independent dominions with military aid. Finally, Whitehall decided to include Pakistan in what came to be called the Middle East Defence Organisation (MEDO), but without military help. This, it was thought, would minimise the risk of losing India to the Soviet Union.[35] Unmoved by Britain's opposition, American officials argued that overtures to Pakistan without any transfers of military equipment would do little for a long-lasting agreement. Pakistan was seen to be 'pro-west', and such sentiments needed nurturing.[36] Yet, with attention focused on the Korean Peninsula, and given the diplomatic assistance provided by India at the UN (as discussed in Chapter 3), this was hardly the opportune time to choose and support one of two nations in a region where both were useful, but in dramatically different ways. India, senior officials argued—much like they do in the present milieu—was important because of long-term interests. Pakistan was seen to be the answer to immediate and mainly security-related issues. In the reading of American officials, Pakistan offered (and perhaps continues to offer) options for the fulfilment of short-term needs.

Nehru, for one, was wary from the start. In November 1953, following a leak in the *New York Times* about the assistance, he wrote to Prime Minister Ali. Nehru made clear that if this were true, India would not be able to 'ignore' it. All 'our problems,' he argued, would 'have to be seen in a new light'.[37] To U Nu, his close friend and confidant, the Indian prime minister confessed that Pakistan would soon become the 'satellite of America' in South Asia.[38] In his usual exuberant style, he argued that if India were offered assistance, it would 'reject it with thanks'.[39] In Parliament, he stated that external assistance of this sort is a 'dangerous thing'. In a particularly emotional outburst, the prime minister made plain that by 'relying on others' a nation could 'lose' its 'spirit'. 'If India,' he continued, 'loses her soul what would it profit her who defends it?'[40]

This was, however, long before the 1962 War; such language would be dropped altogether in its aftermath. For the time being, Nehru rejected an offer by Eisenhower who pledged his administration's 'sympathetic consideration' should India also want military assistance.[41]

By the late 1950s, and while Nehru was clear that the 'latest type of armour in large quantities and plenty of new aircrafts' were being given to Pakistan, he sought to look past what he considered to be America's ill-conceived approach to South Asia as a whole. Yet he was clear that the alliance with Pakistan would have 'far-reaching consequences for India'. It meant that the 'Cold War had come right to our North-Western frontiers.'[42] Indeed, the consequences Nehru spoke of were most palpable in the manner in which Ayub chose to push Washington to support its case with regard to Kashmir.

In 1958, the Eisenhower administration initiated a backchannel effort to bring India and Pakistan to the negotiating table. Two years later, and following the president's visit to India in December 1959, the White House chose only to provide general and symbolic support. It deliberately refrained from offering concrete plans to resolve the dispute. In New Delhi, Eisenhower was greeted by hundreds of thousands of people. India, according to Howard Schaffer, 'presented Eisenhower with a priceless gift—a part of her heart'.[43] There was no way this president was going to mortgage any part of this goodwill for a conflict that had no apparent solution. The US embassy in New Delhi too noted that 'no pressure short of war would force India to relinquish the Valley'.[44] Further, improved relations between India and the Soviet Union provided New Delhi with a handy veto if and when the issue of a plebiscite was to be mooted in the Security Council.[45] Ayub's straw-man thesis, that Pakistan was the only reliable ally against communism in the East, had partially lost its appeal. This remained the case until Kennedy came to office. Determined to find a solution to an issue that, in official American reading, would allow the US to foster closer ties with both South Asian nations, the new Democratic administration made its attempt to strike a balance.

Kennedy and Kashmir

The Kennedy administration came to office in January 1961 with a mission to advance America's relationship with India. As one of his biographers noted, 'Jack' understood 'un-alignment' in India, and 'adopted a live-and-let-live attitude'.[46] That dealing with India meant dealing with the idea of exception hardly unnerved the former senator from Massachusetts. Dialogue between India and Pakistan was considered a means by which America could truly engage India, limiting the risk and hazard of protest from Ayub Khan's Pakistan: a Cold War ally.

In November 1961, Nehru visited Washington. For the US president, and as is well known in the historiography of this period, the meetings with the prime minister were a 'disaster'.[47] The younger Kennedy not only found Nehru to be older and uninspiring, but also withdrawn and uninterested. Only discussions over Kashmir concentrated the attention of the 72-year-old Indian premier. Nonetheless, nothing was concluded. As ever, Nehru was unshakeable when it came to the question of redrawing borders. Indeed, following one of these meetings, when asked how he got on with Kennedy, an irksome Nehru bluntly told journalists: 'I can get on with anybody in this world.'[48] The passion and excitement with which Nehru had approached Washington in 1949 was altogether absent. Kashmir, as Kennedy put it, was a 'bone-deep issue' for Nehru.[49] The president understood this, but, as outlined above, he was somewhat hamstrung by his administration's quest for balance in South Asia.

In January 1962, a solution was proposed by Kennedy. Eugene Black, a 'high-level mediator' known to both Indians and Pakistanis and who had negotiated the Indus Water Treaty,[50] was to serve as an 'impartial' party to talks.[51] The Indian response, as B.K. Nehru intimated to Galbraith even before he consulted the MEA or the prime minister, was that 'earnest consideration' should not be expected in the immediate future. This, according to the Indian ambassador, was what Nehru too would suggest.[52] In fact, Nehru went further. In a four-page note, and while underlining the 'highest regard' he had for 'Mr. Black's personal qualities', the prime minister respectfully argued that public reaction to reports of 'third party intervention' were 'overwhelmingly adverse'. Such an approach, Nehru continued, 'Might make matters worse.' Even 'informal' lines of enquiry on the part of Black would be seen as 'some kind of mediation and arbitration' and would be 'strongly resented'. 'Direct negotiations and discussions' were the only way forward.[53] For the time being, Nehru and his advisors did well to shield their diplomatic preference of dealing with Pakistan through bilateral channels. The choice of strategy rested with Indian elites. As war broke with China ten months later, and throughout the time of combat and despair, pressure from Ayub mounted.

Pakistan and the China War

On 3 January 1962, a newspaper article aptly titled 'The Enemy Of My Enemy' reported that 'the Chinese government is making overtures to Pakistan for a common front against India'.[54] The opinion piece was referring to exploratory discussions around a potential border agreement between the two states. There were no official negotiations yet, but a note was sent by Pakistan to Zhou in 1960.[55] The idea, as it later transpired, was to define and demarcate the boundary roughly along the mountainous Karakoram Range. Official negotiations only began in October 1962, with an agreement being concluded in March 1963. In effect, and as Gundevia later noted, 'a good chunk of the north-eastern frontier of Kashmir' was being 'gifted away to China'.[56] The area in question, totalling around 5,000 square kilometres in and around Hunza and Gilgit, lay on what India considered to be territory that Pakistan had occupied during the First Kashmir War.[57] Clearly, Pakistani elites did not lose view of the slightest opportunity to pressure both Washington and New Delhi to consider talks. The negotiations with China were a mere precursor to a forceful diplomatic move as more and more American planes offloaded hundreds of tonnes of military equipment at Indian airports.

On 16 October 1962, four days before the Chinese onslaught began in full measure, Prime Minister Ali wrote the first of several notes to Dean Rusk, the US secretary of state. Wary that a 'neutral' such as India was to get military equipment or a 'free ride' when it was Pakistan that had sworn to stem the Communist tide, Ali suggested that this was an 'excellent opportunity' for 'ministerial level discussions on outstanding Indo-Pak issues'.[58] At the time, the request was rebuffed.[59] Galbraith simply suggested that Nehru write to Ayub 'to tell him not to do anything disadvantageous'.[60] Otherwise, and for the moment, American eyes were trained on the threat posed by China to a nation widely considered the beacon of democracy in Asia.

On 4 November, the day the first wave of American arms were delivered to Dum Dum airport in Calcutta, Foreign Minister Muhammad Ali Bogra, the former Pakistani governor general, brought up the question of a plebiscite with British diplomats in Karachi. Pakistani officials were furious that the US had provided arms to India without first notifying Pakistan. Ayub maintained that Nehru had exaggerated the Chinese threat. It was vital, he told Walter McConaughy, a career diplomat and the US ambassador to Pakistan, that Nehru make some kind of 'conciliatory gesture' on Kashmir.[61] Ayub himself was no doubt under pressure from a variety of domestic lobbies to use the opportunity of the moment to push for dialogue. The president of the Muslim League demanded that UN forces replace Indian troops in Jammu and Kashmir. The Lahore Municipal Cooperation launched a campaign against aid to India. Former prime ministers also lobbied British officials to push India into talks.[62]

Following the diplomatic blitz, and given India's need for further equipment in the face of a renewed attack in the second week of November, Galbraith, Rusk and South Asia specialists like Robert Komer rethought Ali and Ayub's earlier call to discuss Kashmir. A last-ditch attempt to convince Ayub was made by Nehru. The prime minister assured the president that weapons from abroad would 'not be used for any purpose' other than the 'effective resistance' against 'further Chinese aggression'.[63] This, however, did nothing to placate the self-appointed Pakistani field marshal. The latter needed assurances of support from his Cold War ally, the United States, and not the head of the nation widely considered as the enemy by elites in Pakistan. On the same day that Nehru made an attempt to reason with Ayub, the Pakistani premier appealed to Rusk and Kennedy. By settling the dispute, he argued, India could relocate a bulk of its forces from the border with Pakistan to the east with China. If, according to Ayub, there were to be a 'change of heart' in India, 'an equitable and honourable settlement', he suggested, 'should not be difficult'.[64]

At this point, even Galbraith argued that 'eventually but not too soon the Indians must be asked to propose meaningful negotiations on Kashmir'.[65] He, much like his counterpart in Islamabad, realised the difficulty of providing India with more equipment without giving Pakistan something in exchange. Much like the Americans, the British government also understood the need to pacify Pakistan. On 19 November, the day Tezpur was evacuated and the prime minister requested American military assistance, M.C. Chagla, the Indian high commissioner in London, was asked by Foreign Office officials if Nehru would not 'say something helpful' with regard to Pakistan's demand over Kashmir.[66] The next day, just hours before the unilateral Chinese cease-fire was announced on Peking radio, and at a time when the invasion of eastern India including Calcutta was considered an all-too-real possibility, S.K. Dehlavi, the Pakistani foreign secretary, read the riot act to British officials. Pakistan, according to Dehlavi, had been 'let down by her friends'. The West, he continued, 'failed to place pressure on Nehru on Kashmir'. The Pakistani government, he made clear, was forced to 'take advantage of any situation' that came its way. By this, Dehlavi insinuated that Pakistan would happily befriend China.[67]

Following the call for a ceasefire, Pakistan pressed its case. On 21 November, Muhammad Ali spoke with McConaughy. The foreign minister argued that while Pakistan and China were like 'oil and water', 'some immediate national advantage' was to be gained by engaging with Beijing.[68] This, as might have been imagined, served to convince the likes of Rusk and Galbraith that further assistance to India could not be entertained without talks on Kashmir. Indeed, Booth, the British high commissioner to Delhi, wasted no time. A day after the ceasefire, he pushed Nehru to 'improve relations with Pakistan'. At first, and given that the prime minister was living in the shock of defeat, he said nothing. His 'prickliness and suspicion about everything Pakistan say and do,'[69] Booth recalled, remained intact. Yet, that India would need to discuss Kashmir was soon apparent, regardless of the prime minister's personal and immediate views. As Gundevia notes, 'while we [India] were licking our wounds, came pressures, pressures worth, shall we say, a little more than $60 million', the cost of the 'shopping bill' for the arms given on aid from the US.[70] Talks with Pakistan were the 'price of defeat' and something Nehru ultimately and reluctantly agreed to.[71] Yet, and as was also apparent, India might have been shocked into dialogue, but what went on in the discussions was India's alone to determine.

Preparing for Talks

On 21 November, a team of twenty-four American experts and civilian advisors boarded what was known as the 'McNamara Special', a custom-made KC-135 jet for the US secretary of defence, Robert McNamara. The team was led by Averell Harriman, an assistant secretary of state. A former candidate for the Democratic presidential nomination, and considered the 'Number One elder statesman' by his British colleagues,[72] Harriman was less sure of the task he was set by Kennedy. Paul Nitze, then an assistant secretary of defence and part of Harriman's group, was somewhat clearer about his role. 'My thought,' he wrote more than twenty-five years later, 'was to extract a promise from Nehru to attempt a settlement with Pakistan in return for our military assistance.'[73] This was clearly consistent with guidance provided by the White House. At a news conference a day before the KC-135 left for New Delhi, Kennedy underlined that 'in providing military assistance to India, we are mindful of our alliance with Pakistan'.[74]

The mission arrived in India on 22 November. They were immediately taken to meet with Nehru, although only for a brief courtesy call.[75] Roger Hilsman, director of the State Department's Bureau of Intelligence and Research, recalled how the welcome was anything but warm. 'It was pro forma, it was withdrawn, it was very limited.' Nehru, according to Hilsman, came across as an 'embarrassed and tired man'. Unlike only a few days before, when he had pleaded for American assistance, he was now reluctant to even admit asking for aid. This undoubtedly did little for a group of advisors who had flown for eighteen hours in response to Nehru's appeal.[76]

On 24 November, Duncan Sandys, the overly assertive and less courteous UK minister for Commonwealth relations, arrived to work with Harriman. He immediately agreed with Nitze's 'suggested approach'.[77] In fact, and as Booth records: 'Sandys lost no time in making it clear that one of his chief objects in coming to India was to see whether in the existing fluid situation, some real step could be taken towards solving the Kashmir problem.'[78] The Sandys–Harriman enquiry lasted all of nine days (22–30 November). The aim was to put forth suggestions for a settlement on Kashmir and to arrive at an estimate of India's military requirements. Predictably, and as the mission learnt, it would not be easy to nudge a giant like Nehru.

The first indication of Nehru's hesitation to discuss the Kashmir issue with Pakistan was evident in the four meetings he held with Harriman in the last week of November. Harriman's attempts at discussing a range of options such as the partition of Kashmir or exploring the question of an independent status for Kashmir were immediately shot down.[79] Such stubbornness, which grated those like Nitze, was difficult to understand from an American point of view. After all, and on India's insistence,

Kennedy had authorised the use of a dozen C-130 transport planes for India's use.[80] General Paul Adams, the commander-in-chief of the American Strike Command, and Field Marshall Sir Richard Hull, the British chief of the General Staff, were in India to assess the level and types of assistance to be given to the Indian military, not to mention the arms already provided at a moment's notice. The least Nehru could do, according to those sent to negotiate, was to hear out the options for talks. What, of course, the Anglo-American team could not have then appreciated was that the prime minister was playing his cards close to his chest. He was well aware that the following few months would require careful and cautious negotiation: giving away nothing, not even a smile, was all part of Nehru's strategy. In sum, Nehru's rigid approach was altogether understandable. After all, as the members of the Harriman mission argued following their first call on the prime minister, 'a settlement of the Kashmir issue' was 'fundamental to the problem' before them. India would need to watch each and every step very closely.[81]

Those negotiating on behalf of the US and the UK adopted styles that were equally irksome to Indian elites. Sandys annoyed not only the prime minister, but also Gundevia and Desai. Shortly after his arrival, and less aware of India's discomfort with the very notion of alliances, the minister recommended that India 'come under the protection of a NATO umbrella'. The suggestion was simply 'fuzzed over'.[82] Unable to shake Nehru, the mission approached T.T. Krishnamachari, the prime minister's confidante. Indeed, TTK, as Krishnamachari was commonly known, was recalled from retirement to work with scientists, manufacturers, foreign firms and, most importantly, the Indian military and the MoD to reconfigure what he found to be 'a very leisurely, haphazard, unscientific, and unplanned manner' in which defence production functioned.[83]

TTK made clear to Harriman, whom he had met in the past, that while India was 'prepared to extend the hand of friendship' to Pakistan, 'there must be a basic realisation [on] the part of Pakistan that the position of the Valley of Kashmir cannot be questioned'. Unmoved by TTK's reasoning, Harriman would go on to recommend a variety of ways in which the 'question' of the Valley could be considered. However, where Harriman agreed was that a plebiscite, a Pakistani demand, was simply untenable.[84] Ultimately, and following suggestions by Gundevia and M.J. Desai, Nehru agreed to ministerial-level talks with Pakistan followed by a summit with Ayub. If verbal commitments can be considered useful indicators underlining intent, part of Harriman's job was done: Kashmir was squarely on the table. On 29 November, India and Pakistan issued a joint communiqué. It stated that both nations 'agreed that a renewed effort should be made to resolve the outstanding differences between their two countries'. Importantly, the communiqué continued, this included 'Kashmir and other related matters.'[85] The wording of the last sentence was constructed on India's insistence. This was, and remains, an imperative for Indian insiders. Dialogue needed to be 'comprehensive', a term adopted in the 1990s by Prime Minister Narasimha Rao's government.

The first of six rounds of talks was to be held in Rawalpindi. The task of working with both Indian and Pakistani principals was left to Booth and Gundevia in New Delhi, and McConaughy and Maurice James, the British high commissioner to Pakistan, in Karachi. In a 34-page document, the Harriman Report (as the findings of the mission came to be called) made several recommendations. These included providing India with military and development assistance and most importantly, cooperating with Pakistan. The last paragraph on the final page was moot. It stated: 'the United States and the United Kingdom should give every assistance to the achievement of a Kashmir settlement, including continuing strong pressure on both governments'.[86] Read by Galbraith as repeating much of what was known, the American ambassador passed it off as 'an excellent elucidation of the commonplace'.[87] Yet, much more importantly, what the Harriman Report did was to provide the official reasoning behind the Kennedy administration's chosen approach. This could hardly be ignored by India, especially at a time when Nehru himself recognised the high likelihood of a renewed Chinese offensive in the spring of 1963,[88] when India's defence establishment was in shambles and Khrushchev was less forthcoming than was otherwise believed. Indeed, Nehru was sure that China posed a 'long-term threat', and had made clear its 'open bid for domination'.[89]

The following part of this section briefly examines the conditions underlining the variety of pressures upon Indian negotiators in dealing with a historically unprecedented period of crises. Notably, Indian representatives stood firm on Kashmir. This could well be considered an anomaly given the pressures detailed below. In fact, it speaks to the importance of approaching national change in measure. Indian interests may have changed. China was no longer a friend. The need for arms was evident to everyone in and out of positions of power. Yet non-interference, solidly rooted in the idea of non-alignment, proved less easy to shake.

Assistance for Talks

The 1962 year-end issue of the *Economic Weekly*—later rebranded the *Economic and Political Weekly*—carried an editorial titled 'A New Phase Is Opening.'[90] The article recounted gossip in New Delhi about a new political phase in which India was forced to hear veiled threats from the likes of American and British diplomats. Assistance for talks became a well-known and over-narrated party-line in the Indian capital.

Indeed, the pressure was on. The deal was formally outlined on 20 December 1962 at an Anglo-American conference in the Bahamas.[91] As agreed by Macmillan and Kennedy, military assistance was to be divided into two parts. First, the emergency phase included military aid worth $120 million split between the US, the UK and the Commonwealth.[92] This phase, which had begun with the delivery of US equipment to India in the first week of November, was to have no bearing on India's foreign policy and the question of Kashmir. However, long-term military aid, or phase two, was entirely dependent on talks between India and Pakistan.[93] After all, India's long-term needs were substantial.

TTK requested help to equip six to ten new divisions of the Indian Army, as well as assistance to develop India's armament industry and ammunition production factories.[94] A more formal set of demands was made on 9 December. India asked for air defence and US aircrafts to be stationed in India, and additional US radar installations manned by US personnel to oversee the protection of New Delhi, Calcutta and northeast India.[95] Wary that insiders like Desai, TTK and Gundevia would not take the conditions for talks seriously, Rusk and Macmillan sought to devise what they believed were creative ways to discuss Kashmir. For his part, the US secretary of state asked Galbraith to convince senior officers in the Indian military of the 'direct relationship' between 'US capacity [to] extend military aid and [a] Kashmir settlement.'[96]

Macmillan advised that visiting ministers, generals and prominent personalities could adopt the role of a 'candid friend' and convey the message about military aid and a Kashmir settlement.[97] Accordingly, Booth spoke with Sudhir Ghosh. Soon after, Ghosh wrote to Nehru, requesting the prime minister to consider cooperation with Pakistan.[98] Clearly, Macmillan's plan worked at least with one Indian of some repute. By the middle of December, Nehru and his advisors understood the gravity of the situation at hand. Rather than entering talks for the sake of talks, India was engaging with Pakistan in order to insure itself against the looming Chinese threat. Given the dismal state of India's military preparedness, such an insurance policy was vital.

Defence in Shambles

On 24 November 1962, Pitambar Pant, the chairman of the Planning Commission, authored a twelve-page note outlining India's 'Defence Needs and Economic Policy.' The covering letter, addressed to the prime minister, set the tone for what was to come. 'Everyone seems to be aware that big things have to be done,' Pant wrote, 'but no one seems to be clear as to what needs to be done.' The number of men in the army would have to be increased by 50 per cent. The air force and navy too would have to be increased by 25 per cent. The memo made clear that 'if large scale provision for air warfare was contemplated, the estimates of expenditure and of foreign aid would have to be substantially increased'.[99] There would need to be an increase from the present 2.5 per cent to at least 5 per cent of the national income spent on defence. Tucked into the thick and technical character of the note, Pant highlighted questions that needed urgent answers. First, would the country be 'ready to accept the extra taxation' to meet these demands? Second, given the 'upsurge in military expenditure, including an extra foreign exchange burden', would the acceptance of aid be 'feasible or desirable?' Further, the government was told that 'an effective defence against massive aerial warfare cannot be achieved by indigenous efforts'. In order to deter future Chinese attacks, 'excess of what our [Indian] factories can produce will be obtained from abroad, *free*'.[100]

Much like Pant, TTK conducted his own investigation. The outcome was even more depressing than the Planning Commission's accounts. To pick a few examples, TTK informed Nehru that since 1954, 40,000 military vehicles had stayed inoperative and that many of the 312 Sherman Tanks needed maintenance and replacement. 'No attempt has been made in this direction.' As far as ammunition was concerned, indigenous production could only meet 15 per cent of the need to service sixteen divisions. Alluding to the confusion in post-war defence organisation, the minister wryly wrote, 'I have not met a chemist in the defence organisation or for that matter in the government who can put us right in this matter. With all the vague talk of what we should do, nothing precise has so far happened.' On 26 December 1962, having met with officers concerned with defence production, TTK wrote, 'an atmosphere of complete unreality prevailed … It did not appear that we were discussing these matters at a time when the country is engaged in a war and renewal of hostilities might take place at any time. The atmosphere was one of peacetime.' Key defence officials 'did not have a full picture' of what India needed.[101] The bottom-line was that there was no way in which India could sustain its military forces in the event of a conflict in the next few months. 'We have to frankly admit,' TTK bluntly told Nehru, 'that we have not faced the problem of the defence of the country squarely these years.'[102]

These findings were also highlighted in the Harriman Report. General J.N. Chaudhuri, the new chief of Army Staff, wanted three new divisions to be raised by the end of 1963 and the re-equipment of 'the equivalent of three existing divisions'. Yet precisely how this was to be achieved remained unclear. Chaudhuri, according to the mission, visualised 'effective close air support', but, as the Americans found out, there was 'no acceptable plan' for this.[103] For his part, and notwithstanding earlier demarches about not accepting free assistance from abroad, Nehru told parliamentarians that it was essential to accept foreign military aid.[104] On 22 December, in the first letter to his chief ministers since the border clashes in early October, Nehru once again underlined that indigenous options were simply not tenable.[105] For the moment, the US and the UK were the two main sources for supplies. The much-vaunted Soviet Union was not an option in the immediate term.

The Soviet Union: Not an Option

In radio broadcasts, Russian commentators stressed that unlike 'western imperialists', Moscow did not 'attach political or economic strings to its aid'.[106] What, of course, Soviet propagandists did not and could not admit was that their government was hardly well placed to offer immediate assistance. In the summer of 1962, India and the Soviet Union negotiated a contract for the sale of MiG-21 fighter aircrafts.[107] This trumped an American suggestion for the sale of F-104 fighters manufactured by the US giant Lockheed Martin.[108] India's decision, then, as M.J. Desai put it, was in keeping with its stand to make purchases from wherever it could 'secure the type of equipment we want on the most favourable terms'.[109] However, such terms were less obvious a few months down the line. As outlined in the previous chapter, the first phase of the Sino-Indian border conflict coincided with the height of the Cuban missile crisis. Soviet 'neutrality' was somewhat understandable at a time when Moscow needed Beijing's support. Indeed, as Jagat Mehta, then a mid-career diplomat working on China, argues, 'the USSR reaffirmed its solidarity with China'.[110] Interestingly, from a Chinese perspective, and as Arne Westad puts it, Soviet neutrality did nothing for Beijing: 'Mao was not impressed.'[111] Immediately following the border war, and despite an embargo of oil exports to China,[112] Russian willingness to discuss the delivery of the MiGs or offer other forms of assistance was limited at best.

The record of conversations between T.N. Kaul, the Indian ambassador in Moscow, and Russian elites presents contradictory viewpoints. In his memoirs, Kaul states that, on 24 November, Khrushchev 'criticised China openly and came out with an offer to help in the early supply of defence equipment to India'.[113] Conversely, Kaul's record of the same discussion with Khrushchev on 24 November, archived as part of his private papers, quotes Khrushchev as saying that the Sino-Indian dispute 'is disturbing for all those who want peace; but to us it is a matter of special regret since it has arisen between our ally [China] and our friend [India]. This puts us in a particularly unpleasant situation.' Khrushchev makes no commitment about the 'early supply of defence equipment'. In fact, according to Kaul's own record, Khrushchev was evasive about the MiGs. The Soviet premier stated, 'we will supply you the MiGs, maybe, in December, and if not December, then somewhat later'.[114]

On 29 November, Kaul again argued that the Soviets were 'sympathetic' towards India, and should be 'encourage[ed]' to give India 'symbolic assistance', but this would not be of 'much military value'.[115] TTK also supported Kaul's appraisal. The minister argued that 'the USSR will not take definitely sides with India against China even if their relationship with China worsens'.[116] Indeed, Russia's 'pretence of neutrality', as Henry Kissinger writes, was only 'dropped' much later, towards the end of 1963,[117] following which members of the Politburo openly accused

the PRC of aggression. For the time being, Indian elites set out to negotiate with Pakistan with the knowledge of the limited options available
to India.

Talks

On 26 December 1962, a team of Indian negotiators arrived in
Rawalpindi. The location of the first round of talks was in fact chosen
by the Indians. A new capital—Islamabad—was being built in 'Pindi',
as Rawalpindi is popularly called, and seemed to Gundevia like a welcome opportunity. He had no trouble convincing Sardar Swaran Singh,
the lead Indian negotiator. Singh, a Sikh from Punjab, had recently been
appointed as the Indian railways minister, and, as Gundevia recollects,
he enjoyed the prime minister's 'fullest confidence'. Apart from Singh
and Gundevia, the Indian side included G. Parthasarathi, the new
Indian high commissioner to Pakistan, and B.L. Sharma, officer on special duty in the MEA.[118]

The representatives were received by Zulfikar Ali Bhutto. A Berkeley
and Oxford graduate and founder of the People's Party of Pakistan
(PPP), the then 34-year-old was the minister for industries and Singh's
counterpart in the talks. Personally unconvinced about what discussions
could actually achieve, the soon-to-be foreign minister—Bhutto
replaced the ailing Mohammad Ali Bogra in 1963—appealed to
Pakistani legislators to give talks a chance. As he eruditely put it, 'there
is no force, and there is no argument, which is stronger than the com-
pulsion of events'. Defeat and necessity, Bhutto insinuated, brought
Singh to Rawalpindi. He asked the National Assembly to 'be patient
and cautious', but also to 'take cognisance' of the 'change that has taken
place'.[119] Indeed, testing the extent to which Nehru and his delegates
were serious about discussions, Bhutto orchestrated a Machiavellian plot
that nearly jeopardised the entire Indo-Pakistani enterprise even before
the first round on 27 December.

Round One: Rawalpindi

Put-up in a typically large and 'old-fashioned' government guesthouse,
the Indian delegation was careful not to say anything that would reveal
their talking points. The residence, as Gundevia found out, was bugged.

On the evening of their arrival, the representatives chose to tune into Karachi radio. What they heard horrified them all. Pakistan and China, according to the broadcast, were soon to sign a border agreement.[120] The territory in question, as outlined earlier in this chapter, lay in what India considered Pakistan-occupied Kashmir.[121] This was all part of Bhutto's ploy. Years later, he told Booth that the Pakistani government did this because they knew that the Indians 'were not coming in good faith'.[122] Galbraith was outraged. The irony did not escape the strongest advocate for talks. 'History can be idiotic', he vented. 'A staunch American ally against Communism,' the ambassador continued, 'is negotiating with the Chinese Communists to the discontent of an erstwhile neutral.'[123] For a moment, it seemed as though the hard task of getting Indian and Pakistani principals in the same city, if not yet the same room, would come to nought.

Rather than pack and leave, and despite Sharma's plea to Singh to do exactly this, Sardar chose to stay on. Contrary to the personal prejudices held by Bhutto and also Nehru, who was himself less confident of the outcomes of the talks, Gundevia and others were convinced that 'there was a fair enough chance' to 'persuade' Pakistan to accept a 'new line in Kashmir', which, as the Commonwealth secretary argued, could 'on the whole' be 'favourable to Pakistan'.[124] Apart from the pressures upon India to negotiate with Pakistan, there was a genuine desire to make the most of the opportunity at hand. The next day, or the first day of talks, neither Bhutto nor Singh said anything about the Chinese agreement, and this despite the fact that all major newspapers carried the story.[125] In a meeting with Ayub, the latter simply stated that the announcement was 'provisional', and would be finalised only after an Indian and Pakistani agreement was realised.[126]

In so far as substantive talking points on Kashmir and 'other related matters' were concerned, each side was given the opportunity not only to make their stated, typically bureaucratic and often long-winded cases, but also to offer functional suggestions. Rather than making 'little progress', as Howard Schaffer concludes in his masterful recount of 'America's role in Kashmir', the two-and-a-half days in Rawalpindi did well to set the tone for further debate.[127] This was not an issue where progress was going to be immediately visible. This of course is a point that escaped some American officials at the time. Two issues merit elaboration.

First, the Indian side, and Gundevia specifically, were quick to detect tensions between Bhutto and the Foreign Office represented by Foreign

Secretary Dehlavi, as also between Bhutto and Ayub. The 'pre-arranged drama' with regard to the Sino-Pakistani border was thought to be mainly Bhutto's doing.[128] Ayub, British officials argued, 'urged Indians not to allow this incident to destroy present historic and perhaps unrepeatable opportunity'.[129] For their part, junior officers in the Pakistani Foreign Office were set to 'sabotage the whole effort'.[130] Yet India's visible commitment to talks following the ill-timed radio broadcast appeared to have at least partially impressed Bhutto.

Second, the possibility of progress was made clear in the substantives placed on the negotiating table. On the first morning, Singh stated that there was no question of transferring the Valley to Pakistan, or entertaining discussions with regard to this.[131] All that the Indian delegation was willing to do was discuss the potential of extending the international frontier through the state of Kashmir. In principle, Pakistan also agreed to address the same.[132] As an inducement to Pakistan, the Indian side was open to discuss issues that Pakistan considered vital, including those like self-determination and the much-vaunted issue of a plebiscite.[133]

Following a dinner on 28 December, Bhutto asked Parthasarathi to stay back. The young minister, according to Booth's record, 'spoke of [the] necessity to consider a political solution involving the drawing of the international boundary through Kashmir'. The next morning, and in private, Bhutto discussed the same issue with Singh. The key was to explore and identify specific alterations that could be made along the existing CFL. For the moment, both sides were clueless on how exactly to proceed. Contingencies with regard to such alterations needed deliberations within respective negotiating parties and with their national leaders. This, as well as a re-examination of past attempts for an amicable division, was to serve as the main areas of debate in the next round in New Delhi scheduled for the middle of January. A minor point of enormous public importance, the first round ended with both sides committing themselves to a 'call for a moratorium on adverse propaganda against one another in the news media'. This was underlined in a joint communiqué issued on 29 December,[134] the last day of talks. In the end, there was an objective—to consider alterations along the CFL—and a visible desire on the part of both parties to continue the discussions. This was more progress than almost any principal predicted, and needs to be read in balance and in the context of the period of crises.

Round Two: Delhi

Back in Delhi, two issues most exercised Galbraith and Gundevia. First, while South Asia specialists inside the US State Department agreed that the talks had gained a degree of momentum, they also made plain to Galbraith that a settlement was of paramount importance.[135] The American ambassador went out of his way to stress publicly that 'conditions or pressures' were not a 'very useful way of advancing a cause',[136] but there was little doubt in anyone's mind that aid was linked to progress on talks. Second, the two areas that promised a degree of hope, that is, the question of alterations and the earliest manifestations of what commentators and later Indian Prime Minister Manmohan Singh would refer to as the 'soft-borders' approach, became a major public and private relations issue for India.

The earliest iterations of such an approach were outlined in a memo signed-off by Roger Hilsman. The idea was to consider the possibilities of 'an undivided state of Jammu and Kashmir jointly administered and jointly defended by India and Pakistan'.[137] From the outset, and as a point of discussion, this seemed plausible to elites in both India and Pakistan. Yet, as perhaps most negotiators in a variety of negotiations well understand, a plan of action not only requires convincing those across the border, but equally, leaders inside the principal nation. Nehru, for one, was certain of the impossibility of the task at hand. In fact, the prime minister was 'unalterably opposed' to any plan that required the large-scale migration of non-Muslims in areas given-up by India along the CFL. Thus despite the limited progress in Rawalpindi, Booth notes that officials had 'no success in persuading' Nehru to consider the arrangements under discussion.[138]

Further, and as importantly, Nehru himself was under attack.[139] Following the announcement of the Sino-Pakistani deal, A.B. Vajpayee, then a leader of the Jan Sangh Party, pushed the government to postpone talks. Equally, he appealed to both the US and the UK not to succumb to Pakistan's 'blackmailing tactics'.[140] C. Rajagopalachari, now the founding leader of the recently formed Swatantra Party, launched nothing short of a frontal attack on non-alignment.[141] These were hardly the sort of 'atmospherics', as diplomats like to say, that were conducive to a major bilateral agreement. What also did not help were suggestions—or mere rumour, as it later turned out—made in Washington that India was closely considering a formal alliance with the US.[142] Hence, while forced to negotiate by external powers, Nehru was equally compelled to give away nothing because of internal opposition. To make matters worse, Dehlavi's fiery and provocative choice of rhetoric during a visit to Europe piqued Indian sensitivities. He was found 'gloating publicly over India's misfortune'.[143]

If this were not enough to complicate the task of finding a solution, the plan for soft-borders, which was developed with the help of Galbraith, was difficult to propose. This was not, at this stage, because of the plan itself, but was instead due to how the plan was perceived, as it came to be seen as an American-led 'non-territorial' option.[144] Singh was concerned by the fact that the plan was being bandied about by American officials, making it all that more difficult to accept. Soon, and instead of simply adapting Hilsman's rudimentary outline, an independent approach was considered by Gundevia and Parthasarathi. The scheme was to examine whether or not a common boundary line could be agreed where 'the substance of the Vale including Srinagar' remained with India. As an incentive to Pakistan, India would consent to discuss issues 'across a broad front'. These, it was thought, could include a common customs union, a joint investment effort, a shared World Bank loan for development and the eventual withdrawal of military forces.[145]

In the following days, a two-level approach began to emerge. First, negotiators set out to investigate a plausible settlement proposal. Second, Nehru refused to indicate any willingness to consider a deal either publicly or even privately. Although this apparent disconnect between the approaches adopted by the prime minister on one side and his negotiators on the other was not entirely pre-planned, it was not completely accidental either. In practice, negotiators responded to issues in a flexible way as and when they arose on each day of the negotiations—talks, of course, were ultimately dependent on the prime minister's support, but for the time being what happened inside the negotiating room was left entirely to the negotiators themselves.

The second round in Delhi started on 16 January 1963. The Pakistani team was accommodated in the Rashtrapati Bhavan, the Indian president's residence. Unlike the guesthouse in Pindi, the rooms were not bugged, or so Gundevia claimed. Bhutto met with President Radhakrishnan and Nehru, 'the apple' of the PPP leader's 'bright, political eye'.[146] While Radhakrishnan was cordial, all the Pakistani minister received from the

Indian prime minister was a flat commitment to 'do what he could to be helpful'. In one-on-one meetings with Singh, Bhutto and the lead Indian negotiator reached a roadblock—neither was willing to put forth concrete proposals.[147] For Singh, and apart from the question of popular perception, the difficulty lay in Pakistan's stated position that the 'most obvious' rationale for drawing a line between India and Pakistan was on the 'principle on which the 1947 partition had been based'.[148] With maximalist positions such as this, there was little use in even lightly exploring the most rudimentary variety of the soft-border option. The larger ministerial-level discussions likewise stalled following an exhausting exchange of stated positions. Yet, strangely, both the Indian and the Pakistani delegates seemed to think that the 'atmosphere' of the meetings was 'excellent'. The Pakistanis argued that the 'exercise' of repeating known stances 'had to be gone through before the next step namely exploration of new ideas could be undertaken'.[149] Indeed, this is exactly what happened.

A plan along the lines of a softer border was finally floated by Singh. The first step, he now argued, required discussing parameters around 'complete military disengagement'. This could then lead to 'such things as free movement over the border'. Even Bhutto agreed that this was a 'constructive thought', and believed it could lead to economic cooperation directly relevant to Kashmir. Bhutto, however, insisted that India first outline a proposal defining the altered border as India saw it.[150] For their part, Gundevia and Singh were working under the assumption that limited adjustments could be made along the existing border. A soft-border could then help dampen Pakistan's obsession with the Valley or Srinagar. Clearly, Bhutto did not see it this way. The Indian position that 'territorial readjustment' should involve 'the least possible disturbance to the life and welfare of the people'[151] was construed to mean that a major change such as the division of the Valley was out of the question, which it was. At best, India would consider negotiating a small part of the Valley, but the 'readiness for concessions stopped there'.[152]

Unable to move India to consider a new line favourable to Pakistan, the talks came to an end. However, and less grudgingly than might have been expected, delegates agreed to a third round in Karachi in the second week of February. Indeed, they even authored a joint statement of objectives ad referendum for official use only. This was not published.[153] Further, and back in Karachi, Bhutto made clear to McConaughy that while Pakistan's demand for an undivided Vale remained firm, it was willing to reconsider the question of a plebiscite. The negotiators, Bhutto explained, would explore options such as a transitional period before a plebiscite be put in place. Ayub offered to hold a plebiscite a year later if it would help matters, but, as the president underscored, it would need to be held. Bhutto confessed that the fourth round, to be held in Calcutta in April, would be critical. The discussions in Karachi could be treated as a serious brainstorming session that looked beyond first principles. The idea was to set the frame for substantive discussions. Hence while Bhutto urged McConaughy not to intervene during discussions in Karachi, pressure needed to be applied on India to agree to a settlement in Calcutta.[154] In many ways, the suggestion of third-party intervention coupled with growing dissatisfaction on the part of both Macmillan and Kennedy eventually jeopardised the process as a whole. Nehru and his representatives would not be moved by imperatives other than those shaped by them alone.

Round Three: Karachi

Little known to either the Indian or Pakistani interlocutors, the US State Department was working on what might be called Plan B. State Department officials outlined a partition plan along the soft-borders model. It was, as Robert Komer writes, outwardly possible.[155] The idea, as Schaffer recounts, was to transfer 'substantial territory' on the northwestern side of the Valley and the western portion of Jammu. In exchange, India would get a 'sliver of Pakistan-held territory', allowing it to maintain a buffer between the Valley and Ladakh in the east.[156] This was then to be followed by provisions around the free movement of people and jointly administered bureaucracies. For his part, Galbraith found it to be a 'rather sensible compromise'.[157] Booth, on the other hand, felt that the approach was unlikely to 'lead to an answer'.[158]

Prior to their departure to Karachi, Philips Talbot visited New Delhi. McConaughy and Rusk were also in the capital. The assistant secretary of state reminded Gundevia that the 'aid story was with the Congress, and they were having difficulties'.[159] A deal was imperative. To be sure, Talbot was only communicating what he himself was hearing on Capitol Hill. Senator William Fulbright, chairman of the Senate Foreign Relations Committee, publicly argued that sanctioning aid to India in the absence of a settlement in Kashmir would prove difficult.[160] Clearly, like India, the Americans also had to contend with domestic pressure.

Talbot, obviously briefed on his department's Plan B, pushed Gundevia to consider bartering parts of Jammu and the north-west of the Valley. The answer again was firm. If forced on this issue, Gundevia made clear that the 'talks were doomed to end in disaster'.[161] In Washington, and despite the State Department's initiative, Kennedy intuitively grasped the fact that Nehru was not going to budge. He wrote to Macmillan: 'Nehru is unlikely to settle Kashmir with too obvious a gun at his back.'[162] Yet, as carefully as possible, the US president appealed to the Indian prime minister. On 6 February, two days before the Karachi round was to begin, he wrote that the Kashmir issue was something of a 'painful diversion'. Much like President Barack Obama's efforts to improve relations with India some fifty years later, Kennedy stressed that a solution would 'open new perspectives in terms of India's role on the world stage', and if left unresolved, it would continue to complicate 'US–India relations in ways disadvantageous' to both nations.[163] The note, as might have been predicted, had no impact on the Indian side.

The negotiations in Karachi began on 8 February. Unlike the previous two rounds, the Pakistanis were found to be more forthcoming. Rather than repeating known positions, they asked Singh to identify lines on actual maps that India would find agreeable. The Indian side, and Gundevia and M.J. Desai specifically, worked up four such options. These ranged from maps to be tabled for minimum and maximum concessions. None of these options considered the transfer of the Valley, and Bhutto's position now became more rigid than before. Even the suggestion of a new line giving Pakistan an additional 1,500 square miles of territory along an amended CFL was turned down.[164] The Indian team were back in New Delhi on 10 February.

A *Times of India* headline pithily stated the obvious: 'Talks Heading Towards Roadblock.'[165] Unlike in the past, Singh freely told journalists that the differences were 'considerable'.[166] Unable to reach even a degree of consensus, the last three rounds of dialogue held in the following four months witnessed Anglo-American interference, but with no success. In fact, Kennedy for one was quick to recognise the futility of the process at hand. He soon asked his envoys to dial-back the aid–Kashmir axis. American and British officials did what they could to push a less receptive India, which kept its own pressure on the US for military assistance while refusing to adhere to its sole supplier's key demands. Once again, Indian exceptionalism could not be clearer. The nation may have been recently defeated in war, but its measured approach in international politics informed by the need to remain independent, a hard goal to achieve in this period, was evidently but carefully married with the idea of change.

The Next Two Rounds: Calcutta and Karachi

On 2 March, Chen Yi, the Chinese foreign minister, and Bhutto, now the Pakistani foreign minister, leant their respective signatures to a border pact. They were in Beijing. The Islamic Republic and the People's Republic delimited a 300-mile border between what India considered 'Pakistani occupied Kashmir' and the Chinese province of Sinkiang. For good measure, and as mentioned earlier, Article 6 of the treaty stated: 'after the settlement of the Kashmir dispute between Pakistan and India, the sovereign authority concerned will reopen negotiations with the Government of the People's Republic of China on the boundary'.[167] This did little to convince the MEA, which shot off a letter of protest to the president of the Security Council. The timing of the pact thus served to dim the already faint light of hope in the bilateral discussions between India and Pakistan. Nehru even argued that, in the near future, India could not 'rule out an attack' by 'Pakistan to synchronise with Chinese aggression.'[168]

Duncan Sandys and his staff were livid with Ayub. Falsely optimistic that a 'delineation of [an] international boundary in Jammu–Kashmir' was still possible, the CRO urged the Pakistani president that 'because of Bhutto's visit [to China], the burden will be on them to keep the talks going'. Except, and unnerved by Indian reticence, the Pakistani team were to push the issue of 'internationalisation' of the Valley.[169] Galbraith, far more in tune with what India would or would not accept, rightfully disagreed. In fact, he made his disagreement clear to Selig Harrison— the South Asia Bureau chief of the *Washington Post*—with the view to 'kill the idea'. The next round of talks began in Calcutta on 12 March. Bhutto did not even broach Sandys' ill-conceived initiative.[170] In hindsight, Booth wrote how he had 'underrate' the 'degree to which the steam had gone out of the negotiations'.[171] The Pakistani delegation, who had been guests of Padmaja Naidu, the governor of West Bengal and daughter of Sarojini Naidu, the poet, playwright and Congress activist, departed the Raj Bhavan, or governor's residence, on 14 March with only an agreement to continue the discussions in Karachi in April. 'This set of talks,' as Booth notes, 'came to nothing.'[172]

At the end of March a set of options and counter-options was considered. First, Macmillan, anxious that Kennedy was not doing enough to pressure Nehru, made clear to his American counterparts that unless a settlement was reached his government would find it next to impossible to offer long-term military assistance to India. Rusk noted that, Macmillan might be forced to pull out of the 50/50 arrangement decided in December 1962.[173] Second, and notwithstanding Britain's reluctance, the US secretary of state underlined to his president that settlement or no settlement, 'strategically, we would still need to be in a position to give India some assistance against Chinese Communist pressure'.[174] Kennedy understood that aid, his 'chief leverage', was a 'wasting asset',[175] but pressure from Congress and Ayub required that India do something, or at least make it look like it was doing something to take the talks seriously. This was becoming impossible to achieve. Indeed, the fact that Nehru had delinked the aid–talks nexus came home to the likes of Rusk and Ormsby-Gore, the British ambassador in Washington, during a visit by Biju Patnaik, the chief minister of Orissa. Gore writes:

It seemed clear from the Patnaik discussions in Washington that military plans pre-supposing aid on a vast scale (one billion dollars was mentioned during his visit) were being prepared in Delhi. It was therefore necessary to make clear the difficulties in the way of reaching any decision on aid until there had been an advance towards a settlement between India and Pakistan.[176]

This time, and given the failed attempts in the recent past, the Kennedy administration adopted a different approach. Walter Rostow, from Rusk's policy planning staff, and Komer, who was on Bundy's White House staff, were to visit New Delhi. The more junior staffers were to appeal to Nehru's reason. The argument, as Booth notes, was not: 'no settlement, no US aid at all'. Instead it was: 'if you do reach a settlement on Kashmir see what immense possibilities of aid, otherwise unrealisable will follow'.[177] The Americans were to adopt a softer line couched in the language of inducement rather than the erstwhile coercive spirit in which talks were initiated in the first place. Further, McNamara, the secretary of defence, made plain to Kennedy that the timeline for taking orders from India and delivering assistance required acting immediately.

This was that much more potent if India was to have even a portion of the equipment it asked for—mainly for air defence—in time for a repeat Chinese offensive.[178]

In early April, Rostow and Komer arrived in India to push their brief. They came with a developed version of the State Department's Plan B for talks. This time, the Plan B-plus was co-authored with officials in the CRO. It came to be called the 'Elements of a Settlement Plan.' The idea was for the negotiators in Karachi to stick to the 'political elements of solution' rather than getting bogged down with technical details. Most importantly, the ambassadors in India—Galbraith and Booth—as well as Rostow and Komer were authorised to adapt the plan as necessary to 'avoid break down of talks'. In brief, it was considered to be impossible for either India or Pakistan to 'give-up its claim to the Kashmir Valley'. Both countries, the joint US–UK guidance document noted, 'must have a substantial position in the Valley', as well as 'assured access to and through the Vale'. Further, and resting on the older concept of soft-borders, the idea was to develop bureaucratic 'arrangements for sovereignty' and law and order. Lastly, efforts were to be made for the 'rapid development' of joint approaches to tourism, water and forestry, small industries, health and welfare and communications.[179] In short, the objective was to find a way for both sides to live together and jointly administer what each side considered contested territory. But it was a hare-brained idea from the outset—neither side was willing to recognise basic questions of sovereignty, let alone those of joint sovereign control. Yet, and with the view to keep the pressure on, Macmillan—with Kennedy's prior agreement—wrote to Nehru:

Frankly I have been disappointed at the lack of progress in the talks between India and Pakistan on Kashmir. I recognise the deeply held convictions on both sides ... but progress towards a settlement would produce such great benefits to the defence and peaceful development of the subcontinent as a whole, that I know you will forgive me for urging that every attempt should be made at the next round of talks at Karachi to break the present deadlock.[180]

In India, Rostow and Komer met everyone in a position to influence the talks. This included Nehru, TTK, Y.B. Chavan and a number of joint secretaries in both the MEA and the MoD.[181] Interestingly, and obviously aware of Indian reticence, the 'elements' proposal was given in print to Bhutto, but not to anyone in India. It was only when Parthasarathi visited New Delhi prior to the talks in Karachi that

Gundevia and Singh had sight of what they immediately considered a 'full tilt on the side of Pakistan'.[182] Anglo-American interference had come to naught. In Karachi, during the fifth round of talks (21–25 April), the US–UK leverage plan failed to achieve any of its goals.[183] Nehru's intolerance to both the aid–talks formula and external interference more generally was palpable. Placing the blame squarely on 'intervention of third powers', Nehru wrote to Kennedy that 'these ill-considered and ill-conceived initiatives, however well-intentioned they may have been, have at least for the present made it impossible to reach any settlement on this rather involved and complicated question [of Kashmir]'.[184] The prime minister had spoken, and Kennedy for one understood that this meant the issue was no longer tenable.

The Last Round: Delhi

With little attention to the sixth and last round in Delhi, the inside story in the White House shifted. Komer argued that the US needed to look beyond the Kashmir issue,[185] while Rusk, albeit more bluntly, made the point that the 'US cannot subject our overall strategic objectives to [the] settlement of Kashmir, or any other single problem.' The Chinese could at anytime attempt to expand their influence on the 'free world perimeter'.[186] A day after Nehru's letter arrived in Washington, and in a meeting with his close aides, the president underlined that it was not worth being 'penny wise about India'. He said, 'Let's not let them get into a position where they feel that they can't cope with the Chicoms and Paks on top of their own problems.'[187] By early May, the altered US position had been communicated to India. Rusk, on a visit to New Delhi, told Nehru that long-term military aid was no longer contingent on a Kashmir settlement.[188]

In the last round of discussions (Delhi, 15–16 May), and although Gundevia mentions that thus far, 'talks stalemated meant arms stalemated',[189] it became clear to all concerned parties that India would not shift from its public position on Kashmir.[190] In a meeting between the Earl of Home, the British foreign secretary and Ayub Khan, the Pakistani president rightly concluded that there was little chance of success. He told the foreign secretary that Talbot, Galbraith, Harriman and, to a lesser extent, Rusk were all convinced that this was a 'good opportunity to get India in the bag'. Following the meeting, Home wrote: 'there was little chance of success for the sixth round of negotiations'.[191]

In the discussions between the two sides at the last round, not only was there a complete absence of any indication of progress but the prospect of future discussions also seemed bleak. Bhutto suggested that the Valley could be 'internationalised', or even 'transferred' to Pakistan after India's border problems with China were resolved. This of course was immediately rejected by Swaran Singh. On the evening of 16 May, the talks officially broke down with no conclusive arrangements being worked out between the two sides.[192] On 1 June, in a discussion between McConaughy, Morris and Bhutto in Peshawar, the Pakistani foreign minister was told that neither the US nor the UK was 'prepared to freeze arms aid to India'.[193] By the end of June, the Kashmir aspect of US policy towards India was buried. Whispers around an effort by a third-party mediator similarly petered out.[194] The discussions turned squarely to the manner and method by which the US and the UK were to provide long-term military assistance.

Indeed, at the same time as Singh and Gundevia wrestled with the likes of Bhutto in New Delhi, TTK and M.J. Desai were pushing the case for assistance in Washington. Unwilling to entertain the aid–Kashmir construct, the minister and the foreign secretary 'argued convincingly' that long-term assistance needed to be negotiated 'within the framework of formal non-alignment'. India's envoys also made clear to Kennedy that the free export of military hardware to India should by no means be misunderstood as implying that India would turn down Russian MiGs or that it would be unresponsive to help from Moscow.[195] India's position had changed, but an alliance or anything resembling an alliance was out of the question. Indeed, and as Nehru underlined, Soviet pressure on and criticism of the PRC, which increased incrementally in the early months of 1963, was only possible because India chose to remain unaligned in a time of crises. 'Even if there were no other valid reasons,' the prime minister argued, 'our maintaining our policy of non-alignment is essential for this purpose.'[196]

Further, and as was demonstrably clear, a more flexible approach to the United States was gradually adopted. For instance, the USAF joined the IAF in peacetime training exercises.[197] These 'training exercises' were designed to deter future Chinese attacks. The US squadrons would be camouflaged during the exercises to limit public criticism of foreign intervention on Indian soil. The only reservation to USAF activities in India was that the overall responsibility for the air defence of India would remain vested in 'the appropriate Indian commander'.[198] Over and above the exercises, McNamara authorised the use of two mobile radar installations with related communications equipment. The installations were to be located in New Delhi and Calcutta and manned by US personnel, until such time that Indian personnel were trained. The training would continue until 1964. In the event of a Chinese attack, the DoD agreed to consult with the Indian government 'regarding possible additional United States assistance in strengthening India's air defence'. Further, and according to a general understanding with TTK, American contributions in terms of military aid would include funds for air transport ($2.7 million), road construction assistance ($5.6 million), equipment for Indian troops ($425,902), equipping two Corps ($3,721,624), modernising two mountain divisions ($11,250,888), weapons systems support ($2,490,000), provision of ground control radios ($366,030) and the supply of ground control radars ($1,078,999).[199]

In the end, the actual investment in India's defence sector was by no means substantial.[200] Yet, when taken in the context of the crises at hand, America's offer of assistance was crucial. It was only unfortunate that Kennedy, Macmillan and their respective emissaries, underappreciated and largely misunderstood the centrality of Kashmir. This was not an issue where one or both sides could be coerced into a resolution. As noted by Nehru, the war and the 'changing actualities' of international politics brought to light the need to 'adjust our relations with friendly countries',[201] but this did not mean that India and her envoys would instantly replace their layered and self-determined approach to the United States or diplomacy more generally.

Conclusion

In March 1965, nearly a year after Nehru had died, Sudhir Ghosh publicised the contents of the fateful second letter authored by the prime minister on 19 November 1962. Notably, it was the response to this letter and the more general state of crises that led to the constitution of the Harriman mission and the construction of the aid–Kashmir ensemble. Congress MPs erupted in disbelief. Lal Bahadur Shastri, India's second prime minister, threatened the attention-seeking Bengali with expulsion for accusing India's long-time prime minister of something no one thought possible. It took an intervention by Chester Bowles to save

Ghosh.[202] In a sense, both parliamentarians and commentators alike could well be indicted for hypocrisy and even insincerity. Throughout the crises of 1962–3, reporters, and Congress and opposition elites—mainly from the Jan Sangh and Swatantra—urged the government and Nehru in particular to try to gain as much assistance as possible. Yet in a moment when the invasion of eastern India was considered highly probable, Nehru's response spun legislators into agitation.

Clearly, it would take time for them to get to grips with what Nehru, TTK, Desai, Gundevia and Singh were shocked into internalising. These principals did not have the luxury to absorb the moment they were living in perhaps until it had passed. Equally, they negotiated the idea and substance of change while keeping in mind the need to remain free of any conditions with the potential to constrain India's ability to make independent choices in the future. The fact that the CFL across Kashmir remained intact was no mean feat. It should hardly be taken for granted. The approach adopted by Indian negotiators speaks of a policy informed by the connection of changing ideas around 'autonomy'—weapons from abroad were no longer taboo—and interests. Further, the Sino-Pakistani pact, Anglo-American pressure and the general position adopted by Ayub and Bhutto made clear to elites that Washington's approach to India would be tied to its approach to Pakistan.

As importantly, and notwithstanding the irritation and sheer exasperation of those negotiating the case for both aid and borders, something unusual was forged in this moment of crisis between India and the US. As one commentator succinctly noted, the relationship had 'reached a special depth of understanding', and this was evidently 'achieved without India having to seek admission into any military alliances'. There was a 'new turn' in the approach to the other.[203] The crises at hand allowed representatives and principals from both sides to work closely in a deeply political but human arena where intentions and interests were matters of education for those duly involved in the quest for stability. That both sides read or approached stability in vastly different ways should not take away from the fact that a conversation was underway. The tensions underlying this conversation would be redefined in the decades to come, and were conspicuously underlined in 1971 as Indira Gandhi took India to war.

6

'DIAOYUTAI'

1971

On 3 December 1971, while at a meeting in Calcutta with artists and theatre buffs,[1] Indira Gandhi was informed that at 5.30 p.m. the Pakistani Air Force (PAF) had commenced attacks against Indian cities and air bases along the western border dividing the two largest South Asian nations.[2] Later that evening, and following the prime minister's arrival in New Delhi, a capital that was 'completely blacked out',[3] her Cabinet declared a state of war with Pakistan.[4] A day later, the Indian Army launched operations in both the western sector, bordering present-day Pakistan, and the eastern sector, alongside the soon to be independent nation of Bangladesh. On 15 December, and indicative of India's military superiority, an ultimatum delivered to Lieutenant General Ameer Niazi, the commander of the East Pakistani Army, underlined that the resurgence of violence on the part of his forces would re-invite an Indian offensive 'with the utmost vigour'.[5] On 16 December, Niazi surrendered 90,000 of his soldiers and the whole of East Pakistan to Lieutenant General Jagjit Singh Aurora, the commander of the Indian Army on the eastern front. At 8.00 p.m. on 17 December, India declared a unilateral ceasefire on the western border, formally ending a war that permanently partitioned post-independence Pakistan.

Then fifty-four years old and appointed prime minister in 1966, Gandhi's decision to go to war partially informed her populist caricature as the 'empress of India'. Henry A. Kissinger, President Richard Nixon's national security advisor, also drew similar references when depicting Gandhi.[6] Indeed, Kissinger—a former Harvard professor—found Gandhi a lot more enticing than Nixon, himself something of a 'brooding Irish puritan' as the journalist Gary Wills described the southern Californian Republican.[7] 'They,' the president once said of Indians, 'are the most aggressive goddamn people around.'[8] Of course, such spiteful remarks were hardly the exception when it came to India. Nixon was, as an entire set of biographies recount, known for his 'petty meanness'.[9] As Adlai Stevenson once noted, 'Nixonland' was all about 'hustling, pushing, and shoving'.[10] Yet, and notwithstanding the generalities that defined a statesman who did 'much to damage American public life', as the author Margaret Macmillan put it,[11] when it came to India, Nixon had his reasons to be demonstratively irate. At the same time, in the summer of 1971, as millions of East Pakistani refugees fled to India's north-eastern border states, prompting Gandhi's government to consider intervention, Kissinger prepared to make what is now his well-documented, but at the time clandestine, visit to Beijing.[12]

On 9 and 10 July 1971, Kissinger held two rounds of official negotiations with Zhou in Beijing. The first of these meetings was hosted at Diaoyutai, the state guesthouse once home to Madame Mao. These 'first encounters', as Kissinger titles the crucial chapter in his tour de force, *On China*, laid the groundwork for the game-changing state visit by Nixon in February 1972;[13] of far greater significance for Indian officials, however, was the spectre this raised of American, Pakistani and Chinese collusion. Notably, General Muhammed Yahya Khan—Ayub's successor—was asked by Nixon to facilitate the rapprochement with Beijing as early as October 1969,[14] with Kissinger eventually travelling to Beijing in secret from Pakistan less than two years later.[15] As the Indian leadership had high expectations for a president whom they believed would work in India's interests, the Nixon administration's blanket support to Yahya came as a shock.

Nixon urgently needed Yahya, and made it clear that he shared a 'special relationship' with the military dictator.[16] For his part, Yahya declared a state of martial law following Ayub's resignation on 25 March 1969. Exactly two years later, Yahya's government ordered a military crackdown in the east. The Muslim Bangla-speaking population led by Mujibur Rahman—or Mujib, soon to be the founding president of

Bangladesh—wrestled for greater federal rights following their unwelcome triumph—as far as West Pakistani elites were concerned—in Pakistan's first-ever national elections held in December 1970.[17] The demand for Bangla rights and the consequences of Yahya's concentrated effort to quell the rebellion in the east placed Gandhi's government in a quandary. Military intervention required a diplomatic screen to discourage even the slightest risk of both American and Chinese interference.

The answer was partially found in a Treaty of Friendship signed by India and the Soviet Union on 9 August 1971. Significantly, Article 9 made provisions to 'enter into mutual consultations' if and when either party was 'subjected to an attack or a threat thereof'. Further, each 'High Contracting Party' would take 'appropriate effective measures to ensure peace and the security of their countries'.[18] Hence, while phrased carefully in order to avoid any suggestion of a bilateral security guarantee, the treaty made clear that Soviet support in the event of war was not improbable.[19] With the agreement in hand, Gandhi and her government were freer to prepare the required diplomatic ground while making military preparations to intervene in East Pakistan.

The existing literature and commentary on both India–US relations and the apparent change in India's approach to international affairs largely remains trapped in two sets of narrative. First, the early 1970s is commonly remembered and documented as an era when America—specifically Nixon—tilted in Yahya's favour, a principal needed to fulfil the promise of rapprochement with Mao's China. South Asia more generally was read by the Nixon White House as simply 'another complication', according to Kissinger. It was considered prudent, both Kissinger and Nixon thought, to keep the region as a whole off the 'agenda'. American attention was all but completely focused on the withdrawal of American troops from Vietnam and the need to prop up South Vietnamese forces.[20] Nixon's dogma-like approach to China was the all-important challenge for a president who campaigned in favour of 'taking the long view', as he put it, when it came to the PRC.[21] The 1971 War was as unwelcome a development for him as Mujib's electoral success was to West Pakistani elites, discussed below. Yet, and as will be demonstrated in this chapter, while the institutionalised memory of the so-called 'tilt' is deeply engrained in the minds and hearts of Indian leaders and the public more generally, the cause and consequence of war did not in itself negate the possibilities of a relationship further forged in crises. As

T.N. Kaul, the then Indian foreign secretary, put it, the 'un-tilt' in fact began almost as soon as the war was over. America's 'sloping or leaning position' towards Pakistan could 'only be,' Kaul publicly argued, 'temporary and not permanent'.[22] Notably, the Nixon administration recognised an independent Bangladesh in April 1972.

Second, as mentioned above, the popular caricature of the prime minister as an empress and 'the heroine of the saga of the Bangladesh War', as one confidante put it,[23] has led scholars and commentators to characterise this period in Indian strategic history as one in which idealism—as loosely understood—was replaced by a sure-footed and pragmatic approach to international affairs. The treaty with the Soviets was said to have buried the 'Nehruvian principle' of non-alignment, according to one of Gandhi's biographers, 'once and for all'.[24] As a close observer and family member also argued, it 'represented a complete reversal in foreign policy'.[25] The prime minister's determination, as a poet put it at the time, to 'show courageous anger at the right time',[26] presumably a reference to the difficult decision to go to war, was widely understood to be demonstrative of India's apparent and new found 'realism' in international politics. As established earlier in this book, these simplistic dichotomies of idealism *or* pragmatism do not withstand analytical scrutiny. Moreover, they tell us almost nothing about the struggle to negotiate change in a time of crisis and political succession.

There is little doubt that change was underway. 'A certain quality of non-alignment,' as one insider argues, 'was more attractive' to Gandhi: an advance minus the need for less necessary rhetoric associated with anti-colonial creeds evident in her father's forceful oratory.[27] Further, there is no doubt whatsoever that India's first and thus far only woman prime minister assumed a forthright view on what she considered to be right or wrong. The 'genocide' in East Pakistan, as she was to put it, was wrong.[28] Indeed, Gandhi was not always her father's daughter when it came to tact or language. Yet her instinct for and sense of non-alignment was by no means divorced from Nehru's understanding and approach to foreign policy. This is of course not to suggest, as authorities on Indian foreign policy have, that Gandhi was obsessed with 'anti-colonialism', a preoccupation that was 'never', according to them, 'far from Indira Gandhi's mind'.[29] Rather, and as others maintain, she sought a 'more constructive and cooperative relationship' with both Washington and Moscow, without the sort of hesitation that was evident prior to Nehru's first-ever visit to America in October 1949. Gandhi 'zealously' sought to guard India's 'autonomy', as one author argues,[30] but not because of the potential for entrapment by great powers, something that Nehru and his early advisors were relentlessly wary of, but because such an approach suited Indian interests. In fact, as this chapter shows, her decisions were informed by both the idea and want for non-dependence as much as the need for material security provided by interest-based opportunities—such as the 9 August treaty—to ensure the same. The treaty with the Soviets did not bind India, but freed its hand to prepare for a war of its choosing.

This chapter is divided into four parts. The first—titled 'Resistance'—provides a short background to the crisis in East Pakistan. (Bengali political resistance to West Pakistani authority is well documented elsewhere).[31] The second—'The Need for a Treaty'—looks more closely at the period between 25 March 1971 and 9 August 1971, that is, the period between the onset of the military crackdown in the east to the conclusion of the Indian–Soviet treaty. The third—'From Treaty to War'—examines the initiatives adopted and the decisions taken by Gandhi's government between 9 August 1971 and 4 December 1971, when the Indian Army began ground operations in East Pakistan. This chapter does not aim to provide a military history of the war itself, which, as with the issue of Bengali political resistance, is detailed in existing works.[32] The conclusion analyses Indian and American rapprochement after what was a testing period of crisis.

Resistance

'Urdu will be the only state language of Pakistan', argued Khawaja Nazimuddin soon after he took over as the prime minister of Pakistan. Nazimuddin, the second governor general of Pakistan after Jinnah, switched roles to assume the office of the prime minister following the assassination of Liaquat Ali Khan on 16 October 1951. His remarks about language were surprising not only because they were made in Dacca, the capital city in the East, but also because he himself was a Bengali and a former chief minister of East Bengal. Mujib was shocked. A central 'pledge' to recognise Bengali as an official language, Mujib argued, had been broken.[33] Nazimuddin's comments were immediately followed by riots and protests. According to Richard Sisson and Leo Rose—authors of an excellent account of the 1971 War—the ensuing violence led to the 'creation of the first martyrs,' they argue, 'for a Bengali movement'.[34] The fight for ethno-linguistic rights and greater autonomy from West Pakistan became the rallying cry of the Awami League, a breakaway organisation of the Muslim League created as a party in its own right in 1949. Soon after its creation, West Pakistani elites lost no time in denouncing the Awami League and its demand for greater autonomy. 'I will smash the head,' Liaquat Ali Khan purportedly once stated, 'of anyone who takes part in Awami League activities.'[35] The 'One Unit' plan, or the administrative reforms initiated to consolidate West Pakistan into one provincial unit in 1956, was, as Ian Talbot underscores, arguably designed to 'safeguard the centre from a populist Bengali challenge'.[36]

By the late 1960s it was nearly impossible to continue to discount such a challenge. In 1966, the League outlined what came to be called the six-point programme,[37] demanding greater decentralisation. It was summarily rejected by Ayub.[38] In November 1969, some seven months after Yahya became president and the so-called chief martial law administrator of Pakistan, he issued a Legal Framework Order to transfer power. Finally, in December 1970, Pakistan held its first-ever national elections. The results astonished the West Pakistani elite as well as the military.[39] In fact, as Guha recounts, they 'shocked' Yahya.[40] Crucially, it left Bhutto, the PPP leader, who held a majority of seats in the West, with a minority of eighty-one seats in the 300-member National Assembly. The Awami League secured as many as 167 seats in the East.[41] Yahya found himself in a position for which contingency plans simply did not exist. The Awami League was not supposed to have secured this many seats. Now that they had, the military regime would have to address the issue of East Pakistani autonomy.[42]

In the post-election period, while the military were still seemingly in favour of transferring power to a civilian-led government, the PPP, and in particular Bhutto's resistance to the dominance of the Awami League, led to a convoluted series of negotiations. During the third week of March, and notwithstanding a last ditch attempt to negotiate a settlement between Yahya and Mujib—a process that began in Dacca on 16 March—political violence escalated. The Awami League armed its volunteers and party members.[43] At midnight on 25 March, Mujib declared independence. According to Mujib's eldest daughter, Sheikh Hasina (the Bangladeshi prime minister since 2009 and head of the Awami League), her father was arrested shortly after the declaration.[44] He was flown to an unknown location in West Pakistan.

At 11.30 a.m. on 25 March, the Pakistani military junta launched Operation Searchlight.[45] Its first objective was to disarm Bengali soldiers and policemen suspected of siding with the Awami League. Further, university students and teachers—the Awami's strongest support group—were 'slaughtered in cold blood', writes the veteran journalist Inder Malhotra.[46] The plan backfired almost instantaneously. Bengali officers, regular soldiers, students, intellectuals and policemen mutinied.[47] On 26 March, Yahya banned the Awami League.[48] On the same day, the Voice of Independent Bangladesh, a radio station managed by the leading members of the Awami League, broadcast a unilateral declaration of independence. Subsequently, while some Awami leaders went underground, others fled to Calcutta, where they established the government of Bangladesh in an area of the city that aptly came to be called 'Mujibnagar' or the 'city of Mujib'.

India and the Resistance

Soon after he retired from government service, M.C. Chagla wrote what is perhaps a less-read but crucial record of both his history and that of the nation he served. A jurist, India's envoy to the US and the UK, education minister, and the first of five ministers of foreign affairs to serve under Gandhi, Chagla closely witnessed the virtues of political succession. In his autobiography, published in 1973, the Oxford-educated former vice-chancellor of Bombay University made clear that Gandhi had developed a 'mastery of political strategy' that her father lacked, and which 'finished practitioners' in the 'art of politics', he argued, would find enviable. Gandhi was 'eloquent', 'ruthless', a 'powerful speaker' and a 'master craftsman'.[49] She was also hugely popular, a point Chagla omits. In fact, just as Pakistan's first test with democracy unravelled into chaos and then rebellion, India's democratic credentials as the numerically largest political experiment in the contemporary world was successfully put to test.

In March 1971, India held its fifth General Assembly elections. An electorate of 275 million was eligible to vote. Gandhi and her party won 352 out of 518 seats in the Lok Sabha. The result, Katherine Frank concluded, 'was a Congress landslide—a tremendous mandate for

Indira'.[50] Importantly, it sidelined an older Congress guard and vindicated a less than promising outcome in the last elections. In 1966, following Prime Minister Lal Bahadur Shastri's demise,[51] and after a hard fought battle against some seven contenders for the top job within the Congress, Gandhi was appointed prime minister.[52] A year later, in 1967, and in the fourth General Assembly elections, the Congress under Gandhi—her first-ever elections—won only 283 seats. The party lost ninety-five seats.[53] With a slim majority of forty-four, Gandhi led a minority government with the help of twenty-three seats won by the CPI. For three years, between 1967 and 1970, acute differences between Gandhi and her opponents within the party—who came to represent the so-called 'syndicate'—eventually led to a split within the Congress. Indira's Congress or Congress (R or Requisitionist) went on to receive a colossal mandate from India's voting population in 1971, which left her freer to pursue strategies of action unhindered by internal opposition or the problems inherent in sharing power with allies.

Throughout the election period (December 1970 to March 1971) the emergency in East Pakistan was given scant attention.[54] The only major bilateral India–Pakistan issue discussed at length was the hijacking of an Indian Airlines plane. On 30 January 1971, two individuals from the Kashmir Valley hijacked a plane and landed it in Lahore. Three days later, although the passengers had been released, the plane was bombed.[55] In response, on 2 February, the government of India first banned over-flights by Pakistani military aircraft between West and East Pakistan, and later prohibited over-flights by Pakistani commercial aircraft. Matters were made worse when India's request to Yahya to hand over the hijackers was rejected. For his part, Yahya pushed Nixon to use the president's 'good offices' to resolve the issue. At the time, the State Department's official line was to 'avoid being drawn', as one cable put it, 'into this contentious situation, particularly on one side or the other'.[56] In the end, the matter was referred to the International Civil Aviation Organization.

At this time, India complained that Pakistan was 'clandestinely interfering in India's internal affairs'.[57] After all, the hijackers were thought to enjoy the support of Pakistani officials. In little more than a month, or by the end of March 1971, the tables turned. Pakistan began to complain that India was interfering in its internal affairs in the East. Since the military crackdown on 25 March, tens of thousands of refugees poured into Indian territory, especially in West Bengal, Assam, Meghalaya and Tripura. As noted by P.N. Dhar, Gandhi's confidante who had been appointed an advisor to the Prime Minister's Office in November 1970, this region was deemed to be 'demographically askew, economically retarded, politically unstable, and socially volatile'.[58] India charged Pakistan with 'indirect aggression'.[59] Wary of the increasing numbers of refugees, which, by the middle of April, had jumped to 3.5 million, Gandhi was determined to take matters into her own hands. Her government's response to the crisis required melding military options with a diplomatic offensive. This only added to Nixon's increasing impatience with an obstinate woman prime minister and an emergency in South Asia he would soon need to place at the top of his agenda.

The Need for a Treaty
25 March to 9 August 1971

Largely untouched by the refugee crisis on India's eastern borders, on 1 April, Nixon authorised the relatively trivial sum of $2.5 million for refugee relief. In Washington, L.K. Jha—former governor of the Reserve Bank of India and the Indian ambassador in Washington—kept American officials apprised of the developing crisis caused by the influx of refugees.[60] In New Delhi, Jha's counterpart, Kenneth Keating, met regularly with T.N. Kaul, the Indian foreign secretary. Keating pressed Kaul to exercise restraint. After all, and as P.N. Dhar recorded, by April, some 60,000 refugees were pouring into the less-than-stable parts of eastern India every day.[61]

Finally, on 29 April, the prime minister convened a Cabinet meeting.[62] In addition to the civilians present, General (later Field Marshal) Sam Hormusji Framji Jamshedji Manekshaw or Sam Manekshaw for short, the Indian chief of Army Staff, was also invited.[63] According to Pupul Jayakar, yet another of Gandhi's confidantes, the prime minister made clear to Manekshaw that something needed to be done. 'Refugees are pouring in,' she allegedly stated. 'You [Manekshaw] must stop them. If necessary move into East Pakistan but stop them.'[64] Unflinching, the chief supposedly underlined: 'you know that means war', to which Gandhi's reply was firm: 'I don't mind if that is war.'[65] At this testing time, and as far as Gandhi was concerned, something drastic had to be done in order to reverse the refugees settling in India back to East Pakistan. If this meant war, then so be it. However, others in her council, as also Manekshaw, did not share her enthusiasm for immediate action. Swaran Singh—by then the foreign minister—argued that it would be prudent to garner international support prior to taking military action.[66] For Manekshaw, at least according to secondary accounts of the 29 April meeting, two factors hindered intervention at the time. First, troops and units were dispersed across the country on election duty. 'Time was required to concentrate them,' confirms one of Manekshaw's deputies.[67] Unverified and more popular accounts suggest that the chief went even further to delay military intervention. '100 percent defeat',[68] he apparently stated, was assured unless he was not given a free hand in operational matters.[69] This also included choosing the right time for intervention.

Second, Manekshaw stressed that India's security would be in jeopardy if China decided to intervene.[70] J.N. Dixit writes that, other than Manekshaw, some of Gandhi's civilian advisors were also of the view that India needed to take into account the possibility of Chinese support to Pakistan, which would be separate from the support Nixon might have extended to Yahya.[71] At the end of the 29 April meeting, and according to Dixit, 'an evolutionary policy stance was adopted'. The primary objective, he emphasised, 'aimed at freedom to exercise the military option if interim measures taken did not resolve the East Pakistan crisis'.[72] Hence while the military option was placed squarely on the table, the government was to buy time to convince the international community of the 'genocide' in the east. Equally, Gandhi's envoys were to explore ways by which potential Chinese and American political and military assistance to Pakistan might be deterred, freeing the Indian military's hand in taking direct action in East Pakistan. 'The shield', as one journalist put it, was the Indo-Soviet Treaty of Friendship.[73]

An Offer of a Treaty

In January 1969, the British High Commission in New Delhi noted that the Soviet Union had stepped up its propaganda campaign within India.[74] According to an article cited in the *The Current*, a right-of-centre Indian publication, pamphlets and periodicals printed or imported by the diplomatic missions of the USSR outnumbered those routed to India by the US and the UK by four times.[75] In the same month, a report sent by the US embassy in New Delhi to Christopher

Van Hollen in the US State Department stated that it was felt in India that good relations with the Soviets would help 'defend India against China and Pakistan'.[76] In June 1969, Gandhi made clear to US Secretary of State William Rogers that India was inherently wary of Chinese designs. The US government was increasingly concerned about the PRC's support to tribes in India's north-eastern corridor engaged in rebellion against New Delhi.[77] Indeed, the potential threat posed by the PRC to both India and the Soviet Union, according to Kaul, was the 'main reason' why Moscow was 'keen to come closer to India'.[78] In March 1969, the Soviets proposed a Treaty of Friendship and Cooperation.[79] In a meeting between R. Bhandari, the Indian chargé d'affaires in Moscow, and Nikolai Pegov, the Soviet ambassador to India, Bhandari argued that the Soviets 'saw no prospects in the immediate future of China being friendly to India'.[80] According to Bhandari, once such a treaty was 'solid and firm', it would serve as 'very good insurance against any possible aggression by China or Pakistan'.[81]

In addition, Bhandari made clear that Pegov was given the go-ahead by the likes of Chairman Kosygin.[82] A week after Bhandari met with Pegov, D.P. Dhar, the Indian ambassador in Moscow, spoke with Soviet Defence Minister Marshal Andrei Grechko. According to Dhar, Grechko had in fact told Swaran Singh that the 'Soviet Union would come to India's assistance in case of aggression from China and Pakistan.'[83] Dhar suggested 'cashing in on this offer'. If the Soviets, Dhar argued, were also willing to provide 'defence equipment and know-how on long-term credits', then India, he wrote, 'might agree to enter into a Treaty of Friendship and Cooperation with them'.[84] Yet, at the time, and given Gandhi's political reliance on the left, the potential for a final agreement entrapping India in the Soviet sphere was thought to outweigh the advantages underlined by Dhar. Negotiating and signing an important treaty from a position of strength was seemingly favoured to considering such a treaty in a position of relative domestic weakness. As Sisson and Rose point out, a position of strength would help ensure that the language used in the treaty was carefully constructed while diminishing the likelihood of the CPI's interference, ultimately leaving India free to pursue strategies of her choosing.[85]

By early 1971, British officials were convinced that the 'distrust of China is very deeply rooted in the mind of the Indian masses'.[86] In addition, the Indian government was increasingly concerned about the close nexus between China and Pakistan.[87] In January 1971, Yahya made an official visit to China, rousing further suspicion in India.[88] Consequently, Gandhi's government pursued a diplomatic strategy aimed at detaching Pakistan from China.[89] Following Yahya's visit, Indian officials broached the issue of exchanging ambassadors with China, suspended since 1962. This overture, it was argued, would help normalise relations with China, thereby providing Zhou and Mao with less of a reason to support Pakistan.[90] From the outset, and as British diplomats made clear, this was 'wishful thinking for the Indians'.[91] By the third week of February, the PRC began issuing statements in favour of Pakistan, openly supporting Islamabad's position on Kashmir.[92] Following the crackdown in the East a month later, and given the PRC's obvious obsession with Pakistan, Indian officials re-explored the potential of a treaty with Russia while pressing ahead with a diplomatic offensive designed to push Western principals to consider stemming the extent of the atrocities in the East.

A Diplomatic Offensive

The diplomatic offensive began with Gandhi writing to Nixon. The prime minister, it would appear, sought to pressure Nixon into helping resolve the ensuing crisis in and around Dacca. Gandhi wrote passionately about the 'barbarities which have been committed' in the East. Her concern, she argued, was to draw American 'attention to the gigantic problems which Pakistan's actions in East Bengal have created for India'.[93] Alluding to the 'indirect aggression' inflicted on India, Gandhi wrote that 'Pakistan's war on the people of East Bengal and its impact on us in the form of millions of refugees cannot be separated.'[94] Yet, for the time being, her note did little to entice Nixon.[95] According to Kissinger, the president gave Yahya 'time to follow through his efforts to work out', the then national security advisor wrote, 'his own arrangements transitional to greater Pakistani cooperation or autonomy'.[96] Mindful of Yahya's importance in engaging the PRC, Nixon underlined in a note to the Pakistani president that 'it is to no one's advantage to permit the situation in East Pakistan to lead to an internationalization of the situation'. 'Foreign involvement,' the president made clear, 'could create new problems and compound the difficulty of securing an ultimate settlement.' Nixon further stated that his administration was in touch with the Indian government, and 'stressed the need for restraint'.[97] The less-than-forceful effort on Nixon's part to pressure Yahya infuriated the Indian establishment. At a meeting with Kissinger, L.K. Jha complained that India could no longer absorb the thousands of refugees pouring into India. 'They must find a way to get back into East Pakistan', Jha plainly argued. With a view to force the national security advisor's hand, he also made clear that not only could the situation in the East lead to the total deterioration of India–Pakistani relations, but, as Jha put it, 'it could also result in a backwash effect on Indo-US relations'. Further, the ambassador stressed that India could foresee Chinese involvement in the East, which, he underlined, was beginning to concern the Indian government more seriously than ever before.[98]

For his part, and at the given time, Nixon appeared convinced that India was promoting war with Pakistan.[99] His views, of course, had a lot to do with the special arrangement between him and Yahya, the 'indispensable middle man'.[100] Untouched by Gandhi's appeal, the Nixon administration did almost nothing in the months of April and May to restrain Yahya. Indeed, India's frustration with an unwelcoming and almost deaf White House was heightened between the middle of June and the beginning of August. In June, the *New York Times* reported that Washington was sending arms shipments to Pakistan. This exasperated the Indian government, which accused the Nixon administration of abetting Pakistan's brutal policies in the East. The situation was then further compounded on 7 July, during Kissinger's fleeting visit to New Delhi prior to travelling to Pakistan and Beijing, when he told Gandhi and other Indian officials that Nixon planned on improving relations with the PRC, thereby generating even more anxiety among the Indian leadership.

Arms Shipments to Pakistan

On 22 June, the *New York Times* reported that two shipments of arms were being transported on Pakistani-registered freighters from New York to Pakistan.[101] This was unexpected as it contravened an executive decision on the part of the American administration to embargo military equipment to both India and Pakistan following the 1965 War between the two nations. In 1966, the embargo was modified to permit the sale to both countries of non-lethal items such as communications, medical and transportation equipment. In October 1970, a one-time exception was provided to Pakistan to authorise the sale of 300 armoured personnel carriers and approximately twenty aircrafts.[102] In early April 1971, as the situation in the East became tense, the US government claimed that no further licences had been issued. However, licences and equipment paid for under the one-time exception rule prior to April 1971, American officials maintained, had to be honoured.[103]

Swaran Singh, who visited Washington in the second week of June, was shocked. After all, during the foreign minister's meetings with Kissinger and Nixon he had been told that the president would use his 'influence as effectively as possible' to find a political solution to the East Pakistani crisis.[104] Nobody had told Singh about the arms shipments to Pakistan. In London on 20 June, Singh in fact stated that he was 'precisely' and 'definitely' told that the Nixon White House would pressure Pakistan to find a political solution. He added that the Soviet Union was doing its bit by having stopped all transfers of military aid to Pakistan.[105]

During Kissinger's visit to New Delhi in the first week of July, the arms shipments became a matter of heated discussion. Kissinger blamed the State Department bureaucracy in Washington for not keeping the White House 'fully informed of things already delivered to the docks prior to March 25 1971'. He claimed that both he and Nixon were 'not aware' of these developments when they spoke to Singh in Washington, and thus that they were 'very much surprised of the *New York Times* report'.[106] Kissinger's admissions are disputable. Declassified NSC papers in the US reveal that Kissinger and Nixon had been apprised of the arms shipments as early as May 1971.

In fact, in a note written by Harold Saunders, the State Department official clearly wrote that since the 'non-lethal' items were purchased directly from US commercial suppliers, there was no way of knowing exactly what items were sold and when. Saunders stated that although no significant shipments had been scheduled for delivery since March 1971, 'soon,' he argued, 'specific cases will come up'.[107] Kissinger might not have known exactly when shipments were made or licences bought, but he had been told that there was a possibility that shipments might be made in the post-March period.[108] In fact, on 4 June, Kissinger was further apprised about the arms shipments. It was made clear to the national security advisor that communication equipment worth $2.6 million, heavy vehicles and trainer aircraft worth $11 million, lethal spare parts for F-86 aircrafts and tanks worth $12 million, and ammunition for 106 mm guns worth $3.4 million had been signed off by the Nixon administration.[109] Whether or not these figures were available to Swaran Singh and India officials is unclear, but what is certain is that the potential of shipments during this testing time confirmed Kissinger and Nixon's less-than-forceful attitude towards both the crisis in the East and Yahya.

Testing Rapprochement with India

On 6 July, during the first day of Kissinger's two-day visit to New Delhi, P.N. Haksar made clear to the visiting American envoy that while India 'did not want to go to war', it 'did not know how not to go to war'.[110] After all, the refugee crisis was getting worse by the day. Gandhi ordered the Indian Border Security Force (BSF) to provide assistance and support to the 'freedom fighters' in the East. The so-called Mukti Fauj or armed factions of the Mukti Bahini—the Bengali resistance—were directly supported by India.[111] In his attempt to temper India's war-like footing, Kissinger appeared to have in fact further emboldened India's need for diplomatic cover. On 7 July, during a meeting with Gandhi, he informed the Indian prime minister that the Nixon administration was keen to improve relations with the PRC, a revelation made with indelicate timing given that Gandhi had only recently stated that 'she was afraid of mounting Chinese influence in East Pakistan'.[112] In a following meeting with Jagjivan Ram, the Indian defence minister, Kissinger argued that China may well 'intervene on behalf of Pakistan if there was a war between India and Pakistan'.[113] Whether Kissinger's message was intended to caution India's advance towards intervention or whether it was designed merely to outline his thinking if India intervened in the East is less clear. For Indian officials like Ram, America's renewed approach to the PRC was troubling, to say the least.

In fact, and unlike Kissinger's discussions in New Delhi, his meeting with Jha made clear that American support in case of Chinese interference was hardly assured. On 17 July, according to Jha, Kissinger bluntly stated that if China were to intervene in a war between India and Pakistan 'we would be unable to help you [India] against China'.[114] At a time when war with Pakistan was a very real possibility, these mixed signals from Kissinger did nothing to reassure the Indian establishment.[115] Between 9 and 11 July, Kissinger made his secret visit to China. He held seventeen hours of conversations with Zhou, Mao and other Chinese officials. Kissinger's visit, writes P.N. Dhar, 'had a decisive impact on Indian policy making'. It led Gandhi and her advisors 'to veer in favor of a treaty [with the Soviets]'. Dhar emphasised that 'while the timing and substance of the visit had nothing to do with the crisis in the subcontinent, it nevertheless had an adverse effect on it from our [India's] point of view'.[116]

On 5 August, Andrei Gromyko flew to India, and on 9 August the Indo-Soviet Treaty was signed. As noted by Dixit:

The specific objective was to provide a basis for future support from the Soviet Union in case the US and Pakistan, or Pakistan and China acted in concert to thwart any military operations India might undertake in support of Bangladesh's liberation struggle.[117]

The Treaty and After

Following the signing of the treaty, the Indian government initiated a three-pronged diplomatic strategy. First, Singh briefed Indian ambassadors and MEA delegates in different parts of the world to impress upon the international community that the treaty was not directed against any one country, including China.[118] This initiative was to be strengthened when Gandhi decided to tour the world's capitals in an effort to urge the international community to find a political solution to the impending crisis in the East. Second, having found a shield in the Soviet treaty, India decided to strengthen relations with China. As outlined by Inder Malhotra in *The Guardian* shortly after the treaty was signed, Gandhi was 'willing to start talks with China at any level at any time on any or all problems between the two countries without any preconditions'.[119] Third, and perhaps most importantly, emissaries were told to make clear to both American and British officials that the treaty itself did not mean that India's policy of non-alignment had been abandoned. In fact, Singh made this clear in the Indian Parliament on the day the treaty was signed. Instead of defending the merits of non-alignment when the treaty had raised doubts with regard to India's traditional foreign policy, Singh unabashedly stated that India hoped that 'the policy of non-alignment will be further strengthened and will become an effective instrument for the safeguarding of our national interest'.[120]

Of the twelve articles in the treaty, Article 9 was the most controversial. In essence, and as mentioned above, it made clear that if either the USSR or India were militarily confronted or even threatened, both countries would 'immediately enter into mutual consultations in order to remove such threats and to take appropriate effective measures to ensure peace and the security of their countries'.[121] Kissinger's immediate reaction to the treaty was that it could not be reconciled with India's policy of non-alignment.[122] As far as Nixon was concerned, Gandhi had taken the diplomatic measures necessary to break-up Pakistan.[123] In keeping with India's strategy to convince the international community otherwise, Jha met with Kissinger on 9 August to impress upon him that India was not going to be anyone's diplomatic satellite. The Indian ambassador claimed that all India was looking for was 'a counter-weight to Pakistan's repeated claims that in a new war China would be on its side'.[124]

By the end of August, Kissinger's initial reactions to the treaty seemed to have tempered. He argued that, in effect, the treaty 'seem[ed] to do little more than record formally the existing Indo-Soviet relationship'.[125] Comparing the text of the treaty with the one signed between the United Arab Republic (UAR) and the Soviets, Kissinger stated that 'the Indian treaty seems a degree less strong in that it calls only for consultation if hostilities threaten while the UAR treaty calls for the two sides to "concert" their positions'.[126] He made it clear to Nixon that 'the Indians do not seem at all prepared to write off the US'.[127] Kissinger at one point even argued that Gandhi was 'cold blooded and tough and will not turn into a Soviet satellite merely because of pique'.[128]

As far as British officials were concerned, the treaty came as a 'surprise'.[129] Like Jha in Washington, Kaul in India tried to convince British diplomats that the treaty 'respects the Indian policy of non-alignment'.[130] Indeed, Article 4 of the treaty, inserted on the insistence of the Indians, clearly stated that nothing in the treaty would undermine India's policy of non-alignment. According to Kaul, the treaty gave 'greater credibility' to the policy of non-alignment, which, he argued, was seen to be 'dynamic and flexible and to conform to changes in the situation in the world'.[131]

The rhetoric chosen by Jha, who claimed that the treaty served as a 'counter-weight', and by Kaul, who stated that the policy of non-alignment was 'flexible', indicated a clear change in the manner and method in which Indian diplomats parcelled Indian foreign policy. This change was not only limited to mere rhetoric, but very clearly manifested itself in the body of a treaty, which, by any measure, meant that India as a nation was no longer free to negotiate a completely independent approach to international affairs. The fact remained that India was obligated to consult the Soviet Union in the event of a threat emanating from a third party. By signing the treaty, India sought to balance the perceived threat emanating from a so-called US–Pakistan–China conglomeration. But this did not mean that India had sacrificed her independence, a point accepted back in 1971 by diplomats in both the US and the UK.[132]

From Treaty to War

On 10 August, a day after the treaty with the Soviets was concluded, Gromyko laid out the Soviet Union's position on the crisis in the East. During official talks with the Indian prime minister, he told Gandhi that India should follow a policy of restraint. He stated:

We [the Soviet Union] believed it would be very good if your government continues the restraint and regards the situation in a cold blooded way. We know the emotions of your people which are justified. It would be good if they could be kept under control. The heart should be warm but the mind should be cool.[133]

Restraining India was by no means the sole purpose of the treaty. As mentioned above, the Soviets first presented Indian diplomats in Moscow with the idea of a treaty or channel for cooperation in 1969, years before the crisis in East Pakistan came to absorb India's attention. Initially, Kosygin argued that the USSR wanted to bring about better relations between India and Pakistan so that they could 'jointly tackle China'.[134] Further, and less recognised in the existing literature, the treaty with India was to cover cooperation in all fields—technical, scientific and economic—allowing Russia to tap into an emerging market.[135] In short, in the summer of 1971 both countries found themselves in a position where they could take advantage of each other's interests.[136]

However, British and American interpretations of the Soviet Union's motives for going ahead with the treaty in 1971 indicate that the Soviet leadership actually believed that it could restrain India.[137] Following a meeting between British diplomats and Vadim Sopriakov, the first secretary in the Soviet embassy in New Delhi, officials in the British High

Commission in New Delhi estimated that the 'Russians had been extremely worried over the "smell of war" in the air.' They were anxious, one cable argued, 'to take some practical measure to defuse the situation'. According to a telegram wired from the high commission to London on 17 August, the treaty 'had greatly reduced the chances of conflict in the coming months'. 'But,' it continued, 'in the long term there was still a considerable risk of war.'[138] That the treaty with the Soviets bought time to discuss a political solution in the East appears to have been the generally accepted line of argument, at least for British officials in New Delhi.[139] The Americans too bought the thesis at hand. In a paper presented by the US delegation to NATO on 25 August, the Americans were convinced that Moscow had thrown its weight 'demonstratively on one side of the Indo-Pakistani conflict'. Soviet officials, it argued, planned 'to help keep the lid on the situation in the short-run, and encourage Islamabad to acquiesce in a political settlement'. The US embassy in New Delhi also conveyed a similar analysis to the State Department. Like their British counterparts, Keating and his team accepted that, as far as the Soviets were concerned, the treaty would prevent conflict by serving as a deterrent. In Washington, Anatoly Dobrynin, the Soviet ambassador to the US, confirmed Keating's analysis. He passionately argued that the treaty provided the pretext by which the Soviets could restrain Indian actions.[140] Following a meeting with Dobrynin, Kissinger wrote: 'the Soviets seemed to have gambled that, by simultaneously strengthening India's position and making New Delhi more beholden to Soviet counsel, they can best restrain India and also deter Pakistan from taking steps likely to lead to war'.[141]

However, events between the end of September and the beginning of November indicate that while the Soviets exerted pressure on the Indians to exercise restraint, the Indian government followed its own approach to the crisis at hand, emboldened rather than hindered by Soviet counsel. There was no question of curtailing India's independent judgement.[142] This was recognised by a number of British diplomats, who vociferously argued that although the Soviet–Indian treaty was 'dubiously compatible with the strict doctrine of non-alignment', it did not mean, as one telegram put it, that Britain 'considered India to have cut herself off from her other friends and to be wholly committed to the Soviet Government'.[143]

In a meeting held between Gromyko and Kissinger at the end of September, Gromyko continued to argue that the Soviet Union had faith in Gandhi and that India would not precipitate war.[144] However, events on the subcontinent had begun to move at a rapid pace. The Indian government, while having received the assurance it needed from the Soviets, upped the ante. On 8 October, Jha met with Kissinger. The Indian ambassador told Kissinger that there was not much time for a political settlement. The Indians expected the number of refugees to increase to 10 million. Further, Jha made clear that Gandhi was wary that Maoist insurgent groups in the eastern border regions might find in the refugees fresh recruits, further destabilising the East. Kissinger warned Jha of taking unilateral action, but Jha, for his part, stated that if a political settlement was not reached soon India might have to take military action by the end of the year.[145]

By the second week of October, Indian and Pakistani troops reinforced their respective positions in the western border.[146] In a last ditch attempt to apply pressure on the international community to broker a political solution Indira Gandhi toured a number of European capitals. In London, she told the British prime minister that 'she did not know how to hold back the great pressures in India'.[147] She claimed that India was hosting some 9.5 million refugees as of 25 October. Although unable to verify this figure independently, a document authored by the UN reported that it was 'satisfied that the system of registration, ration cards and recording inoculations provides the Indians with the basis of a very fair estimate of the refugee figures including those not in camps'.[148] In fact, eyewitness accounts claimed that between 5,000 and 7,000 refugees from the East were entering India at a single crossing. The Foreign Office in London concluded that 'an influx of over 100,000 a week at the present time does not appear exaggerated'.[149] In Brussels, Gandhi claimed that India could not foresee any solution other than independence for East Pakistan; 'only then,' she argued, 'would the refugees go back'.[150] Similarly, at a press conference in Vienna, she stated that only a 'settlement acceptable to the elected representatives of East Bengal could lead to a solution of the crisis'.[151]

While Gandhi toured Europe, Keating approached T.N. Kaul in India to agree to a mutual withdrawal of forces from the border areas.[152] Alarmed by an increase in Pakistani and Indian troop deployments in both the western and eastern border regions, the US ambassador stressed the need to agree to a withdrawal.[153] In Moscow, US officials were asked by the State Department to approach Gromyko. American officials believed that perhaps Moscow would be able to exert some amount of pressure on India, forcing it to withdraw its forces if and when the Pakistani military withdrew theirs.[154] In the beginning of November, Gandhi paid a visit to Washington. Nixon once again suggested a troop withdrawal. Gandhi was hardly interested[155]—the prime minister appeared to have made up her mind to intervene. Soviet calls for restraint had done little to influence the Indian government. On 23 November, Gandhi wrote the last official letter to Nixon before the war with Pakistan commenced. Once again, she described the dire situation in the East.[156]

As far as the government of India was concerned, diplomatically, it had done everything possible to find a peaceful solution to the East Pakistan crisis while making sure that it had acquired the shield necessary to assure US and Chinese non-interference in the event of war. By the end of November, Kosygin argued that 'under existing circumstances', a request for a mutual withdrawal of troops is 'scarcely feasible'.[157] Unwilling and unable to convince the Indians otherwise, by the beginning of December Kosygin seemed to have understood that India would not be swayed by external advice, but would make its own foreign policy-related decisions based on its own calculations.

On 5 December, following Pakistani military attacks in the Western Frontier, and the publication of a *gazette extraordinaire* by Yahya's government on 4 December declaring a state of war against India, Gandhi notified Nixon that she was left with no option but to put her country on a war footing. With a tone of defiance and confidence, she wrote, 'the grave consequences that should follow Pakistan's unprovoked attack on us all shall be the sole responsibility of the Government of Pakistan'.[158] The consequence of Yahya's actions led ultimately to the dismemberment of Pakistan and the birth of an independent state: Bangladesh.

Conclusion

Towards the end of the crisis, Kissinger ordered the American Seventh Fleet to the Bay of Bengal. The Indians read US actions as not only hostile, but as having the potential to internationalise India's intervention into East Pakistan. In the end, while the Indian Army reached Dacca, forcing the Pakistanis to surrender, the cessation of hostilities no longer required the American fleet to remain in the region.[159] Nevertheless, this show of strength would not be forgotten by the Indian strategic elite or the general public. The event would be remembered as the US 'tilt' towards Pakistan.[160] However, post-1971, relations between India and the US had, to an extent, been rectified. The Americans did not view India as a satellite state of the Soviet Union. In fact, they seemed convinced that India would not allow the 'consolidation of Soviet influence'.[161]

By the summer of 1972, Kissinger told L.K. Jha that US actions in 1971 were 'reactions to a tactical situation and were not in accordance with any fundamental US interests'.[162] In the following year, Jha wrote that although 'relations between India and the United States are at fairly low ebb', he estimated that some analysts in the State Department believed that the US had been 'backing the wrong horse on the sub-continent'.[163] Jha recognised that the Washington bureaucracy chose not to harp on the merits and demerits of the treaty in both official and unofficial parleys. Instead, the Nixon administration, according to Jha, sought 'some improvement in bilateral relations'.[164] At the same time, and given America's backing for Pakistan during the crisis, Indian leaders focused more on a militarised nuclear weapons programme with the aim of creating a deterrent able to shield India from the threat of future conflagrations.[165]

In 1973, when T.N. Kaul was appointed the Indian ambassador to the US, relations between the two countries seemed to have again been on the upswing. In one of the first public speeches made by Kaul, he argued that a tilt 'can only be temporary and not permanent'.[166] He made clear that a 'strong and stable India will not be the stooge or satellite of any other power or group of powers nor try to dominate any region or gang up against any power or group of powers'.[167]

Following a meeting with Kissinger in late 1973, Kaul wrote that Kissinger gave him the impression that the US was not 'panicked by closer Indo-Soviet friendly relations'.[168] Both circumstance and a new prime minister led to an advance less thinkable during Nehru's early years in office. Yet this did not mean that idealism—wrongly associated with the Nehru years—was replaced by pragmatism, a term scholars loosely use but seldom define. As Gandhi herself argued, 'international relations have entered an era of rapid change', leading nations to 'seek new ties' and cut 'across old rigidities'.[169] To remain relevant, India needed to change too. Greater engagement was the need of the hour. Cooperation was essential to safeguard its interests. Yet older ideas underlying the need to remain unaligned were not altogether dropped, but injected with new vigour, a process started in 1962.

These newer ideas would be built not in situ of older ideas, but alongside them, giving rise to tensions that became much starker at the turn of the century, some sixty years after Nehru had claimed that 'if India is to survive, India will survive by her own strength, self-help and self-confidence, not by relying on others'.[170] India had now begun to rely on others, but as this chapter has shown, that did not mean that it had jeopardised its own strength, self-help or self-confidence. The shift from non-alignment to engagement is not a clear-cut story about older and newer ideas, but the interlinking and meshing of older and newer ideas, as well as the tensions that lie therein.

PART III

NEGOTIATING ENGAGEMENT

7

'NINDA'

2003

On 14 July 2003, Yashwant Sinha, the recently appointed foreign minister, told journalists that the government of India would 'consider the deployment of our troops in Iraq' *if* there was an 'explicit UN mandate for the purpose'.[1] In effect, and given that an 'explicit' UN mandate was seemingly impossible, India had rejected America's request to contribute troops to the US-led intervention in Iraq. The comments followed a ninety-minute meeting of the Cabinet Committee on Security (CCS), the top committee on security-related matters, which was chaired by the then Prime Minister Atal Bihari Vajpayee. The remarks put an end to a four-and-a-half-month debate on both the merits and limits of military intervention and its resultant effect on India's relationship with the US. After all, military involvement in Iraq, as one distinguished commentator put it, had the potential not only to 'raise New Delhi's military profile in the Persian Gulf', but equally, to 'lay the foundations for long-term security cooperation with Washington in the Indian Ocean Region'.[2]

Some in the Indian Cabinet held similar positions. In fact, Sinha argued that the government had arrived at its decision after having carefully considered Indian domestic interests, those of the 'people of Iraq', 'long standing ties for the people of the Gulf' and, as importantly, India's 'growing dialogue and strengthening of ties with the US'.[3] That the US and President George. W. Bush were high on the minds of

Indian elites could not be denied. In fact, the words used to construct the parliamentary response to the intervention clearly demonstrated the government's need and inclination to tread carefully. Having deliberated over some half a dozen iterations, the final resolution stated that 'the house deplores the military action'.[4] Crucially, the government was able to avoid using the language of 'condemnation', which the Congress— the lead opposition party—favoured.[5] Interestingly, it took lengthy, painstaking meetings in the Speaker's Chamber and a close review of Hindi and English dictionaries to agree on the word 'deplore', the English translation of the Hindi word *ninda* that all parties were able to agree upon.[6] Seen by some as a mere dispute over semantics, the choice of rhetoric was vital to a government anxious to avoid irritating the Republican administration over an issue that had already alienated many of Washington's closest allies. 'Diplomatic astuteness', or pragmatism, as Sinha argued, required conditioning Indian imperatives.[7] These practitioner views were also echoed in more general commentary. The prior emphasis on the idea of non-alignment, after all, was hardly something that continued to take precedence in the twenty-first century.

Academic texts argue that this chapter in India's history witnessed the introduction of something 'new'. Phrases such as India's 'new foreign policy' or 'the shock of new' became commonplace in the titles of scholarly works discussing India's contemporary approach to the US.[8] 'Non-alignment', as somewhat superficially understood to mean a product of 'Nehruvian laurels' or 'anti-colonialism', is often assumed to have become 'something of an oxymoron' given the end of the Cold War.[9] As one writer argued, it was time to 'shed' India's 'magnificent obsession' with these dated ideas.[10] In short, an apparent shift away from idealism began to dominate the academic discourse surrounding Indian foreign policy, and this continues to be case. In a sense, and given the popular but untestable descriptions of non-alignment used in the majority of work on Indian foreign policy, disassembling the popular discourse around a term many use, but which very few test through investigational reasoning, is likely to prove an exhaustive, if not impossible, task. Instead, the intent behind this chapter is to push readers to think beyond the accepted rationales for change in Indian foreign policy. Indeed, and as was argued in Part II, change in Indian foreign policy could well be traced to 1962 or 1971. It is hardly 'new'.

Rather, it is a process that was accelerated by the fall of the Soviet Union, the reforms that led to economic liberalisation and the introduction of nuclear weapons. This course of change convinced those in government that the moment of transformation in both economics and foreign policy was underway. Indeed, as Kuldip Nayar makes clear, it was in this context that Manmohan Singh, the Oxford-educated former bureaucrat and finance minister in P.V. Narasimha Rao's Congress-led government, opened his budget speech with the words of Victor Hugo. The then 59-year-old minister argued: 'no power on earth can stop an idea whose turn has come'.[11] He was, of course, referring to the need for financial liberalisation. In time, and in the arena of international affairs, the mood for change found a brand name in what Brajesh Mishra, the national security advisor during the Vajpayee era, called 'engagement'. 'Engaging the world', and especially the US, according to Mishra, was an objective from the start.[12] It did not mean or signify a clean break from the past. It instead meant focusing more on one end of an imaginary line of tension drawn between the more guarded practices of the past and the ability to engage world actors and leaders on equal terms in the present, and the latter was only possible because India had remained watchful in the initial decades following independence. The freedom to make independent choices at a time when the world was experiencing a structural transformation was hardly something that could be taken for granted.

Further, a state of tension, by definition, is reflective of a state of unsettlement. Reconciling policy decisions, such as sending troops to Iraq, necessarily required dealing with a preoccupation with the past and the promise of the future as seen and lived by those making and shaping the choice of strategy at hand. Indeed, and as those known to have pushed the case for 'engagement' and 'pragmatism' also realised, while the foundations of a 'new' foreign policy needed to be 'premised on establishing good relations with the West', the 'traditional Indian resistance to change', as one scholar argued, had prevented 'a total rejection of non-alignment'.[13]

Ideas do not, of course, always change as fast as interests. Somewhat astutely, Donald Rumsfeld, the former US secretary of defence and a lead agent in pushing India to send troops to Iraq, argued that the debate in 2003 was 'educational' for both India and the US. It made clear, he continued, that India was a country open to 'engaging in the world'. That it ultimately refused to send troops should not, in his view, take away from the reality that this was a country 'coming out of tension'. The fact, Rumsfeld concluded, that India was 'getting comfortable' with pressing questions such as intervention was itself noteworthy.[14] Apart from what American leaders noticed and recorded, in some ways, the adoption of '*ninda*' could well be read as a manifestation of this period of change. Indeed, as Shashi Tharoor writes, India was and continues to be 'in a position to graduate from a focus on our own sovereignty to exercising a vision of responsibility on the world stage'. While Tharoor and a whole host of writers omit or simply overlook India's history of engagement in cases such as Korea, as detailed earlier in this book, there is little doubt that the ability to accept 'strategic autonomy' as a 'fact of life' has allowed Indian elites somewhat broader cerebral and bureaucratic space in dealing with the world.[15] How exactly India understands and implements the terms of 'responsibility'—its renewed approach to the US—while simultaneously reconciling changing ideas and interests is detailed below in an analysis of the debate for and against the Iraq intervention.

This chapter is divided into five parts. The first part provides a background to some challenging, if not decisive, moments in the last decade of the twentieth century. It briefly outlines a number of turning points in the 1990s, such as the nuclear tests in 1998, the War in Kargil in 1999 and India's reaction to the US-led intervention in Afghanistan in 2001, which served to encourage the US and India to make progress on a dialogue that had previously lacked structure, and at times even a clear intent. This section is designed simply to establish the context for the larger issues under consideration. Further details regarding this important period and key issues such as the impact of America's renewed offer of military assistance to Pakistan and the 2002 crisis following a terrorist attack on the Indian Parliament are available elsewhere.[16] The issues surrounding nuclear non-proliferation and India's approach to non-proliferation regimes are discussed in the following chapter. The second part of this chapter introduces some of the central Republican characters involved in shaping policy towards India following George W. Bush's electoral victory. The third section looks carefully at the arguments and initiatives adopted in India between February 2003, when the debate over Iraq began to gain momentum in India, and April 2003, when the government set out to 'deplore' or evoke *ninda* in a parliamentary resolution. The fourth section examines the manner in which elites on both sides chose to negotiate the terms for India's potential military involvement. The conclusion introduces the new and present (as of 2013) Congress-led government and its attempts at deliberation over the Iraq question.

India and the Clinton White House

In 1994, a year into his presidency, Bill Clinton confessed that Washington had 'bad relations with both' India and Pakistan. The latter, argued the 47-year-old former governor of Arkansas, felt 'screwed on Kashmir'.[17] These recollections were recorded via Dictaphone over the course of seventy-nine meetings between the highly imaginative historian Taylor Branch and President Clinton while the latter was travelling home from the White House. In many cases, Branch was able to capture views and emotions that would have been impossible to grasp in more formal settings. As Branch argued, his approach was one of a 'participant in a memoir', depicting the president 'candidly in texture'.[18] The fact that Clinton was clearly irritated over South Asia is more than apparent in the relevant pages of Branch's best-selling narrative. Most of these select pages refer to Clinton's reading and reaction to the nuclear tests by India—on 11 and 13 May 1998—and Pakistan—on 28 May 1998—and the War in Kargil in 1999.

The question then arises: did South Asia and India more specifically come to occupy a position of significance for the US only because of the overt introduction of nuclear weapons? The short answer is yes. As the president underlined to Branch, there was 'no greater responsibility' for him 'than to reduce conflicts that threaten nuclear war'. 'This one,' or the conflict between India and Pakistan, Clinton continued, 'certainly does'.[19] Given the select focus of the Clinton White House on a specific range of foreign policy issues, the significance attached to the Indian and Pakistani nuclear tests is thus hardly surprising. As one biographer argued, this Democrat came to Washington with an 'insatiable curiosity'[20] that was to lead him to examine and oversee agreements between the Israelis and Palestinians, to play the role of an honest broker in the conflict in Northern Ireland and attempt to resolve the humanitarian crisis in the Balkans. India was not on the top of his agenda. While a twelve-day tour of South Asia by Hillary and Chelsea Clinton in 1995 had captured the imagination of Indian elites,[21] it still left a lot to be desired for a relationship that lacked bureaucratic enthusiasm.

For the five years prior to the tests, incremental steps towards more public, high-level initiatives were being taken in the background. In many ways, such smaller, less visible and seldom reported forms of diplomacy helped increase the levels of contact between two sides that had invested much more time interacting with each other during the Cold War than in the early and mid-1990s. In the spring of 1995, the chief of the Indian Air Force made a state visit to Washington to enter into dialogue with the American Joint Chiefs of Staff. Two years later, General Joseph Ralston, the then vice chairman of the US Joint Chiefs of Staff, visited India, the first chairman or vice chairman to visit since 1953. For his part, and obviously enthused by what he saw and heard in India, Ralston returned to Washington with a message to 'build closer bonds' with a nation seen to be crucial to many in the Pentagon. Yet as Ralston subsequently put it, for the moment, such zeal, even if it came from the second highest-ranking military official in the US, was simply 'glazed over'.[22] At this stage, prior to the nuclear tests, American misgivings around India's desire for nuclear weapons served to limit both the scope for testing and the ability to widen talking points in bilateral discussions.

In December 1995, a *New York Times* story claimed that India was about to conduct nuclear tests. Frank Wisner, the eighteenth US ambassador to India, reportedly showed Rao satellite pictures by way of confirmation. Rao denied the claims. Yet as the senior journalist and scholar C. Raja Mohan argues, the fact was that 'India had been coaxed into not going ahead with the tests, which were due in less than seventy two hours.'[23] A year later, Prime Minister Deve Gowda, the Janata Dal (Party) leader who took over as prime minister after Rao but lasted less than a year, also queried the possibility of tests. He asked I.K. Gujral, the foreign minister, if tests were conceivable. To his surprise, according to Gujral's account of events, he was immediately asked by the US State Department to speak with Warren Christopher, the US secretary of state. The Americans, according to Gujral, had an insider in the Indian Cabinet. Both Christopher and Wisner were determined to ensure that Indian elites understood this.[24] The pressure was clearly on. Testing was simply unfeasible.

Indeed, the one piece of advice given to Vajpayee by Rao, as the former led the BJP to power in 1996, was: 'I could not do it [test nuclear devices] though I wanted very much to, so it is really up to you now.'[25] Secrecy was of paramount importance. In the view of some Indian elites, it would be more than possible to manage the expected backlash from countries like the US and the UK in the aftermath of any tests. But going ahead with nuclear tests when the US had made it known that it was aware of Indian intentions could well serve as a direct and provocative affront to the Clinton White House and international society more generally. Although this distinction may seem to be of marginal significance, in the universe of diplomacy it mattered a great deal.

Tests and a Backchannel

On 19 March 1998, Vajpayee was sworn-in as prime minister for the second time in two years. However, in contrast to his first premiership, he now headed the BJP-led National Democratic Alliance (NDA), a coalition of more than a dozen political parties. He would be re-elected for a third time in the autumn of 1999, remaining in office until May 2004. Almost immediately, as Bruce Riedel, special assistant to President Clinton in the NSC, recounts, change was evident. It was clear, he stated, 'that the BJP wanted to engage the United States in a way none of its predecessors wanted to engage us'.[26] Shortly after the elections, Riedel accompanied Ambassador Bill Richardson to New Delhi. Richardson, then the US ambassador to the UN, was on his way to meet with the Afghan Taliban. Somewhat unexpectedly, Jaswant Singh, a senior BJP leader, conveyed to these dignitaries that he was authorised by Vajpayee to initiate a backchannel dialogue with the US. 'Nothing like that had been proposed by the Indian government,' Riedel noted. Indeed, and notwithstanding the fact that the Foreign Ministry portfolio was held by Vajpayee, it was clear that 'Jaswant quickly established himself as the principal spokesman on foreign policy.'[27] This was all good news as far the Americans were concerned. Thus despite the threat of nuclear tests, the Clinton White House also began to consider rapprochement. Albright, the US secretary of state following Clinton's re-election in 1996, visited India a year before Richardson. A presidential trip was on the cards. Yet generating momentum for such a visit became next to impossible due to the rapid changes in government within India outlined above, and ultimately,[28] the nuclear tests in 1998.

The tests came as a complete shock to the US administration, and indeed to many within the Indian government. According to Jaswant Singh, the anger this generated among Clinton and his advisors was not solely due to the fact that the tests had been conducted. What had 'riled them more' was that:

Their intelligence agencies and satellite surveillance, indeed an entire array of technical gadgetry, had failed to get even an inkling of the tests. That is why, long after they had been conducted, seismic monitors all over the world, including in the United States, kept arguing against and querulously refuting what was an irrefutable scientific fact.[29]

As mentioned earlier, secrecy was of overriding importance, and Vajpayee and his coterie of advisors pulled-off what Rao could not. As Clinton admitted to Branch in one of their less formal meetings, India knew the US 'had only three spy satellites in rotations, and they timed the orbits shrewdly to conceal the test preparation'.[30] As Strobe Talbott, Clinton's friend from Oxford, a Russia specialist and the deputy secretary of state under Albright, recounts in his diary-like narrative on India, everyone was caught unawares. Key figures in both the State Department and the CIA were receiving what little information they could from CNN.[31]

Clinton was personally irked. This was obvious in the tone of his public statement on 13 May. He lamented:

They're a very great country … But to think that you have to manifest your greatness by behaviour that recalls the very worst events of the 20th century on the edge of the 21st century, when everybody else is trying to leave the nuclear age behind, is just wrong. It is just wrong. And they clearly don't need to maintain their security, vis-à-vis China, Pakistan, or anybody else.[32]

Indian leaders of course saw it very differently. China had tested nuclear weapons for the first time thirty-four years earlier. Pakistan had the required capability. In a letter explaining India's decision to Clinton, Vajpayee made it clear that the threat posed by China and its assistance to Pakistan had pushed India into testing. That there were symbolic and normative reasons too—such as evoking a sense for a particular strain of nationalism—were, unsurprisingly, omitted in this letter between principals. Vajpayee ended his note with some conciliatory remarks that were designed to help soften the backlash of sanctions and the disenchantment that would inevitably follow. That India would work to 'promote the cause of nuclear disarmament' was highlighted in the concluding paragraph.[33]

Following the tests, and as had been expected, the US imposed economic and military sanctions on India. Other than targeting food aid and humanitarian initiatives, the Clinton administration imposed sanctions on everything from defence sales to export licences. It opposed IMF and World Bank loans, and conducted a sweeping review of all scientific exchange programmes, including recalling and cancelling visas issued to Indian scientists in the US. Somewhat inexplicably, the chairman of the Senate Foreign Relations Committee stated that India 'clearly constitute[d] an emerging nuclear threat to the territory of the United States'.[34] Yet despite his clear anger over what had happened, Clinton soon came to accept that the tests themselves had been largely inevitable.[35]

In fact, as Ralston recollected, the tests 'did more to bring our two nations [the US and India] together than anything else'.[36] The sanctions notwithstanding, Riedel argued that the tests only temporarily 'undercut the credibility of the backchannel'—the US and India, he asserted, 'recover[ed]' from this temporary interlude fairly quickly.[37] Talbott likewise concluded that one of the expected consequences of the tests was that the US would 'pay them [India] serious, sustained, and respectful attention of a kind the Indians felt they had never received before'.[38] This is exactly the sort of attention India now received. Where some Indian elites would slightly disagree with Talbott, however, was that they too were now willing to provide America the space for a type of dialogue that differed from anything in the past. The energy for conversation was generated not only out of necessity—as an unanticipated consequence of the tests—but equally because principals like Singh, Riedel and Talbott had come to recognise that engaging with each other was imperative for both countries.

Accordingly, and in what turned out to be a captivating set of meetings, Talbott and Singh entered into a backchannel dialogue. The overarching aim, from an American point of view, was to address the interrelated issues underlining India and its approach to non-proliferation. After all, India refused to sign the Nuclear Non Proliferation Treaty (NPT). The first meeting took place on 12 June 1998, a month after the tests. Singh and Talbott met fourteen times in ten locations in seven different countries. The exchanges that took place were recorded in two monographs, one authored by Talbott and the other by Singh, both of which provide a number of highly revealing insights regarding diplomacy in practice.[39] For Talbott, he and his counterpart 'were dealing with each other' with a 'shared desire to fix something that had been broken for a long time: the US–India relationship'.[40] For Jaswant Singh, this dialogue not only gave him the opportunity to put across India's point of view on contentious issues such as the Comprehensive Test Ban

Treaty (CTBT) and non-proliferation more generally, but perhaps much more importantly, it also provided him and Talbott the ability to 'intellectually exchange thoughts with each other'. It was, as Singh put it, about 'making a connection'.[41] The Jaswant–Talbott dialogues, as they have come to be called, began to bear fruit in 1999.

Kargil and 'Normalisation'

On 4 July 1999, Nawaz Sharif, the Pakistani prime minister and leader of the Pakistan Muslim League (Nawaz) or PMLN, arrived in Washington. The visit, which was unplanned, was prompted by an escalating conflict in and around the Kargil district of Kashmir. In the beginning of May, Pakistani Army regulars, belonging mainly to the Northern Light Infantry, led a smaller group of infiltrators or mujahidin fighters across the Line of Control (LoC) or the erstwhile CFL that divided AJK and Jammu and Kashmir. The intrusion was directed and managed by General Pervez Musharraf, the Pakistani chief of Army Staff. There was no doubt in the minds of American observers and those in the Clinton administration that the attack and the resultant war were caused and stage-managed by the Pakistani Army. Almost all notable secondary sources suggest the same.[42] Indeed, the details of the war itself can easily be found in the existing literature.[43] Notably, and consistent with the arguments pursued in this book, Clinton's reaction to the crisis proved to serve as a game-changer in India's perception of the United States.

Having accepted that the Pakistani Army had covertly infiltrated Indian territory, for the first time in history a US president unequivocally took India's side in an India–Pakistan conflict. Moreover, Clinton made clear to Sharif that he would 'not agree to intervene in the Kashmir dispute'. There was no question of using America's good offices at a time when the president was clear that Pakistan was in the wrong. American non-intervention was one of the two conditions put to the Pakistani prime minister prior to agreeing to his self-invitation. The other was simply to withdraw the Pakistani Army back across the LoC. Clearly, and apart from the fact that any alternative course of action would be near impossible to justify given the obvious evidence of Pakistani aggression, the backchannel between India and the US began to pay dividends. Throughout the conflict, Jaswant Singh and Talbott were on the phone exchanging updates as they came in. Sandy Berger—Clinton's national security advisor—and Mishra, India's first ever national security advisor and also the principal secretary to Vajpayee, were on what might be considered an unofficial hotline, created as a result of the Jaswant–Talbott dialogue.[44]

Washington insiders were clear that Clinton's unambiguous and uncomplicated position on the war had led, as Walter Andersen remarked, 'to an immediate change of perception in India'. Additionally, Andersen, the former head of the South Asia Division in the US State Department, argued that what did not help Sharif was that Pakistan was seen to be doing little to 'reign-in' the Afghan Taliban or help corner Osama Bin Laden. The mood in Washington or at least in the White House was hardly one of sympathy for either Sharif or for Pakistan.[45] Indicative of this intolerance, Clinton told Sharif that 'unless he did more to help', he 'would have to announce that Pakistan was in fact supporting terrorism in Afghanistan'.[46] In short, and notwithstanding America's self-rationale for castigating Sharif and the obvious case of aggression in Kargil, the Indians, argues Stephen Cohen, were 'flabbergasted that the US supported them'.[47] Nothing like this had happened in the past. There were no attempts at creating leverage for future bargaining or any effort to listen carefully to the Pakistani position. Clinton, according to Mishra, agreed with India's stance on the inviolability of the LoC.[48]

In the meeting of 4 July with Sharif, and as was obvious, the US 'brief', according to Riedel, 'was simple'. The senior NSC staffer was the only other person in the meeting between the two premiers.[49] Sharif, Riedel recalls, 'had to commit to withdraw with no quid pro quo'.[50] There would be no face-saving strategy, an especially potent point given that the prime minister, wary that he would be deposed on his return to Islamabad, had brought along his wife and children on the plane to Washington. Indeed, Sharif, according to Branch, 'blamed the whole Kashmir gambit on Musharraf'.[51] As a result, or at least partially so, he was ousted from power in a coup spontaneously orchestrated by Musharraf and his military loyalists, but only much later, in October 1999.[52] In July, and on the eve of Sharif's meeting with Clinton, the president spoke with Vajpayee. He updated the prime minister about the upcoming meeting. Vajpayee, according to Riedel, said nothing. 'There was a pause in the conversation.' For Riedel, 'that pause was reflective' of Vajpayee saying to himself: 'We'll see when it happens.' The US, after all, seldom took India's side in an armed conflict with Pakistan. Sharif's agreement to withdraw troops from Indian territory 'provided the transformation' in the minds of Indian elites.[53] Suggestive of the acceptance of change, Jaswant Singh, in a phone call with Talbott, made clear that 'something quite new and good has happened'. This, Singh continued, concerned 'the matter of trust'.[54] The conflict finally ended on 26 July 1999. Less than a year later, Clinton visited India, the first US president to do so since Jimmy Carter in the late 1970s.

The trip, organised by Riedel, was nothing less than a success. The BBC reported that 'Clinton mania' had engulfed both elite and popular India.[55] Vajpayee stated that the visit 'marks the beginning of a new voyage in the new century by two countries which have all the potential to become natural allies'.[56] The speech echoed that which had been made by the Indian prime minister in New York in 1998, except on that occasion he had stressed the importance of engagement 'on an equal footing'.[57] Now less guarded in his approach, Vajpayee appeared to have embraced what he and his advisors believed was a change in American disposition when it came to South Asia and India specifically. By the end of 2000, the sanctions regime was relaxed. Clinton, according to Cohen, was eager for the rapid dismantlement of the same.[58]

As a new US president of a completely different ideological colour stepped in to the White House, India's relations with the US had clearly been 'normalised'. As Riedel put it, American insiders 'came to the conclusion that non-proliferation objectives were less important than broader bilateral relations'. 'The architecture of the non-proliferation regime,' Riedel clarified, 'was less important than the *spirit* of the non-proliferation regime.'[59] This, according to Lalit Mansingh, the Indian ambassador to Washington during the initial stages of the intervention in Iraq, was 'clear' to Clinton's successor from the very beginning.[60]

Republicans and India

'I was not impressed,' argued George Fernandes, the Indian defence minister and political giant in the NDA government, following a visit to the US. His conclusion: 'America is for itself' and is a naturally expansionist state.[61] In many ways, these were unusual views, given that many of his Cabinet colleagues held a less pessimistic outlook of an America that they believed was beginning to better understand and appreciate

India. It is important to note, of course, that Fernandes represented a BJP ally, the Samata Party, and that he held a somewhat negative perception of a nation he had been wary of for at least the last three decades. Thus on the whole, and while perhaps not necessarily impressed, India's ruling elites were initially far from hostile towards the new Republican administration led by President George W. Bush. Bush's preference for personal diplomacy, and, as the journalist Frank Bruni notes, 'Informal banter',[62] struck a chord with Indian leaders involved in the business of foreign policy. As will be discussed below, this was most obvious during Deputy Prime Minister L.K. Advani's visit to Washington just as the debate over Iraq began to dominate press coverage in India.

Initially, it was one of Bush's key advisors who had sold the idea of India to the new US administration. Condoleezza Rice, a highly regarded Sovietologist and former provost at Stanford University—a significant accomplishment at the age of thirty-eight—who had served as foreign policy advisor during the 2000 presidential campaign was quickly appointed Bush's national security advisor.[63] According to Andersen, she wasted no time in pushing the importance of policy towards India. It was not for nothing that she was compared to the likes of Robert Komer, the NSC staffer who had received Nehru's critical letter in 1962, and was widely considered the 'the inside father on India–US relations'.[64] Rice's views on India were openly available for scrutiny in a 2000 article in *Foreign Affairs*. India, she argued, was 'not a great power yet', but it had the 'potential to emerge as one'. For Rice, India offered a sensible but latent means to balance growing Chinese influence in South Asia.[65] Rather than ponder the past, and as she makes clear in her memoir, the new national security advisor was informed by the likes of C.V. Wedgwood. 'History', as the poet Wedgwood wrote, 'is lived forwards.'[66] This was certainly the view taken on India.

Bush, as a result, was quickly convinced of the merits of engaging with India. In his frank autobiography, the president wrote that India had the 'potential to be one of America's closest partners'.[67] That this rhetoric was supported by substance is evidenced in the next chapter. Less enthusiastic about this potential,[68] the secretary of state, Colin Powell, as well as the State Department more generally, chose caution over expediency. Pakistan and the politics of balancing in South Asia were obviously on top of the minds of those dedicated to dealing with the task of diplomacy.

The one unlikely figure who also favoured the position adopted by Rice, and who would play a role in attempting to persuade India to contribute troops to Iraq, was Donald Rumsfeld. As secretary of defence, a position he held for the first time under President Gerald Ford, Rumsfeld was to meet with Indian officials in the Pentagon some twenty-six times, and another sixteen times with the Indian leadership in Washington. Indeed, he met with Mishra in Munich in February 2001 only a month after the new administration had taken office.[69] Two key figures in the Bush administration vis-à-vis India, Robert Blackwill, the newly appointed US ambassador to India, and Douglas Feith, the US undersecretary of defence for policy, were convinced of India's importance to the US well before they took up their respective posts.[70]

Blackwill, the twentieth American ambassador to independent India, was something of an enigma. He was Rice's superior in the NSC under George H.W. Bush. In July 2001, when he arrived in India, at sixty years of age, he had spent the last twenty-two years in the Foreign Service. As Bob Woodward puts it, 'he was a prickly, demanding boss, who often referred to himself as Godzilla'. Indicative of his apparently less than appealing personality, a report for the NSC following his departure from India in July 2003 plainly stated: 'People don't want to work with him.'[71] These were, of course, the opinions held mainly by bureaucrats and those forced to deal with his demanding style on an everyday basis. There was little doubt that Blackwill was a 'forceful presence', as one official on the South Asia desk at the State Department argued, whose pro-India views were well known.[72] Yet officers who berated his style of management were also quick to state that he 'was a brilliant man'.[73] Indeed, while the ambassador was unsuccessful in selling the Iraq War to his Indian audience, there was no doubt that he was personally responsible for initiating the path that underscored transformative changes in America's approach to India. Following his posting in India, Blackwill was put in charge of strategic coordination for Iraq in the NSC under Rice. Again, though his manner may have been considered 'overbearing' and 'imperious', he was to prove vital in questioning the less than convincing assumptions held by American officials regarding Iraq.[74]

Dealing with War

A decade after the US-led intervention in Afghanistan began in October 2001, a former minister in the erstwhile Taliban-led government argued that Indian involvement in this war-torn nation had 'complicated matters'.[75] But it was not that the minister in question was inherently averse to India. Rather, for him, Pakistan's reaction was paramount. Somewhat paradoxically, such views were, at least in a limited sense, shared by the likes of Rumsfeld. The secretary made it clear that 'India was not critical' for the US with regard to Afghanistan. Pakistan, on the other hand, 'was critical', and 'still is'. Quite simply, as Rumsfeld clarified, 'the fact India had a reasonably good relationship with the Northern Alliance was a complicating factor because [of] our need to get cooperation from Pakistan'[76] which had historically opposed the Northern Alliance.

The Vajpayee government, according to Raja Mohan, 'communicated to the American Mission in New Delhi it would extend whatever support the United States wanted'. This, Mohan continues, included 'military bases, in its global war against terrorism'.[77] American observers went further. Enders Wimbush, a consultant at the Pentagon who worked on several projects with the Indian military, argues that 'India offered-up all kinds of things, over flights, basing, and logistics', and that they also 'offered things they had never offered before'.[78] That this was indeed a changing nation was abundantly clear. So much so that Musharraf, now the self-appointed president of Pakistan, convinced himself and his corps commanders that if Pakistan 'did not join the United States, it would accept India's offer'.[79] The late Hilary Synnott, the British high commissioner in Islamabad at the time, also confirmed that the idea of an 'Indian hand in Afghanistan' was very much on Musharraf's mind.[80] In November, Rumsfeld travelled to New Delhi. As Howard Schaffer writes, the idea was to emphasise 'that the new US support for Pakistan would not come at India's expense'.[81] Jaswant Singh seemed satisfied.[82]

Clearly, at this stage, and notwithstanding the apparent change of attitude within India, these offers of assistance received little or nothing by way of return from the Bush administration. Instead, Washington chose to develop an alliance with Pakistan. In the case of Iraq, and as discussed below, the scales tilted. This time, America led the efforts to involve one of the world's largest armies in a war of its choosing. For their part, Indian elites began to consider the merits and limitations of a non-UN mandated intervention at a scale unlike any other in India's past.

To 'condemn' or to 'deplore'
February to April 2003

On 28 January 2003, Yashwant Sinha, the Indian foreign minister, reportedly held a meeting in Abu Dhabi with eleven Indian ambassadors from across the Middle East. The idea, as one diplomat told news sources, was to discuss Iraq. It seemed clear to these Indian officials, as one of them was quoted as saying, that 'the great scenarios prepared in the seminar houses in Washington that everything will have neat consequences [following intervention in Iraq] and neat endings is completely bogus'. The diplomat continued, 'You will have violence and you will have refugees. This is where India will have a role.'[83] Clearly, much like diplomats and civil servants in different parts of the world, India was also considering its options. The strategy, if there was one, was to stride with caution rather than sprint to conclusions.

Erring on the side of prudence, Kanwal Sibal, the then foreign secretary, was careful to push the case for multilateralism and the need for a clear UNSC resolution during a visit to Washington in 2003. He did so without labouring the point around unilateralism, which he believed would unnecessarily exasperate his American counterparts. To be clear, Sibal held 'deep personal reservations' about the entire Iraq enterprise,[84] but, as a senior representative of the government, and as one report put it, the official remained 'restrained' in his views, and this was noted in Washington.[85] In fact, between February and March, Bush spoke with Vajpayee three times requesting assistance. The prime minister rejected these requests outright.[86] At the end of February, and fittingly at a Non-Aligned Movement (NAM) Conference in Kuala Lumpur, the then 78-year-old Vajpayee brazenly argued that 'the US role is such that it cannot be supported'.[87] Much like his foreign secretary, the prime minister pressed the Bush administration to either give serious consideration to gaining a UNSC resolution that would mandate the intervention or to back down. Interestingly, and again, just like Sibal's tight-rope exercise in Washington, Vajpayee made clear that India would take an official decision only 'in case of outbreak of war'.[88]

In the Indian capital, the government, according to commentators who were sympathetic to the political left, turned 'soft under US pressure'.[89] In Parliament, senior Congress leader Mani Shankar Aiyar turned almost acerbic. India, the author, diplomat and Congress stalwart argued, had 'become something of a lap-dog'.[90] As far as the government was concerned, and as was made clear by Jaswant Singh, the then finance minister, India stood by the ill-fated UNSC Resolution 1441 adopted in November 2002.[91] Accordingly, President Saddam Hussein was to comply with UN-regulated disarmament guidelines. The five-page resolution did not authorise the use of force.[92] In official parley, and as Vajpayee stressed, India pushed for a solution shaped by way of consensus through the UN. Regime change, the prime minister told journalists, is 'wrong and cannot be supported'.[93] Yet there was no doubt that the government, as one notable journalist observed, had 'tempered its stand'.[94] While the thrust of India's thinking was more or less clear, in practice New Delhi's approach remained flexible. Taking something of an absolutist stance—supporting or opposing the war—seemed unnecessary to a set of elites who were keenly aware that this was a core issue for the Bush administration. As Sinha underlined, 'the developments' with regard to the war and Iraq were 'moving so fast that anything said today' 'may become stale tomorrow'.[95] To be clear, the BJP seemed certain that military intervention was inevitable. On 16 March, B.B. Tyagi, the Indian ambassador in Baghdad, was moved to Amman. Other diplomats also left.[96]

Apart from the fact that the issues under consideration were demanding and would have far-reaching consequences no matter which way India turned, domestic opinion also remained something of a consideration. According to a poll conducted in the beginning of February, 59 per cent of Indians stated that 'under no circumstances' could war be justified. Another 29 per cent would agree to intervention 'only if sanctioned by the United Nations'. Importantly, 62.4 per cent expressed opposition to India supporting the war effort.[97] In another poll conducted at the end of February, 87 per cent of respondents—from within New Delhi—did not think war was justified, while 75 per cent were sceptical that the US could 'pull-off a quick victory'.[98] Moreover, as J.N. Dixit, the former foreign secretary, highlighted in the first of a number of op-ed pieces on the war, the impact of intervention on India's Muslim minority could not be overlooked.[99]

Whether or not domestic political opposition and the perceived views of Indian Muslims played an important role in the decision-making process remains unclear at best, and is a matter for further investigation. What is clear is that at the highest echelons of government, domestic factors, as verified by Mishra, did shape elite views, at least to a certain extent.[100] After all, the BJP was to fight a General Assembly election almost exactly two years later. In fact, and as a means to prolong providing a clear-cut answer for or against the war, one rather irate State Department officer mentions that Indian officials often used the 'election card' when pressed for an answer.[101] Whether the Iraq question had electoral resonance or not, what was clear was that this was an issue openly and closely monitored in the public domain.

A Public Debate

The MEA's position and messaging appeared to be carefully choreographed. A day or two prior to the intervention, a statement read: 'we are deeply disappointed by the inability of the Security Council to act collectively'.[102] A declaration short of an official protest was clearly registered. Yet a day after American-led troops moved into Iraq, MEA officials, while making plain that the war lacked 'justification' and was 'avoidable', also stated that India was 'ready to play its part' in humanitarian initiatives. Importantly, the slight censure evident in the pre-written text did not once name the US.[103] In a telephone call with Bush, the prime minister was reported to have expressed only 'deep anguish' rather than outright frustration with US policy.[104] On the whole, as a number of reporters argued, policy insiders were careful not to anger their American counterparts. It was crucial, argued one such reporter, 'that the government's carefully nurtured relationship with the US is not destroyed'.[105] V. Sudarshan, a journalist then writing for India's *Outlook Magazine*, argued that India 'acquiesced in favour of the US'. Sudarshan's piece, aptly titled 'Age of Consent', carried interviews with two former Indian ambassadors to Iraq. Neither seemed rattled by the intervention. In fact, they both highlighted the need to foster closer ties with the US.[106]

Unlike like his message at the NAM conference in Malaysia, Vajpayee made clear in an all-party meeting that 'whatever the rights and wrongs of the Iraq situation, our relationship with others [presumably the US] cannot be defined by a single issue'. 'Quiet diplomacy,' he added, 'is far more effective than public posturing.'[107] This is of course not to suggest that Vajpayee had even momentarily considered sending troops to Iraq. Rather, the need to work with America in the long term, and not *for* America in the immediate term, was self-evident for someone senior

American officers considered 'smarter than the rest'.[108] Indeed, as Marc Grossman, then the US undersecretary of state for political affairs (he was subsequently appointed President Obama's special representative to Afghanistan and Pakistan in early 2011), had underlined, the fact that India was not 'as outspoken in its opposition to the war as might have been expected' was clear from the start.[109]

By the beginning of April, and just as Parliament was to reconvene on the 7th, public–elite debate on both Iraq and the US dominated mainstream newspapers and magazines. Political India was clearly polarised. On one end of the spectrum, those who were more willing to consider the imperatives of sending troops argued that a 'new pragmatic strain', as one renowned international affairs journalist put it, had 'taken root in India's foreign policy'.[110] India, he argued in another report, 'needs to think creatively about new international coalitions' to deal with the menace of terrorism and the 'spread of weapons of mass destruction to irresponsible regimes and extremists groups'.[111] The bottom line was that India needed to 'deal purposefully with the dynamic war situation and its potential aftermath in Iraq'.[112]

Similarly, for these observers, it was time India took 'realistic positions'. The need for a 'mature' and 'dignified' response—i.e. one that was not anti-American—was commonplace in the popular press. The key, it would seem, was to construct a narrative that would allow India to 'have a role to play' in the reconstruction of Iraq,[113] which many assumed would happen fairly shortly. That the intervention would lead to an insurrection and eventual civil war was predicted by only a few. Prem Shankar Jha, the veteran journalist, editor and author, for example, argued that 'in the day of the satellite phone and the Kalashnikov' an insurrection is not hard to start.[114] This, of course, as was evidenced later in Iraq, rang all too true. On the other end of the spectrum, commentators branded the government as 'camp followers' of America or what they called the 'militarily muscular'.[115] Others berated the BJP for adopting the 'law of the jungle' rather than adhering to that of the UN, and for being seduced by the 'gratuitous advice of bogus realists'.[116]

Not unlike the public discourse around intervention, the debates in Parliament also highlighted the deep divisions between the government and the opposition as also those within the BJP-led coalition. Fernandes for one was hardly enthralled by what he argued to be the 'unprincipled' position taken by his Cabinet colleagues.[117] In fact, his party made this point publicly.[118] Further, and much like in early February, polling towards the end of February suggested that the public—or at least those polled—were hardly convinced. A total of 65 per cent of respondents said that the government should condemn the war, while 56 per cent wanted India to risk 'annoying' the US 'by criticising its actions in Iraq'; 69 per cent of respondents even called Bush a 'warmonger'. In all, 86 per cent of those polled opposed the war in Iraq.[119] Even the Rashtriya Swayamsevak Sangh (RSS), a close ally of the BJP, argued that 'at the people's level, there is complete opposition to the war'. 'No one,' a party member argued, 'In the *Sangh* can support what is happening.'[120]

Evoking 'ninda'

In Washington, a good distance away from the commotion in India, Lalit Mansingh, the Indian ambassador to the US, argued that he was being 'fully briefed on Iraq'. A former foreign secretary, the ambassador stated that 'in the beginning' he had been 'interested' in the Iraq debate. However, and all the same, he was unclear what exactly American officials meant when they bandied around terms like 'military stabilisation' and 'post-conflict reconstruction'. Such officials, Mansingh suggests, were also interested in India's participation, but the terms of reference were vague at best.[121] For the moment, and apart from the somewhat casual requests or queries made by Bush directly to Vajpayee, there was no real push to bring India on-side. Indeed, within India, the first important step was to pass a unanimous parliamentary resolution in response to the intervention.

For two days, 7 and 8 April, the Indian Parliament intently debated whether to 'condemn' or 'deplore' the war in Iraq. Leading the charge, Priya Ranjan Dasmunshi, a senior Congress leader and spokesperson, made his party's position clear: the 'war against Iraq', he stated, violates all accepted canons of international law, and therefore, 'needs to be condemned'.[122] The opposition were in no mood to prolong the government's wait-and-see approach, which, it argued, was a 'weak, inadequate, and ambiguous policy'.[123] Indeed, the Congress' own Working Committee resolution called for an 'immediate end to hostilities' and for the 'United Nations system' to be given a second chance.[124] Speaking for the CPI (M), Somnath Chatterjee likewise lambasted the government. He demanded that it condemn what he called 'this naked aggression'.[125] For their part, government ministers held their nerve.

On the following day, and after at least two all-party meetings in the Speaker's Chamber, a unanimous resolution was confirmed. There was no mention of condemnation. As discussed earlier in this chapter, the Hindi word *ninda* saved the day. As peculiar as it might seem, *ninda* created some middle ground. The resolution stated that the House 'deplores the military action by the Coalition forces led by the USA against a sovereign Iraq'. This, the resolution made clear, was 'unacceptable'. In the crucial last line, it added, 'the House also calls upon the UNO to protect the sovereignty of Iraq and ensure that the re-construction of Iraq is done under UN auspices'.[126] In a sense, and while Congress speakers continued to warn against the 'lengthening shadow' of America's 'militaristic unilateralism',[127] the resolution provided a degree of justification to examine Indian involvement as long as it was 'done under UN auspices'. This, of course, could have meant many things and could have been read in multiple ways. Sinha, for one, made it absolutely clear that a role for India could not be discounted. In a rare case of fluster prior to the debate in Parliament, and clearly irritated with the opposition's demand that the government condemn the war, Sinha told journalists: 'If tomorrow, suppose we use that word, will everything become alright? Will the war in Iraq end if we condemn it? If tomorrow we want to play a role there, then will it help us? I myself have said that the world after the Iraq war will be different than the world before the Iraq war.'[128] Notably, following the two-day debate in the Lok Sabha and having passed a resolution, the House went silent on this critical issue. The next tête-à-tête would not be before the third week of July.[129]

The point in the resolution about the UN was crucial. Indeed, only a few months following the intervention, Bush too considered ways to bring in more nations *and* the UN. The president, according to Rice, finally agreed with what was Powell's view from the start: that the US would need 'substantial UN presence' to establish 'post war order in Iraq'.[130] UN cover, it turned out, would not be as difficult to obtain after having intervened in a country that desperately needed assistance, reconstruction and plenty of aid—all of which Indian diplomats had discussed in some detail weeks prior to the intervention. The question was thus what kind of contribution could India actually make, or at the very least, consider? That the government of the day embraced engagement was clear, but did this mean that it would be comfortable sending troops—even in small numbers—to operate in a theatre under

American-led command? This after all was not a blue-helmet operation. The following part of this chapter shows how exactly the alleged and so-called pro-American party in power married the changing ideas underpinning the very concept of independence with Indian interests. The fact that a discussion with regard to an intervention of this kind was even taking place was shocking, but that the government of the day would continue to press the case of exceptionalism soon became clear to the likes of Rumsfeld and perhaps even Blackwill. As Sinha bluntly put it, 'Neither will we [India] sell our souls to others nor will we pursue blindly antagonistic policies for the sake of antagonism.'[131] The key was maintaining a sense for balance in these changing times.

'A Bridge Too Far'
May to July 2003

The proposition of sending troops to Iraq gained momentum soon after the parliamentary resolution was passed. In fact, and somewhat shrewdly, Blackwill tried hard to soft-sell the 'Case for War', which was also the title of one of his op-eds in the *Indian Express*. 'Iraqis are welcoming Coalition Forces into their cities, towns and villages',[132] wrote the ambassador, someone Rice considered to be 'one of the best policy engineers' she knew.[133] On the second and last day of the debate in the House, Blackwill stressed that the US and its fifty Coalition partners 'did not seek, did not want' war. Again, in a boldly titled piece— 'Defence of an Invasion'—in the *Hindustan Times*, he highlighted that the legality underlying the intervention had come from UNSC Resolution 1441. This was and still is, of course, a matter of considerable dispute among international lawyers.[134] In all, the ambassador, widely considered the 'greatest cheerleader for New Delhi' in Washington,[135] authored some half a dozen such appeals.[136] As far as he was concerned, joining the Coalition could well transform both India's potential in the world and its relationship with the US. As those on the receiving end of Blackwill's cables noted, 'He couldn't have been more enthusiastic about what India meant for the United States'. The State Department, one official asserted, both knew this and remained wary.[137]

Powell was hardly enthused by what he was reading in the cables from the mission in New Delhi. His deputy and 'best friend', Richard Armitage, was also suspicious.[138] In fact, Powell, according to an insider, 'discounted' Blackwill's cables 'heavily'. Ordinarily, and especially in the days of Henderson and even Galbraith, such disagreement would pose a problem for envoys. After all, the secretary of state was technically their boss. Yet in Blackwill's case, an open line to the White House and the Pentagon went some distance in involving these vital institutions in convincing India to deploy. The fact that the ambassador had 'close working relations' with Richard Hass, the director of policy planning in the State Department, was also to prove useful.[139]

The Indian press soon caught wind of these points of tension. That the State Department had 'anti-Blackwill bureaucrats', as one journalist argued, was common knowledge.[140] Indeed, and for one reason or another, Blackwill soon left his post for a more prestigious position working on Iraq. In his last public plea, titled 'A Passage from India', he made clear that Bush's goal to 'forge' a 'concentrated strategic collaboration' between 'the world's oldest and largest democracies' was well under way.[141] Notwithstanding the difficulty his bureaucracy had in dealing with him, he made a case for New Delhi—as *he* saw it—with fervour. At least some of the ruling elites within India, as the discussion below shows, were enthused by both the idea of America and highly curious about the prospect of Iraq.

The MEA Moves

By the end of April, the government of India returned its erstwhile ambassador, who had been moved temporarily to Amman, back to Baghdad. B.B. Tyagi, the diplomat in question, was said to be in 'close touch with the situation as it unfolds'.[142] In neighbouring Kuwait, Indian Ambassador Swash Pawansingh reportedly met with Jay Garner, a former US general designated to lead the post-war reconstruction effort, and Ambassador Barbara Boudine, a senior State Department official who had been appointed coordinator for central Iraq. R.M. Abhyankar, the MEA's Arab hand and secretary-in-charge of West Asia (Middle East), was scheduled to visit Amman, Damascus and Ankara to gauge regional perspectives following the intervention.[143]

Clearly, the MEA lost no time. Indeed, its diplomatic manoeuvring was impressive to say the least. In parallel, 'India Inc.' also began to eye what was an oil-rich Gulf state. As Mishra confirmed, the corporate sector was 'most interested' in both the government's decisions on Iraq and in American plans for reconstruction.[144] A joint delegation of private sector and government officials prepared to depart for the US. As one report stated, the aim was to 'secure contracts from the US authorities in [the] $80 billion reconstruction of Iraq'. The secretary general of the Federation of Indian Chambers of Commerce and Industry (FICCI), Amit Mitra, who later became the finance minister for the Indian state of West Bengal, openly argued that India's interest was to 'get contracts on the level of execution'. Indian companies, he argued, had experience with reconstruction efforts.[145] In addition, according to reports, the Indian Oil and Natural Gas Cooperation (ONGC), private sector firms and conglomerates were intent on oil contracts. It was argued that they were 'using their clout to somehow get into Iraq'.[146] The approach was plainly clear to J.N. Dixit. The government, he underlined, 'initiated a diplomatic and political interaction with the US and its allies in order to participate in Iraq's reconstruction'.[147]

On 26 May, the CCS met to discuss the options on Iraq. What exactly took place in the first of at least two such crucial meetings remains unclear. The nuances underlying the tensions at this time will only become apparent from analysis of the Indian archives, and as with archival norms in most other nations, at least twenty years are required to have passed before the relevant documents can be released. Accordingly, the purported 'inside' story, at least on the basis of what is publicly known, is as follows: the principal decision taken at the 26 May meeting, according to official announcements, was for the MEA to 'obtain clarifications' from Rafeeuddin Ahmed,[148] a former Pakistani Foreign Service officer and the recently appointed UN special advisor to Iraq. Ahmed's portfolio, according to an official press statement, was to help determine the 'potential role for the United Nations in post-war Iraq'.[149] The MEA was pushed to examine the legal frameworks in place for UN member states to contribute troops to a predominantly US-led mission. After all, and as was discussed by Cabinet ministers, the UN appeared to have adopted a somewhat ambiguous position with regard to the contribution of troops. UNSC Resolution 1483, which was passed on 22 May, encouraged member states to 'contribute to stability and security in Iraq by contributing personnel, equipment, and other resources under the Authority'.[150] The problem, as Fernandes underscored, was with the term 'authority'.[151] According to 1483, this 'authority' rested with what came to be called the Unified Command directed by the US and the UK. In effect, contributing states would need to work under their Command.

Curiously, some reports suggested that a paragraph in the 1483 preamble was inserted at the behest of American representatives in the UN to assuage India's obvious reservations. The paragraph in question distinguished between 'occupying powers'—the US and the UK—and 'those' countries that 'may work in the future', but 'under the authority'.[152] Whether these amendments were made with India in mind is unclear. Interestingly, within India, and following the government's call for clarifications on 26 May, commentators came up with all sorts of permutations to intervene. Some fervently pressed the government to abandon its apparent obsession with the UN. 'An India that ducks for UN cover,'[153] suggested one writer, 'will become marginal to Gulf security.' Others considered a 'rotational command' or a 'joint command' led by a two-star general but shifted between contributing nations.[154] There is little to suggest that these viewpoints were closely considered by decision-makers.

Further, and apart from the technicalities underlying the question of involvement and the media coverage, fissures within the Cabinet were also apparent, at least according to those interviewed for this book. In the CCS meeting, Mishra stated, 'I was opposed to sending troops.' He told those who were slightly more convinced by the imperatives of intervention (Mishra did not mention who these were) that 'there was no consensus in the country on sending troops'. In addition, he urged his colleagues that it was important to remember the Indian experience in Sri Lanka, where Indian soldiers were caught between two warring sides. It was highly possible, he added, that there would be a 'similar situation in Iraq if Indian troops be shot at'.[155]

Jaswant Singh argued that 'India cannot and must not be in Iraq as part of an occupying force'. Yet his position on whether or not troops should have been sent in accordance with the guidelines in Resolution 1483 was less clear.[156] Others, however, forcefully argue that the then finance minister 'definitely supported some role' for India in Iraq.[157] Indeed, as one senior Indian military officer put it, 'Jaswant Singh was a leader among them [those who supported Indian troops being sent to Iraq].' 'He,' the officer continued, 'would have got us sunk in a deep morass and we would have never got out of it.'[158] While these assertions are extremely difficult to verify, the discussions between Indian and

American elites in the beginning of June—discussed below—strongly suggest that intervention was indeed considered at the highest levels of the Indian government. Furthermore, and interestingly, while ideas around alliance formation and collective security gained a greater degree of acceptance, the chief stumbling block for Indian interlocutors had to do with the command structure in Iraq. Much like Nehru's and Pannikar's views on Korea—where Macarthur rather than the UN was perceived to be in charge—India could not be seen to intervene in a conflict or post-conflict state under an American flag.

Washington and Back

In the second week of June, the Indian deputy prime minister L.K. Advani visited Washington. Meetings with American counterparts were held at the Willard Hotel, close to the White House. Advani, accompanied by the Indian home secretary, the director of the IB and two joint secretaries in the MEA,[159] met almost everyone in a position of authority. According to an American DoD official present at some of the meetings, Advani's visit 'was seen to be of critical importance by the [American] administration'.[160] Indeed, the Bush administration, according to one reporter, 'courted him [Advani] and extended courtesies they normally don't do to others'. The president himself dropped in for a thirty-minute discussion while the deputy prime minister was speaking with Rice.[161] Rumsfeld, US Attorney General John Ashcroft and Homeland Security Secretary Tom Ridge all exchanged notes with their Indian counterparts.[162]

As expected, the two issues that reportedly exercised Advani and his team, both of which were communicated directly to Bush, had to do with the modalities and limitations underlying Resolution 1483 and the question of the command structure in Iraq.[163] Notably, and as advisors in Rumsfeld's office confirmed, the fact that discussions around military arrangements were taking place was itself encouraging.[164] Moreover, Douglas Feith, responsible for developing the DoD's international relations, and someone who would play a key role in fostering defence ties with the Indian MoD in the following years, was 'hopeful' that India would send troops, or at least that was what he was 'hearing'.[165] More junior US officials were also of the opinion that the Indian military saw deployment to Iraq as a 'huge opportunity'. In fact, meetings held with

Advani gave Pentagon officials the 'feeling' that the Indian military and civilian bureaucracy was open to taking the discussion forward.[166] Anderson confirms that these were certainly seen as 'very successful meetings'.[167] To journalists, Advani made it clear that he was under no pressure to commit troops.[168]

In India, some found Advani's public declarations less believable. Congress stalwarts like Natwar Singh, who became India's foreign minister a year later, argued that 'Mr. Advani during his visit to Washington almost committed troops.'[169] Senior foreign affairs journalists covering this moment of change and crisis suggest that the foreign minister, Yashwant Sinha, 'swung in favour' of sending troops once Advani returned.[170] Again, whether these accounts are merited or not is of course debatable. What is verifiable is the fact that, following the Washington visit, Bush decided to send Peter Rodman, the assistant secretary of defence for international affairs, to New Delhi to iron-out questions with regard to the vaunted issue of a command structure and Resolution 1483.[171] Rodman worked directly for Rumsfeld. One of his primary work-related objectives was to travel with the secretary of defence 'to gather allies for the war on terrorism'.[172] The fact that he was to visit India was no coincidence. Indeed, American officials took India's flexible, and hence, in their reading, promising, disposition seriously.

While Rumsfeld stresses that he 'never publicly pressured countries to do anything', 'privately', the secretary made clear, he 'talked to them about what they might do'. In a vague and carefully phrased comment, as he himself acknowledges, he says: 'I do think it was important for countries to participate in international coalitions which are doing things that have good reasons to be done.' With regard to India, he conceded, 'We were interested in help.'[173] Daniel Markey, then starting out as a policy planning staffer in the State Department, commented that his team 'felt that they [India] were taking this [sending troops] seriously at very high levels'.[174] Bruce Riedel seemed almost convinced that the DoD expected India to join the mission. He states: 'the Bush administration, particularly the Pentagon, were so confident that they were going to get Indian troops, that the planning documents for post war occupation already had three divisions in AOR (Areas of Responsibilities)'.[175] While no other available source indicates that the US made a request for three divisions, there is no doubt that the military aspect of the debate gathered attention. Following Advani's visit, and as one official recollected, the likelihood of India contributing troops 'was real'.[176]

A Division

On 15 June, Sonia Gandhi and the Congress leadership met with the prime minister. The leader of the opposition made it clear that the 'Congress would be totally opposed to the deployment of Indian troops under any arrangement other than a United Nations command.' As Natwar Singh told journalists following the meeting, a 'national consensus' needed to be 'evolved' before any major decision could be taken.[177] Within the Congress, Singh argues, there was no appetite for intervention whatsoever. Both Pranab Mukherjee, a senior Congress leader who was elected president of India in July 2012, and Manmohan Singh, elected prime minister for a second term in 2009, were 'opposed' to even the suggestion of sending troops.[178] Yet, as Fernandes asserts, within both the NDA and the Cabinet there 'were very serious, strong positions' developing.[179] This was most palpable in the short yet wide-ranging discussion around the force structure to be prepared in the seemingly unlikely event of a political decision acceding to America's request for troops.

According to press reports, an infantry division of between 15,000 and 20,000 soldiers was identified.[180] If deployed, according to Raja Mohan, the Indian division would have been the second largest contingent—after the US—in Iraq.[181] Senior Indian officers mandated to speak with their American counterparts confirm that the question of Indian intervention was discussed at some length. Brigadier Gurmeet Kanwal, then the deputy assistant chief of what is known as the Integrated Defence Staff (Training and Doctrine) and one such senior officer made clear that following the fall of Baghdad, 'the US asked for one Indian Division to be sent to Iraq'. They, he argues, 'offered the North', in the Kurdish-dominated areas of Kirkuk and Mosul.[182]

A team from the MEA was even said to have visited these northern areas.[183] As was later revealed, according to press reports, the VI Division—a reserve division based in Bareilly, a district in the north Indian state of Uttar Pradesh—was assigned for deployment under the command of Major General P.K. Mahajan.[184] American observers close to Pentagon officials stress that the Indian military 'wanted to go [to Iraq] in a big way'. This is what they were purportedly hearing from US officers dealing with India.[185] Yet much like the discussion points highlighted by Advani, the military were also—at least allegedly—sensitive to the issue of command. The designated division commander, as the journalist V. Sudarshan has underlined, would need to be the 'boss' in the sector given to India.[186] However, prior to any serious discussion around the distribution of military force, the question of legality and the extent to which UN Resolution 1483 provided the explicit cover India demanded needed to be addressed. From this viewpoint, the Rodman visit was crucial.

The Rodman Visit

On 16 June, a four-member team led by Rodman was reported to have held two rounds of talks with Indian officials and representatives from the Indian military. The Indian delegation was reportedly led by a joint secretary—B.S. Prakash—responsible for 'UN Political'.[187] Further, Rodman and his entourage met separately with Foreign Secretary Kanwal and the national security advisor, Mishra. Interestingly, and again according to news reports, a group of three Indian brigadiers from the armed forces medical corps accompanied by an MEA official was in Iraq during the same week to assess the humanitarian crisis.[188] The group, it was reported, were assessing the feasibility of setting up a field hospital on the border of Iraq and Jordan. The government also pledged $20 million towards reconstruction.[189] In the meantime, the prime minister, highly sceptical and largely silent in public on the issue of troops, asked the convenor of the National Security Advisory Board (NSAB), an ad hoc body associated with the NSC, to draft a report on the merits and demerits of intervention and the need for a mandate.[190] Clearly, at some level, both India and America sought to examine the contours underlying the potential for involvement of troops and support.

As might have been expected, the discussions with Rodman, Fernandes argues, got 'stuck' around the issue of a clear mandate.[191] Indian officials, reports at the time also suggest, were adamant about the need for a clear mandate with regard to the 'stabilisation force' and the rules guiding the exact nature of the relationship between a deploying force and the UN. 'The parleys', according to one report, were very much held in the 'context of the UN Security Council Resolution 1483.'[192] The key question for the Indian civilian bureaucracy, suggests one American official who accompanied Rodman, had to do with Command. 'The principle of Command,' he argues, and the 'deep reservations' around the less-than-clear UN directive, proved difficult to resolve or clarify. As a form of inducement, the American team even considered offering Basra in Southern Iraq rather than Mosul and Kirkuk. Members of the State Department were also aware of this.[193] At the time Basra was understood to be a 'quieter area of operations'.[194] That it was anything but became all too real to the British contingent finally deployed in and around the port city close to Iran. As Hilary Synnott, the British diplomat and regional coordinator for Southern Iraq (including Basra) quickly found out, it was a disaster with an insurgency in the making.[195] However, Indian military officers who trained Saddam Hussein's air force in Basra also preferred this particular AOR for Indian soldiers. Unsurprisingly, the only condition, as a former Indian military trainer and highly placed strategic affairs expert states, was that the AOR be offered with 'the required UN resolutions'. The latter, Air Commodore Jasjit Singh made clear, 'was an absolute necessity'.[196]

When the team led by Rodman returned to Washington with India's demands, analysts and experts who were partial to the idea of deploying Indian forces made their case once again. 'Sending a division-sized force', argued one well-known commentator, could only help Indian interests in the Persian Gulf and in strengthening maritime relations with the US.[197] In an op-ed titled 'Why We Should Say Yes', retired General Satish Nambiar wrote that India 'will get a chance to become a global player' by 'sending a force to Iraq'. Yet the command structure clearly remained an important issue, one which, Nambiar suggested, could be resolved by creating a 'command mechanism' in which Indian 'forces do not take orders from Washington'. Clearly, and despite the expressed desire to send troops, taking orders from an American-led Command continued to be out of the question.[198] Others underlined that Iraq was 'a chance', as a former senior admiral argued, 'of being accepted as a regional power'.[199]

No doubt, and apart from the attempts to influence insider thinking in the government, the pressure of American requests to contribute Indian troops was evident. As the conservative Beltway commentator Dana Dillon stressed, the US 'offered India an opportunity to help, and whatever decision they make will show us [US] how India defines better relations with the US'.[200] William Triplett, a former Republican counsel to the Senate Foreign Relations Committee, underlined: 'Showing that the Indian army are rolling up their sleeves to help out now will pay dividends with the Americans later.'[201] Indeed, as Sibal made clear, there was 'a lot of pressure to send troops'. The arguments around the so-called 'opportunity to work closely with the US', the then foreign secretary stated, were 'common ones'.[202] Having interacted with senior officers in the Indian Army, one Pentagon consultant concluded that the Indian military saw a 'much larger picture'. They, the quasi-official felt, 'wanted to play and they wanted to play on a much larger stage', and this was an opportunity in waiting.[203]

Yet apart from what might be considered the somewhat premature reading of both the situation in Iraq and the apparent importance connected to Indian involvement, senior officers in the army made their displeasure clear to American counterparts. Sitting with an American brigadier general sent to New Delhi, an Indian one-star general recollects asking his counterpart: 'What are the pay-offs? Why should we help you to pull your chestnuts out of the fire, and burn our fingers in the process?' Somewhat irritated, and obviously asking questions outside the said officer's remit, the general persevered: 'Would the US commit to helping India get a permanent seat in the Security Council or lift technology denial regimes?' There was no clear answer to any of these questions.[204] Indeed, during an all-party meeting following the Rodman visit, Fernandes, in his capacity as the defence minister, informed opposition leaders that discussions were concluded, and 'key clarifications [around 1483 and Command] have remained unanswered by Washington'. Some in the government, Sibal confirms, were 'completely indifferent' to the visit.[205] Despite the mounting pressure, which mainly emanated from the Pentagon, India stood its ground. Its key demands remained unaddressed, leading to an outcome that the prime minister had been certain of from the very beginning.

'Saying No'

On 14 July, the CCS met for the last time to discuss Iraq. The decision, as outlined in the introduction to this chapter, was less than clear. 'Were there to be an explicit UN mandate', argued Foreign Minister Sinha, then the government 'could consider the deployment of troops in Iraq'. Unsurprisingly, and given the amount of bureaucratic time spent discussing intervention and the relative importance of India's relationship with America, Sinha's official comments were clearly tailored to avoid, as Fernandes put it, bluntly 'saying no'.[206] As news reports had also suggested prior to the meeting, the idea was to communicate room for manoeuvre in the event of a UN mandate being extended in the future.[207] In the end, and as Harish Khare, the veteran journalist and later the media advisor to Prime Minister Manmohan Singh, stressed, the Vajpayee government was 'willing to risk certain American displeasure'.[208] Although Vajpayee, according to Mishra, was 'never in favour of sending troops', he still did his part to 'entertain debate'. The prime minister was adamant that sending troops to Iraq was simply an 'unworkable idea', not least because of the issues related to Command and the absence of an explicit UN mandate. 'What would happen,' the then national security advisor recollects Vajpayee repeatedly saying, 'If our [Indian] soldiers are shot at?' The prime minister was also certain that 'saying no' would not destroy, or even seriously affect, the progress made in India's deepening relations with the US.[209]

As far as Mishra was concerned, the Bush administration 'came with a clear position that it wanted to improve relations'. This 'position', Mishra suggested, was not contingent on India saying yes or no to a specific US foreign policy decision with regard to Iraq. If anything, it said something to the question of 'balance' in India's desire to 'engage with major powers'.[210] The Americans, Mishra and what Shivshankar Menon, appointed India's fourth national security advisor in January 2010, calls an 'old fashioned patriot',[211] was in fact confident that the US was provided with a 'real' picture of New Delhi's approach to 'balance' in international affairs. India would never be an ally as traditionally understood, nor would it become involved in anything like the relationship between the US and the United Kingdom. That, he stressed, was a 'different agenda'. Those who think otherwise, according to Mishra, and as was conspicuous in the commentary in the Indian press, tend to 'go over-board'.[212] Interestingly, many argued that Mishra was at the very least 'sympathetic' to the idea of sending troops. Whether this was true or not, by the time Rodman's visit ended it seems safe to conclude that the then national security advisor was no longer interested.[213]

Equally, as underlined by Menon, as one among a few to have witnessed Mishra in action or negotiating for India, the 'quintessential realist' took a simple and sensible view of diplomacy. 'Always give the other man something to take away from the table,' Menon recollects. 'Otherwise,' Mishra argued, 'he has no interest in doing what he has promised you.' Although these remarks were made in reference to talks the then national security advisor had held with counterparts in Pakistan, they could very easily have referred to his approach for the negotiations with the US in 2003. The blatant change in approach to discussing intervention was evident. That the UN mattered more to this partner or so-called 'natural ally' only meant that the world's two largest democracies did not see eye-to-eye on matters such as the utility of force in international politics. Further, that the Indian Army could not be seen taking orders or working directly under an American-led Unified Command spoke to the continuing if not aggressive approach to the sort of non-dependence Nehru, TTK, Y.D. Gundevia, M.J. Desai and Indira Gandhi would not find unusual. The BJP-led government's approach to change was riddled with tensions that were in part informed by India's historical approach to non-alignment as re-interpreted in the first chapter of this book.

While allowing for debate within the Cabinet, Vajpayee did not hesitate to state publicly that 'India will never become a lackey of even the most powerful country in the world.'[214] The prime minister went on to emphasise that India is 'following an honest non-aligned policy'.[215] In fact, as one senior Indian official intently involved in the negotiations claimed, 'Sonia Gandhi and the opposition at large were encouraged' by Vajpayee 'to make their reservations heard in public.' It 'helped', the official asserted, 'to give the Prime Minister cover' to make his case for resistance within both the Cabinet and the party.[216] In fact, as a former Indian special envoy and academic recounted, Vajpayee and Mishra's question to the parties of the left was quite straightforward. They asked: 'why don't you bring people on the streets and protest?' The 'indication', according to this envoy, and as he learnt from those among the left, was to 'give the impression that there was tremendous public opposition to the war and sending troops'. This again was to help embolden those wanting to say no, but for whom it was as important to make an evidence-based case.[217] After all, there were those in Cabinet who were in favour of intervention until the very last CCS meeting. Mansingh, the Indian ambassador in Washington, argued that for some ministers 'this was the first big offer that any of the superpowers gave India in the Middle East'. It was, according to some, 'the first big break for India', and its respective merits or otherwise were the subject of intense debate behind closed doors.[218]

Advani, although more convinced by the apparent virtues of working with the US in Iraq during his state visit to Washington, 'changed his tune back in India', according to one senior Indian official.[219] Yet until the very end, the deputy prime minister reportedly kept his mind open in case the US was able to modify Resolution 1483. Sinha's position, according to Khare, was now found to be 'ambivalent'. Fernandes, as always, was squarely in the 'no-troops' camp.[220] Jaswant Singh, adamant that those making decisions for India 'will always be careful of its strategic autonomy',[221] was clearly partial to the idea of India assuming some kind of role in Iraq until the last CCS meeting.[222] Ultimately, as one journalist who had followed the Iraq story from the beginning to the end recounted, the inability to reach a consensus within the country and within the Cabinet 'finally broke the back of those who had been arguing in favour of such a foreign policy gamble'.[223] Thanks to the 'superb wisdom' of the prime minister, one observer noted,[224] India had retained the ability to say no.

Disappointed and Changing

When asked if India's final decision adversely affected both America's approach to India and those championing its case in Washington, Rumsfeld empathically stated: 'Oh my goodness no, India–US relations were not damaged in any way because they did not send troops to Iraq.'[225] Riedel, however, argues that 'Rumsfeld was personally quite irked that the Indians didn't send troops.' The soon-to-be South Asia and Afghanistan advisor to President Barack Obama claimed that the bureaucracy continued to seek ways to strengthen relations without 'his [Rumsfeld's] enthusiastic support'.[226] Indeed, whether or not Riedel's views are substantiated, public statements indicate that US officials were disappointed to say the least.

In Washington, Mansingh claimed that although 'nobody at the first level [the top echelon of the Bush administration] mentioned it; I was given to believe that there was anger in Washington'. The then ambassador argued, 'I had a feeling that we led them to believe that we will send troops'.[227] According to reports, 'key US divisions were promised that they would be sent back at once the Indian contingent shipped in'. Richard Boucher, the US State Department spokesman at the time, made it clear that although he did not 'predict' any problems for the relationship, his government very much 'hoped the [Indian] troops would have been able to go [to Iraq]'. 'I think,' Boucher stressed, 'it is in our interests and what we perceive as their [India's] interests as well.'[228]

Paul Wolfowitz, the US deputy secretary of defence, reportedly once remarked that India's reasons for not sending troops were 'devious' and 'ingenious'.[229] Wolfowitz at one point 'strongly appealed' to Sibal, during one of the latter's visits to Washington, to send troops.[230] For Feith, someone who invested considerable time in furthering India–US military relations, Iraq 'would have set the pace for assuming global responsibilities'. This, according to Feith, 'was the big ticket to major power status'. He appreciated that the Iraq issue was controversial, but he made clear that 'if India had worked with the US it would have contributed a lot more to US–India relations'.[231]

The lesson for Markey, then at the State Department, was that 'this [asking India to contribute troops] was asking too much of the Indian Government'.[232] In hindsight, Rumsfeld recognised that although today India is a country that is 'engaging the world, as a country in its importance should', he was hardly surprised that 'there are competing arguments of *how* India should approach the world'.[233] For those designated to convince India of the apparent merits of intervention, the change in 'attitude' in New Delhi was 'unmistakable'. As one of Rodman's team members recounts, this was a 'strategic moment' for India and the US, and the eventual result apart, the tensions underlying this 'moment' indicated to American principals, and as importantly, the bureaucracy, that they were dealing with a 'changing India'.[234] It was not that intervention in Iraq was a 'bridge too far', as one insider noted, but rather that India only chose to cross those bridges it saw fit for its purposes. India might have been changing, but the architecture of its shifting imperatives could not but be rooted somewhere between the history of the past, the realities of the present and the way in which Indians debated the potential of the future.

Conclusion

In May 2004, the Congress-led United Progressive Alliance (UPA) came to power in the General Assembly elections, the fourteenth to have been held since 1951, when Nehru was first elected to office. The Congress alone won 141 out of the 543 elected seats in the Lower House or the Lok Sabha. The BJP leadership were nothing less than shocked out of power. Most elites belonging to the erstwhile centre-right coalition could not have predicted that they would be sitting in the opposition.

Indeed, the BJP, confident about victory, called for elections six months before it needed to. The Congress, with a slim majority of its own—it only won seven more seats than the BJP—relied primarily on what was widely called the left bloc—of four parties—to help reach 272 seats.[235] This is the required figure—the rounded half of 543 seats—to satisfy the prerequisite to form the government in the first-past-the-post system of direct parliamentary elections.

The left's support, with fifty-nine seats in total, was crucial both to placing the Congress in the lead and—as it later turned out—in setting very real limits to the exercise of executive power in matters of international affairs. This was palpable in the negotiations leading to a major and historic nuclear agreement between India and the US, which is discussed in the following chapter. Indeed, and to a lesser extent, that such limitations would shape and even check the choices made by Congress elites was clear barely a month after the new government was sworn in. In June 2004, Natwar Singh attended President Reagan's state funeral. What was perhaps meant to serve as a less formal and potentially less significant visit quickly turned into a matter of much debate in India. In a meeting with Colin Powell, Foreign Minister Singh reportedly stated that he and the Cabinet would take a 'fresh look' at the question of sending troops to Iraq.[236]

This was shocking to say the least. After all, the Congress had strongly and unfailingly opposed the mere suggestion of sending troops to Iraq while in opposition. Vajpayee had even banked on the centre-left party to make its differences public. In the summer of 2004, the controversy was quickly put to rest. The leadership, under Manmohan Singh, the thirteenth prime minister of India, and Sonia Gandhi, the UPA chairperson, resolved the issue without further controversy. The left demanded this. In Parliament, the Congress' reply was simple: it stood by the April 2003 all-party resolution and the collective sentiment underlying *ninda*.[237] In person, the then foreign minister made clear, he had told American elites that Iraq was hugely contentious, but that—as with the BJP—the government's reservations would remain private. To the Indian Cabinet, Natwar Singh argued that the past five years had indeed 'led to huge and important changes' in the US–India relationship.

Following his contentious visit, the former secretary general of the NAM argued that the Americans appeared to have 'accepted that India will not be pushed around'. Washington, he continued, 'better under-

210

stood the importance India attached to an independent foreign policy'. As Vajpayee predicted, a clear rejection of US policy towards Iraq would only irritate, certainly not shake, the Bush administration's conviction in the political, economic, social, cultural and strategic design India came to represent in the American imagination. Natwar Singh was quick to pick this up. The relationship, he stressed, needed to be 'managed with great skill'.[238] It was, after all, one between two colossal democracies *and* their polities, something that rang all too true in negotiating the nuclear deal.

8

'4.30 A.M.'

2005–8

On 18 July 2005, reporters and former and current officials from both India and the US were seated with anticipation in the East Room of the White House. They were soon to be addressed by Prime Minister Manmohan Singh and President George W. Bush, the first of a handful of joint appearances, each of which was preceded by a great deal of suspense. 'Word began to filter in the crowd,' stated one distinguished former American official, that 'there was this nuclear agreement being discussed.' Nobody, he stressed, 'knew much about what was to come'.[1] Earlier that day, just after 9.00 a.m., the president officially welcomed the Indian prime minister in the South Lawn of the 200-year-old Executive Mansion, as the White House was officially known prior to the turn of the twentieth century. There was no indication whatsoever that a nuclear agreement was to be announced. Manmohan Singh's veiled suggestion in his official rejoinder that morning gave away little. 'There is vast potential,' he argued, for 'our countries to work together on an ambitious agenda of cooperation.'[2]

Two hours later, back in the East Room, the oblique opening comments by the president only outlined that both nations had begun a 'bilateral energy dialogue to find ways to work together'.[3] Such initiatives were hardly earth-shattering. Left unsatisfied by this, C. Raja Mohan, who was then the strategic affairs editor of the *Indian Express,*

213

began to look for further clues. Mohan turned, as he writes in the most detailed account of the early negotiations behind the nuclear deal to date, and saw David Mulford, the then American ambassador to India. Mulford, according to Mohan, 'smiled broadly and gestured that things had gone well'.[4] What most of the audience were of course unaware of was that, behind the scenes, interlocutors and officials from both sides were 'hammering out as fast but carefully as possible',[5] as one such official put it, a joint statement. It was released a little after the interaction in the East Room. For those previously in the know, especially Clinton administration representatives like Strobe Talbott, who spent months in his unofficial meetings with Jaswant Singh trying to convince his counterpart to accept at least aspects of the mainstream non-proliferation regime, the statement that afternoon was 'simply disbelieving'.[6] 'What they laid out,' Raja Mohan wrote, 'was the deal of the century.'[7]

According to the carefully worded, three-and-a-half page statement, the president 'told the Prime Minister that he will work to achieve full civil nuclear energy cooperation with India as it realises its goals of promoting nuclear power and achieving energy security'.[8] This was the first time since the Indian nuclear test in May 1974 that an American administration had committed itself to rescuing India from what Lalit Mansingh, the former ambassador to the US, had labelled the 'nuclear dog house'. Treated as nothing less than a 'pariah' because of its refusal to sign the 1968 Nuclear Non-Proliferation Treaty (NPT), India, Mansingh stressed, was essentially 'circumscribed'.[9] It did not have access to international nuclear markets. As emphasised in the last paragraph of what was a historic statement, 'international institutions', Bush reiterated to the Indian prime minister, were 'going to have to adapt to reflect India's central and growing role'. Such 'institutions', the statement went on, 'reflect changes in the global scenario that have taken place since 1945'.[10] In essence, India's position, role and determination to shape both its fortune and that of cross-national regimes—like those associated with non-proliferation—were not only acknowledged by an American incumbent, but in fact endorsed by him. What is more, and characteristic of the down-to-the-wire nature of each and every step of negotiations over the following three years, it took a last minute bid by Condoleezza Rice, an American diplomat and the newly appointed secretary of state, to salvage the arbitration at 4.30 a.m. that 18 July morning.[11]

Over the next thirty-nine months, and until the 'nuclear deal' was concluded on 10 October 2008, Indian and American negotiators would need to contend with and eventually overcome a crisis of trust. Unlike the past six crises examined in this book, the nuclear deal is of a separate character altogether. That the Bush administration was intent on providing the necessary waivers required for India to take part in international nuclear commerce was, of course, immediately welcomed by Indian officials. Yet actually realising these objectives through a series of laborious and highly technical negotiations required striking a common sense of trust in a process and with individuals sitting across a negotiating table. In short, it required believing in the other's motivations. In the words of Foreign Secretary Shyam Saran, who played a central role in the negotiations and later became Manmohan Singh's advisor on nuclear-related matters, 'This was a learning process like none other.' Every budding Indian diplomat, Saran underlined, 'needs to understand how this happened' and 'why it worked for India'.[12]

Above and beyond the crisis of negotiations, Indian principals and the government as a whole would need to deal with the political backlash in New Delhi. The left bloc, the Congress' key allies in the UPA coalition, was fervidly against any such arrangement. In one commentator's interpretation of the left's view, the deal was thought to haul India into 'imperialist America's global power game and would jeopardise, the country's independence'.[13] For the Communist Party of India (Marxist) or CPI (M), the largest of four such parties with forty-three crucial seats in support of the UPA, the deal was quite simply 'a part of American design'. As one of their letters of protest noted, it was designed to tie India into 'a wide-ranging strategic alliance'. It would, according to this particular strain of argument, 'adversely affect the pursuit of an independent foreign policy and our [India's] strategic autonomy'.[14]

Those on the political right, most notably the BJP, adopted what might, at best, be described as an inarticulate response to a process many of their own leaders had initiated only six years earlier. The primary concern, the force underlying which dipped at different periods of debate, had to do with India's nuclear deterrent. It had been 'surrendered', argued Yashwant Sinha, the former foreign minister who had once reportedly been partial to the idea of sending troops to Iraq. The negotiations, he asserted, would limit India's ability 'to do a third Pokhran'—test nuclear weapons again.[15] Similarly, commentators and scholars also underlined that 'the deal', as one such writer states, 'Mortgages India's future security at the altar of US non-proliferation interests.'[16] In fact, so vituperative did their criticisms become that the newspaper which some of these commentators wrote for came to be understood as 'anti-Congress and anti-American'.[17] The debate within India—both in Parliament and beyond—was consequently vocal to say the least. This perhaps explains why Rice, during the concluding ceremony for the signing of the deal, stressed that 'many thought this day would never come'.[18]

Yet despite the opposition from certain sections of the media and among the Indian elite, the nuclear deal did not serve to entrap India into a network of American alliances, as many had argued; nor did it lead to an irreparable rupture in Indian policy between the idea of independence and the material need to work more closely and even intimately with the American government. Indian interests, as this chapter shows, remain India's alone to determine and advance. They have hardly been substituted by those nurtured elsewhere, least of all in Washington. This, it can be concluded, remains the vital contribution of those negotiating at a time of engagement, and who, much like Gundevia and Swaran Singh in the early 1960s, were determined not to give away anything that might have in fact undermined India's ability to think and act for itself in both the present and the future. This was most clear in India's dealings with the democratic administration under President Barack Obama in the few testing months following the first of his two presidential terms, and is highlighted in the conclusion to this book.

For the sake of clarity, this chapter is divided into four parts. The first—'Dealing with Non-Proliferation'—introduces why the so-called 'nuclear deal' was indeed groundbreaking. Hence it very briefly outlines the history and restrictions placed upon India as a result of its nuclear tests and failure to sign the NPT. In addition, it introduces some of the key characters who engineered the shift in American focus when it came to India. In a second section, the chapter examines the negotiations between the end of 2004, when the discussions around nuclear trade were initiated, and March 2006, when the first major step—or what was called the Separation Agreement—was finally realised during President Bush's state visit to India.

The third section—titled 'Negotiating Contest'—scrutinises the pressures and conditions upon India's negotiating team as they contended with the political fall-out within India from what came to be called the Hyde Act. This was a crucial piece of American domestic legislation that was needed to provide India with the necessary waivers from the US Atomic Energy Act of 1954. Without this piece of enabling legislation, it would have been legally impossible for any American administration to cooperate with a state like India that had tested nuclear weapons but which refused to sign the NPT. This section also outlines the debates following the finalisation of what was known as a 123 Agreement, or a bilateral cooperation agreement between India and the US. Indeed, it was only following the conclusion of the 123 Agreement at the end of July 2007 that the sharp political disagreements among the Congress' coalition partners, supporters and the opposition more generally began to dominate Indian television channels and the print media. Such opposition came precariously close to breaking the UPA. Further, this section looks at India's positions and objections during the final phase of negotiations with the International Atomic Energy Agency (IAEA) and the Vienna-based, forty-six member Nuclear Suppliers Group (NSG), which took place between the summer of 2008 and October of the same year. The fourth and concluding section of this chapter returns to the larger argument in this book regarding ideas and interests at a time of transformation.

Dealing with Non-Proliferation

In October 1974, five months after India conducted its first nuclear test, Adlai Stevenson, the American ambassador to the UN during the Cuban missile crisis, argued that the explosions had 'set its [India's] door ajar'.[19] After all, it conducted a nuclear test after having refused to sign the NPT, adopted on 12 June 1968.[20] According to Article IX of the treaty, only those states that 'manufactured and exploded' nuclear explosive devices prior to 1 January 1967 were to be considered legitimate Nuclear Weapons States (NWS).[21] This included all five permanent members of the UN Security Council. The Indian tests, of course, came after this deadline. Indira Gandhi's government claimed that the explosion in Pokhran, the testing site in the deserts of the West Indian state of Rajasthan, was a Peaceful Nuclear Explosion (PNE) since the device that was being tested had not been weaponised.

Yet as Raja Ramanna, the celebrated nuclear physicist in charge of the so-called PNE and then director of the Bhaba Atomic Research Centre—India's top nuclear research facility housed in a suburb in Mumbai—

underlined, 'an explosion is an explosion' just like 'a gun is a gun'. The test, he argued, 'was not at all peaceful'.[22] For all practical purposes, as Strobe Talbott stresses, 'Terminology aside, India now had the bomb.'[23] India forcefully opened a 'door ajar' voluntarily locked by sixty-one non-nuclear weapons states or founding members of the NPT as the treaty came into force on 5 March 1970.[24] Notably, France and China, which tested a nuclear device in 1960 and 1964 respectively, were not founding signatories and only joined in 1992.

An Indian Case

In many ways, India came to represent something of an anomaly in the world of non-proliferation norms. By 1998, albeit in a limited sense, it was to be joined in this by Pakistan and, reportedly, Israel: states with nuclear weapons, or allegedly so in the case of Israel, but who were non-signatories to the NPT. The key difference, of course, between India and Pakistan was that the latter was known to have indulged in extensive proliferation. As is well documented, a far-reaching black market programme had been overseen by the architect of the state's nuclear agenda, the iniquitous Abdul Qadeer Khan. Rice would refer to Khan as *the* 'nuclear proliferation entrepreneur'.[25]

India's justification for non-membership had been made long before the treaty was signed.[26] In short, as Jaswant Singh argued in a widely read and oft-quoted article in *Foreign Affairs* soon after the 1998 tests, the NPT 'arbitrarily divided nuclear haves from have-nots'. As Singh underlines in the provocatively titled piece, 'Against Nuclear Apartheid', this was hardly prudent for a nation such as India. After all, India was sandwiched between China, a nuclear-weapons state and perceived foe, and Pakistan, a proliferator of weapons of mass destruction that was known to have had the capability to test by the late 1970s, or certainly by 1980. Moreover, Indian elites were convinced that China was sharing—or proliferating—nuclear weapons-related technology and resources with Pakistan.[27] This was in direct contravention of Article I of the NPT, which prohibited 'transfer' of such technologies to 'any non-nuclear weapons state'.[28]

Further, and as Ramanna and a whole host of Indian scientists, practitioners and scholars have convincingly argued, India's refusal to sign the NPT did not mean that it was opposed to nuclear disarmament or non-proliferation. India voluntarily banned 'prospective' plutonium production, a key ingredient for a nuclear arsenal.[29] Nehru's government called for an end to nuclear testing in 1954, just as Eisenhower was to make his compelling case of 'atoms for peace'. In fact, C. Rajagopalachari, the founding member of the Swatantra Party and former Congress leader, made a bid for universal disarmament long before the objectives underlying the same were outlined in the preamble to the NPT. This is, of course, a crucial point, which, as Jaswant Singh underlines, went unheeded. The five so-called nuclear-weapons states, he argues, were largely found 'busily modernising their nuclear arsenal', and this while India called for the creation of a non-discriminatory treaty on non-proliferation in 1965 and the non-use of nuclear weapons in 1978.[30]

If these characteristics underscoring India's approach to matters nuclear were not enough to convince those more sceptical of Indian motivations—mainly American principals like Clinton—or what Ramanna called those invested in 'the all-or-nothing attitude attributed to India',[31] India's role in the creation of the International Atomic Energy Agency (IAEA) ought to have provided at least a degree of pause. After all, the IAEA's fate, structure and mandate were determined by an exclusive seven-member scientific committee including Homi J. Bhabha, the Bombay-born nuclear physicist and founder of the first privately funded nuclear research institute in India. Of the seven, Bhabha emerged as the uncontested presidential candidate at the First Geneva Conference in August 1955, a meeting attended by more than 1,500 delegates and scientists. The conference helped to further the idea of an international agency, and, as importantly, to bridge the Cold War disharmony between the East and the West.

Adding to what was clearly the Indian state's and representatives' commitment to non-proliferation, even if not to a regime of non-proliferation, India fervently championed the cause and need for disarmament at the UN. Rajiv Gandhi, Nehru's grandson and India's sixth prime minister, pushed forward a forceful proposal in the Third Special Session on Disarmament of the General Assembly in June 1988. Making the case for an 'action plan' for 'ushering in a nuclear-weapon free and non-violent world order', the younger Gandhi might well have been said to have established the kernel for the endeavour that has come to be called Global Zero in the twenty-first century. Notably, the objectives set out by Rajiv Gandhi continue to embody those pressed by Indian diplomats in the present day, a point clearly made in the 2012 Substantive Session of the UN's Disarmament Commission.[32]

The Non-Proliferation 'Barn'

Despite the many initiatives taken by India before and after the PNE, for the most part, and as Teresita C. Schaffer, former American diplomat and authority on South Asian security, argues: 'India was treated by the non-proliferation system mainly as an object of controls' rather than a 'country that could contribute to non-proliferation' or 'help shape the controls'.[33] Indeed, the Nuclear Suppliers Group (NSG) was created in direct response to the 1974 Indian nuclear test. Its main objective is 'to ensure that nuclear trade for peaceful purposes does not contribute to the proliferation of nuclear weapons'.[34] Further, and as was reiterated at the May 2010 NPT Review Conference in New York, the primary objective of NSG participating governments is to oversee the trade and use of nuclear-related goods and technologies among all 'NPT states'.[35]

Until 2008, or when the NSG granted India a waiver with regard to its rules, this meant that India could not legitimately attract such goods and resources from NSG member states. Further, the then American administration under President Jimmy Carter instituted what was called the 1978 Nuclear Non-Proliferation Act (NNPA). This piece of legislation prohibited the Carter White House and successive US administrations from engaging in nuclear trade with any non-nuclear weapons state that did not have 'full scope safeguards' or international inspections on *all* its nuclear activities.[36] The bill, Rice later argued, 'cut off all nuclear trade with India'.[37]

As suggested above, India represented something of an anomaly in the world of nuclear non-proliferation. It had nuclear weapons capabilities, but had not signed the NPT. Further, while India certainly did not qualify as a non-nuclear weapons state, it was not and could not be considered a legitimate nuclear weapons state as determined by the NPT. For the better part of three decades, India remained outside and further apart from a club of nations shaped by rules embodied in what Indian representatives insisted and continue to maintain is an 'unequal nuclear regime'.[38] Following the 1974 test, Stevenson, a two-time contestant for the Democratic nomination for president, argued that scientists and American civil servants more generally realised that 'the cows', as he put it, 'have started out of the barn and may soon be gone'. Yet for the most part, practitioners were almost blinded by what Ashley Tellis would later call the 'non-proliferation straight-jacket', which, in his words, 'doomed all efforts at bilateral rapprochement'.[39]

The latter point might well be considered something of an exaggeration. If, for instance, the Talbott–Singh talks had not gained a degree of momentum, or Clinton personally had not taken what was a clear and uncompromising position on Kargil in 1999, there is little doubt that rapprochement in the post-Bush era would have been that much harder. On the other hand, and as pointed out by Tellis—a crucial insider widely understood to have 'made the deal happen' in 2008[40]—Clinton's unbending resolve for non-proliferation regimes could at best normalise the relationship with India, but take it no further.

For instance, the last and fourteenth meeting between Talbott and Jaswant Singh was, unsurprisingly, dominated by discussions around non-proliferation objectives. The American deputy assistant secretary of state was clearly told that India could not sign the Comprehensive Test Ban Treaty (CTBT). Adopted by the UN General Assembly in September 1996, an Indian signature was long considered an imperative for Talbott. He was hardly surprised by the outcome. Soon after, as Talbott himself recounts, Bush's campaign spoke to themes 'that were music' to Indian 'ears'. Unlike the Democrats, Bush made clear, as Talbott writes, 'that he had little use for traditional non-proliferation measures'.[41] This included the CTBT that Clinton had signed, but which failed to be ratified due to a dissenting Republican majority in the US Congress. For India, the distinction between the two administrations could not have been clearer.

The Vulcans

From the start the Bush White House approached India as a 'part of the solution to non-proliferation', as Tellis notes, rather than the problem.[42] Moreover, as established in the last chapter, policymakers like Rice were certain that the Vulcans—a name given by Rice after a giant statue of a Vulcan in her hometown to a team of Bush's foreign policy advisors including Blackwill prior to the 2000 campaign[43]—were determined to 'change the terms of US–Indian engagement'.[44] Aside from Rice's and Bush's determination, what helped in this was the fact that the Republican team was directed and aided by experts in the science of both diplomacy and technical minutiae. Such a combination of people would prove vital in a set of negotiations that sought to free India from the restrictions embedded in both international regimes and American domestic law. American negotiators and advisors needed to tread cautiously, but at the same time with a sense of daring for something new: a deal with India.

Three such actors, whose 'ambition and purpose' kept an often exasperated series of dialogues going, as one State Department official put it,[45] were Nicholas Burns, Ashley Tellis and Philip Zelikow. Burns was the undersecretary of state for political affairs, and took the lead in negotiations sometime in April or May 2005, a few weeks before Manmohan Singh's visit to Washington. Further, crucial in at least the initial stages of negotiations and prior to Burns' taking charge, was the role played by Philip Zelikow, the former, and, according to Bob Woodward,[46] 'aggressive', executive director of the 9/11 Commission. Zelikow was Rice's counsellor, one-time co-author, confidant and deputy. He was someone the former national security advisor refers to as 'brilliant but baroque',[47] and who Indian counterparts found 'forthcoming and accessible'.[48] Zelikow left office in 2007.

Burns was assisted by Tellis, a senior advisor to the undersecretary and previously Blackwill's advisor during the ambassador's spell in New Delhi. Author of what is perhaps the most influential monograph on Indian nuclear strategy, and a long-time proponent of a more 'nuanced non-proliferation agenda',[49] Tellis sought to bolster America's relationship with India. The latter, he testified—to the House of Representatives Committee on International Relations a month prior to the release of the Joint Statement—was nothing less than a 'strategic asset to the United States'. To forge this relationship, Tellis made clear, India would require 'liberal access', as he put it, 'to a variety of high-technologies in the areas of civilian nuclear energy'.[50] Indeed, much like Tellis, Burns also argued that he wanted 'a more effective non-proliferation regime', one that would make space for India. By 'resolving' the nuclear issue, the undersecretary of state argued, India and the US would be better placed to 'define a more truly ambitious partnership'.[51] What helped in 'resolving' such pressing questions was the Republican Party's general drift towards an 'antipathy to nuclear arms control agreements', and 'realist and neo-conservative factions' that, Tellis recounts, 'took a more relaxed view of New Delhi's emerging nuclear capabilities'.[52]

Such 'realist' practitioners included Donald Rumsfeld, Robert Zoellick—then the deputy secretary of state and later the president of the World Bank—and Stephen Hadley, a deputy national security advisor who later became the president's national security advisor when Rice moved to head the State Department. As discussed in the previous chapter, Rumsfeld was nothing less than enthusiastic about India. In fact, the defence secretary's interest in India—specifically its market size and business potential—can be traced as far back as the early 1970s. Then the American ambassador to the North Atlantic Treaty Organization (NATO) in Brussels, the young Rumsfeld received unclassified and promising updates on India authored by Patrick Moynihan, the tenth American ambassador to New Delhi. Three decades later, and as defence secretary for the second time since 1975, Rumsfeld plainly argued: 'I did not think it made any sense for us to be at odds with them [India].'[53] His interest in an India no longer 'fencing' the US,[54] as he put it, was no doubt obvious to his immediate subordinates in the Pentagon.[55] After all, as Rice later argued, one of the key selling points of the nuclear deal and for allowing India access to American technologies was the hope that the country would 'become a customer for US military hardware'. This, as Rice clarifies, was an 'exciting prospect for the defence industry',[56] and predictably the US Defence Department. Douglas Feith for one found the argument compelling.[57] Zoellick and Hadley—both fellow Vulcan constituents—were also seemingly convinced by Rice's approach.

Further, and at least in the initial period of negotiations, 'key decisions', according to Glenn Kessler—a senior correspondent for the *Washington Post* and author of an unflattering biography of Rice—were made 'by Rice and a handful of close aides'. These included Zelikow, Zoellick, Hadley and later Burns, with Tellis by the undersecretary's side. Many in the State Department were simply 'cut out of the loop'. After all, and as what might be considered something of a truism, noted by Kessler, 'established bureaucracies tend to resist new ideas'. This was certainly the case for a bureaucracy that had, for a long time, hyphenated India and Pakistan in America's approach to South Asia. Equally, individuals in the State Department were fixated by the non-proliferation ideals peddled by Talbott and Washington's effective non-proliferation lobby more generally. Blackwill's attempts, as early as October 2001—barely three months after he had arrived in New Delhi—to refocus this approach was initially ignored by his direct line manager, Powell. As far as the latter was concerned, 'red lines' needed to be maintained when it came to India and non-proliferation.[58] As a result, bureaucrats within the State Department continued to press the case for 'hyphenation', whereby each and every initiative taken in respect to one of the two large South Asian nations would require careful consideration of US interests with regard to the other.

Trumping these time-tested advances, the Vulcans, much like Kennedy's 'Team India' in the early 1960s—as discussed in Chapter 4—sought to find ways to connect directly with New Delhi's political elite.[59] However, while Kennedy, Galbraith and Nitze strove to find a balance—partially because of their preoccupation with hyphenation—between Washington's relationship with India and Pakistan, the Bush team adopted an entirely different approach. It was given the inelegant title of 'de-hyphenation'.[60] The idea, as Burns put it, was to seek 'highly individual relations with both India and Pakistan'.[61] By doing so, the Bush administration, according to Raja Mohan, 'reconceived the framework of engagement with New Delhi'.[62] The 'oppositionists' in the State Department, argued Blackwill, were challenged by an exclusive team of advisors around Rice. 'The old bureaucrats', Blackwill continues, were to be met by those who were 'more than their match'.[63]

The Bush team managed to tailor an approach to each South Asian nation that abandoned the previous pattern of first needing to address the question of Kashmir. Unlike Ayub's one-time bidding with Kennedy, Bush was free to engage both India and Pakistan on their individual merits. It led to an 'entirely new and comprehensive engagement,' as Burns writes, 'between the United States and India'.[64] This point was immediately acknowledged by the likes of Brajesh Mishra, the former Indian national security advisor.[65] Rice made sure that Prime Minister Manmohan Singh was fully briefed on what at the time was seen to be an innovative approach. In addition, what helped in convincing India of America's change of tact was that Bush and Singh immediately took to each other. The latter, as one scholar puts it, proved an 'articulate but deliberate interlocutor'.[66] The former, who once blanked when asked the name of the Indian prime minister following his announcement to stand for president,[67] was absolutely convinced by the imperatives underlying both de-hyphenation and the need for a deal. The stage was thus readied for what would be a three-year-long battle of nerves and patience in the pursuit of answers to questions previously unaddressed.

A Statement and the Need for Separation
November 2004 to July 2006

In November 2004, Prime Minister Manmohan Singh attended the fifth summit to be held between India and the European Union (EU) at The Hague in the Netherlands. It led to the announcement of a 'strategic partnership' between India and the EU. New Delhi had been one of the first nations to establish formal diplomatic relations with the European Economic Community (EEC) in the early 1960s.[68] Of the thirty or so points of agreement and action outlined in a Joint Statement, the nineteenth seemed particularly curious. It spoke to the need for developing 'multilateral consultations' when it came to the proliferation of Weapons of Mass Destruction (WMD).[69] This was perhaps the first time since India had tested nuclear weapons in 1998 that the EU had demonstrated a willingness to open discussions—on nuclear-related matters—with a country long shunned by some of its member states. In constructing the strategic partnership, Indian interlocutors pushed the case for a dialogue on energy security more broadly. As Shyam Saran, the then Indian foreign secretary argued, India was bent on 'expanding its nuclear industry', and thus, as Saran asserted, it was time for the EU to look beyond what might have been considered 'philosophical and theological' questions informed by the almost dogmatic wording of the NPT. The response 'was cautious, but positive'. EU officials 'skirted the heart of nuclear nonproliferation', as Saran underlines, but at the same time, they were open to inviting India to join a major nuclear fusion project that only select nations were allowed access to. The so-called ITER (International Thermonuclear Experimental Reactor) project, which was established in the mid-1980s, sought to find ways to produce sustainable energy. Inviting India, with American support and consent, was hardly 'dramatic', but at the same time, as those negotiating for India asserted, it was a 'significant breakthrough'.[70] In preparation for Manmohan Singh's visit to Washington in July 2005, it provided MEA officials with an exemplar of the growing international acceptance and need to enter into a dedicated dialogue on nuclear energy with a consumer as large as India.

Setting the Tone for Talks

As established above, in Washington, Indian representatives were knocking on an open door. Apart from the renewed vision of the so-called

225

Vulcans, Tellis and Blackwill did their part to lay 'the ground work', as one scholar put it,[71] well before Bush's second term in office. In 2002, Blackwill, along with Sir Rob Young, the then British high commissioner to India, authored joint cables to both Washington and London urging their bureaucracies to consider nuclear cooperation with India. 'Changing the status quo', as Tellis argues, was the key objective. During a visit by Hadley in 2002, the Blackwill–Tellis duo convinced the then deputy national security advisor of the merits of 'shifting the nuclear debate altogether'. In an outreach meeting hosted by the Washington-based Aspen Institute in the Lake City of Udaipur, in the Indian state of Rajasthan, Blackwill, Tellis and Henry Kissinger—a chief guest—were intent on persuading Zelikow, who was also to attend the five-day meeting.[72] Zelikow, then in government but not as yet with Rice, was converted.[73] Hence, importantly, the views of many of those who would later play crucial roles both in the administration and on the nuclear deal were already shaped by what might be considered change engineers embedded in the American embassy in New Delhi in the early 2000s.

This was eminently clear to Saran. In his first meeting following Bush's return to power, with Rice and Zelikow in November 2004, the former Indian ambassador to Nepal and Myanmar suggested setting up an energy dialogue like the one with the Europeans. While such proposals were not new—similar ideas had first been mooted by Mishra in 2002—they had earlier been rejected by Powell.[74] Further and intently aware of the change in the Bush administration's approach to India, Saran pushed Rice to look at ways to 'overcome' the 'matter of Tarapur'.[75] This was a reference to the two American-supplied reactors housed in the Tarapur Atomic Energy Plant in the Indian state of Maharashtra. As a result of the 1974 nuclear test and the subsequent passage of the US NNPA under Carter, not only did the US cut off fuel supplies—or low enriched uranium (LEU)—to the reactors but he also prohibited India from reprocessing spent fuel. The latter posed a significant safety hazard as successive American administrations refused to take back accumulating nuclear waste. In 2004, and given that serious discussions on nuclear energy were only beginning, Saran limited his pitch to a 'legacy issue' that almost irreparably piqued both the MEA and the Indian Department of Atomic Energy (DAE). After all, as far as Indian bureaucrats and scientists were concerned, America had 'reneged' on its Tarapur commitments.[76]

To Saran's surprise, Rice went further than either he or India's political elites expected. That the newly appointed secretary of state's visit to New Delhi in March 2005 was going to be 'critical' was known, 'but no one,' Raja Mohan makes clear, 'was sure just how big it would turn out to be'.[77] Natwar Singh, two years junior to Mishra in the IFS and then the Indian foreign minister, was 'slightly taken aback' too, as he put it.[78] Rice spent two days in the Indian capital between 15 and 16 March 2005.[79] In a meeting with the prime minister, she made it clear that the Bush administration was willing and even eager to consider civil nuclear cooperation with India. Clearly, the secretary was looking for something 'beyond Tarapur', as Saran recounted.[80] During her meeting with Natwar Singh, Rice's 'presentation', as one American reporter asserted, was 'still vague about the specifics'.[81] In public, nothing was given away either during the secretary's interactions with the American press corps on board her plane, or in the joint remarks with Natwar Singh on 16 March.[82] Not one reporter, at least among the Americans, 'followed up'.[83] Indian insiders knew more, but they too had little by way of detail.[84]

In private, one of the key objectives in the meetings with Indian representatives, as one official underlines, was to make sure that India successfully completed the Next Steps in Strategic Partnership (NSSP).[85] The two-phase process was launched in January 2004 by Bush and Vajpayee.[86] It was intended to ease export controls for nuclear-related and what is commonly known as 'dual-use' technology sales to India. The first phase was concluded on 17 September 2004, providing India with very limited 'modifications to US export licensing policies', as an official Joint Statement put it.[87] In the press conference with Natwar Singh, Rice stated that she 'look[ed] forward' to Phase II of the NSSP being 'completed'.[88] In fact, this was a priority. Three aspects of the NSSP needed completion to enable broader civil nuclear cooperation with America or any other state willing to deal with India.

Importantly, all three were also considered necessary steps by Indian officials. There was no contradiction yet between what Rice and her team placed on the table and what Indian negotiators were willing to consider.[89] These included, first, passing a bill in the Indian Parliament to prevent the proliferation of WMD and their delivery systems, which India did on 13 May 2005.[90] Second, harmonising export controls of 'sensitive technologies', including those used for reprocessing and enrichment practices, in accordance with UNSC Resolution 1540.[91] This was to convince international partners that nuclear-related material imported by India 'would not be diverted to third countries'.[92] Third, and mirroring the substance of Resolution 1540, India was required to sign a bilateral 'end user agreement' with the US to ensure there was no potential for the leakage of nuclear-related and imported technology to any third country. This was signed between Saran and Marc Grossman, Burns' predecessor, in early 2005. In exchange, the US State Department moved fast to remove thirteen so-called 'entities'—including the Indian Defence Research and Development Organisation (DRO)—from the so-called 'entities list', which had imposed sanctions upon these organisations. Clearly, the rhetoric of change was swiftly realised and supported by substance.

Playing 'hardball' in Washington

Following Rice's short but essential visit, Saran, at the heart of the obvious and fast-moving changes, was clearly emboldened by the secretary's forward-looking initiative. Yet he emphasised to his American counterparts that for a partnership to mean something: 'you have to treat India as a partner and not a target'. 'Both,' the foreign secretary underlined, 'cannot be done together.'[93] Interestingly, notwithstanding the fact that an American administration was finally coming around to address what Adlai Stevenson once called the half-opened door in the nuclear 'barn', Saran and Indian negotiators more generally were clear not to give anything away. Negotiations, as far as they were concerned and as outlined below, were largely to their favour, even if it meant going 'past the wire', as Daniel Markey put it. The State Department, Markey recollected, was soon convinced that the 'Indians were going to play hardball.'[94] The irony underlying the fact that India had few aces in a game of cards fashioned to address its nuclear status was not lost on anyone, not even Saran, the chief Indian negotiator.[95]

The mandate received from the prime minister and observed by the Indian team was clear from the start. The twin objectives were to negotiate India's way out of 'nuclear apartheid' and the restrictions imposed by the NSG with the aim of expanding India's civil nuclear energy capacity. In doing so, negotiators were clearly told that India's strategic programme, including maintaining the right to test nuclear weapons, was to remain untouched. Such a right was sacrosanct. On these counts, nothing was to be given away, even if it meant, as one official recounted, 'losing the prospect of [an] agreement'.[96] With this in mind, Natwar Singh led a team of negotiators to Washington on 14 and 15 April. The expressed purpose was to prepare the basis for Prime Minister Manmohan Singh's scheduled visit in the middle of July.

The meetings in April were truly groundbreaking. Unlike Rice's approach in New Delhi, where the secretary merely outlined her administration's desire to consider civil nuclear cooperation with India, in Washington her team converted aspirations into clearly defined goals. Zelikow, in a meeting with Indian bureaucrats, and according to one official, made it clear that the Bush administration was intent on 'changing India's nuclear status'. These were no longer matters for exploration, but for action. Rice no doubt notified both Bush and his administration prior to Zelikow's call.[97] She called Musharraf too.[98] Although it had taken the Bush administration the better part of the first presidential term to place what diplomats like to call 'substantials' on the table, something Blackwill and Tellis had first advised in 2002, the deed was now done. This, Zelikow allegedly argued, is how the Republican administration was going to 'alter' the relationship with India.[99]

A six-page note proposing the alteration was reportedly dictated to Zelikow by Rice on the plane following the secretary's departure from New Delhi. The idea was simple: 'go for broke and cut a broad deal'. The cautious and incremental steps taken so far, as useful as they were to socialise the idea of a deal among Rice's inner circle and within a handful of Indian elites privy to the discussions, were to be trumped by something much bigger.[100] As Saran himself underscored, the Indian team quickly realised that the Americans were looking for something 'much more ambitious'.[101]

Once again, in public, the foreign minister gave away little.[102] Natwar Singh merely outlined that part of his delegation, led by Montek Singh Ahluwalia, the deputy chairman of the Indian Planning Commission, was staying back to lead on an energy dialogue with Sam Bodman, the American secretary of energy.[103] Notably, apart from Saran, the Indian team also included a representative from the DAE, R.B. Grover.[104] Grover was to address technical questions on nuclear-related matters and, according to one insider, he was also to watch over a process that was viewed with a high degree of suspicion by DAE officials.[105] After all, it was these scientists who had faced the brunt of the US-led sanctions regime for decades following the 1974 test.

Significantly, so far, this was a 'top driven process', with limited media and legislative scrutiny in both nations. When Manmohan Singh landed in Washington, the hard work of finding agreeable language for a Joint Statement was to be conditioned by two factors. First, what Singh perceived he could sell back home in the Lok Sabha and within the Congress-led coalition. The latter, Natwar Singh argued, was an all-important consideration for the prime minister. Many within the Congress, let alone the UPA, were less convinced about working closely with the Bush administration.[106] Next was what MEA and DAE officials would insist on including in a statement that otherwise had every opportunity to force limits on India's strategic weapons programme.

An Indian Joint Statement

On 15 July, two days prior to Manmohan Singh's arrival, Saran reached Washington.[107] The objective was to finalise the language in the Joint Statement. The American side, apart from a battery of lawyers that the Indians found baffling—the Indians had none—were represented by Burns.[108] Given the contemporary nature of the discussions at hand, what went on in these meetings is hard to determine. What can be verified, and as indicated in the introduction to this chapter, is that the final wording was agreed a little after the Indian prime minister and President Bush began their official remarks to journalists on 18 July in the East Room of the White House. Indeed, as Rice recounts in her memoir, earlier that morning Natwar Singh made clear that despite his beckoning, the prime minister would not go ahead. As the foreign minister put it, he could not 'sell' the statement—as it stood earlier that morning—back 'in New Delhi'.[109] Clearly, the politics of perception, not to mention the risk of being seen as selling out India, weighed heavily on Singh's mind. The prime minister was determined to accept only what he felt he could stand by. Nothing could be taken for granted.

In the windowless Roosevelt Room in the White House, and at the same time as Singh and Bush addressed their public audience, the negotiators painstakingly agonised over five key issues. Some of these, as Raja Mohan recounts, were decided earlier on 17 July, but needed finalisation. Notably, Anil Kakodkar, the chairman of the Indian Atomic

Energy Commission (AEC), who had been invited to join the prime minister's entourage and M.K. Narayanan, India's third national security advisor, held 'serious reservations', according to Raja Mohan, on the nature of the agreement.[110] That both, but especially Kakodkar, were sceptical from the start was understood and taken into consideration by Saran and Grover during their meetings with Zelikow, Burns and Rice between April and June.[111]

In essence, and with the view to provide a degree of context, the final statement would make clear that the US was to work towards 'full civil nuclear energy cooperation with India'. Washington would also 'work with friends and allies to adjust international regimes'. Importantly, as Saran stressed in November 2004, the statement emphasised that 'expeditious consideration' would be given to 'fuel supplies' to reactors such as Tarapur. It also highlighted India's desire to contribute to the ITER project. In exchange, India would need to adopt the practice of 'identifying and separating civilian and nuclear facilities', and placing these under IAEA safeguards. Its military programme, as outlined in the initial directive or mandate given to negotiators, was completely out of bounds. Further, India would be required to continue its self-imposed moratorium on nuclear testing—announced immediately after the 1998 tests—and work with the US towards a multilateral Fissile Material Cut Off Treaty (FMCT). Lastly, India was to follow standard non-proliferation norms of 'refraining from transfer of enrichment and reprocessing technologies' and working towards harmonising its export control legislation.[112] As mentioned above, the latter two points were taken into consideration as India passed the required legislation to conclude Phase II of the NSSP.

On the morning and afternoon of 18 July, in the Roosevelt Room, apart from dealing with American demands, Saran and Ronen Sen, the then Indian ambassador to the US, were left to deal with the AEC's reluctance—to put it mildly—to separate its nuclear facilities. Unlike the meetings of the Sunday before or those held on 17 July, Kakodkar was absent. According to one account, Narayanan was to represent both Kakodkar and the AEC.[113] This was imperative—they were, at least in their view, protecting India's interests as they understood them. Indeed, the reservations held by the likes of Kakodkar perhaps added a greater sense of balance to India's approach. Tellingly, four key issues holding back the agreement were shaped according to Indian imperatives and only one by Burns and his team—the latter had clearly been told by the president to reach an agreement.

First, the word 'full'—as in 'full civil nuclear energy cooperation'—was reportedly insisted upon by Kakodkar. There was to be no opportunity afforded to the American side to later make a case for limited civilian cooperation.[114] Second, another issue, which, according to Glenn Kessler, took an 'hour to resolve', had to do with the word 'voluntarily'.[115] Burns was reportedly insistent that the US would choose which of India's twenty-two nuclear facilities were to be branded as 'civilian' or 'military'. This was of course vital—as the American team saw it—as only civilian reactors were to be placed under IAEA safeguards. As determined earlier, India's strategic programme was a clearly demarcated no-go area. The Indian team again prevailed. India reserved the right for itself to separate its nuclear facilities 'voluntarily' as its negotiators saw fit. Third, Saran and his team were adamant that the separation was to be conducted 'in a phased manner', and not immediately as per American preferences. This was crucial, giving India enough time to separate facilities that had long worked in tandem. Fourth, with regard to the FMCT, Saran was resolute that India would only accept 'working *with* the United States' towards its conclusion. There was no question of India outlining its intent to consider the said treaty if the Americans backed-down. After all, in the recent past and notwithstanding Bill Clinton's determination to pass the CTBT, the US Congress voted against its ratification.

The one essential point—and the fifth matter of contention—left to Burns and his team was with regard to the term 'advanced nuclear technology'. Indian negotiators were purportedly assured in the meetings with Zelikow in April and later in May that India would be unambiguously recognised as a 'de facto nuclear weapons state'.[116] This was, of course, seen to be crucial given that the language of the NPT—as outlined above—was largely determined by the division between 'nuclear weapons states' and 'non-nuclear weapons states'. India, as Tellis later remarked, was 'neither fish nor fowl'.[117] Its negotiators demanded the same level of legal and normative acknowledgment as given to the five accepted nuclear weapons states or those that had tested nuclear weapons prior to 1 January 1967. In the end, and despite the 'roll back', as Saran later recounted, the best Indian negotiators could do on this single point of concession was to make sure that India was seen and approached as a 'unique case'.[118] It did so by committing to enter what later came to be called 'India specific safeguards' with the IAEA.[119] In some measure, negotiators carved a distinctive persona for India in a world of non-proliferation largely divided between what Jaswant Singh once called the 'nuclear have and have-nots'.[120] Ultimately, and satisfied with the text, the 'nuclear section', as one commentator put it, was 'squeezed in the joint statement in single space format', and readied at 1.00 p.m. on 18 July. There was no doubt in anyone's mind that this was a 'last minute addition'.[121]

Indeed, if there ever were a case for exceptionalism in international politics, as discussed in different moments of crisis in the previous chapters, the urgent few hours in the Roosevelt Room epitomised Indian imperatives, which were nothing less than clear to at least those arguing for and with India. The fact that Indian principals were 'willing to take this to the eleventh hour', as one former State Department official pointed out, or 'push our [the Bush administration's] buttons hard' could hardly be understated; 'the regular feedback I got,' the official continued, 'was that this was miserable, the Indian side was impossible'.[122] In short, 'a careful reading of the Joint Statement should leave no one in any doubt', as Tellis later put it, 'that this agreement is wholly beneficial to India'. Crucially, Tellis underscored, it allowed India to continue to produce materials needed to sustain its strategic and military programme untouched by the guidelines outlined in the Joint Statement.[123] The wording, as one negotiator argued, needed to be 'both clear and rigid'. It was the foundational framework for the negotiations ahead. The next step was to finalise a separation plan with a view to implementing those tricky and carefully negotiated aspects of the Joint Statement.

'India's Separation Plan'

In his memoirs, George W. Bush wrote that 'In the Presidency, there are no do-overs. You have to do,' he argued, 'what you believe is right and accept the consequences.'[124] The deal with India was clearly one that he believed in and one which he thought was right, and for which he—much like but to a lesser extent than Manmohan Singh—risked the near lethal consequences of legislative and political inspection. Indeed, as Tellis points out, for the president and members of his administration like Rice, 'the main motivation was strategic'.[125] Much to the chagrin of the 'techies' in the State Department, who had clearly warned Rice against the legal obstacles that were soon apparent,[126] the secretary pushed for 'simplification', as one insider put it.[127] Further, with regard to separating India's nuclear facilities, the role played by Bush and Singh would prove paramount. They outline how and why strategic imperatives prevailed over what were largely considered technical impediments in the case of the former, and the degree to which those living and breathing the 'legacy' of Tarapur would require momentary reassurances from the latter. As Rice makes clear, 'the effort almost failed several times'.[128]

On 1 March, Bush landed in New Delhi. The day after, a Joint Statement stated that both the president and Prime Minister Singh 'welcomed the successful completion of discussions on India's separation plan'.[129] From the outset, the letter of the Separation Agreement was fairly straightforward. As outlined in the Joint Statement, but now with a commitment for implementation, in exchange for 'full civil nuclear energy cooperation', India would identify and separate 'civilian and military nuclear facilities and programmes in a phased manner'. This was highlighted in some detail in a nine-page note tabled in the Indian Parliament on 11 May 2006.[130] As Bush asserted, it led to an agreement that was nothing less than 'historic'. According to newspaper reports in both India and the US, the pact 'would help India satisfy its enormous civilian energy needs while allowing it to continue to develop nuclear weapons'. To sceptics back home, an elated Bush argued that 'some people just don't want to change and change with the times'.[131]

Neither he nor the prime minister, as officials on both sides argued, had any idea of the resistance they were subsequently to face. This was undoubtedly about much more than simply changing attitudes; it was about challenging accepted norms and the laws of non-proliferation. That India stood its ground—on each and every issued outlined in the 18 July 2005 statement—was soon clear to American counterparts in the months leading up to Bush's India visit. As Tellis later argued, this was 'India's separation plan, not ours.'[132] In fact, the Joint Statement and the Separation Agreement were produced as soon as they were possibly *because* negotiations continued to be top-driven with the prime minister driving a four-seated car along with only Saran, Kakodkar and perhaps Grover.[133] Narayanan, although present in the key moments of dialogue, was largely divorced from the detailed discussions held between the American and Indian sides.[134]

That the Separation Agreement would in itself receive scathing criticism later within India was, to put it mildly, an understatement. Yet the derisive arguments under the full glare of India's print and visual media gained momentum only after the Hyde Act was passed in July 2006 and more importantly once the so-called 123 Agreement was made public in August 2007. Given that the disparagement which the deal as a whole received encompasses points of debate negotiated in the Separation Agreement, the 123 Agreement and the Hyde Act, the subsequent part of this chapter consequently delineates the latter two pieces of legislation, before outlining the major points of criticism that were levelled at the agreement. It then returns to the negotiations, outlining how exactly Indian interlocutors sought to safeguard the separation of India's nuclear facilities. Switching from the so-far sequential method of examination—or arguing India's case in the chronological order in which the deal was negotiated—is intended to provide a degree of context underlying why the Separation Agreement was vital and, in the end, to India's benefit.

This period of change hardly meant that ideas once more closely associated with non-alignment, as interpreted and advanced in this book, would simply disappear. The barriers that threatened the quick promotion of the deal were not assembled because of the Indian elite's preoccupation with the past, as Rice erroneously suggests,[135] but an unusual passion for a future where India's interests were to be determined by India alone. Nothing was to be taken for granted. As Mishra argued only days after the 123 Agreement was concluded, the question is 'not whether this agreement' will 'constrain India', rather, 'it is about negotiating something [whereby] saying "no" in the future', he underlined, "is not difficult."[136] Getting to this point required unravelling a cerebral knot tied on the one end by those less inclined to embrace engagement—like the left and elements within the DAE—and on the other by those convinced about the urgency for engagement—such as the prime minister—but not without a clear and uncompromising view of sovereignty and what it meant to India and for Indians more generally.

Negotiating Contest
August 2007 to August 2008

On the morning of 18 December 2006, exactly five months after Rice's burst of inspiration at 4.30 a.m. in July of that year, President Bush signed into law a bill to enable civil nuclear cooperation with India. The legislative proposal known as H.R. 5682 was passed in both the US House of Representatives and the Senate respectively on 26 July and 16 November 2006.[137] Sponsored by Henry J. Hyde, the late Republican congressman and one-time Democrat, who switched parties to support Eisenhower,[138] the bill was aptly titled the 'Henry J. Hyde United States–India Peaceful Atomic Energy Cooperation Act.'[139] In common parlance, it would be called the Hyde Act, and was entered into force in the presence of the then 83-year-old representative from Illinois. Interestingly, the congressman, Mr Hyde, was initially less convinced by the virtues of exempting India from American domestic legislation, which is what the act did. In his last meeting with Saran prior to the signing ceremony, Hyde, not unknown to oppose his own party on key policy issues,[140] said he was 'hugely honoured' to have his name attached to this 'piece of legislation'. For Saran, this indicated that 'American lawmakers were coming around to nuclear cooperation.'[141] As Bush put it that December morning, the act was central 'to help clear the way for us [the US and India] to move forward with this process [deal]'.[142]

Crucially, the act exempted India from clauses embedded in the US Atomic Energy Act of 1954. Specifically, Section 128—that established the criteria and procedures for the export of nuclear material—clearly outlined legally coded principles for cooperating with 'non-nuclear weapons' states. India did not figure in its carefully worded brief.[143] This was prior to the constitutional amendments and waivers offered in the decisive Section 104 of the Hyde Act.[144] For the first time in American constitutional history, at least since the 1954 act was passed, the US Congress authorised the executive branch to enter into a 'proposed agreement for cooperation with India', a state that had not signed the NPT but which had tested nuclear weapons. This agreement was a requirement as per Section 123—outlining the merits of 'cooperation with other nations'—in Chapter 11 of the 1954 act.[145] Accordingly, and following multiple rounds of forceful discussions,[146] the bilateral agreement between India and the US was signed on 1 August 2007. The text of the 'Agreement for Cooperation' or what popularly came to be known as the '123 Agreement' was released for legislative scrutiny in both Washington and New Delhi a few days later.[147]

Almost immediately, political uproar engulfed India. For a select group of Indian elites and commentators, the deal had 'given away the store to the United States'.[148] In their view, it paralysed India's military nuclear programme. For the four left parties then in support of the Congress-led coalition, the agreement with the US drew India into a strategic eddy shaped and controlled by those in Washington. For almost a year, since the 123 Agreement was completed, Manmohan Singh's government was forced to stall further negotiations—first with the IAEA, then with the NSG—because of the critical veto that was held, at least for a limited period, by the left bloc. The challenge of domestic opposition introduced an added dynamic less obvious in moments of crises over the preceding six decades. For perhaps the first time, an Indian government was found negotiating its way through a crisis of confidence shaped by domestic opposition, but over an issue broadly understood as one of foreign policy. More forcefully than in the past, it made clear that bilateral relationships forged between principals were hardly devoid of elite scrutiny, shaping to some extent the nature and imperatives of the relationship in question.

Interestingly, for those in Washington, and contrary to the argument promoted by the voices of dissent within India, this was a 'bomb-friendly deal', as Michael Krepon, a staunch and notable critic put it.[149] Hence while commentators in India labelled the prime minister a 'strong anti-nuclearist',[150] those in Washington were convinced that the deal was in fact a 'huge loss' to the promotion of non-proliferation.[151] In the end, and as one American observer put it, the 'Indian nuclear establishment' was 'the big winner'.[152] As discussed in some detail in the section below, the nuclear 'store' was in fact painstakingly negotiated to India's advantage, a point unambiguously acknowledged by American detractors. At the same time, the process of permanently opening the doors to Stevenson's 'nuclear' barn, which were nudged ajar as far back as 1974, was far from straightforward. The final text of the 123 Agreement undoubtedly required forceful and near-impossible fortitude on the part of the Indian negotiators.

In all, as one reporter who followed the developments more closely than most made clear, it took 'nine rounds and 300 hours of talks over two years' to arrive at this point.[153] Notably, Saran retired from the Foreign Service in September 2006. He was soon appointed the prime minister's special envoy for India–US civil nuclear issues more broadly. Shivshankar Menon was appointed as the new foreign secretary, and later the national security advisor in early 2010.[154] Further, Foreign

Minister Natwar Singh was replaced by Pranab Mukherjee, who first held this post more than a decade ago, in 1995. Mukherjee, often called the 'other Prime Minister' would play a vital part in maintaining governmental unity throughout this period.[155] Indeed, Menon and Saran may have led the charge in Vienna—with the IAEA Board of Governors and the member states of the NSG—but the decisive task of keeping the government together rested with the West Bengal-born Mukherjee. In July 2012, he was elected the president of India.

The Departing Left

On 9 September 2007, the CPI (M) authored an open letter to all parties outlining the implications of the Hyde Act as the members of its Politburo saw it. In the main, the note emphasised that the nuclear deal 'should not be seen in isolation from the overall context of Indo-US strategic relations'. This, it stressed, included the 'impact' on India's 'foreign policy and our strategic autonomy'.[156] In a Joint Statement, all four left parties argued that the deal would 'entangle India' in a 'complex web' of 'relationships' determined by the US. Reinforcing what might be considered the dogmatic views of those on the left, Prakash Karat, the general secretary of the CPI (M) similarly argued that the deal, as he was to put it, drew India into a 'strategic alliance with the US'. From the outset, Karat made it unambiguously clear that taking the deal forward would invite 'heavy political consequences'.[157] As another journalist closely following the story argued, this was a 'basic issue' for the left.[158] Karat knew that the UPA was 'running', as he often stressed, 'on [the] Left's critical support'.[159] Further, and unlike the BJP, discussed below, the left's position might have been considered irritatingly—at least for officials—unbinding but consistent.

For the most part, all four left parties peddled and shared an almost identical outlook. A.B. Bardhan, general secretary of the Communist Party of India (CPI), categorically stated that 'the US has no business in our country'.[160] Abani Roy, a leader in the Revolutionary Socialist Party (RSP), demanded that the left immediately review their ties with the Congress.[161] The Forward Bloc, with three seats, also agreed.[162] Even Sitaram Yechury, long considered a moderate leftist, argued that the deal would make India a 'subordinate ally of the US'. By and large, the narrative was informed by the popular language of 'anti-imperialism'.[163] As outdated as such ideas might have seemed to elites in both the Prime Minister's Office (PMO) and in Washington, the fact was that these parties held fifty-nine critical seats. The Congress-led UPA, without these fifty-nine seats, would be left with 219 of their own. They desperately needed the left to continue to enjoy the confidence of the Lok Sabha and to maintain 272 seats, a number guaranteeing a majority in the House.[164] Further, and apart from the issues associated with electoral numbers and entrenched creeds, the left highlighted a seemingly crucial point. In a letter to the Congress dated 14 September 2007, it made clear that in the event of a clash between the substance of the 123 Agreement and the Hyde Act, the latter would prevail.[165] Indeed, the Hyde Act, and specifically Section 102 (Clause 6), pointed out that India was not to follow a 'foreign policy that is incongruent to that of the United States'.[166] That this act was US domestic law, and hence, as the prime minister repeatedly claimed, was 'not binding on us just like our laws are not binding on them [the US]' was rejected outright by the left.[167]

In the following few months, the CPI (M)-led objections became more pronounced. The deal was quickly brandished the 'brainchild of the BJP', removing any opportunity for speculation that the left agreed with the right. At the end of November, the CPI (M) stated that the 123 Agreement did not assure 'uninterrupted fuel supplies' in the event of India testing a nuclear weapon in the future.[168] This was an odd claim, given that the left had historically opposed nuclear tests. A nine-hour-long debate in the Rajya Sabha, or the Upper House, did little to satisfy leaders like Yechury.[169] A left–UPA Coordination Committee convened by Mukherjee and made up of nine Congress and non-Communist UPA allies on one side and six representatives from the left including Karat and Yechury on the other was constituted in September to negotiate an agreement.[170] It met eight times between September 2007 and June 2008.[171] The last meeting, scheduled for 18 June 2008, was cancelled. The prime minister reportedly saw little reason to bargain with those who were intent in their approach.[172] Finally, and despite Mukherjee's optimism—he was 'hopeful of sorting out this issue', as he often argued[173]—the left pulled its fifty-nine seats from the UPA. However, the loss in seats was almost immediately replaced by the Samajwadi Party (SP), which had thirty-nine seats of its own. Indeed, the Congress had had the SP in its 'pocket', as one headline asserted, at least a week before the left withdrew its support.[174]

That Amar Singh, a senior SP leader who once equated 'nuclear fundamentalism', as he called the deal, to 'religious fundamentalism',[175] a jab at the communal politics his party firmly stood against, mattered little. The SP had earlier even gone public in its support for the left, assuming the latter's strategic language in their seething criticism of the US. 'It is the powerful corporate lobby of USA,' Amar Singh argued, 'which is behind the nuclear deal, not the interests of the country.'[176] Clearly, and as one editorial stressed, the 'tentative demeanour' of the prime minister notwithstanding, his 'steely resolve' was soon obvious to all. Entering into an alliance with one-time critics and detractors was hardly considered unusual for a prime minister who was widely believed to have invested incredible 'personal capital', as one Congress minister argued, in a deal he believed in.[177] Much like Viscount Palmerston, the nineteenth-century British prime minister who emphasised the importance of interests over relationships in politics, and in an obvious defence of allying with a party that until recently had stood against both the Congress and the deal, Manmohan Singh pithily stated: 'In politics, there are no permanent foes.' An agreement was imperative, he argued, if India was not to be seen as an 'unreliable partner'.[178] In sum, the prime minister, as one Congress insider told journalists, was simply 'unmoved by the Left's objections'.[179] This was the all-important context forcing backroom deals to keep the Congress comfortably afloat, and in a position, at least as far as Manmohan Singh was seemingly concerned, to complete the deal. With the SP by its side, the newly constituted Congress-led UPA won a motion of confidence in the Lok Sabha with a slim majority.[180] Singh and his team were free to conclude two separate agreements with the IAEA and the NSG.

A Shifty Right

The BJP's position was ambiguous from the start. In July 2007, the party argued against the deal in its entirety. In September, party leaders suggested that the deal needed to be 'scrapped'. According to them, it restricted India's strategic nuclear programme.[181] Further, and to protect India from the Hyde Act, Advani, then the leader of the opposition, suggested amending the Indian Atomic Energy Act.[182] The Hyde Act, his party argued at the end of October, would trump the 123 Agreement and lead to the eventual collapse of the deal.[183] In December, Yashwant

Sinha, making no mention of the Hyde Act, argued that 'the main issue is credible minimum deterrent', which, the former foreign minister suggested, 'the government does not understand'. Somewhat less believably, Sinha also stated that 'if we [BJP] come to power,' which, it failed to do in the 2009 General Assembly elections, 'we will renegotiate the deal'.[184] In Parliament, Advani claimed that the Congress had 'surrendered' to the US. By entering this deal, the 'government', he asserted, 'is willing to give in writing that it will never do a third Pokhran'.[185]

In the end, the party's position was less convincing and largely inarticulate. Its 'obstructionist attitude' in Parliament, as Sonia Gandhi— the Congress chairperson—argued, was evident in the BJP-led and staged walk-outs from the Lok Sabha, making it all the more difficult to delineate the merits of the opposition's key arguments.[186] In total and as the then Speaker of the Lok Sabha calculated, 423 hours or 24 per cent of the House's legislative time was wasted because of 'disruptions and adjournments' between 2004 and 2009.[187] Obviously irritated by this, a scathing editorial in the *Times of India* argued that 'The BJP doesn't have any real case against the nuclear deal.' 'Let's not,' the piece continued, 'allow it to be derailed.'[188] Talbott, who dealt closely with the BJP and specifically Jaswant Singh, was clearly unimpressed by the BJP's less than sure-footed approach, and told the *Indian Express* that if the Clinton administration offered 'half of' what 'Bush was willing to make with Manmohan Singh', the Vajpayee government 'would have gone for it'. I 'can't understand', the former deputy secretary of state argued, how the 'BJP could oppose the deal as it obviously does'.[189]

Indeed, in an effort to reach out to the nationalists, Ambassador Mulford called on BJP leaders like Advani and Yashwant Sinha soon after the deal was placed on hold.[190] Kissinger, who was in India to help promote the deal, was also invited to speak to the BJP's top brass.[191] The BJP, it would seem, was seeking to score political points which it believed had traction with the public. Yet the few polls conducted at the time provided contradictory and often confusing conclusions. In August, one poll revealed that 96 per cent of the 'public', or at least those included and considered in representative samples, thought that the deal was in India's interest.[192]

A month later, and following the first UPA–left coordination meeting, a much larger survey concluded that 63 per cent of 'urban voters' supported the deal, but 51 per cent argued that the government ought not go ahead without the left's support; 70 per cent urged against working too closely with the Bush administration. At the same time, 44 per cent endorsed the tough stance taken by the Congress against the left. Importantly, 58 per cent stated that the prime minister could have handled the crisis better.[193] The latter point was crucial, and something that officials in the MEA also thought needed greater attention.[194] In the end, and as both Mishra and Natwar Singh argued in the testing days following the release of the 123 Agreement, the deal would prove less important in the actual elections.[195]

Their predictions were proved right. In the 2009 General Assembly elections, the Congress won a total of 209 seats, sixty-eight more than it had secured in 2004. The BJP won 116 seats, eighteen less than what it had before the polls. The four left parties together managed twenty-four, a staggering thirty-five seats less than had been the case only five years previously.[196] This is not to suggest that the elections in 2009 in anyway validate the merits of the nuclear agreement. As officials involved in the negotiations suggested, the deal was a 'non-issue'.[197] In fact, that domestic politics seldom shape electoral outcomes is a point underscored in the limited academic works on internal politics and Indian foreign policy more broadly. At the time, and as far as Mishra was concerned, the merits and demerits of actual negotiation points needed to be 'spelt out',[198] not for electoral reasons but to better understand a game-changing agreement. These points of negotiations, as outlined below, considered the opposition's concerns well before the latter had sight of the agreement. They hardly, as one sceptic put it, 'mortgaged' India's 'nuclear crown jewels'.[199]

Three central points of negotiation might be kept in mind when reading or following the criticisms put forward by both the left and the right. These 'negotiating points', as one official argued, were 'hardly straightforward'.[200] Indeed, they required a degree of give and take. After all, India was negotiating for something unheard of and largely unconsidered until Bush's second term in office. The push-and-pull tension between what Indian envoys were mandated by the prime minister to accept and what American negotiators wanted India to accept was revealing to say the least. It unmistakably exposes the complexities of dealing with elites mindful of the need for a nuclear agreement but not if it meant surrendering India's ability to determine its future.

Back to Separation

First, the separation of India's nuclear reactors into those labelled for civilian and military use was, as one official argued, itself a 'major concession'. Moreover, it would be a 'costly affair'.[201] Dividing reactors, or making sure that resources and material used for civilian purposes are restricted from military or strategic objectives, was bound to affect the full potential of a so-far undivided nuclear establishment. Commentators also made this clear.[202] In fact, on this point, Tellis argued that the Separation Plan, while no doubt a primarily 'Indian' scheme, *did* strengthen non-proliferation efforts.[203] Yet, as Indian officials recognised, the separation agreement was essential. In fact, in early 2005 the British Foreign Office had told J.N. Dixit—the national security advisor prior to Narayanan—that such a plan, much like India's space programme, would need to be divided. This was the only way India was going to receive the concessions it demanded from the IAEA and the NSG, given its unique position as a state with nuclear weapons that was outside the NPT.[204]

A note tabled in the Indian Parliament on 11 May 2006 made it clear that the 'overarching criterion' of placing reactors in the civilian category 'would be a judgement' taken by the government of India and the DAE. The central measure of 'subjecting a facility to IAEA safeguards', the note underlined, would depend on the relative and perceived impact it may have on 'India's national security.' A 'civilian facility,' it argued, would be 'one that India has determined not to be relevant to its strategic programme'.[205] This was of course the definition provided by Manmohan Singh from the outset and—as detailed earlier—painstakingly negotiated into the Joint Statement and later the Separation Agreement by Saran, Narayanan, Sen, Grover and Kakodkar. The latter reiterated India's position in the press once the note was read in Parliament. He clearly stated that India, and not the US, would decide which facilities would be branded as civilian and military. The process of identification would be 'determined at different points in time' in a 'phased manner'—as again negotiated by Saran and his team—keeping India's national security needs in mind.[206] Importantly, Burns and his advisors pushed hard to separate not only material but also human resources. Personnel were to be strictly divided between those allowed into civilian and military facilities. For the Indian team, as one insider argued, 'This was a deal breaker.' The DAE, the national security advisor and the

MEA were unanimously opposed to this. Burns and Tellis were clearly told that if the question of personnel was pursued, India would walk away from the agreement. In the end, and because of India's unbending position, Burns eventually relented by allowing personnel to shift between facilities without restrictions.[207]

In Washington, anti-deal campaigners vociferously argued that the Separation Agreement was a 'minimalist plan'.[208] The fact that India could choose which facilities would be placed under international safeguards and in a 'phased manner' was balked at. Labelling it a 'bomb-friendly' deal,[209] for Washington's non-proliferation lobby, the separation plan 'sold out core American non-proliferation values and positions'. 'By opening up the spigot for foreign nuclear fuel supplies to India,' argued the Arms Control Association, the deal allowed India to use its domestic reserve of uranium for the sole purpose of arms production.[210] With this in mind, such lobbies made a case to at least place India's prototype Fast Breeder reactor—capable of producing greater amounts of fissile material than it consumes—and future reactors under international safeguards. Indeed, and according to negotiators, 'a fair bit of pressure' was put on the Indians to accept this.[211] Yet, and while the Indian team accepted that fuel for such reactors would be placed under safeguards as they were to be imported, the reactors themselves were not safeguarded. In addition, according to the implementation plan, all future reactors, whether they are thermal power or Fast Breeder reactors would be labelled either civilian or military by the government of India. This remained the latter's 'sole right', a point negotiated and included in the 11 May note to Parliament.[212]

Further, lobbyists on the outside and lawyers working with Burns on the inside pushed Saran and his team to place more than the eventual figure of fourteen of India's twenty-two reactors under inspections. The more the better, was the argument seemingly pursued by American interlocutors. The then Indian foreign secretary and especially the DAE resisted. In the end, and just as Bush landed in New Delhi in March 2006, the president, according to a State Department official, told his envoys: 'This is not a matter of two or four reactors, I'm not going to hold up the deal because of this: get it done.' Clearly, according to this insider, Bush saw the deal 'from day one as a strategic whole picture'— the technical details were not of central concern. What also helped was that Rice was able to 'change' the 'weight' of the argument in the State Department away from the 'techies'.[213]

Treaty Obligations

Second, the least Burns could do, detractors in Washington argued, was to ensure that India put an end to fissile material production and sign the FMCT. Indeed, throughout the discussions on the Separation Plan and the 123 Agreement, Indian negotiators made clear that this was 'impossible'.[214] New Delhi would 'work with the United States' to help conclude an FMCT,[215] but, as mentioned above, it would take no responsibility for initiating treaty obligations without American support. Further, while the Americans tried hard to get India to state explicitly that it would 'not stand in the way of the CTBT', as one negotiator put it,[216] India made it clear that this was a no-go area. This was crucial. Despite American attempts to pull India closer and closer into the so-called non-proliferation vortex, and in spite of the allegations made by the BJP suggesting the same, the Indian team left no room for ambiguity whatsoever. Nothing was left to chance when it came to treaty obligations. There is no mention of the CTBT in official documentation including in the 123 Agreement. In the end and notwithstanding that the Bush administration had taken 'a game-changing step', as Krepon put it, 'not playing at the margins, but getting in there and shifting a lot of pieces on the [non-proliferation] table',[217] the Indian team were determined to avoid 'non-proliferation traps'. After all, they were continually watchful of the sharp political debates within India.[218]

That the agreement was 'so controversial from the word go',[219] as a Washington-based South Asia watcher argued, mattered little to a small group of Indian officials willing only to agree to what the prime minister would accept back in New Delhi. So forceful were Indian demands that Burns was compelled to admit publicly that 'India will continue, obviously, with its strategic programme. The agreement [the separation plan],' he argued, 'will not have an impact on that strategic programme.'[220] Robert Joseph, the US undersecretary of state for arms control and international security, even warned the Senate Foreign Relations Committee that demands to get India to cease fissile material production would be 'deal breakers'.[221] Similarly, Rice made plain to the Senate that the White House 'didn't set out to constrain the [Indian] strategic programme in this agreement'.[222] For his part, Saran bluntly maintained to the American press that the Separation Agreement 'emerged from exceedingly complex and tough negotiations' and the result was a 'very, very delicate state of balance'. 'Now,' he continued, 'if you start making revisions and changes, that balance is likely to be off-set.'[223] Ultimately, neither the Senate nor the House supported amending the Separation Plan to limit India's fissile production capabilities, in spite of the fact that the five NPT-recognised nuclear weapons states have all suspended the production of fissile material. Pointedly, Krepon noted that the deal avoided the choice in India 'between electricity and bombs',[224] a choice made by 183 NPT member states who had followed the so-called rules of the 'N' game.

Testing and Reserves

The third crucial issue had to do with the question of nuclear testing. At different points of time, both the left and the right in India insisted that India's nuclear deterrent, or ability to test weapons in the future, was limited. Various parts of the Hyde Act strongly suggest that nuclear testing was out of the question. Section 103 (E 5) states that the US should 'seek to halt the increase of nuclear weapons arsenals in South Asia', promoting their 'reduction and eventual elimination'. Section 104 (5 G) makes clear that the US president is to report any 'significant changes in the production by India of nuclear weapons'. Section 104 (3 B) strongly makes the case that cooperation with India would be terminated if India resumed nuclear testing.[225] Yet, and notwithstanding the somewhat prescriptive wording of the Hyde Act, three points need to be kept in mind. Indeed, it is these that purportedly convinced both Manmohan Singh and Indian negotiators of the fact that while future testing would no doubt lead to unwelcome consequences, it could not be deemed illegal. Further, and according to the 123 Agreement, no American administration could—at least according to the carefully negotiated technical language in the agreement—cut off all supplies to India following nuclear tests.

First, the Hyde Act was US domestic law. It had 'no bearing on India at all', as Indian negotiators saw it. Indeed, as far as the PMO was concerned, and according to officials, while the prime minister and the national security advisor 'did not like the legislation', they were convinced that it could not be used by American legislators to push or shape India's approach to international affairs. Further, the act allowed the executive branch to cooperate with India even though India was a non-NPT signatory. It clearly acknowledged that India's strategic programme

246

was off-limits, and made provisions for unconditional waivers to cooperate with India.[226] Second, in a legal battle, Indian officials were clear that the 123 Agreement, and not the Hyde Act, would prevail. Hence, notwithstanding the left's critique, this was hardly a case of tying India into the 'NPT through the backdoor', as a CPI (M) spokesperson put it.[227] International lawyers with extensive experience authoring 123 agreements also argued that the latter almost always superseded US domestic law; for these lawyers, the '123 agreement is the law of the land'. In the case of India, the 123 Agreement would clearly 'override any inconsistencies it might have with the Hyde Act'. Anti-deal lobbyists agreed.[228]

Lastly, while most 123 agreements make provisions for the return of technologies or the call for an 'automatic trigger to cease cooperation' in the event of a nuclear test, in the agreement with India, the word 'test' is not once mentioned in the sixteen-page agreement.[229] This was, as an insider put it, watchfully avoided. Burns, the said official argued, was intent on 'including at least a few lines on testing'. The Indian side were adamant. 'Testing,' as they saw it, had no place in a 'legal and binding document'.[230] The idea was to incorporate ambiguous language that could be used to each side's advantage. Hence Article 14—dealing with the 'termination and cessation of cooperation'—stated that 'Parties' would consider the other's 'concern about a changed security environment' prior to terminating the agreement.[231] This could of course mean any number of things, presumably including motivations underlying the need to test nuclear weapons.

Further, according to Articles 2 (2 e), 5 (6 iii) and 5 (6 b IV) of the 123 Agreement, the US would help India develop a 'strategic reserve of nuclear fuel to guard against any disruption of supply over the life time of India's reactors'. If disruptions were to occur, Washington was legally required to 'convene a group of friendly supplier countries' like Russia, France and the UK to 'pursue such measures as would restore fuel supply to India'.[232] In short, as US Congressman Edward Markey argued, the agreement 'was nuclear capitulation to India's every wish'.[233] In the case of India, and as American negotiators quickly learnt, the reality was that 'the harder we [Americans] push: the lesser we get'. There was no doubt in any American negotiator's mind that their counterparts not only knew what they wanted—an almost restriction-free waiver in nuclear commerce—but that they were also willing to walk if they did not get it.[234] India may have changed, her interlocutors may have emerged as the early captains in the times of transformation and engagement, but the idea of autonomy stood firm in the granular matter of negotiations.

In Vienna

Having embedded the above-mentioned negotiated points in legal documents, and with a narrow trust vote to the Congress-led UPA's favour, Indian representatives travelled to the IAEA and then the NSG. An India-specific facilities agreement with the former and a waiver from the latter were not only essential to conclude the bilateral arrangement with the Bush administration but also, crucially, to enable international nuclear commerce with NSG member states. In the case of Washington, the administration was desperately keen to conclude an agreement, which it was thought the Obama administration, elected in November 2008, would 'scuttle' in the event of it being delayed. Indeed, as an old India hand in Washington put it, 'if you leave it to the Democrats, then they are going to keep losing the files'.[235] With the sense of urgency in mind, Kakodkar negotiated an agreement between India and the IAEA Board of Governors on 7 July 2008.[236]

Kakodkar and his team from the DAE had in fact begun negotiating in Vienna and with the IAEA—a 144-nation organisation—as early as September 2007.[237] In October, Mohamed ElBaradei, the Cairo-born IAEA director general, visited New Delhi. Otherwise dismayed by the Bush administration and absolutely convinced that Iraq was a 'needless war', ElBaradei had no hesitation in accepting and even endorsing the imperatives underlying the nuclear deal with India. As he put it, 'I viewed the agreement as a win–win situation, good for development and good for arms control.'[238] In New Delhi, ElBaradei reportedly made clear to Narayanan and the prime minister that he favoured the deal.[239] In the final meetings in July 2008, Indian exceptionalism was once again obvious. Unusually for the IAEA, the safeguards agreement with India underscored that in the event of termination—because of nuclear weapons testing, for example—India would be allowed to take 'corrective measures' to 'ensure uninterrupted operation of civilian nuclear reactors'.[240]

As Grover told the Indian press, such measures might be described as 'unspecified sovereign actions'. Further, safeguards would be considered valid only so long as fuel supplies from abroad were uninterrupted.[241] While states like Austria, Ireland and Switzerland were said to 'barely disguise their unhappiness' with an agreement they all found distasteful, India got its way.[242] A unanimous decision to enter into agreement with India was signed. Suspicious that the deal may falter in the US Congress prior to the final sign-off by Bush, India would sign the agreed documents with the IAEA following the full passage of the US–India nuclear deal. The twenty-three-page piece of international legislation was finally entered into force on 11 May 2009.

At the NSG

On 6 September 2008, the NSG approved what came to be called a 'clean waiver' allowing India to enter into nuclear-related trade and commerce with all forty-six members of the consensus-based organisation. Critically, and while the process of considering such a waiver was clearly prompted by, and because of, the entrepreneurship on the part of Washington and New Delhi, the waiver permitted India to deal with any NSG member state. As Manmohan Singh repeatedly told critics and the political opposition in the Indian Parliament, it 'marks the end of India's decades-long isolation from the nuclear mainstream and of the technology denial regime'.[243] In fact, only days after the NSG waiver, India signed its first nuclear agreement with France, and this before the US–India deal was finally passed by the US Congress.[244] On 6 December, India signed a 'mega uranium' deal with Russia.[245]

Yet, and these bilateral agreements notwithstanding, getting to this point was anything but simple. Along with American support, Menon—with Saran sitting-in on the meetings but not always leading them—set out to convince member states, which otherwise followed the same 'non-proliferation straight jacket' Clinton was said to champion in the 1990s. As Siddharth Varadarajan—an Indian journalist who followed the latter period of negotiations more closely than any of his contemporaries—argued, the fact was that the first session of the NSG did nothing for India. 'The session,' Varadarajan wrote, 'degenerated into a free-for-all with amendments and suggestions flowing thick and fast.'[246] Most of these sought to constrain India's strategic programme. After all, India was to be allowed an exception that was not available to other states: a guarantee to trade with the NSG without signing the NPT.

Making a case for India in Vienna required delicate diplomacy with the premiers of at least twenty seeming detractors, and personal interventions on the part of Singh, Bush and senior Indian diplomats. The Bush administration was even said to have 'rubbished its conservative credentials by strong-arming' member states.[247] Those that required further persuasion were individually contacted by Indian representatives. Crucially, according to NSG protocols, a decision needed to be unanimous. Hence, in practice, New Zealand's or Mexico's votes counted as much as those of the United Kingdom or Canada.

Among those that required personal interventions were Brazil, where Manmohan Singh spoke directly with President Lula da Silva, and Argentina, where Indian officials working with their counterparts from Buenos Aires at the UN in Geneva were able to use their personal accord. Bush spoke directly with the premiers in New Zealand, Australia and Sweden. MEA officials 'worked' Switzerland and the Netherlands. The latter seemed satisfied following an orchestrated statement by the Indian foreign minister outlining that India fervently stood for nuclear disarmament. In all, Indian and American elites battled-off some fifty amendments attached by the above-mentioned nations to the NSG waiver. Only China held back its support until the very end. The 'game' for Beijing, as one insider argued, was not to be seen as the sole opposition. The Chinese delegation communicated their intention to vote in favour of the waiver at the last minute and directly to the Indian team in Vienna.[248]

In the end, in each and every case, India managed to move the nations in question without giving in to non-proliferation demands. These included avoiding signing the FMCT, the NPT or placing all its reactors under safeguards, a point disparagingly highlighted by advocates of non-proliferation in Washington.[249] As Krepon noted, the 'NSG even declined to clarify penalties in the event of a resumption of nuclear testing by India.'[250] As the discussion above demonstrates, the rules of nuclear commerce were tailored to suit India's interests. India today is the only non-NPT state with nuclear weapons that produces fissile material, has an active nuclear weapons programme and can still trade with the NSG.

Conclusion

Following the completion of the deal, the late K. Subramanyam—the 'doyen' of India's strategic fraternity[251]—made clear to detractors in

New Delhi that rather than curtailing India's nuclear sovereignty, the deal and the NSG waiver in fact made India less vulnerable. Mishra, someone once less convinced about the merits of the 123 Agreement, had become a 'great advocate of the deal' by the time the IAEA had approved the safeguards agreement.[252] After all, India could now engage more of the world on a wider array of subjects without having to worry about a nuclear 'barn' constructed by those states once on the more advantageous side of 'nuclear apartheid', a regime that was unravelled to make way for a determinant but watchful India. On 10 October 2008, moments before the nuclear deal was finally signed by Rice and Mukherjee, the secretary of state could honestly argue that rather than an end to a long-fought process, the 'most valuable' aspect of this agreement, as she put it, 'is how it unlocks a new and far broader world of potential' for India and America.[253] That the agreement and the process of negotiating with future partners altered one of the definitive bilateral relationships in the twenty-first century is beyond doubt. At the same time, that this relationship, like any association between two ever-growing democracies, would be almost necessarily riddled with contradictions and disagreements was soon apparent to those invested in the task of changing India.

In the immediate aftermath of the deal, disagreements rose when Rice pushed the NSG to renege on the transfer of ENR or 'enrichment and reprocessing technology and equipment' to India. Hence the so-called 'clean waiver' provided to India did not look as 'clean' as Indian counterparts had hoped, and proved a matter of concern and considerable irritation for Indian envoys.[254] On the other hand, as far as American companies and Congress were concerned, the Indian government's unwillingness to adhere to liability laws that often suit the supplier—or American firms wanting to sell reactor technology to India—has made it all the more difficult to implement an agreement signed only in principle.[255] There is no doubt that the above-mentioned points require a great deal of introspection. Yet the latter issues notwithstanding, it is important to note that game-changing measures and trade at this scale take time to absorb. It in no way takes away from the fact that nuclear commerce is a possibility today and in the future, an option that was simply non-existent for India between 1974 and 2008.

Further and perhaps much more importantly than the agreement at hand, the negotiations were vital for at least two less visible reasons.

First, as Shyam Saran put it, 'It exposed India and officials to something unlike anything in the past.' The negotiations, the former foreign secretary argued, 'were an experience in themselves', allowing a careful look at what far-reaching and international negotiations might look like. After all, as India seeks to find a place for itself in a whole range of international regimes and structures, the practice of such negotiations will surely be paramount. Second, this particular exercise—both with the US and in Vienna—made it clear that while this was a nation convinced of the imperatives underlying engagement and change, it eloquently and necessarily struggles to maintain an extreme and even irritatingly—for American officials like Rice—sacrosanct understanding of independence obvious in each and every round of negotiations in New Delhi, Washington and Vienna. Not even a nuclear deal could hustle its negotiators or the prime minister of the day into accepting anything even vaguely resembling restrictions to its sovereignty. This is, of course, not to say that New Delhi will resist making decisions that suit the political needs of the hour at the calculated cost of India's general drift in international politics. An Indian vote in 2005 against Iran at the IAEA, for example, was without doubt associated, at least at some level, with the objective of not wanting to further alienate already mistrustful Congressional elites in Washington.[256]

Indeed, the idea of non-alignment, as articulated by Nehru and interpreted in this book, may not have informed Saran, Menon, Sen, Grover, Kakokdar, Narayanan, Natwar Singh, Pranab Mukherjee and Manmohan Singh's approach, but there is nothing to say that the cerebral strands that once shaped non-alignment had simply disappeared. Non-alignment was and continues to be as much about ideas as interests. The material need for a deal did not in any way undermine the efficacy of uncompromising autonomy from what scholars erroneously—and as mentioned earlier in this book—casually label 'pragmatism'. India's so-called 'pragmatism', if one prefers, was premised on a set of beliefs that only mesh further with the needs of the present rather than disappear into the abyss of the past. Indeed, that such an approach was palpable in the years following the deal is briefly outlined in the conclusion to this book, which looks at the policies and prerogatives conceived by the new Democratic administration in Washington.

CONCLUSION

Ending Nonalignment?

An article in the March 2013 edition of *The Economist* magazine argued that 'India needs to give up its outdated philosophy of non-alignment.' Frustrated by what the article refers to as a 'modest power', it assertively advocated that India join 'Western-backed security alliances.' Doing so, its authors suggest, would introduce India to the rank and file of 'great powers'.[1] Other commentators and scholars have similarly advocated the end of non-alignment. The mere use of the term serves to excite a wide range of detractors. A 2012 strategy document on Indian foreign policy, titled 'nonalignment 2.0', invited scathing criticism.[2] What appeared to grate the reviewers most was the fact that the document paid little attention to the US. How could any outline of India's future not consider allying with the US? Moreover, why non-alignment, a label that continues to be read as one rooted in 'post-independence creeds of semi-pacifism'?[3]

Yet the fact that non-alignment lives on within India—or at least that part of India engaged in international affairs—cannot be ignored. Abandoning non-alignment is akin to separating the mind from the soul. It is impossible. Wishing for its deletion from popular discourse and official lexicon is futile. The idea of non-alignment is necessarily entrenched in the vocabulary of India's past, present and future. But this does not mean that non-alignment is inevitably anti-Western or anti-American. This book has sought to revise this less-tested term. It has done so by tracing and examining the practice of Indian foreign policy—and the changes therein—in a series of crises where Indian and American officials play the role of protagonists.

Its findings in part revise the diplomatic and contemporary history of Indian–US relations and Indian foreign policy more generally. Three principal conclusions are outlined below. Further, I sketch-out some necessarily untested observations about the future of India's relationship with the US. Crucially, these democracies have come to represent two opposing but necessary sets of arguments that in turn promise to further shape the system of international relations in an ever more associated world of so-called 'rising' and risen powers.

Conclusions

First, India's relationship with the US has been the most comprehensive association the country has had since independence. Indeed, as this book finds, the more popular reading of the relations between these two democracies is erroneously described as inherently fractious and necessarily in conflict. Marred by disagreements, vastly different approaches to international affairs and the less-than charitable view of the other held by principals and officials—most notably Nixon's view of Mrs Gandhi and Nehru's perception of Eisenhower—has given rise to an entire body of literature that treats the India–US relationship as one characterised by mutual 'estrangement'. The so-called 'transformation' in US–Indian relations, commentators contend, took place only after the collapse of the Soviet Union. To some extent, the dissolution of the USSR provides a clear and obvious marker for scholars and writers. After all, it brought an end to bipolarity, leaving India—according to this line of argument—with little choice other than to reach-out and engage America: the sole superpower to have survived the Cold War. The road to *ninda*, as examined in Chapter 7, bears-out the early attempts at renegotiating a relationship that is said to have been in a state of decline for much of the time that the Iron Curtain was drawn closed.

Nonetheless, the invocation of *ninda* on the floor of the Lok Sabha and later the strategic agreements reached between India and the US—as discussed in Chapter 8—were not solely the product of initiatives launched in the 1990s or the early 2000s. In fact, as this book argues, these were only made possible because India and the US had long engaged each other in a series of crises that gradually forged a deeper sense for each other's motivations and aspirations. This is truly a relationship forged in crisis. The first fifty years—as detailed in Part I and II of this book—were hardly a period of time that was lost to two countries that were eventually destined to find common ground. The lengthy series of arbitrations leading to the nuclear deal in 2008 serve as a clear example of how officials on both sides managed to remain sure-footed but resilient. This resilience was not assembled in a decade or two. It rested on the successes and failures of the past sixty years, programming a degree of trust and a sense for each other into a relationship that was in fact considerably more cooperative than otherwise believed. This is as true of the Nehru years as it is of Mrs Gandhi's early years as prime minister. Neither Nehru nor his daughter was anti-American. If anything, as made clear in Part I of this book, India's first prime minister was excited about the idea of America. Much was simply lost in translation between Nehru's less than palpable thinking on America, and what American envoys and officials considered to be the prime minister's tough and even impossible position on a variety of issues. Difference and opposition were misunderstood as manifestations of anti-Americanism, a term that has little intelligible meaning. That Nehru rejected an offer by Eisenhower to enter into a series of international alliances or refused to be pressured by Kennedy administration officials into negotiating away parts of J–K should not take away from the fact that a conversation was underway. This exchange, as mentioned in the first chapter, began well before independence and is continuing today.

There was no time in Nehru's seventeen years as prime minister when he or others in his Cabinet chose to ignore or end a discussion with American counterparts. Krishna Menon might have been seen to represent the 'symbol of anti-Americanism'—as Kennedy once told his envoy John Galbraith—but this did not mean that the broader relationship was foundering. In fact, as outlined in Chapter 3, even the likes of Dulles—known for his irritation with the very term non-alignment—came to respect Menon's politicking at the UN and the contribution India made to ending the war on the Korean Peninsula. Similarly, Eisenhower may have offered Patton Tanks and Sabre-class jets to Pakistan, but this did not cause India to abandon the process of improving its relations with the US. For his part, Eisenhower soon came to admire India, a country whose elite citizenry he once referred to as 'funny people' whom he did not think he could trust.

In sum, this book offers a critical corrective on Nehru and India's approach to the US during and after the Cold War. It remedies the staid and somewhat untested reading of a relationship that for too long has suffered from uncritical labelling and unsubstantiated conclusions. Importantly, it has sought to tell a series of stories relying not only on American and British archives and sources, but also on those available in India. To some extent, the book has sought to produce the first 'Indian' reading of a relationship historically trapped in the worldviews and impressions held by American protagonists that have been so far recorded in a single source collection: that of American papers and records.

Second, this book breaks away from the simplistic analytical dichotomy of explaining India's motivations as a product of either ideas *or* interests. As discussed in the introduction to each chapter, for the most part, scholars and commentators read non-alignment—in its various guises—as either a creation informed by India's memory of colonial rule or as an approach predesigned to strike unobvious alliances. In the case of the former, non-dependence is given primacy because of an apparent desire to remain uncompromisingly free. Idealism is said to have moved or informed India's approach to the world. Nehru's exciting rhetoric during his first two terms as prime minister did much to contribute to such interpretations. The latter school of thought, on the other hand, speaks to India's Machiavellian schemes of forging an alliance-like relationship with either one of two superpowers. Nehru is portrayed as an undeclared realist. Non-alignment and the ambiguous language surrounding independence, autonomy and sovereignty, was, according to this line of thought, nothing more than a disguise to strengthen external partnerships with the view to ensure economic and military assistance.

The central problem with both schools of thought is an obvious one: they tell us only one part of the story of India and its approach to the world. In most cases, such selective recounting does little more than express the biases inherent in those drawn to either ideas *or* interests. Such unsophisticated analyses, empirically substantive though they often are, frequently lose sight of nuance. Admittedly, the chosen approach of explaining behaviour by way of multi-causality—where ideas *and* interests matter—might not satisfy theoreticians. But this book is not about theory-building. In fact, too much theory has the potential to kill the appetite for new knowledge, or hitherto unexplored explanations.[4] This book has thus sought to adopt a novel approach, rather than one based purely on expediency, in identifying how ideas about statehood intersected with the need for material power, or capabilities.

CONCLUSION

As Chapters 1 and 2 show, both the edifice and practice of non-alignment was intended to seek-out material needs—such as economic and military assistance—while at the same time ensuring that India remained free to pursue its own foreign policy goals. The key lay in negotiating the tension between the idea of autonomy and the need to survive and remain autonomous. As with the case of food aid in the mid-1950s and the more complex issue of military assistance in the early 1960s, Indian leaders well understood the need for give and take.

This is not to say that Indian leaders followed a doctrine situated between a chosen set of ideas and predetermined interests. It is instead to make the point that non-alignment itself was a layered and highly introspective conception. It made allowances for ensuring non-dependence while carving a distinct persona for a nation unimpressed by the somewhat dogmatic ideological policies underpinning containment during the Cold War. Both material and ideational drivers shaped an approach that took the relationship with the US more seriously than any other. India got the assistance it needed when it could—like in the late 1940s, in 1963 following defeat against the PRC and later in the twenty-first century when it entered into a major nuclear agreement with both the US and the NSG. India adjusted and amended its approach—such as during the Korean crisis—when it was considered vital to do so. Most importantly, Indian leaders were able to say no—as was the case in 2003 when India considered sending troops to Iraq—when it did not suit its security objectives. In most cases, India made decisions based on well-thought-out considerations—at least as far as the crises at hand would allow—without resorting to blatant anti-Americanism.

A difference in approach did not mean turning away from dialogue, but instead to engage American officials in a way that was designed to articulate India's rationale for opposing US policy. Such an approach as well as the changes therein—from non-alignment to engagement—simply means that the tension between the need to engage with the world and the desire to remain free from alliances has grown stronger. In short, as this book suggests, much like the impossible task of separating India from non-alignment, it is equally impossible to divide ideas and interests.

Third, that India's approach to international affairs is not scripted in a written document frustrates commentators and scholars as much as the invocation of non-alignment in the twenty-first century. India's so-called obsession with 'utopianism' rather than prudent decision-making and the unscripted nature of India's approach appears to have pushed some scholars to call India's very approach to foreign policy into question. In fact, this is exactly the sort of loose, un-interrogated and dubious myth-making—around both Nehru and non-alignment—that appears to have inspired the empirically untested scholarship on Indian foreign policy in more recent times. With little or no evidence, commentators conclude that 'an intellectual vacuum' has allowed Indian foreign policy 'to drift without any sense of direction'. India, according to this line of argument, 'has little to offer except some platitudinous rhetoric that does great disservice to its stature'.[5] Indeed, such claims are commonplace in the study of Indian strategic history and analysis.[6]

Some scholars have focused on ideational aspects of behaviour in relation to India's varied political landscape, attributing behavioural characteristics in accordance with particular streams of political contemplation.[7] Others have chosen to offer more generalist accounts of India's apparent inability to think carefully about strategy. Analysts point to the timeless characteristics of Hinduism,[8] the lack of political energy to think carefully about strategic affairs[9] and the absence of a tradition of historical recording that makes it all that harder to craft meaningful strategy in the present, which inherently requires some understanding of the past.[10]

The existing critiques no doubt bring to light the serious problems faced by a country that is said to have 'arrived'. Yet they do little to highlight what possible influences shape the strategic decision-making process. For the most part, the analyses do not do enough to test the criticisms empirically. As mentioned above and argued in each chapter of this book, the lack of a clear and published set of Indian foreign policy priorities should in no way be mistaken for a lack of direction. This is not to say that the direction and practice of Indian foreign policy is seamless. It is not. Or that that the Indian government, the MEA and private partners could not do more to achieve this end. Collective decision-making—between and within ministries—is in dire need of attention. Indeed, the Indian Foreign Service bureaucracy finds itself naturally handicapped due to its small size and relative lack of personnel.[11] However, as empirically tested in the crises analysed in this book, there is considerable evidence to show that India thinks, strategises and delivers. This was more than clear in the crises of 1963 in negotiating

Kashmir with Pakistan, in preparing for war in 1971, saying no to war in 2003 and in bargaining for nuclear freedom in 2008.

Unless writers re-trace steps of change, they are unlikely to uncover for themselves the direction that only the detail of history can provide.[12] There is an imagination that guides India. It can loosely be called non-alignment. This may irk contemporary elites, irritate those commentators narrowly in search of national 'stature'—whatever it is that means—and even serve to reinforce what many consider a cliché. Yet, as established in this book, non-alignment ought to be re-studied. The motivation underlying its less than certain formulation requires revisiting the past. It is only then that the clear sense of direction that commentators strive for will become more obvious in the present, serving to guide Indian leaders as they seek to chart their nation's future.

The Future

Extrapolating generic lessons for the future of India and the US is in many ways a lazier form of scholarship. It is necessarily untested. Hence, rather than engage in detail in such an endeavour, I very briefly outline some general observations with regard to this all-important relationship. While doing so, I hint at a point or two about the Obama years in office.

First, India will never be an ally of the US. Comparing India to the UK or even France is pointless. The UK depends on America for its military and economic freedom. France may have once chosen to slip away from its Cold War security blanket and even oppose a major US-backed intervention in the early part of 2003, but it remains reliant on American support. The campaign against Libya only demonstrated France's need for American cover. Every American administration from Eisenhower onwards (at least after he was re-elected) understood India's need to remain non-aligned—insiders in the Obama administration appear to understand this as well. This should not, of course, be read to mean that India is or will turn inherently opposed to American desires and objectives. It will not. Cooperation on a whole range of issues—on Iran and the deliberations over humanitarian interventions in 2012 and 2013—suggests that dialogue and debate—much as before—will continue and strengthen unimpeded.

Relations between India and the US in the current milieu might not have reached and may never reach a point at which leaders can take the relationship for granted. Democracies of these sizes can ill afford such complacency. Such a relationship remains vital exactly because of its less than predictable character, where a general sense and support for each other's approach outweighs momentary disagreements over a whole range of issues. The sharp divide over climate change, rules of nuclear commerce, free trade and India's necessarily undedicated approach to defence procurement only serves to strengthen the tenor of argument between two oversized polities. Yet such differences can no longer undermine a momentum that far outpaces narrower bureaucratic biases. India's growing market size, geographic location, spirit for enterprise and well-founded democratic credentials, and America's ability to continue to shape and inform world politics seems to have convinced elites that the once 'new world'—as Bowles put it to Truman—has indeed been embraced—an objective Bowles set out with in 1951.

Apprehension of course remains. America's less-than-clear approach to Pakistan continues to irk Indian leaders. The Obama administration's reserved approach to nuclear commerce irritates those who spent years negotiating a deal that was said to help transform relations. The occasional screening of Indian diplomats and elected officials in American airports still makes headlines in Indian newspapers, and for good reason. But notwithstanding the typical trials and tribulations experienced in a relationship between any two nations, especially two of the world's most populous democracies, a well-founded strain for elasticity has not only taken root, but much more importantly and much less evidently makes allowances for temporary incidents of botched diplomatic forays.

Second, as commonly recognised—but worth repeating—public pronouncements on the part of any US administration declaring an intention to 'solve' the dispute over Kashmir do far more harm than good to both India and Pakistan. The atmospherics could not have been more different between when Obama was first elected to office and when he was re-elected. A resilience of sorts, forged over a period of six and a half decades, trumped what had seemed to Indian officials and commentators as a return to the policies pursued in the time of Kennedy.

During the 2008 election campaign, Obama publicly underlined that Kashmir was 'obviously a potential tar pit diplomatically'. He mentioned the need to 'figure-out' what he called a 'plausible approach', and even raised the question of the need for a 'special envoy'. He asked the 'Indians, you guys are on the brink of being an economic superpower, why do you want to keep on messing with this?'[13] As expected, the mere suggestion of third-party intervention in Kashmir raised alarm bells in New Delhi. Following Obama's inauguration on 20 January 2009, the late Richard Holbrooke, Obama's special representative to Afghanistan and Pakistan, was, according to Washington insiders, to include India in his brief.[14] For the Obama White House, and specifically the president, a resolution to the Kashmir crisis, he argued, would help Pakistan 'stay focussed not on India, but on the situation with those militants [camped on the border with Afghanistan]'.[15] White House insiders went further. They argued that following the completion of the nuclear agreement, Washington was potentially in a 'strong position in the subcontinent'. The US, such advisors made clear, 'should now try to quietly press the parties to find a solution to the Kashmiris' desire for greater self-rule'. It would 'require', they well understood, 'very delicate diplomacy but the pay-off would be great'.[16]

This somewhat short-sighted, ill-conceived and poorly advised policy initiative emboldened both New Delhi and India's well-established lob-byists in Washington.[17] Apart from the fact that diplomatic intervention of this nature lost its appeal once and for all following Kennedy and Macmillan's attempts in 1962 and 1963, the fact that such initiatives were purportedly being discussed only weeks after the devastating attacks in Mumbai in November 2008 did little for Indian leaders. After all, the gunmen arrived in India from Pakistan, and were supported in their heinous efforts by those inside Pakistan. How could American interlocutors have misread and misunderstood the pulse of a nation recently under siege? These were of course burning questions in the minds of Indian officials.

Yet, demonstrative of the hardiness programmed into a relationship as rooted in history as that between India and the US, the matter drowned in the light of future cooperation. Obama's visit to Mumbai and New Delhi in November 2010 was indicative of the promise of a relationship entrenched in a more established standing. On the floor of the Indian Parliament, the president made clear that it was no 'coinci-dence' that India was his first stop on a visit to Asia. Equally, he stated, 'it has been my longest visit to another country since becoming President'. Making sure to add what is nothing less than a truism, that 'only Indians can determine India's national interests and how to advance them on the world stage', he also added that he was 'convinced that the interests of the United States—and the interests we share with India—are best advanced in partnership'. For the first time in public, Obama indicated his nation's support for India's quest to 'take its seat on the United Nations Security Council'.[18]

Such strong and timely appeals appear to have tempered the frenzy over earlier comments on Kashmir. Of course, the entire episode might have been averted had those advising the president more carefully read their own nation's history with India. Public pronouncements and campaigning, as Eisenhower, Kennedy and Clinton grudgingly learnt, were hardly useful in dealing with an issue as deep-seated and personal as that of Kashmir. Indeed, Obama's own writings, which query 'whether men and women in fact are capable of learning from history', were perhaps worth reflection. His self-critical appeal to 'listen to other points of view' was equally worth recalling.[19]

Third and lastly, as difficult as it may seem to those—both in India and the US—tirelessly working towards on alliance-like relationship or even a deeper 'partnership,' an alliance of sorts would do little good for international politics. It is in fact in the interest of the larger international community—including Britain, Japan and Australia, all of which share particularly close relations with Washington—to keep the fires of argument between India and the US burning. This point may not be immediately obvious, but it is in fact essential. India represents and advocates an alternative set of arguments in an international system where the pursuit of foreign policy is increasingly challenged by opposition from within nation-states themselves. This is most apparent with regard to the issue of international intervention and the utility of military force. Branded a 'sovereignty hawk', India has come to be seen as what the historian A.J.P. Taylor calls a 'troublemaker': relentlessly representing the virtue of dissent. This of course irritates American officials in New York and Geneva who appear more determined than others to consider the use of military force. This was most evident following the rebellion that marked the downfall of Muammar Gaddafi in Libya. In the summer of 2013, both America and Britain were keen to consider some form of military assistance to 'stabilise' Syria.

In such cases, India is seen to turn inherently averse to suggestions of force. Much is said to have to do with its obsession with sovereignty. Yet, as in the case of Syria, Indian representatives at the UN have sought to find a middle path to end the violence. In the six or so statements on

CONCLUSION

Syria between January 2012 and February 2013, India's position has been far more flexible than otherwise understood. While each and every intervention in the Security Council highlights the need to evolve an approach 'anchored in state sovereignty' (12 February 2013) that is 'Syrian-led and Syrian-owned' (31 January and 30 August 2012), Indian representatives remain cognisant of changing ground realities. India first pushed for the League of Arab States to pressure the Assad regime and the opposition to negotiate. It then worked through IBSA (India–Brazil–South Africa), and supported the effort on the part of Kofi Annan—in his capacity as the joint special envoy—to implement a six-point plan. Once the latter initiative failed, India threw its weight behind Lakhdar Brahimi—the UN's joint special representative—to engage with both the ruling government and the Free Syrian Army. In short, there is no doubt that India actively supported, and continues to support, proposals authored by the Security Council. What it opposes are a series of measures—such as arming rebel groups—unilaterally mooted by the US.

Clearly, such debates are not going to end. The question of humanitarian intervention is one of the most potent matters of interstate argument. India's active role and determination to temper the anger over the use of force may not satisfy or impress American and even British officials at the UN, but it promises to invite the need for balance in a world in which rebellion and revolt shake and at times displace the very notion of sovereignty. For its part, India of course needs to do a lot more to articulate dissent, if it is indeed to maintain a sense for international balance. Leadership requires a dictionary of its own. Those producing the language for argument are inherently better placed to shape new grammar. Trouble-makers need finer language to emphasise dissent, if not to be heard by those deafened by the noise of their own jets and bullets, then by those on the divided streets of Syria and elsewhere who desperately require their oppressors and leaders to pay heed to the responsibility to protect.

NOTES

INTRODUCTION

1. Howard B. Schaffer, *Chester Bowles: New Dealer in the Cold War*, Cambridge, MA: Harvard University Press, 1993, pp. 1–37.
2. Nehru Memorial Museum and Library [hereafter NMML], Chester Bowles, oral history interview with B.R. Nanda, New Delhi, 7 Mar. 1971.
3. Jawaharlal Nehru, 'Free India's Role in World Affairs', 7 Sep. 1946, in *Selected Works of Jawaharlal Nehru*, Second Series [hereafter *SWJN*, SS], vol. 1, New Delhi: Jawaharlal Nehru Memorial Fund and Oxford University Press, 1984, p. 405. Note: the interim government was formed on 2 Sep. 1946.
4. Sarvepalli Gopal, *Jawaharlal Nehru: A Biography*, vol. 2, *1947–1956*, New Delhi: Oxford University Press, 1979, p. 43.
5. Robert Scalpino, 'Neutralism in Asia', *The American Political Science Review*, 48, 1 (Mar. 1954), p. 49.
6. Second oral history interview with Loy W. Henderson, Washington, DC, 5 July 1973, by Richard D. McKinzie, Harry S. Truman Library and Museum, available online: http://www.trumanlibrary.org/oralhist/hendrson.htm#transcript
7. Gopal, *Nehru: A Biography*, vol. 2, p. 43.
8. NMML, Albert Einstein to G.L. Mehta, 10 Apr. 1953, G.L. Mehta Papers, file no. 4
9. 'US Leaders Pay High Tribute to Mr. G.L. Mehta', *Times of India*, 2 May 1958.
10. Note: while the BJS and later the BJP participated in a number of coalition governments in the period following the fourth General Assembly elections in 1967, it first came to power in May 1996 but was ousted in less than a fortnight. It returned to power as the lead party in the NDA in Feb. 1998 for thirteen months, and again (as the lead coalition party) in Oct. 1999 following India's thirteenth General Assembly elections. For a succinct summary see Paranjoy Guha Thakurta and Shankar Raghuraman, *Divided We Stand: India in a Time of Coalitions*, New Delhi: Sage, 2001, pp. 178–83.

11. Jaswant Singh's commission in the Central India Horse, formed in 1857 as a cavalry regiment, lasted between 1957 and 1966. For a detailed account of his turn to politics see: Jaswant Singh, *A Call to Honour: In Service of Emergent India*, New Delhi: Rupa & Co., 2006, pp. 3–76.

12. Author's interview with Bruce Riedel, Washington, DC, 28 Aug. 2008. For a detailed account of the backchannel discussions see Strobe Talbott, *Engaging India: Diplomacy, Democracy and the Bomb*, Washington, DC: Brookings Institution Press, 2006, and Singh, *Call to Honour*. For a more recent analysis see Bruce Riedel, 'South Asia's Nuclear Decade', *Survival*, 50, 2 (Apr.–May 2008).

13. Author's interview with Brajesh Mishra, New Delhi, 11 Aug. 2007.

14. Bill Clinton, *My Life*, New York: Arrow Books, 2005, p. 597.

15. For a brief analysis see Paul Kapur and Sumit Ganguly, 'The Transformation of U.S.–India Relations: An Explanation for the Rapprochement and Prospects for the Future', *Asian Survey*, 47, 4 (July–Aug. 2007).

16. Author's interview with K. Natwar Singh, New Delhi, 24 July 2007.

17. 'US Aid to Pakistan is Intervention', *Times of India*, 2 Mar. 1954.

18. The agreement was signed in June 2005. See K. Alan Krondstadt, 'India–US Relations', CRS Issue Brief for Congress, the Library of Congress, 9 Nov. 2006, p. 4.

19. For a background analysis see C. Raja Mohan, *Impossible Allies: Nuclear India, the United States, and the Global Order*, New Delhi: India Research Press, 2006, pp. 1–10.

20. 'Full Text of Obama's Parliament Speech', 8 Nov. 2010 (available at: http://ibn-live.in.com/news/full-text-of-obamas-parliament-address/134649-3.html).

21. For details on India's rise see C. Raja Mohan, 'India and the Balance of Power', *Foreign Affairs*, 85, 4 (July–Aug. 2006).

22. For an eloquent note on the same see Yasuhiro Izumikawa, 'Explaining Japanese Anti-Militarism: Normative and Realist Constraints on Japan's Security Policy', *International Security*, 35, 2 (Fall 2010), pp. 123–60 and T.V. Paul, *The Tradition of Non-Use of Nuclear Weapons*, Stanford: Stanford University Press, 2009, pp. 17–36.

23. Paul W. Schroeder, 'History and International Relations Theory: Not Use or Abuse, But Fit or Misfit', *International Security*, 22, 1 (Summer 1997), p. 65.

24. Condoleezza Rice, *No Higher Honour: A Memoir of My Years in Washington*, New York: Simon and Schuster, 2011, p. 437.

25. Manjari Chatterjee Miller, 'Recollecting Empire: "Victimhood" and the 1962 Sino-Indian War', *Asian Security*, 5, 3 (2009).

26. Harsh V. Pant, 'Indian Foreign Policy Challenges: Substantive Uncertainties and Institutional Infirmities', *Asian Affairs*, 40, 1(2009).

27. Shashi Tharoor, *Reasons of State: Political Development and India's Foreign Policy under Indira Gandhi, 1966–1977*, New Delhi: Vikas, 1982, p. 26.

28. For a review and critique see Srinath Raghavan, *War and Peace in Modern India*, New Delhi: Permanent Black, 2010, pp. 1–21.

29. Shashi Tharoor, *Nehru: The Invention of India*, New York: Arcade Publishing, 2003, p. 183.

30. For instance, see Dennis Merrill, 'Indo-American Relations, 1947–50: A Missed Opportunity in Asia', *Diplomatic History*, 11 (1987), pp. 203–26. For a more detailed analysis see: Dennis Merrill, *Bread and the Ballot: The United States and India's Economic Development, 1947–1963*, Chapel Hill: University of North Carolina Press, 1990, Chapter 2; M.S. Venkataramani's three-part series, 'An Elusive Military Relationship', *Frontline*, 16, 7, 16, 8 and 16, 9 (9 Apr., 23 Apr. and 7 May 1999).

31. Robert McMahon, *The Cold War on the Periphery: The United States, India, and Pakistan*, New York: Columbia University Press, 1994, p. 49.

32. Mohan, *Impossible Allies*, pp. 1–10.

33. Ashton Carter, 'America's New Strategic Partner?' *Foreign Affairs*, 85, 4 (July–Aug. 2006).

34. Author's interview with Douglas Feith, Washington, DC, 10 Oct. 2008. Note: Feith was the US undersecretary of defence for policy in 2003. He worked closely with the Indian military and Ministry of Defence.

35. Mohan, *Impossible Allies*, pp. 29–36.

36. Talbott, *Engaging India*, p. 6.

37. Dennis Kux, *India and the United States: Estranged Democracies, 1941–1991*, Washington, DC: National Defense University Press, 1992, p. xii.

38. David Cameron, 'We Must Forge a New Special Relationship—With India', *The Guardian*, 5 Sep. 2006.

39. George W. Bush, *Decision Points*, New York: Virgin Books, 2010, p. 214.

40. Sunil Khilnani, 'India as a Bridging Power', Author's personal copy.

41. Harsh V. Pant, 'The Trials of a Rising Power', *Livemint.com* and *The Wall Street Journal*, 29 Dec. 2009.

42. These included the *Foreign Relations of the United States* [FRUS] series, *Selected Works of Jawaharlal Nehru* [SWJN] and the *Letters to Chief Ministers*, consisting of a series of letters written by Nehru to Indian chief ministers from 1947 to 1964.

43. Paul Kapur, *Dangerous Deterrent: Nuclear Weapons Proliferation and Conflict in South Asia*, Stanford: Stanford University Press, 2008, p. 200.

1. 'NEW INDIA'

1. Nehru to K.P.S. Menon, 17 Nov. 1946, in *Selected Works of Jawaharlal Nehru*, Second Series [SWJN, SS], vol. 1, New Delhi: Jawaharlal Nehru Memorial Fund and Oxford University Press, 1984, p. 543.

2. Nehru to Pandit, 14 Nov. 1946, ibid., p. 539.

3. National Archives, Kew Gardens, London [Hereafter NA], KV2/2512, note, untitled, 31 May 1949.

4. Sunil Khilnani, 'Nehru's Evil Genius', *Outlook* (19 Mar. 2007).

5. Nehru to Pandit, 25 Nov. 1952, *SWJN*, SS, vol. 20, p. 430.

6. Roosevelt to Churchill, Washington, 29 July 1942, in Francis Loewenheim, Harold D. Langley and Manfred Jonas (eds), *Roosevelt and Churchill: Their Secret Wartime Correspondence*, London: Barrie and Jenkins, 1975, p. 230.

7. Kenton Clymer, *Quest for Freedom: The United States and India's Independence*, New York: Columbia University Press, 1995, p. 206.

8. Dennis Kux, *India and the United States: Estranged Democracies, 1941–1991*, Washington, DC: National Defense University Press, 1992, p. 8.

9. Clymer, *Quest for Freedom*, p. 287.

10. Ibid., p. 207.

11. Harold A. Gould, *The South Asia Story*, London: Sage, 2010, p. 23.

12. A detailed discussion of Roosevelt's attempts to advocate India's freedom can be found in Kux, *India and the United States*, pp. 4–38.

13. Arthur Herman, *Gandhi and Churchill*, London: Hutchinson, 2008, p. 474.

14. Churchill to Roosevelt, London, 31 July 1942, Lowenheim, Langley and Jonas (eds), *Roosevelt and Churchill*, pp. 230–1.

15. Nehru Memorial Museum and Library [NMML], interview with Chester Bowles by B.R. Nanda, 17 Aug. 1972, oral history section, file no. 286.

16. The instructions to allow Pandit to travel came directly from Summer Wells, the US assistant secretary of state. See Vijayalakshmi Pandit, *The Scope of Happiness*, London: Weidenfeld and Nicolson, 1979, p. 187.

17. Churchill to Roosevelt, 9 Aug. 1942, Lowenheim, Langley and Jonas (eds), *Roosevelt and Churchill*, p. 234.

18. The National Archives, College Park, Maryland, [hereafter TNA], Memorandum of Conversation [hereafter MoC] between the president and secretary of state, 3 Apr. 1949, Records of Robert Komer, Department of State Papers, box no. 1.

19. Churchill to Roosevelt, London, 9 Aug. 1942, Lowenheim, Langley and Jonas (eds), *Roosevelt and Churchill*, p. 234.

20. Cited in Herman, *Gandhi and Churchill*, p. 475.

21. Roosevelt to Churchill, 10 Mar. 1942, Lowenheim, Langley and Jonas (eds), *Roosevelt and Churchill*, pp. 191–2.

22. Kux, *India and the United States*, p. 38.

23. Note: while Roosevelt supported India's independence, he refused to intervene in a resolution drafted by the INC on India's freedom. See Sarvepalli Gopal, *Jawaharlal Nehru: A Biography*, vol. 1, *1889–1947*, New Delhi: Oxford University Press, 1979, p. 290.

24. Roosevelt to Churchill, 10 Mar. 1942, Lowenheim, Langley and Jonas (eds), *Roosevelt and Churchill*, pp. 191–2.

25. Liddel Hart Archives, King's College London [hereafter LHA], National Security Council [hereafter NSC] Files, 'United States Policy towards Asia', 10 June 1949, NSC 48/MF 72.

26. LHA NSC Files, 'The Position of the United States with Respect to Asia', 23 Dec. 1949, NSC 48/1/MF 72.

27. John T. McNay (ed.), *The Memoirs of Ambassador Henry F. Grady: From the Great War to the Cold War*, Columbia: University of Missouri Press, 2009, p. 117.

28. J.N. Dixit, *India's Foreign Policy 1947–2003*, New Delhi: Picus Books, 2003, p. 22. A counter-argument can be found in Anita Inder Singh, *The Limits of British Influence: South Asia and the Anglo-American Relationship 1947–56*, London: Pinter, 1993, pp. 47–57.

29. NMML, Joseph Baker, 'Is India our Business?', undated, 1945, V.L. Pandit Papers, 2nd instalment, subject file 1.

30. Papers of Harry S. Truman, President's Secretary's Files, Document 76, *Documentary History of the Truman Presidency Volume 2: Planning for the Postwar World*, Washington, DC: University Publications of America, 1995, pp. 556–7.

31. Elizabeth Edward Spalding, *The First Cold Warrior: Harry Truman, Containment, and the Remaking of Liberal Internationalism*, Kentucky: University Press of Kentucky, 2006, p. 227.

32. Kux, *India and the United States*, pp. 47–8.

33. NMML, Vijayalakshmi Pandit, memorandum submitted to the secretary general of the United Nations Conference on International Organisation, San Francisco, 2 May 1945, V.L. Pandit Papers, 2nd instalment, subject file no. 1.

34. Singh, *The Limits of British Influence*, p. 55.

35. Nehru, 'Free India's Role in World Affairs', 7 Sep. 1946, *SWJN*, SS, vol. 1, p. 405.

36. K. Shankar Bajpai, 'Engaging With the World', in Atish Sinha and Madhup Mohta (eds), *Indian Foreign Policy: Challenges and Opportunities*, New Delhi: Academic Foundation, 2007, p. 83.

37. Robert Beisner, *Dean Acheson: A Life in the Cold War,* New York: Oxford University Press, 2009, p. 506.

38. K.R. Narayanan, *In the Name of the People*, New Delhi: Penguin, 2011, p. 61.

39. K. Shankar Bajpai, 'NAM and the Pitfalls of Revisiting it', *Business Standard* (Mar. 2012).

40. Indira Gandhi, 'Foreword', 18 Jan. 1972, *SWJN*, SS, vol. 1.

41. Sunil Khilnani, *Idea of India*, New Delhi: Penguin, 1997, p. 39.

42. Cited in Narayanan, *In the Name of the People*, p. 61

43. Nehru to Pandit, 14 Nov. 1946, *SWJN*, SS, vol. 1, pp. 539–40.

44. M.J. Akbar, *Nehru*, New Delhi: Rupa-Viking, 1988, p. 482.

45. Cited in Gopal, *Nehru: A Biography*, vol. 1, p. 201.

46. Gopal, *Nehru: A Biography*, vol. 2, p. 56.

47. Srinath Raghavan, *War and Peace in Modern India*, New Delhi: Permanent Black, 2010, p. 20.

48. Note: Norm entrepreuners are those who take the lead on institutionalising new ideas in governance or society alike. For an eloquent description of norm entrepreneurs see Martha Finnemore and Kathryn Sikkink, 'International Norm Dynamic and Political Change', *International Organization*, 52, 4 (Autumn 1998), p. 889.

49. Gopal, *Nehru: A Biography*, vol. 1, p. 98.

50. Nehru, 'Statement to Press', Brussels, 9 Feb. 1927, *Selected Works of Jawaharlal Nehru* [hereafter *SWJN*], First Series [hereafter FS], vol. 2, p. 271.

51. Nehru, 'A Foreign Policy for India', Allahabad, 13 Sep. 1927, *SWJN*, FS vol. 2, p. 348.

52. Ibid., p. 353.

53. Cited in Raghavan, *War and Peace*, p. 20.

54. Shashi Tharoor, *Nehru: The Invention of India*, New York: Arcade Publishing, 2003, pp. 183–4.

55. Nehru to Asif Ali, 21 Dec. 1946, *SWJN*, SS, vol. 1, p. 556.

56. Nehru to Pandit, 14 Nov. 1946, ibid., pp. 539–40.

57. Gopal, *Nehru: A Biography*, vol. 1, p. 100.

58. Nehru, 'Report on the Brussels Congress', Brussels, 19 Feb. 1927, *SWJN*, FS, vol. 2, pp. 278–93.

59. Nehru, 'A Note on the Development of Contacts Between China and India', Chungking, 29 Aug. 1939, *SWJN*, FS, vol. 10, p. 103.

60. Nehru, 'Whither India?', 9, 10, 11 Oct. 1933, *SWJN*, FS, vol. 6, p. 5.

61. Nehru, 'A Foreign Policy for India', Allahabad, 13 Sep. 1927, *SWJN*, FS, vol. 2, pp. 352–3.

62. Nehru, 'India and the Need for International Contacts', *The New Era*, 13 May 1928, *SWJN*, FS, vol. 3, pp. 380–1.

63. Nehru, 'Whither India?', p. 15.

64. Nehru to Tagore, 9 Jan. 1938, *SWJN*, FS, vol. 8, p. 734.

65. Nehru, 'India and the Need for International Contacts', pp. 380–1.

66. Togore to Nehru, 17 Aug. 1939, cited in Krishna Dutta and Andrew Robinson, *Selected Letters of Rabindranath Tagore*, Cambridge: Cambridge University Press, 1997, p. 512.

67. B.G. Verghese, *First Draft: Witness to the Making of Modern India*, New Delhi: Tranquebar, 2010, p. 63.

68. Nayantara Sahgal, *Civilising a Savage World*, New Delhi: Penguin, 2010, p. 85.

69. Nehru, 'On Framing India's Foreign Policy', Allahabad, 26 May 1938, *SWJN*, FF, vol. 8, pp. 744–7.

70. Nehru, 'The Defence of India', Ahmedabad, 9 Sep. 1931, *SWJN*, FF, vol. 5, pp. 556–60.

71. Cited in Rajmohan Gandhi, *Mohandas: A True Story of a Man, his People and an Empire*, London: Penguin, 2006, p. 583.

72. Nehru, note, 'Defence Policy and National Development', 3 Feb. 1947, *SWJN*, SS, vol. 2, p. 364.

73. Cited by Nehru in Max-Jean Zins, 'The Policy of Non-alignment: 1947–1971', in Christophe Jaffrelot (ed.), *India since 1950*, New Delhi: Yatra Books, 2011, p. 168.

74. Nehru, 'A Note on the Development of Contacts Between China and India', p. 103.

75. Cited in Stanley Wolpert, *Gandhi's Passion: The Life and Legacy of Mahatma Gandhi*, New York: Oxford University Press, 2001, pp. 200–2.

76. Nehru, 'Interview to the Press, Visit to Malaya', 23 May to 4 June 1937, *SWJN*, FS, vol. 8, p. 665.

77. Nehru, 'The Defence of India', pp. 556–60.

78. Nehru, 'Interview to the Press, Visit to Malaya', p. 665.

79. Nehru, 'Report on the Brussels Congress', pp. 278–93.

80. Nehru, 'Statement to Press', Brussels, 9 Feb. 1927, p. 276.

81. Nehru, 'Interview to the Press, ND', 15 Mar. 1946, *SWJN*, FS, vol. 15, p. 525.

82. Ibid.

83. NMML, V.L. Pandit Papers, 'An Article on the Policy of Non-Alignment', undated, 2nd instalment, subject file 16.

84. Cited in Ramachandra Guha, *India After Gandhi*, New York: Harper Collins, 2007, p. 153.

85. For a brief discussion of the ethics of non-alignment see Gopal, *Nehru: A Biography*, vol. 1, pp. 44–5. Also see Khilnani, *Idea of India*, pp. 15–42.

86. Nehru to chief ministers, 15 Aug. 1949, in G. Parthasarthy (ed.), *Jawaharlal Nehru: Letters to Chief Ministers*, vol. 1, 1947, London: Jawaharlal Nehru Memorial Fund and Oxford University Press, 1985, p. 433.

87. A. Appadorai (ed.), *Select Documents on India's Foreign Policy and Relations*, vol. 1, London: Oxford University Press, 1982, p. 11.

88. Nehru on non-alignment, 22 Mar. 1949, cited in Appadorai (ed.), *Select Documents on India's Foreign Policy*, p. 14.

89. Nehru to chief ministers, 15 Aug. 1949, in Parthasarthy (ed.), *Letters*, vol. 1, p. 433.

90. Werner Levi, 'Indian Neutralism Reconsidered', *Pacific Affairs*, 37, 2 (Summer 1964), p. 137.

91. For an analysis see Appadorai (ed.), *Select Documents on India's Foreign Policy*, p. xii.

92. Cited in Nehru, note, undated, *SWJN*, vol. 4, p. 596.

93. Ibid.

94. Malcolm House, 'India: Non-Committed and Non-Aligned', *The Western*

Political Quarterly, 13, 1 (Mar. 1960), p. 72. For an eloquent analysis of 'neutralism', see Robert Scalpino, 'Neutralism in Asia', *The American Political Science Review*, 48, 1 (Mar. 1954), p. 50. For a later analysis see T.A. Keenleyside, 'Prelude to Power: The Meaning of Non-Alliance before Independence', *Pacific Affairs*, 53, 3 (Autumn 1980), pp. 461–83.

95. NMML, V.L. Pandit Papers, 'An Article on the Policy of Non-Alignment', undated, 2nd instalment, subject file 16.

96. Pandit, *The Scope of Happiness*, p. 254.

97. Vincent Shean, 'The Case for India', *Foreign Affairs*, 30 (1951–2), p. 77.

98. NMML, Y.D. Gundevia Papers, 'Some Interesting Aspects of Nehru's Policies', speech delivered to the Poona branch of the Indian Council on World Affairs, subject file no. 7.

99. See Pandit, *The Scope of Happiness*, pp. 190–1.

100. Jane C. Loeffler, *The Architecture of American Diplomacy: Building America's Embassies*, 2nd edn, New York: Princeton Architectural Press, 2010, p. 7.

101. LHA, NSC Files, 'The Position of the US with Respect to South Asia', 23 Dec. 1948.

102. Robert Stimson, 'Goodbye to India', BBC, 10 Mar. 1949, cited in John Elliot, Bernard Imhalsy and Simon Denyer (eds), *Fifty Years of Reporting South Asia*, New Delhi: Penguin, 2009, p. 4.

103. Gerald Priestland, 'With Nehru around India', BBC, 1954–8, cited in Elliot, Imhalsy and Denyer (eds), *Fifty Years of Reporting South Asia*, p. 21.

104. James Cameron, 'The Death of Nehru', *Daily Herald*, 28 May 1964, cited in Elliot, Imhalsy and Denyer (eds), *Fifty Years of Reporting South Asia*, p. 60.

2. 'MAXIMUM HARDSHIP POST'

1. The 'Tryst with Destiny' speech was delivered by Nehru on the eve of India's independence. The full text can be found in Subimal Dutt, *With Nehru in the Foreign Office*, New Delhi: Minerva Associates, 1977, p. 9.

2. For a brief note on the crisis in the Mediterranean see Harold Gosnell, *Truman's Crisis: A Political Biography of Harry S. Truman*, London: Greenwood Press, 1980, pp. 341–66. For a detailed account of the origins of the Marshall Plan and the ensuing strategy of containment see Charles Kindleberger, 'Note on Marshall plan Origins', Washington, 22 July 1948, *Foreign Relations of the United States* [hereafter *FRUS*], vol. 3, pp. 241–7.

3. 'Report of the Special Ad Hoc Committee of the State–War–Navy Coordinating Committee', 21 Apr. 1947, *FRUS*, vol. 3, pp. 206–8.

4. Elizabeth Edward Spalding, *The First Cold Warrior: Harry Truman, Containment, and the Remaking of Liberal Internationalism*, Kentucky: University Press of Kentucky, 2006, p. 2.

5. Note: British Foreign Secretary Ernest Bevin made this point to Loy Henderson, who stopped over in London on his way to India to begin his stint as the US ambassador. See H.W. Brands, *Inside the Cold War: Loy Henderson and the Rise of the American Empire 1918–61*, New York: Oxford University Press, 1991, p. 198.

6. Dennis Kux, *India and the United States: Estranged Democracies, 1941–1991*, Washington, DC: National Defense University Press, 1992, p. 55.

7. The National Archives, College Park, Maryland, [hereafter TNA], 'Department of State Assessment of Press Reports', 28 June 1948, document no. 451, RG 59 General Records of the Department of State [hereafter RG 59], lot file no. 53 D 211, Office Files of Ambassador-at-Large-Philip C. Jessup, 1946–52, box no. 14.

8. Robert McMahon, *The Cold War on the Periphery: The United States, India, and Pakistan*, New York: Columbia University Press, 1994, p. 11. For an overview of US interests in South Asia see Vernon Hewitt, *The New International Politics of South Asia*, Manchester: Manchester University Press, 1997, pp. 89–99.

9. TNA, Loy Henderson to Major General Harry Vaughan (military aide to the president), 13 June 1949, RG 59, lot file no. 67044, box 1, Office Files of Ambassador Loy Henderson 1945–59 [hereafter RG 59/file no.].

10. Nehru to Asia Ali, 21 Dec. 1946, *Selected Works of Jawaharlal Nehru*, Second Series [hereafter *SWJN*, SS], vol. 1, p. 556.

11. Sarvepalli Gopal, *Jawaharlal Nehru: A Biography*, vol. 2, *1947–1956*, New Delhi: Oxford University Press, 1979, pp. 42–43.

12. Quoted in Spalding, *The First Cold Warrior*, p. 1.

13. Nehru Memorial Museum and Library [hereafter NMML], Nehru to V.L. Pandit, 8 June 1948, V.L. Pandit Papers, subject file 1, no. 54.

14. Robert Beisner, *Dean Acheson: A Life in the Cold War*, New York: Oxford University Press, 2009, p. 507.

15. Meghnad Desai, *The Rediscovery of India*, London: Bloomsbury Academic, 2011, pp. 1–3 and p. 317.

16. David Malone, *Does the Elephant Dance? Contemporary Indian Foreign Policy*, London: Oxford University Press, 2011, p. 47 and pp. 154–6

17. Dennis Merrill, 'Indo-American Relations, 1947–50: A Missed Opportunity in Asia', *Diplomatic History*, 11 (1987), pp. 203–26. For a detailed analysis see Dennis Merrill, *Bread and the Ballot: The United States and India's Economic Development, 1947–1963*, Chapel Hill: University of North Carolina Press, 1990, Chapter 2.

18. McMahon, *The Cold War*, p. 49.

19. Ibid., pp. 46–51.

20. A.G. Noorani, 'Balance of Power in South Asia', *Frontline*, 22, 8 (Apr. 2005).

21. Bharat Karnad, *Nuclear Weapons and Indian Security: The Realist Foundations of*

Strategy, London: Macmillan, 2002, p. xxix; Bharat Karnad, 'Habit of Free Riding', *Seminar*, 599 (July 2009), pp. 61–6.

22. See A.P. Rana, *The Imperatives of Non-Alignment: A Conceptual Study of India's Foreign Policy Strategy in the Nehru Period*, New Delhi: Macmillan, 1976.

23. NMML, Nehru to Pandit, 8 June 1948, V.L. Pandit Papers, subject file 1, no. 54.

24. National Archives, Kew Gardens, London [Hereafter NA], DO 35/2921, 'South East Asia: Economic Aid to India as Part of Counterattack against Communism'.

25. NA, DO 35/2921, Archibald Nye to Percivale Liesching, 21 June 1949.

26. NA, DO 35/2921, CRO to Sir Oliver Franks (British ambassador to the US), 9 Sep. 1949.

27. Note: Iengar was acting secretary general for external affairs in Girja Shankar Bajpai's absence.

28. Grady to secretary of state, 20 Mar. 1948, *FRUS*, vol. 5/part 1, p. 498.

29. MoC of a meeting between Girja S. Bajpai, Henderson and others, Washington, 2 Apr. 1948, *FRUS*, vol. 5/part 1, pp. 502–3.

30. MoC of a meeting between Girja S. Bajpai, Lovett and others, Washington, 2 Apr. 1948, ibid., p. 507.

31. Note: Indian military expenditure (on procurement alone) in 1950 was approximately $800 million. See Glynn. L. Wood and Daniel Vaagenes, 'Indian Defence Policy: A New Phase', *Asian Survey*, 24, 7 (July 1984), p. 728.

32. MoC of a meeting between Bajpai, Lovett and others, Washington, 2 Apr. 1948, *FRUS*, vol. 5/part 1, p. 507.

33. MoC prepared by Joseph Sparks of a meeting with Chopra and others, Washington, 10 May 1948. Ibid., pp. 509–10.

34. Ibid. Note: this request was turned down by US officials in July 1948, see MoC by Joseph Sparks, Washington, 28 July 1948, ibid., p. 523.

35. Ibid.

36. TNA, Elbert Mathews to Loy Henderson, 17 May 1950, RG 59/file 67044/box 1.

37. Vallabhai Patel to Nehru, 7 Nov. 1945, cited in Durga Das (ed.), *Sardar Patel's Correspondence* [hereafter *SPC*], vol. 2, Ahmedabad: Navajivan Publishing House, 1972.

38. Nehru to Asif Ali, 21 Dec. 1946, *SWJN*, SS, vol. 1, p. 556.

39. Cited in Kux, *India and the United States*, p. 51.

40. Ibid.

41. MoC by secretary of state, 26 Feb. 1947, *FRUS*, vol. 3, pp. 147–9.

42. Nehru to Bajpai, 5 Dec. 1946, *SWJN*, SS, vol. 1, p. 549.

43. Grady to secretary of state, 3 Sep. 1947, *FRUS*, vol. 3, pp. 165–6.

44. Nehru to V.L. Pandit, 6 Aug. 1949, *SWJN*, SS, vol. 12, p. 402.

45. Gopal, *Nehru: A Biography*, vol. 2, pp. 57–9.

46. Nehru to Pandit, 24 Aug. 1949, *SWJN*, SS, vol. 13, p. 288.

47. Marshal to Truman, 11 Mar. 1948, *FRUS*, vol. 5/part 1, p. 496. Note: Truman signed off on the embargo on 12 Mar. 1948.

48. For details on the initial intervention and subsequent military operations see Srinath Raghavan, *War and Peace in Modern India*, New Delhi: Permanent Black, 2010, pp. 121–41. For details on the role of the US and the UK in the UN see Howard B. Schaffer, *The Limits of Influence: America's Role in Kashmir*, Washington, DC: Brookings Institution Press, 2009, pp. 9–35.

49. For details on Henderson's discussions with Bajpai on the matter of the embargo see H.W. Brands, *Inside the Cold War: Loy Henderson and the Rise of the American Empire, 1918–1961*, New York: Oxford University Press, 1991, p. 201.

50. MoC prepared by Joseph Sparks, 10 May 1948, *FRUS*, vol. 5/part 1, p. 509.

51. Baldev Singh to Nehru, 14 Apr. 1947, *SWJN*, SS, vol. 2, p. 370.

52. Anita Inder Singh, *The Limits of British Influence: South Asia and the Anglo-American Relationship 1947–56*, London: Pinter, 1993, p. 57.

53. Howard Donovan (Charge in India) to secretary of state, 26 Jan. 1948, *FRUS*, vol. 5/part 1, p. 496.

54. For details see Schaffer, *The Limits of Influence*, pp. 23–4.

55. Note: General Roy Butcher was the first commander-in-chief of an independent Indian army (1948–9).

56. TNA, MoC between Loy Henderson and Prince de Ligne, Belgian ambassador to India, 4 May 1949, RG/59/lot file 67044/box 1.

57. Gopal, *Nehru: A Biography*, vol. 2, p. 45.

58. Grady to secretary of state, 27 June 1947, *FRUS*, vol. 3, pp. 157–8.

59. TNA, Henderson to secretary of state, 18 Nov. 1948, RG/59/lot file 67044/box 1.

60. Grady to secretary of state, 27 June 1947, *FRUS*, vol. 3, pp. 157–8.

61. Nehru to Patel, 21 May 1948, *SWJN*, SS, vol. 6, p. 454.

62. NA, FO 371/76102, acting high commissioner to CRO, 25 July 1949.

63. NMML, Nehru to Pandit, 8 June 1948, V.L. Pandit Papers, subject file 1, no. 54.

64. Nehru and Baldev Singh, 'The Armed Forces in the New Perspective', 22 Nov. 1946, *SWJN*, SS, vol. 1, p. 412.

65. Baldev Singh to Nehru, 14 Apr. 1947, *SWJN*, SS, vol. 2, p. 370.

66. Nehru to Baldev Singh, 8 Apr. 1947, ibid., p. 369.

67. Ramachandra Guha, *India after Gandhi*, New York: Harper Collins, 2007, p. 152.

68. Patel to Nehru, 4 June 1949, *SPC*, vol. 8, p. 135.

69. Nehru, note, 'Defence Policy and National Development', 3 Feb. 1947, *SWJN*, SS, vol. 2, p. 363.

70. Note to foreign secretary, 'Implications of Special Treaty with the USA', 12 Aug. 1948, *SWJN*, SS, vol. 7, p. 630.

71. Nehru, 'Disapproval of Alignment', 21 Aug. 1948, cited in ibid., p. 630.

72. Stephen P. Cohen, *India: Emerging Power*, Washington, DC: Brookings Institution Press, 2002, p. 128.

73. Howard Donovan to secretary of state, 21 Sep. 1948, *FRUS*, vol. 5/part 1, p. 515.

74. Secretary of state to the acting secretary of state, 16 Oct. 1948, ibid., p. 517.

75. Nehru to chief ministers, 20 Feb. 1948, in G. Parthasarthy (ed.), *Jawaharlal Nehru: Letters to Chief Ministers*, vol. 1, 1947, London: Jawaharlal Nehru Memorial Fund and Oxford University Press, 1985, p. 69.

76. Nehru to George Bernard Shaw, 4 Sep. 1948, *SWJN*, SS, vol. 6, p. 715.

77. Grady to secretary of state, 10 Nov. 1947, *FRUS*, vol. 3, p. 171.

78. Note: this is based on the author's survey of Grady's correspondence with Marshall between 15 June 1947 and 1 Nov. 1948.

79. See Grady to secretary of state, 2 Sep. 1947, *FRUS*, vol. 3, pp. 164–5; Grady to secretary of state, 3 Sep. 1947, ibid., pp. 165–6; acting secretary of state to embassy in India, 3 Oct. 1947, ibid., p. 166.

80. For details see Raghavan, *War and Peace*, pp. 105–7.

81. Grady to secretary of state, 2 Sep. 1947, *FRUS*, vol. 3, pp. 164–5.

82. Note: on 26 Jan. 1950, Rajagopalachari relinquished the position of governor general to Rajendra Prasad, who became the first president of India.

83. John T. McNay (ed.), *The Memoirs of Ambassador Henry F. Grady: From the Great War to the Cold War*, Columbia: University of Missouri Press, 2009, pp. 2–4; NMML, Mountbatten to Rajagopalachari, London, 14 Jan. 1950, C. Rajagopalachari Papers, 5th instalment, correspondence with Mountbatten of Burma.

84. Grady to secretary of state, 10 Nov. 1947, *FRUS*, vol. 3, p. 171.

85. Nehru told Grady this on 9 July 1947, *FRUS*, vol. 3, p. 58.

86. Grady to secretary of state, 2 Sep. 1947, *FRUS*, vol. 3, pp. 164–5.

87. Nehru, note, 'Food Grains from Russia', 6 Sep. 1946, *SWJN*, SS, vol. 1, pp. 481–2.

88. NMML, Rajeshwar Dayal to A.Y. Vyshinski (deputy minister of foreign affairs, USSR) (exact month and day unmentioned), 1948, V.L. Pandit Papers, 2nd instalment, subject file no. 3.

89. Nehru to Krishna Menon, 26 June 1948, *SWJN*, SS, vol. 6, p. 463.

90. TNA, MoC between Pandit and Loy Henderson, 30 Apr. 1949, RG59/file 67044/box 1.

91. TNA, MoC between John Mathai and Henderson, 12 Sep. 1949, ibid.

92. NA, DO 35/2921, CRO to Washington, 2 Sep. 1949.

93. NA, FO 371/76102, UK chancery in Washington to South East Asia Department, 23 Aug. 1949.

94. NA, FO 371/76102, UK high commission in India [hereafter HC] to CRO, 25 July 1949.

95. NA, FO 371/76102, acting high commissioner in India to CRO, 25 July 1949.

96. NA, DO 35/2921, UK HC in India to CRO [discussion on talks with US ambassador to India], 8 Sep. 1949.

97. Note to the foreign secretary on the implications of a Special Treaty with the US, 12 Aug. 1948, *SWJN*, SS, vol. 7, pp. 629–30.

98. Donovan to secretary of state, 26 Jan. 1948, *FRUS*, vol. 5/part 1, pp. 495–6; Nehru to Asif Ali, 16 Feb. 1948, *SWJN*, SS, vol. 5, p. 494.

99. For details see Navnita Chadha Behera, *Demystifying Kashmir*, Washington, DC: Brookings Institution Press, 2006, pp. 30–44; Raghavan, *War and Peace*, pp. 124–30.

100. Nehru to Pandit, 16 Feb. 1948, *SWJN*, SS, vol. 5, p. 218.

101. Nehru to Kishna Menon, 16 Feb. 1948, ibid., p. 219.

102. NA, FO 371/76102, CRO to G. Bowen (Commercial Relations and Export Department), 20 Dec. 1949.

103. NA, FO 371/76102, 'Treaty of Friendship, Navigation and Commerce Between the United States and India, Enclosed in S.A. Midgley (High Commission in India)', 28 Nov. 1949

104. NA, FO 371/76102, High Commission in Karachi to CRO, 30 Sep. 1949.

105. NA, FO 371/76102, 'Treaty of Friendship, Navigation and Commerce Between the United States and India, Enclosed in S A. Midgley (High Commission in India)', Delhi, 28 Nov. 1949.

106. Nehru to Menon, 12 Aug. 1948, *SWJN*, SS, vol. 7, pp. 627–30.

107. Nehru to Mathai, 7 Feb. 1949, *SWJN*, SS, vol. 9, p. 61.

108. TNA, MoC between Henderson and Pandit, 28 Apr. 1949, RG59/67044/box 1.

109. TNA, MoC between Henderson and Mathai, 12 Sep. 1949, ibid.

110. Patel to Nehru, 4 June 1949, *SPC*, vol. 8, p. 135.

111. NA, DO 35/2921, UK HC to CRO, 17 Sep. 1949.

112. NA, DO 35/2921, record of meeting in the Foreign Office, London, 20 July 1949.

113. NA, DO 35/2921, UK HC to CRO, 27 Sep. 1949.

114. Robert Beisner, *Dean Acheson: A Life in the Cold War*, New York: Oxford University Press, 2009, p. 506.

115. TNA, Henderson to Major General Harry H. Vaughan, 13 June 1949, RG 59/lot file 67044/box 1.

116. NA, FO 371/76100, MoC between Nye and Sir O. Franks, 20 July 1949.

117. Kux, *India and the United States*, p. 70.

118. *Time Magazine*, 54, 16 (17 Oct. 1949).

119. Ramachandra Guha, 'What's left of Nehru?', *Outlook* (18 Aug. 2003).

120. Kux, *India and the United States*, p. 70.

121. McMahon, *Cold War*, pp. 55–6.

122. Nehru to Pandit, 24 Aug. 1949, *SWJN*, SS, vol. 13, pp. 288–90.

123. MoC between Nehru and Acheson, 12 Oct. 1949, ibid., pp. 295–7.

124. McMahon, *Cold War*, pp. 56–7. Also see: Nehru to Pandit, 8 June 1949, *SWJN*, SS, vol. 11, p. 356; Nehru to Mathai, 14 Aug. 1949, *SWJN*, SS, vol. 12, p. 404; Nehru to Pandit, 24 Aug. 1949, *SWJN*, SS, vol. 13, pp. 288–9.

125. TNA, MoC between Pandit and Henderson, 30 Apr. 1949, RG59/lot file 67044; NA, FO 371/76100, MoC between Nye and Franks, 20 July 1949.

126. Foreign policy resolution passed by Nehru at Jaipur Congress, 19 Dec. 1948, *SWJN*, SS, vol. 8, p. 341.

127. Nehru to Patel, 21 May 1948, *SWJN*, SS, vol. 6, p. 454.

128. Nehru to Henderson, 8 Jan. 1949, *SWJN*, SS, vol. 9, p. 441.

129. Nehru to Pandit, 15 Mar. 1949, *SWJN*, SS, vol. 10, pp. 491–2.

130. Nehru to Pandit, 31 May 1949, *SWJN*, SS, vol. 11, p. 355.

131. Nehru to Pandit, 8 June 1949, ibid., p. 356.

132. Nehru to Radhakrishnan, 7 May 1949, ibid., p. 363.

133. Nehru to Pandit, 22 June 1949, *SWJN*, SS, vol. 12, p. 397.

134. Nehru to Mathai, 14 Aug. 1949, ibid., p. 404.

135. Nehru to Pandit, 23 Sep. 1949, *SWJN*, SS, vol. 13, p. 290.

136. Nehru, 'A Voyage of Discovery', address to US House of Representatives, Washington, 13 Oct. 1949, ibid., pp. 301–4.

137. NA, DO 133/70, Nye to CRO, 19 Oct. 1949.

138. MoC between Nehru and the US delegation to the UN, *SWJN*, SS, vol. 13, p. 307.

139. Nehru, 'Building a New India', address to the Indian residents of New York, 15 Oct. 1949, ibid., pp. 310–11.

140. NA, DO 133/70, Nye to CRO, 19 Oct. 1949.

141. Nehru to Radhakrishnan, 24 Oct. 1949, *SWJN*, SS, vol. 13, p. 399.

142. Inder Singh, *Limits of British Influence*, p. 65 and Vijaya Lakshmi Pandit, *The Scope of Happiness*, London: Weidenfeld and Nicolson, 1979, p. 253.

143. Pandit, *Scope of Happiness*, p. 253.

144. Nehru to Bajpai, 3 Nov. 1950, *SWJN*, SS, vol. 15, pp. 524–30.

145. Nehru to Krishna Menon, 24 Oct. 1949, ibid., p. 410.

146. TNA, MoC between Henderson, G.D. Birla and others, Delhi, 23 Mar. 1949, RG59/lot file 67044/box 1.

147. TNA, George McGhee to Henderson, 20 Dec. 1950, ibid.

148. NA, DO 133/70, Nye to CRO, 20 Mar. 1950.

149. Nehru to chief ministers, 2 Oct. 1949, in Parthasarthy (ed.), *Letters*, vol. 1, p. 484.

150. McMahon, *Cold War*, p. 55.

151. Inder Singh, *Limits of British Influence*, p. 65.

152. J.N. Dixit, *India's Foreign Policy 1947–2003*, New Delhi: Picus Books, 2003, p. 44.

153. James Chace, *Acheson: The Secretary of State who Created the American World*, London: Simon and Schuster, 1998, pp. 10, 292.

154. Nehru to Bajpai, 3 Nov. 1950, *SWJN*, SS, vol. 15, pp. 524–30.

155. NA, DO 133/70, Nye to CRO, 20 Mar. 1950.

156. Nehru to Dorothy Norman, 25 June 1951, *SWJN*, SS, vol. 16/part 1, pp. 97–100.

157. Ibid.

3. 'FUNNY PEOPLE'

1. Jane C. Loeffler, *The Architecture of American Diplomacy: Building America's Embassies*, 2nd edn, New York: Princeton Architectural Press, 2010, pp. 27, 185.

2. Cited in ibid., p. 189.

3. Ibid., p. 183.

4. H.W. Brands, 'The Spectre of Neutralism: Eisenhower, India and the Problem of Neutralism', in Joan P. Krieg (ed.), *Dwight D. Eisenhower*, New York: Greenwood Press, 1987, p. 202.

5. Harold Strassen and Marshal Houts, *Eisenhower: Turning the World Towards Peace*, St. Paul: Magnus Publishing, 1990, p. 132.

6. Robert McMahon, *The Cold War on the Periphery: The United States, India, and Pakistan*, New York: Columbia University Press, 1994, p. 81.

7. Sarvepalli Gopal, *Jawaharlal Nehru: A Biography*, vol. 2, *1947–1956*, New Delhi: Oxford University Press, 1979, pp. 104–5.

8. Vijayalakshmi Pandit, *The Scope of Happiness*, London: Weidenfeld and Nicolson, 1979, p. 258.

9. Nehru Memorial Museum and Library [hereafter NMML], Y.D. Gundevia Papers, 'Some Interesting Aspects of Nehru's Policies', speech given to the Poona branch of the Indian Council of World Affairs, subject file no. 7.

10. Cited in Brands, 'The Spectre of Neutralism', p. 198.

11. Ibid., p. 202.

12. Diers Brendon, *Ike: His Life and Times*, New York: Harper and Row Publishers, 1986, p. 5.

13. Nehru to B.N. Rau, 1 July 1950, *Selected Works of Jawaharlal Nehru*, Second Series [hereafter *SWJN*, SS], vol. 14, part 2, p. 312.

14. American ambassador in Korea to secretary of state, 25 June 1950, *Foreign Relations of the United States* [hereafter *FRUS*], vol. 8, p. 127.

15. For a detailed account of China's approach to the Korean War see Chen Jian, *China's Road to the Korean War: The Making of the Sino-American Confrontation*, New York: Columbia University Press, 1994.

16. Nehru to Menon, 27 June 1950, *SWJN*, SS, vol. 14/part 2, p. 307.

17. Shiv Dayal, *India's Role in the Korean Question*, New Delhi: S. Chand & Co., 1959, pp. 73–4.

18. Nehru to Rau, 1 July 1950, *SWJN*, SS, vol. 14/part 2, pp. 310–12.

19. Nehru to chief ministers, 2 July 1950, in G. Parthasarthy (ed.), *Jawaharlal Nehru: Letters to Chief Ministers*, vol. 1, 1947, London: Jawaharlal Nehru Memorial Fund and Oxford University Press, 1985, pp. 118–22.

20. Nehru to Menon, 27 June 1950, *SWJN*, SS, vol. 14/part 2, p. 307.

21. National Archives, Kew Gardens, London [Hereafter NA], KV2/2512, E.R. Kitchin to Secret Intelligence Service, 4 Aug. 1950.

22. Nehru to Stalin and Acheson, 12 July 1950, *SWJN*, SS, vol. 14/part 2, p. 347.

23. Nehru to Thakin Nu, 2 July 1950, ibid., p. 316.

24. Nehru, 'Fifty–Fifty Possibility of a World War', 7 July 1950, ibid., p. 321.

25. Nehru to Radhakrishnan, 8 July 1950, ibid., p. 343.

26. Nehru to Rau, 1 July 1950, ibid., p. 311.

27. Nehru to Pandit, 8 July 1950, *SWJN*, SS, vol. 14/part 2, pp. 340–3.

28. UNSC Resolution 83 (50), 27 June 1950, text available at: http://daccess-dds-ny.un.org/doc/RESOLUTION/GEN/NR0/064/96/IMG/NR006496.pdf? OpenElement

29. Nehru to Rau, 1 July 1950, *SWJN*, SS, vol. 14/part 2, p. 311.

30. Text available in Dayal, *India's Role in the Korean Question*, pp. 74–5.

31. Nehru to Rau, 1 July 1950, *SWJN*, SS, vol. 14/part 2, p. 313.

32. NMML, Office of the High Commissioner for India, drafted by S.W. Zaman, London, 15 July 1950, report no. 13, P.N. Haksar Papers, 3rd instalment, subject file no. 27 (b).

33. Text available in Dayal, *India's Role in the Korean Question*, p. 80.

34. Nehru to Pandit, 29 June 1950, *SWJN*, SS, vol. 14/part 2, p. 309.

35. Note: the 'Unified Command' was placed under American charge according to Security Council resolution passed on 7 July 1950. Text available at: http:// www.unhcr.org/refworld/publisher,UNSCKOR,3b00f1e85c,0.html

36. The National Archives, College Park, Maryland, [hereafter TNA], Hare to Acheson, 3 July 1950, office files of Philip C. Jessup, RG59/lot file no. 53, D 211/ box no. 3.

37. Henderson's record of conversation with Nehru, 28 June 1950, *SWJN*, SS, vol. 14/part 2, pp. 307–8.

38. Note: this is clearly brought out in Acheson's detailed note on Korea as the crisis unfolded on 25 June. See secretary of state to embassy in Moscow, 25 June 1950, *FRUS*, vol. 8, pp. 14–155.

39. Anita Inder Singh, *The Limits of British Influence: South Asia and the Anglo-American Relationship 1947–56*, London: Pinter, 1993, p. 72.

40. TNA, 'Exchanges of Messages between Secretary of State Acheson (18 July)

and Prime Minister Nehru (13 July)', Washington, 19 July 1950, office files of Philip C. Jessup, RG59/lot file no. 53, D 211/box no. 4.

41. TNA, MoC between Pandit and Dulles, Washington, 15 Aug. 1950, office files of Philip C. Jessup, RG59/lot file no. 53, D 211/box no. 3.

42. TNA, Jessup to Rusk, 21 July 1950, office files of Philip C. Jessup, RG59/lot file no. 53, D 211/box no. 4.

43. Nehru, 'The Psychology of Indian Nationalism' (article in *The Review of Nations*), Geneva, Jan. 1927, cited in *Selected Works of Jawaharlal Nehru*, First Series [hereafter *SWJN*, FS], vol. 2, p. 267.

44. Nehru, 'Report on the Brussels Congress', 19 Feb. 1927, ibid., pp. 279–82.

45. For a brief but excellent introduction to Mao see Andrew Bingham Kennedy, *The International Ambitions of Mao and Nehru*, Cambridge: Cambridge University Press, 2012, pp. 43–67.

46. Nehru's interview with Robert Trumbull (*New York Times*), *SWJN*, SS, vol. 15/part 1, pp. 363–4.

47. Note to secretary general, 12 Aug. 1950, ibid., pp. 367–8.

48. Note: Burma recognised the PRC on 9 Dec. For details see Jonathan D. Spence, *The Search for Modern China*, London: W.W. Norton and Company, 1990, p. 525.

49. Nehru to Pandit, 30 Aug. 1950, *SWJN*, SS, vol. 15/part 1, pp. 380–2.

50. Spence, *The Search for Modern China*, p. 524. For a detailed account of Stalin's approach to Mao see Kathryn Weathersby, 'Soviet Aims in Korea and the Origins of the Korean War,' *Cold War History Project*, Working Paper 9, Washington, DC: Woodrow Wilson Center, Nov. 1993.

51. Odd Arne Westad, *The Global Cold War*, Cambridge: Cambridge University Press, 2007, p. 65.

52. NMML, Office of the High Commissioner for India, drafted by P.N. Haksar, London, 20 June 1950, report no. 12, P N. Haksar Papers, 3rd instalment, subject file no. 27 (b).

53. NMML, Office of the High Commissioner for India, drafted by S.W. Zaman, London, 15 July 1950, report no. 13, P.N. Haksar Papers, 3rd instalment, subject file no. 27 (b)

54. Nehru to Thakin Nu, 2 Aug. 1950, *SWJN*, SS, vol. 15/part 1, pp. 331–2.

55. Nehru to Rau, 21 Aug. 1950, ibid., p. 372.

56. NA, DO 35/2838, Nye to CRO, 9 Aug. 1950.

57. Nehru to Rau, 27 Aug. 1950, *SWJN*, SS, vol. 15/part 1, p. 380.

58. TNA, MoC between Pandit, Dulles, Rusk and others, Washington, 15 Aug. 1950, office files of Philip C. Jessup, RG59/lot file no. 53 D 211/box no. 4.

59. TNA, MoC between Pandit, McGhee, Rusk and others, Washington, 5 Sep. 1950, office files of Philip C. Jessup, RG59/lot file no. 53 D 211/box no. 4.

60. TNA, MoC between Pandit, McGhee, Jessup and others, Washington, 6 Sep. 1950, office files of Philip C. Jessup, RG59/lot file no. 53 D 211/box no. 4.

61. NA, DO 35/2838, Nye to CRO, 27 Sep. 1950. For a Chinese viewpoint see: S.J. Weng, *Peking's UN Policy: Continuity and Change*, New York: Praeger, 1972, pp. 84–92.

62. Henderson to secretary of state, 23 Sep. 1950, *FRUS*, vol. 8, p. 763.

63. Henderson to secretary of state, 27 Sep. 1950, *FRUS*, vol. 8, pp. 790–3.

64. Nehru to secretary general, 24 Sep. 1950, *SWJN*, SS, vol. 15/part 1, pp. 395–7.

65. Text available at: http://www.un.org/depts/dhl/landmark/pdf/ares377e.pdf

66. Dayal, *India's Role in the Korean Question*, pp. 100–2.

67. Henderson to secretary of state, New Delhi, 28 Sep. 1950, *FRUS*, vol. 8, pp. 809–10.

68. Nehru to secretary general, 24 Sep. 1950, *SWJN*, SS, vol. 15/part 1, pp. 395–7.

69. US delegation at the UN to the UN General Assembly, 28 Sep. 1950, *FRUS*, vol. 8, pp. 799–803.

70. NA, DO 35/2838, Nye to CRO, 29 Sep. 1950.

71. Henderson to secretary of state, 4 Oct. 1950, *FRUS*, vol. 8, pp. 869–73.

72. William Stueck, *The Korean War*, Princeton: Princeton University Press, 1997, p. 94.

73. Nehru to Zhou, 27 Sep. 1950, *SWJN*, vol. 15/part 1, p. 398.

74. Nehru to Bevin, 27 Sep. 1950, ibid., pp. 400–1.

75. NA, DO 35/2838, Nye to CRO, 27 Sep. 1950.

76. Acting secretary of state to Henderson, 28 Sep. 1950, *FRUS*, vol. 8, pp. 820–1.

77. Henderson to secretary of state, 29 Sep. 1950, *FRUS*, vol. 8, p. 823.

78. William Head, 'The China Policy of the Truman Administration and the Debate over the Recognition of the People's Republic of China, 1949', in William F. Levantrosser (ed.), *Harry S. Truman: The Man from Independence*, New York: Greenwood Press, 1986, p. 102.

79. NMML, oral history section, B.R. Nanda interview with Chester Bowles in 1972, file no. 286.

80. Nehru to Panikkar, 4 Oct. 1950, *SWJN*, SS, vol. 15/part 1, p. 409.

81. British embassy in Washington to Department of State, undated, *FRUS*, vol. 8, p. 814.

82. NA, DO 35/2838, Nye to CRO, 14 Oct. 1950.

83. NMML, Y.D. Gundevia Papers, 'Some Interesting Aspects of Nehru's Policies', speech given to the Poona branch of the Indian Council of World Affairs, subject file no. 7.

84. Nehru to Rau, 30 Aug. 1950, *SWJN*, SS, vol. 15/part 1, p. 383.

85. NA, DO 35/2838, Nye to CRO, 29 Sep. 1950.

86. Nehru to Rau, 30 Aug. 1950, *SWJN*, SS, vol. 15/part 1, p. 383.

87. Nehru to Panikkar, 4 Oct. 1950, ibid., p. 409.

88. Nehru to chief ministers, 1 Oct. 1950, in Parthasarthy (ed.), *Letters*, vol. 1, pp. 217–18.

89. Chen Jian, 'The Sino-Soviet Alliance and China's Entry into the Korean War', *Cold War History Project*, Working Paper 1, Washington, DC: Woodrow Wilson Center, June 1992, pp. 27–9.

90. NA, DO 35/2838, Nye to CRO, 3 Oct. 1950. Note: recent evidence suggests that Zhou's warning to Panikkar might have been made to buy time for military preparedness or to rally nationalist fervour. For an explanation, see Jian, *China's Road to the Korean War*, pp. 180–1.

91. NA, DO 35/2838, Nye to CRO, 4 Oct. 1950.

92. McMahon, *Cold War*, p. 86.

93. Nehru to chief ministers, 18 Feb. 1951, in Parthasarthy (ed.), *Letters*, vol. 1, p. 331.

94. NA, DO 35/2838, Nye to CRO, 13 Oct. 1950.

95. Stueck, *The Korean War*, p. 94.

96. Jian, *China's Road to the Korean War*, p. 186.

97. Ibid., pp. 211–13.

98. National Intelligence Estimate, Washington, 8 Nov. 1950, *FRUS*, vol. 8, pp. 1101–2.

99. Ibid.

100. Inder Singh, *Limits of British Influence*, p. 84.

101. Dennis Kux, *India and the United States: Estranged Democracies, 1941–1991*, Washington, DC: National Defense University Press, 1992, p. 74.

102. NMML, Chester Bowles, oral history interview with B.R. Nanda, New Delhi, 9 Mar. 1971, record no. 288.

103. McMahon, *Cold War*, pp. 82–6.

104. Cited in Kux, *India and the United States*, p. 74.

105. Nehru to Pandit, 27 Oct. 1950, *SWJN*, SS, vol. 15/part 2, p. 517.

106. Stated by McGhee in McMahon, *Cold War*, pp. 88–9.

107. Kux, *India and the United States*, p. 74.

108. Cited in McMahon, *Cold War*, p. 87.

109. MoC by director of the Office of Chinese Affairs to the assistant secretary of state for Far Eastern affairs, *FRUS*, vol. 8, Washington, 4 Oct. 1950, p. 865.

110. Ibid., p. 865.

111. TNA, MoC between Keskar, Pandit, Jessup and others, Washington, 23 Oct. 1950, files of Philip C. Jessup, RG59/lot file no. 53 D 211/box no. 3.

112. Henderson to secretary of state, 5 Oct. 1950, *FRUS*, vol. 8, pp. 880–3.

113. Nehru to Rau, 25 Oct. 1950, *SWJN*, SS, vol. 15/part 1, p. 460.

114. Nehru to Pandit, 30 Oct. 1950, *SWJN*, SS, vol. 15/part 2, p. 521.

115. David Malone, *Does the Elephant Dance? Contemporary Indian Foreign Policy*, London: Oxford University Press, 2011, pp. 154–5.

116. Ibid., p. 156.

117. Note, Nehru to secretary general, 27 Oct. 1950, *SWJN*, SS, vol. 15/part 2, p. 519.

118. T. Ramakrishna Reddy, *India's Policy in the UN*, Rutherford, NJ: Fairleigh Dickinson University Press, 1968, p. 149.

119. Cited in: Inder Singh, *Limits of British Influence*, p. 85.

120. NA, DO 35/2838, Nye to CRO, New Delhi, 3 Dec. 1950.

121. Nehru to Bevin, 30 Nov. 1950, *SWJN*, SS, vol. 15/part 2, p. 414.

122. Nehru to Attlee, 22 Dec. 1950, ibid., p. 457.

123. Note to secretary general, 30 Nov. 1950, ibid., pp. 415–16.

124. Nehru to Rau, 30 Nov. 1950, ibid., p. 416.

125. Nehru to Rau, 9 Dec. 1950, ibid., pp. 45–452.

126. Stueck, *The Korean War*, p. 139.

127. Nehru Panikkar, 2 Dec. 1950, *SWJN*, SS, vol. 15/part 2, p. 420; Nehru to Panikkar, 7 Dec. 1950, ibid., p. 435.

128. Nehru, 'Record of talk with Henderson', ibid., pp. 421–2.

129. Dayal, *India's Role in the Korean Question*, p. 118.

130. Stueck, *The Korean War*, p. 141.

131. TNA, note by Ernest Gross, New York, 8 Dec. 1950, office files of Philip C. Jessup, RG59/lot file no. 53 D 211/box no. 3.

133. Nehru to Rau, 9 Dec. 1950, *SWJN*, SS, vol. 15/part 2, pp. 451–2.

133. Note: this was communicated to Krishna Menon in London. NA, DO 35/2838, MoC between secretary of state for Commonwealth relations and Menon, London, 11 Dec. 1950.

134. TNA, 'Statement by Wu Hsiu-Chuan to the General Assembly', 16 Dec. 1950, office files of Philip C. Jessup, RG59/lot file no. 53 D 211/box no. 4.

135. NA, DO 35/2838, Nye to CRO, 8 Dec. 1950, 'Text of GoI Telegram to Panikkar'.

136. NA, DO 35/2838, Nye to CRO, 19 Dec. 1950, 'Text of Panikkar Talk with Chou'.

137. Nehru to Rau, 12 Dec. 1950, *SWJN*, SS, vol. 15/part 2, p. 453.

138. William Stueck, *The Korean War: An international history* (Princeton: Princeton University Press (1997), p. 141.

139. NA, DO 35/2838, 'Text of Nehru's Telegram to PM, Delivered by Menon', New Delhi, 22 Dec. 1950.

140. TNA, MoC between Harry Howard (US delegation to the UN), Charles Malik (Lebanese delegation to the UN) and others, office files of Philip C. Jessup, RG59/lot file no. 53 D 211/box no. 4.

141. Stueck, *An International History*, p. 142.

142. Nehru, 'Statement to the Press', 12 June 1951, *SWJN*, SS, vol. 16/part 1, p. 96.

143. Cited in McMahon, *Cold War*, p. 101.

144. Nehru to Pandit, 13 Dec. 1950, *SWJN*, SS, vol. 15/part 2, pp. 530–1.

145. McGhee to Acheson, 30 Jan. 1951, *FRUS*, vol. 6/part 2, pp. 2095–107.

146. Nehru to Pandit, 13 Feb. 1951, *SWJN*, SS, vol. 15/part 2, pp. 533–4.

147. 'Dissentient Views on US Food Aid to India', *Times of India*, 6 Mar. 1951.

148. Cited by Senator Theodore Green in 'US Food for India Bill in Senate', *Times of India*, 28 Apr. 1951.

149. According to former Ambassador William Bullit, see 'India Asked to Join West', *Times of India*, 1 Oct. 1951.

150. Stated by William C. Foster, cited in McMahon, *Cold War*, p. 93.

151. Henderson to Acheson, 28 Jan. 1951, *FRUS*, vol. 6/part 2, p. 2092.

152. Henderson to secretary of state, 27 Jan. 1951, *FRUS*, vol. 7/part 1, pp. 140–1.

153. Nehru to Rau, 12 May 1951, *SWJN*, SS, vol. 16/part 1, p. 431.

154. Nehru to B.N. Chakrabarty (secretary general for Commonwealth relations, MEA), 14 June 1951, ibid., p. 434.

155. Nehru to K.P.S. Menon, 17 Apr. 1951, ibid., pp. 429–30.

156. Henderson to secretary of state, 21 Feb. 1951, ibid., p. 2127.

157. Nehru, 'Broadcast to Nation', 1 May 1951, *SWJN*, SS, vol. 16/part 1, pp. 39–41.

158. Henderson to Acheson, 2 Feb. 1951, *FRUS*, vol. 6/part 2, p. 2109.

159. Gopal, *Nehru: A Biography*, vol. 2, p. 138.

160. Nehru to K.P.S. Menon, 27 May 1951, *SWJN*, SS, vol. 16/part 1, p. 434; Nehru to Radhakrishnan, 23 Mar. 1951, ibid., pp. 70–1.

161. Nehru to Pandit, 22 Mar. 1951, *SWJN*, SS, vol. 16/part 1, p. 69.

162. Nehru to secretary general, New Delhi, 10 Apr. 1951, ibid., pp. 71–2.

163. Nehru to Pandit, 11 Apr. 1951, ibid., pp. 72–3.

164. Nehru to Pandit, New Delhi, 12 Apr. 1951, ibid., pp. 74–5.

165. Nehru to Pandit, New Delhi, 17 Apr. 1951, ibid., pp. 82–4.

166. Ibid.

167. 'Draft Statement of Policy Proposed by the National Security Council on South Asia', enclosure to NSC 98/1, 22 Jan. 1951, *FRUS*, vol. 6/part 2, Washington: United States Government and Printing Office, 1977, p. 2148; Henderson to secretary of state, 17 Apr. 1951, ibid., p. 2146.

168. Henderson to Acheson, 12 Apr. 1951, *FRUS*, vol. 6/part 2, pp. 2142–3.

169. MoC by the directors of the Office of South Asian Affairs, Washington, 21 May 1951, ibid., p. 2153.

170. NA, KV2/2513, note, 'The Present Position and Views of Krishna Menon', 19 July 1952.

171. Nehru to Deshmukh, 31 Oct. 1950, *SWJN*, SS, vol. 15/part 2, p. 522; Nehru to Pandit, 13 Dec. 1950, ibid., pp. 530–1.

172. 'Dangerous to Depend on Other Countries', *Times of India*, 14 Apr. 1951.

173. 'Dissentient Views on US Food Aid to India', *Times of India*, 6 Mar. 1951.

174. 'India Will Follow Independent Line', *Times of India*, 23 Feb. 1951.

175. Nehru to Dorothy Norman, 25 June 1951, *SWJN*, SS, vol. 16/part 1, pp. 97–100.

176. 'Draft Statement of Policy Proposed by the National Security Council on South Asia', enclosure to NSC 98/1, 22 Jan. 1951, *FRUS*, vol. 6/part 2, pp. 1651–2.

177. NMML, Chester Bowles, oral history interview with B.R. Nanda, New Delhi, 7 Mar. 1971.

178. Howard Schaffer, *Chester Bowles: New Dealer in the Cold War*, Cambridge, MA: Harvard University Press, *1993*, pp. 3–4.

179. Ibid.

180. Robert Beisner, *Dean Acheson: A Life in the Cold War*, New York: Oxford University Press, 2009, pp. 506–508

181. Nehru to Panikkar, 20 Mar. 1952, *SWJN*, SS, vol. 17, p. 512.

182. Gopal, *Nehru: A Biography*, vol. 2, p. 162.

183. For details on the dismissal see Stueck, *The Korean War*, pp. 178–203.

184. Nehru to Menon, 17 Apr. 1951, *SWJN*, SS, vol. 16/part 1, pp. 429–30.

185. Gopal, *Nehru: A Biography*, vol. 2, p. 139.

186. Nehru to secretary general, 11 Dec. 1951, *SWJN*, SS, vol. 17, p. 519.

187. Nehru to Panikkar, 7 Apr. 1952, *SWJN*, SS, vol. 18, p. 531.

188. 'South Asia Regional Conference of US Diplomatic and Consular Officers', 26 Feb. to 2 Mar. 1951, Nuwara Eliya, *FRUS* 1951, vol. 6/part 2, pp. 1666–8.

189. Russell Freedman, *Eleanor Roosevelt: A Life of Discovery*, New York: Clarion Books, 1993, pp. 1–4 and p. 159.

190. Eleanor Roosevelt, *India and the Awakening East*, London: Hutchinson, 1954, p. 89.

191. Nehru to Panikkar, 22 May 1952, *SWJN*, SS, vol. 18, pp. 537–8.

192. NA, FO371/105481, FO to embassy in Washington, 30 Dec. 1952.

193. Nehru to Pandit, 7 May 1952, *SWJN*, SS, vol. 18, p. 533; Nehru to Pandit, 15 May 1952, ibid., p. 535.

194. Secretary of state to Bowles, 25 Apr. 1952, *FRUS*, vol. 9/part 1, p. 47; Charge in India to State, 12 June 1952, ibid., p. 63.

195. Nehru to Panikkar, 22 May 1952, *SWJN*, SS, vol. 18, pp. 537–8.

196. Nehru to Panikkar, 27 June 1952, ibid., p. 546.

197. Aparna Basu, *G.L. Mehta: A Many Splendoured Man*, New Delhi: Concept Publishing, 2001, pp. 15, 139.

198. NA, KV2/2512, Delhi to Secret Intelligence Service, 14 Aug. 1950.

199. James Barron, 'W.K. Harrison, 91, Army General, Dies', *New York Times*, 29 May 1987.

200. Nehru to Raghavan, 1 Oct. 1952, *SWJN*, SS, vol. 19, pp. 592–3.

201. Nehru to Raghavan, 26 Oct. 1952, *SWJN*, SS, vol. 20, p. 407.

202. Nehru to Pandit, 26 Oct. 1952, ibid., pp. 407–9.

203. NA, FO371/105481, 'Statement by Lester Pearson to the Canadian House of Commons', 8 Dec. 1952; Dayal, *India's Role in the Korean Question*, pp. 168–70.

204. Nehru to Raghavan, 2 Nov. 1952, *SWJN*, SS, vol. 20, p. 415.
205. Ibid., pp. 415–18.
206. Nehru to Menon, 8 Nov. 1952, ibid., p. 420.
207. Nehru to Raghavan, 20 Nov. 1952, ibid., p. 426.
208. Dayal, *India's Role in the Korean Question*, pp. 177–8.
209. NA, FO371/105481, 'Statement by Lester Pearson to the Canadian House of Commons', 8 Dec. 1952.
210. Nehru to Raghavan, 25 Nov. 1952, *SWJN*, SS, vol. 20, p. 429.
211. Nehru to Pandit, 26 Nov. 1952, ibid., p. 433.
212. NA, FO371/105481, Zhou to Pearson, 14 Dec. 1952.
213. NA, FO371/105481, R.H. Scott to Far East Department, 1 Jan. 1953.
214. NA, FO371/105481, CRO to India, 13 Jan. 1953.
215. Nehru to Pandit, 26 Nov. 1952, *SWJN*, SS, vol. 20, p. 433.
216. Nehru to Raghavan, 28 Nov. 1952, ibid., p. 441.
217. Nehru to Raghavan, 14 May 1952, ibid., pp. 438–9.
218. NA, FO371/105481, British embassy in Peking to FO, 23 Dec. 1952.
219. Leonard Mosley, *Dulles: A Biography of Eleanor, Allen, and John Foster Dulles*, London: Hodder and Stoughton, 1978, p. 5.
220. Townsend Hoopes, *The Devil and John Foster Dulles*, London: André Deutsch, 1973, p. 3.
221. Strassen and Houts, *Eisenhower*, p. 132.
222. Stueck, *The Korean War*, p. 309.
223. Nehru to Menon, 13 Apr. 1953, *SWJN*, SS, vol. 22, p. 425.
224. NMML, Pandit's interview with Ambassador Henry Cabot Lodge, New York, 25 Feb. 1953, V.L. Pandit Papers, subject file no. 4, 3rd instalment.
225. NA, FO371/105491, Washington to FO, 9 May 1953.
226. NA, FO371/105491, Delhi to CRO, 8 May 1953.
227. NA, FO371/105491, Delhi to CRO, 27 May 1953.
228. NA, FO371/105491, Washington to FO, 5 May 1953.
229. NA, FO371/105491, Delhi to CRO, 27 May 1953.
230. NMML, Chester Bowles, oral history interview with B.R. Nanda, New Delhi, 7 Mar. 1971.
231. NA, FO 371/105532, UK delegation in New York to FO, 12 Oct. 1953.
232. NMML, 'The Korean Question: Reports of the Neutral National Repatriation Commission', 9 Sep. 1953 to 21 Feb. 1954, UN General Assembly Eight Session/Official Records, P.N. Haksar Papers, 3rd instalment, file no. 40.
233. Loeffler, *The Architecture of American Diplomacy*, pp. 184–5.
234. Roosevelt, *India and the Awakening East*, pp. 99–100.
235. LHA, NSC Files, 'United States Policy towards Asia', Washington, 10 June 1949, NSC 48/MF 72.
236. LHA, NSC Files, 'The Position of the United States with Respect to Asia', Washington, 23 Dec. 1949, NSC 48/1/MF72.

237. LHA, NSC Files, 'A Report to the President', Washington, 30 Dec. 1949, NSC 48/2/MF72.

238. LHA, NSC Files, 'A Report to the NSC', Washington, 17 May 1951, NSC 48/5/MF72.

239. 'Means to Combat India's Policy of Neutralism', Washington, 30 Aug. 1951, *FRUS*, vol. 6/part 2, pp. 2172–3.

240. LHA, NSC Files, 'United States Policy towards South Asia', Washington, 19 Feb. 1954, NSC 5409.

241. Roosevelt, *India and the Awakening East*, p. 90.

4. 'SHAKEN'

1. Theodore C. Sorenson, *Kennedy*, London: Hodder and Stoughton, 1965, p. 663.

2. State to the embassy in Delhi, 27 Oct. 1962, *Foreign Relations of the United States* [hereafter *FRUS*], vol. 19, p. 352

3. Tape recording of B.K. Nehru's meeting with Kennedy, Washington, DC, 26 Oct. 1962, transcribed in Philip Zelikow and Ernest May (eds), *The Presidential Recordings, John F. Kennedy: The Great Crisis, Volume 3*, New York: W.W. Norton & Company, 2001, p. 339.

4. Ibid.

5. Cited in 'US Military Aid to Pakistan', *The Hindu*, 24 Dec. 1953.

6. John F. Kennedy Presidential Library and Museum [hereafter JKLM], Nehru to Kennedy, 19 Nov. 1962, NSC box 111. Note: the contents of this letter were only revealed in 1965. See Sudhir Ghosh, *Gandhi's Emissary*, London: Cresset Press, 1967, p. 309.

7. Inder Malhotra, 'Letters from the Darkest Hour', *Indian Express*, 17 Nov. 2012.

8. 'Nehru Vows to Fight On: May Accept Arms Help', *The Washington Post*, 26 Oct. 1962.

9. Ramachandra Guha, *India After Gandhi*, New York: Harper Collins, 2007, p. 336.

10. P.B. Sinha and A.A. Athale, *History of the Conflict with China, 1962*, New Delhi: History Division, Ministry of Defence, Government of India, 1992, p. 412. Note: only two and a half divisions of the Indian Army and five to six divisions of the Chinese army were involved in the confrontation.

11. Guha, *India after Gandhi*, p. 336.

12. Other works in the early period include: Werner Levi, 'Indian Neutralism Reconsidered', *Pacific Affairs*, 37, 2 (Summer 1964); T.A. Keenleyside, 'Prelude to Power: The Meaning of Non-Alliance before Independence', *Pacific Affairs*, 53, 3 (Autumn 1980).

13. Neville Maxwell, *India's China War*, London: Jonathan Cape, 1970, p. 11.

14. B.K. Nehru, *Nice Guys Finish Second*, New Delhi: Viking, 1997, p. 408.

15. D.K. Palit, *War in the High Himalayas: The Indian Army in Crisis, 1962*, London: Hurst, 1991, p. 343.

16. Dennis Kux, *India and the United States: Estranged Democracies, 1941–1991*, Washington, DC: National Defense University Press, 1992, p. 204.

17. Levi, 'Indian Neutralism Reconsidered'; Keenleyside; 'Prelude to Power'; Crabb, 'The Testing of Non-Alignment'; Klaus H. Pringsheim, 'China, India, and their Himalayan Border (1961–1963)', *Asian Survey*, 3, 10 (Oct. 1963), p. 493; Apurba Kundu, *Militarism in India: The Army and Civil Society*, London: Taurus Academic Studies, 1998, p. 87.

18. J.N. Dixit, *India's Foreign Policy 1947–2003*, New Delhi: Picus Books, 2003, p. 75.

19. Ibid., p. 75.

20. Quoted in Maxwell, *India's China War*, p. 76.

21. For a detailed analysis, see Alastair Lamb, *The China–India Border*, Oxford: Oxford University Press, 1964, pp. 11–13.

22. John W. Garver, *Protracted Contest: Sino-Indian Rivalry in the Twentieth Century*, Seattle: University of Washington Press, 2001, p. 42.

23. Cited in Srinath Raghavan, *War and Peace in Modern India*, New Delhi: Permanent Black, p. 234.

24. For a detailed and eloquent background to the border dispute see ibid., Chapter 7.

25. Nehru Memorial Museum and Library [hereafter NMML], oral history of R.K. Nehru, file no. 324.

26. Chen Jian, 'The Tibetan Rebellion of 1959 and China's Changing Relations with India and the Soviet Union', *Journal of Cold War Studies*, 8, 3 (Summer 2006), pp. 80–8.

27. For details see Chattar Singh Sharma, 'Panchsheela and After: Sino-India Relations in the Context of the Tibetan Insurrection', *Asian Survey*, 21, 3 (May 1962), pp. 426–8.

28. Guha, *India after Gandhi*, p. 303.

29. Jian, 'The Tibetan Rebellion', pp. 85–6.

30. Gaver, *Protracted Contest*, pp. 55–58.

31. NMML, oral history of the Dalai Lama, file no. 295.

32. NMML, oral history of K.P.S. Menon, file no. 363.

33. A detailed report on India's boundaries in these sectors can be found in Sinha and Athale, *History of the Conflict with China*, pp. 1–5.

34. Details on other territorial issues in the western sector can be found in Lamb, *The China–India Border*, pp. 7–8.

35. Ibid., pp. 7–13.

36. John Kenneth Galbraith to Kennedy, 17 Apr. 1961, cited in John Kenneth Galbraith, *Ambassador's Journal: A Personal Account of the Kennedy Years*, Boston: Houghton Mifflin Company, 1969, p. 64.

37. Paul Gore-Booth, *With Great Truth and Respect*, London: Constable, 1974, pp. 274–5.

38. McGeorge Bundy, 'The Presidency and the Peace', in Aida Dipace Donald (ed.), *John F. Kennedy and the New Frontier*, New York: Hill and Wang, 1966, p. 99.

39. Robert Dallek, *John F Kennedy: An Unfinished Life, 1917–1963*, New York: Allen Lane, 2003, p. 165.

40. Michael O' Brien, *John F. Kennedy: A Biography*, New York: Thomas Dunne Books, 2003, p. 233.

41. Kennedy, excerpt from interview, 8 July 1962, in Ernest K. Lindley (ed.), *The Winds of Freedom*, Boston: Beacon Press, 1963, pp. 233–4.

42. Galbraith, *Ambassador's Journal*, p. 1.

43. Dean Rusk, *As I Saw It: A Secretary of State's Memoirs*, London: I.B. Tauris, 1990, p. 133.

44. Warren I. Cohen, *Dean Rusk*, New Jersey: Cooper Square, 1980, p. 206.

45. Chester Bowles, *Promises to Keep: My Years in Public Life, 1941–1969*, New York: Harper and Row, 1971, p. 439.

46. The National Archives, College Park, Maryland, [hereafter TNA], Department of State, 'Guidelines for Policy and Operations', Apr. 1962, box 7, lot 67D396, RG 59.

47. McGeorge Bundy, *Envoy to the Middle World: Adventures in Diplomacy*, New York: Harper and Row, 1983, p. 297.

48. Bowles, *Promises to Keep*, pp. 310–12.

49. NMML, Desai to B.K. Nehru, New Delhi, 3 Jan. 1962, B.K. Nehru Papers, subject file no. 17.

50. B.K. Nehru, *Nice Guys Finish Second*, p. 387.

51. Note: this was most evident in discussing Kashmir with Kennedy. NMML, B.K. Nehru to Desai, 19 Jan. 1962, B.K. Nehru Papers, subject file no. 17.

52. Y.D. Gundevia, *Outside the Archives*, Hyderabad: Sangam Books, 1984, pp. 200–15.

53. Gore-Booth, *With Great Truth and Respect*, p. 274.

54. National Archives, Kew Gardens, London [Hereafter NA], FO 371/164913, Peking to Foreign Office, Peking, 22 Sep. 1962.

55. D.R. Mankekar, *The Guilty Men of 1962*, Bombay: Tulsi Shah Enterprises, 1968, p. 45. Note: the location of the Indian Army's post at Dhola has been disputed. For a debate see Maxwell, *India's China War*, pp. 296–301.

56. Raghavan, *War and Peace*, pp. 294–5.

57. Maxwell, *India's China War*, p. 304.

58. For a note on the organisation of the Indian Army in 1962 see *India 1962: A Reference Annual*, New Delhi: Publications Division, Ministry of Information and Broadcasting, Government of India, 1962, pp. 66–7.

59. Mankekar, *The Guilty Men of 1962*, p. 46.

60. Maxwell, *India's China War*, p. 305.

61. Mankekar, *The Guilty Men of 1962*, p. 46, also see B.N. Kaul, *The Untold Story*, New Delhi: Allied Publishers, 1967, p. 358.

62. B. N. Mullick, *My Years With Nehru*, Bombay: Allied Publishers, 1973, p. 345.

63. Kaul, *The Untold Story*, p. 358. Note: while Kaul writes that Daulat Singh was heard by Krishna Menon, Mankekar states that Daulat Singh had made these comments only to Thapar. Mankekar, *The Guilty Men of 1962*, p. 46.

64. Palit, *War in the High Himalayas*, pp. 219–21. Also see Maxwell, *India's China Wars*, p. 313.

65. Mankekar, *The Guilty Men of 1962*, p. 47.

66. Note: the 33 corps was taken away from the NEFA to be in command only in Sikkim, Nagaland and the East Pakistan front. Palit, *War in the High Himalayas*, p. 221. Also see Maxwell, *India's China War*, p. 324.

67. NA, 371/164913, Delhi to War Office, 5 Oct. 1962. Also see Kaul, *The Untold Story*, pp. 367–8.

68. Romesh Thapar, 'Handling the Chinese', *Economic Weekly*, 14, 41 (13 Oct. 1962), pp. 1611–12.

69. Ibid.

70. Apurba Kundu, *Militarism in India: The Army and Civil Society in Consensus*, London: Tauris, 1998, pp. 101–2.

71. NMML, oral history with B.M. Kaul, file no. 93.

72. Sarvepalli Gopal, *Jawaharlal Nehru: A Biography*, vol. 3, *1956–64*, London: Cape, 1984, p. 210.

73. NMML, oral history with B.M. Kaul, file no. 93.

74. Note: based on a survey of newspaper articles (on a daily basis) in *The Hindu*, *The New York Times* and *The Washington Post* between 1 Aug. 1962 and 22 Sep. 1962.

75. Gundevia, *Outside the Archives*, p. 15

76. B.G. Verghese, *First Draft: Witness to the Making of Modern India*, New Delhi: Tranquebar, 2010, p. 37.

77. 'Desai to Meet US Senators', *The Hindu*, 23 Sep. 1962.

78. John P. Dalvi, *Himalayan Blunder*, Dehra Dun: Nataraj Publishers, 1969, p. 157.

79. Galbraith, *Ambassador's Diary*, p. 352.

80. Mullick, *My Years*, p. 341.

81. Palit, *War in the High Himalayas*, pp. 209–24.

82. Mullick, *My Years*, p. 360.

83. Guha, *India after Gandhi*, p. 309.

84. Maxwell, *India's China War*, p. 325.

85. Sinha and Athale, *History of the Conflict with China*, p. 98

86. Ibid., p. 99.

87. Ibid.

88. Mullick, *My Years*, p. 359.

89. 'Indians in Border Clash', *The Times*, 11 Oct. 1962.

90. Kaul, *The Untold Story*, p. 382

91. Note: the attack left seven Indians killed, seven missing, eleven wounded and thirty-three Chinese killed. Maxwell, *India's China War*, p. 339.

92. Mullick, *My Years*, p. 361.

93. Palit, *War in the High Himalayas*, p. 225.

94. Maxwell, *India's China War*, p. 338.

95. Mankekar, *The Guilty Men of 1962*, p. 50, also see: Gopal, *Nehru: A Biography*, vol. 3, p. 220.

96. Mullick, *My Years*, pp. 361–2. The attendees to this meeting have been confirmed by other sources, see: Maxwell, *India's China War*, p. 340; Kaul, *The Untold Story*, p. 386.

97. Mullick, *My Years*, p. 362

98. Kaul, *The Untold Story*, p. 386, also see: Palit, *War in the High Himalayas*, p. 227.

99. Kaul, *The Untold Story*, p. 386.

100. Maxwell, *India's China War*, p. 340.

101. B. K. Nehru, *Nice Guys Finish Second*, p. 344.

102. Kaul, *Untold Story*, p. 320; read with B.K. Nehru, *Nice Guys Finish Second*, pp. 344–5; NMML, oral history with B.M. Kaul, file no. 93.

103. B.K. Nehru, *Nice Guys Finish Second*, p. 345.

104. NMML, note by M.J. Desai, 4 May 1962, B.K. Nehru Papers, subject file no. 17.

105. Note: there has been some debate with regards to the final orders given on 11 Oct.: (1) Kaul states that he was told to hold present positions, which he accepted (see Kaul, *The Untold Story*, p. 386); (2) according to Palit, Thapar ordered Kaul to go ahead with offensive operations in Thag-La (see Palit, *War in the High Himalayas*, p. 232); (3) it should be noted that Thapar and Sen did not agree with Kaul's assessment of Chinese strength, but nevertheless in the meeting adhered to the prime minister's directive that offensive operations should be ceased for the time being (Sinha and Athale, *History of the Conflict with China*, p. 101); (4) Mullick, like Kaul, claims that the decision taken was that Indian positions would be held but no offensive action would be taken (Mullick, My Years with Nehru, p. 363); (5) Mankekar states that Nehru had said to hold positions as they were (Mankekar, *The Guilty Men of 1962*, p. 50); (6) Maxwell's account corroborates those by Kaul and Mankekar (Maxwell, *India's China War*, pp. 34–342).

106. Romesh Thapar, 'NEFA and All That', *Economic Weekly*, 14, 42 (20 Oct. 1962), p. 1649.

107. Gopal, *Nehru: A Biography*, vol. 3, p. 220.

108. Sinha and Athale, *History of the Conflict with China*, pp. 101–4.

109. Jawaharlal Nehru, *Jawaharlal Nehru: Letters to Chief Ministers*, vol. 5, 1958–64, London: Jawaharlal Nehru Memorial Fund and Oxford University Press, 1989, distributed by Oxford University Press, pp. 534–6.

110. A list of losses and time sequences can be found in Sinha and Athale, *History of the Conflict with China*, pp. 436–9.

111. Palit, *War in the High Himalayas*, p. 242.

112. Sinha and Athale, *History of the Conflict with China*, pp. 436–9.

113. Palit, *War in the High Himalayas*, p. 268.

114. Thapar, 'NEFA and All That', p. 1650.

115. 'UK Support on Border Issue', *The Guardian*, 1 Oct. 1962.

116. MoC from Stat to Bundy, 15 Oct. 1962, *FRUS*, vol. 19, pp. 57–8.

117. Memorandum from president's deputy special assistant for national security affairs (Kaysen) to President Kennedy, 26 Oct. 1962, *FRUS*, vol. 19, pp. 351–2.

118. A.M. Rosenthal, 'India Searching for Aid in Fight', *New York Times*, 22 Oct. 1962; 'India Reported Seeking Allied Modern Weapons', *Washington Post*, 22 Oct. 1962.

119. NA, FO 371/164914, Delhi to CRO, 21 Oct. 1962.

120. NA, FO 371/164914, Delhi to CRO, 20 Oct. 1962.

121. Galbraith to Kennedy, 16 Oct. 1962, in Galbraith, *Ambassador's Journal*, p. 268.

122. JKLM, Galbraith to Kennedy, 16 Oct. 1962, Galbraith correspondence with Kennedy, NSC box 118 a. Also see Galbraith to State, 24 Oct. 1962, in *FRUS*, vol. 19, p. 350.

123. 'Nation Must Unite to Face Grave Peril', *The Hindu*, 23 Oct. 1962.

124. NA, FO 371/164914, Delhi to CRO, 21 Oct. 1962.

125. Kaul, *The Untold Story*, pp. 396–7.

126. Palit, *War in the High Himalayas*, p. 273.

127. Ibid.

128. Ibid.

129. S.S. Khera, *India's Defence Problem*, New Delhi: Orient-Longman, 1968, p. 230.

130. John Lall, *Aksaichin and the Sino-Indian Conflict*, New Delhi: Allied Publishers, 1989, p. 282; also see Mullick, *My Years*, pp. 403–4.

131. Galbraith to State, 24 Oct. 1962, *FRUS*, vol. 19, p. 350.

132. Galbraith, *Ambassador's Journal*, pp. 355–78; Galbraith to State, 24 Oct. 1962, *FRUS*, vol. 19, p. 350.

133. See: (1) Galbraith to State, 24 Oct. 1962, *FRUS*, vol. 19, 350; (2) Galbraith to State, 25 Oct. 1962, ibid., p. 351; (3) memorandum from Kaysen to Kennedy, 26 Oct. 1962, ibid., pp. 351–2.

134. NA, FO 371/164914, Delhi to CRO, 22 Oct. 1962.

135. NA, FO 371/164914, Nehru to Macmillan, 24 Oct. 1962.

136. NA, FO 371/164914, W.I. McIndoe to J.O. Wright, 24 Oct. 1962.

137. Galbraith, *Ambassador's Journal*, p. 381.

138. Anatol Lieven, *Pakistan: A Hard Country*, London: Allen Lane, 2011, pp. 64–5.

139. NA, FO 371/164914, Macmillan to Ayub Khan, 25 Oct. 1962.

140. Marc Trachenberg, David Rosenberg and Stephen Van Evara, 'Interview with Carl Kaysen', available at: http://www.sscnet.ucla.edu/polisci/faculty/trachenberg/cv/Kaysen%28MIT%29.pdf.

141. Tape recording of B.K. Nehru's meeting with Kennedy, Washington, DC, 26 Oct. 1962, transcribed in Zelikow and May (eds), *The Presidential Recordings, John F. Kennedy*, pp. 337–44.

142. Sorenson, *Kennedy*, p. 662.

143. Note: B.K. Nehru relayed this to Kuldip Nayar, see Kuldip Nayar, *Beyond the Lines: An Autobiography*, New Delhi: Roli Books, 2012, p. 117.

144. Tape recording of B.K. Nehru's meeting with Kennedy, Washington, DC, 26 Oct. 1962, transcribed in Zelikow and May (eds), *The Presidential Recordings, John F. Kennedy*, pp. 337–44.

145. Michael Malloy, 'India Calls a National Emergency', *Washington Post*, 27 Oct. 1962.

146. Easwar Sagar, 'Nehru Asks for Arms: Indian Envoy Apprises President of Serious Border Situation: Favourable Response Expected', *The Hindu*, 28 Oct. 1962.

147. A.M. Rosenthal, 'US Arms Sped at Nehru Plea as China Gains', *New York Times*, 30 Oct. 1962.

148. Henry Bradsher, 'Nehru Agrees India Needs American Arms', *Washington Post*, 29 Oct. 1962.

149. Rusk to Galbraith, 27 Oct. 1962, *FRUS*, vol. 19, p. 353.

150. State to Galbraith, 28 Oct. 1962, ibid., p. 360.

151. Galbraith to State, 29 Oct. 1962, ibid., p. 361.

152. Maxwell, *India's China War*, pp. 384–5.

153. Galbraith, *Ambassador's Journal*, p. 387, also see NA, FO 371/164916, Booth to CRO, 29 Oct. 1962.

154. Galbraith, *Ambassador's Journal*, p. 394.

155. 'US Speeding Airlift of Arms to Assist India', *Washington Post*, 2 Nov. 1962.

156. A.M. Rosenthal, 'US to Send India Light Artillery in Turks Arsenal', *New York Times*, 2 Nov. 1962.

157. 'America Airlifts Arms to India', *The Hindu*, 3 Nov. 1962.

158. NA, FO 371/164915, Gore to Foreign Office, Washington, 29 Oct. 1962.

159. *Lok Sabha Debates*, 8 Nov. 1962, p. 104.

160. The Praja Socialists had twelve, the Socialists six and the Jan Sangh fourteen.

For a complete breakdown of the distribution of seats in the Lok Sabha see: 'Statistical Report on General Elections, 1962, to the Third Lok Sabha', vol. 1, Election Commission of India: New Delhi, p. 82.

161. NA, FO 371/164915, Delhi to CRO, note, 'Situation in India', 26 Oct. 1962.

162. Rajmohan Gandhi, *Rajaji: A Life*, New Delhi: Penguin, 1997, pp. 402–3.

163. Romesh Thapar, 'Moment of Truth', *Economic Weekly*, 14, 44 and 45 (10 Nov. 1962), p. 1713.

164. Kux, *India and the United States*, p. 204, also Palit, *War in the High Himalayas*, p. 277. For a brief account of the Kennedy administration's views on Menon see: Robert McMahon, *The Cold War on the Periphery: The United States, India, and Pakistan*, New York: Columbia University Press, 1994, p. 288.

165. Galbraith, *Ambassador's Journal*, p. 395.

166. Cited in Paul M. McGarr, '"India's Rasputin?" V.K. Krishna Menon and Anglo-American Misperceptions of Indian Foreign Policy Making, 1947–64', *Diplomacy & Statecraft*, 22, 2 (2011), p. 254.

167. Inder Malhotra, *Indira Gandhi: A Personal and Political Biography*, London: Coronet Books, 1990, pp. 71–3.

168. JKLM, Galbraith to Kennedy, 16 Oct. 1962, Galbraith correspondence with Kennedy, NSC box 118 a.

169. Zareer Masani, *Indira Gandhi: A Biography*, New York: Thomas Crowell, 1976, pp. 119–20.

170. Katherine Frank, *Indira: The Life of Indira Nehru Gandhi*, London: Harper Perennial, 2001, p. 266.

171. Michael Brecher, *India and World Politics: Krishna Menon's View of the World*, London: Oxford University Press, 1968, pp. 140–55.

172. Ibid.

173. NA, FO 371/164915, Foreign Office to Delhi, 25 Oct. 1962.

174. NA, FO 371/164915, Foreign Office to Delhi, 5 Nov. 1962.

175. Raghavan, *War and Peace*, p. 309.

176. Henry Kissinger, *On China*, New York: Allen Lane, 2011, pp. 190–3.

177. NA, FO 371/164915, Moscow to Foreign Office, 29 Oct. 1962.

178. According to Galbraith. See Galbraith, *Ambassador's Journal*, p. 394.

179. NMML, Kaul to Nehru, 16 Nov. 1962, T.N. Kaul Papers, correspondence with Nehru, 2nd instalment.

180. NA, FO 371/164915, Moscow to Foreign Office, 29 Oct. 1962.

181. B.K. Nehru, *Nice Guys Finish Second*, p. 453.

182. Tape recording of B.K. Nehru's meeting with Kennedy, Washington, DC, 26 Oct. 1962, transcribed in Zelikow and May (eds), *The Presidential Recordings, John F. Kennedy*, pp. 337–44.

183. Galbraith, *Ambassador's Journal*, p. 397.

184. Note: the equipment sent to India included 40,000 anti-personnel mines;

1,000,000 rounds of calibre .30 ammunition; 200 rounds of calibre .30 machine guns with mounts and accessories; fifty-four 81 millimetre mortars with mounts and accessories; 100,000 rounds of 81 millimetre ammunition; and 500 ANGRC-10 radios. See memorandum from Kaysen to Kennedy, 3 Nov. 1962, *FRUS*, vol. 19, pp. 364–68.

185. JKLM, Galbraith to Kennedy, 9 Nov. 1962, Galbraith correspondence with Kennedy, NSC box 118 a.

186. Galbraith to Kennedy, 13 Nov. 1962, *FRUS*, vol. 19, pp. 381–2.

187. 'Text of Notes Exchanged between the US Assistant Secretary of State and Indian Ambassador', 14 Nov. 1962, cited in *Foreign Affairs Record*, vol. 8, New Delhi: Government of India Publication, 1962, pp. 300–30.

188. According to Surendranath Dwivedy, *Lok Sabha Debates*, 12 Nov. 1962, vol. 9/4, New Delhi: Government of India Press, pp. 920–2.

189. According to Shivaji Rao Deshmukh, ibid., pp. 938–44.

190. According to N.G. Ranga, *Lok Sabha Debates*, vol. 9/I, 8 Nov. 1962, pp. 152–155.

191. According to Renu Chakravarty, *Lok Sabha Debates*, vol. 9/3, 10 Nov. 1962, pp. 635–45.

192. *Lok Sabha Debates*, vol. 9/I, 8 Nov. 1962, pp. 83–130.

193. Palit, *War in the High Himalayas*, pp. 301–2.

194. Ibid., p. 302.

195. T.N. Kaul, *My Years through Raj to Swaraj*, New Delhi: Vikas Publishing House, 1996, p. 408.

196. Galbraith, *Ambassador's Journal*, p. 417.

197. Ibid., p. 419.

198. Sinha and Athale, *History of the Conflict with China*, pp. 439–40.

199. Note: the accounts of events on the 17/18th night remain contradictory: (1) Palit argues that the 4th division had been given an order to withdraw. He states that he does not know who gave the order, and that initially, he actually stopped the order from being sent, but could not stop the order from being sent the second time. Palit, *War in the High Himalayas*, p. 315; (2) Kaul claims that Pathania asked to withdraw, but at 19.45 hours, Kaul advocated holding on to the 4th division's position. Contradicting himself, Kaul states that later that night he told Pathania to use his judgement with regards to withdrawing, but when he learnt that Pathania had actually withdrawn, the decision went against the 'spirit' of what Pathania had been told by Kaul. Kaul, *The Untold Story*, pp. 412–14; (3) Maxwell states that Kaul had given the order to the 4th division to withdraw, but then later cancelled the signal due to pressure from Palit. Later that night, however, the 4th division was given an order to withdraw, and Maxwell does not specify who might have given this order. Maxwell, *India's China War*, pp. 402–4.

200. Kaul, *The Untold Story*, p. 416.

201. Palit, *War in the High Himalayas*, p. 321.

202. Ibid., p. 327.

203. Gore-Booth, *With Great Truth and Respect*, p. 296.

204. Galbraith, *Ambassador's Journal*, p. 419.

205. Gundevia, *Outside the Archives*, p. 220.

206. Maxwell, *India's China War*, p. 405.

207. Note: B.G. Verghese was one of these two Indian journalists. See Verghese, *First Draft*, pp. 72–3.

209. Galbraith, *Ambassador's Journal*, pp. 424–5.

209. A.G. Noorani, *Our Credulity and Negligence*, Bombay: Krishna S. Kurwar, 1963, p. 99.

210. Palit, *War in the High Himalayas*, p. 332.

211. Nayar, *Beyond the Lines*, pp. 115–16.

212. Kux, *India and the United States*, p. 207.

213. Frank, *Indira*, p. 266.

214. Verghese, *First Draft*, pp. 72–3; Meghnad Desai, *The Rediscovery of India*, London: Bloomsbury Academic, 2011, p. 336.

215. Galbraith to State, 19 Nov. 1962, *FRUS*, vol. 19, p. 397.

216. Galbraith, *Ambassador's Journal*, p. 423.

217. Galbraith to Rusk, 17 Nov. 1962, *FRUS*, vol. 19, p. 389.

218. JKLM, New Delhi to State, 19 Nov. 1962 (telegram no. 1891), Nehru's correspondence with Kennedy, NSC box 111.

219. Thomas Brady, 'Chinese Drive Into India', *New York Times*, 20 Nov. 1962.

220. B.K. Nehru, *Nice Guys Finish Second*, p. 453.

221. JKLM, Nehru to Kennedy, 19 Nov. (telegram no. 1891), Nehru's correspondence with Kennedy, NSC box 111.

222. B.K. Nehru, *Nice Guys Finish Second*, p. 453.

223. Sarvepalli Gopal, *Jawaharlal Nehru: A Biography*, New Delhi: Oxford University Press, 1989, p. 433.

224. JKLM, Nehru to Kennedy, 19 Nov. 1962 (telegram no. 1891), Nehru's correspondence with Kennedy, NSC box 111.

225. NA, FO 371/164920, Montgomery to Homes, 19 Nov. 1962.

226. M.C. Chagla, *Roses in December: An Autobiography*, Mumbai: Bhartiya Vidya Bhavan, 2011, pp. 310–11. Also see: NA, FO 371/164920, MoC between Saville Garner and Chagla, London, 19 Nov. 1962.

227. JKLM, Galbraith to State, 19 Nov. 1962 (telegram no. 1889), Nehru's correspondence with Kennedy, NSC box 111.

228. K. Subramanyam, 'That Night of November 19', *Indian Express*, 18 Nov. 2010.

229. Note: this list is based on the author's survey of texts and biographies.

230. Subramanyam, 'That Night of November 19'.

231. Nehru, *Nice Guys Finish Second*, pp. 453–4.

232. Brecher, *India and World Politics*, p. 173.

233. Mullick, *My Years*, pp. 450–1.

234. Brecher, *India and World Politics*, p. 173.

235. Gundevia, *Outside the Archives*, p. 233.

236. JKLM, Nehru to Kennedy, 19 Nov. 1962 (telegram no. 2167), Nehru's correspondence with Kennedy, NSC box 111. Also see: K. Subramanyam, 'That Night of November 19', and State to embassy/New Delhi, 19 Nov. 1962, *FRUS*, vol. 19, p. 398.

237. Nehru, *Nice Guys Finish Second*, pp. 453–4. Note: B.K. Nehru states in his memoirs that the letter was received and delivered on 22 Nov. This is possibly a typo or a mistake. It is fairly clear from multiple sources that the letter was authored, delivered and received by Kennedy on 19 Nov.

238. JKLM, Nehru to Kennedy, 19 Nov. 1962 (telegram no. 2167), Nehru's correspondence with Kennedy, NSC box 111.

239. State to Galbraith, 19 Nov. 1962, *FRUS*, vol. 19, p. 399.

240. Rusk to Galbraith, Washington, 20 Nov. 1962, ibid., pp. 400–1.

241. NA, FO 371/164921, Peking to Foreign Office, 20 Nov. 1962.

242. NA, FO 371/164919, note by Zhou to heads of states, 15 Nov. (filed in the UK on 19 Nov.) 1962.

243. NA, FO 371/164921, Peking to Foreign Office, 21 Nov. 1962.

244. NA, FO 371/164921, Booth to CRO, 21 Nov. 1962. Note: the ceasefire was implemented on 21 Nov.; Lorne J. Kavic, *India's Quest for Security*, Berkeley: University of California Press, 1967, p. 182; Gopal, *Nehru: A Biography*, vol. 3, pp. 234–9.

245. Note: for an analysis of the Chinese ceasefire from an Indian perspective see Palit, *War in the High Himalayas*, pp. 349–50.

246. Galbraith, *Ambassador's Journal*, p. 427.

247. Romesh Thapar, 'Peace or War', *Economic Weekly*, vol. 17/84, 1 Dec. 1962, p. 1841.

248. A.M. Rosenthal, 'Nehru's Two Battles', *New York Times*, 12 Nov. 1962.

249. CIA Briefings, 'The Sino-India Conflict: Outlook and Implications', National Intelligence Estimate, no. 13/14 Dec. 1962

250. Kux, *India and the United States*, p. 204.

251. Maxwell, *India's China War*, pp. 384–5.

252. 'US Military Aid to Pakistan', *The Hindu*, 24 Dec. 1953.

253. Jawaharlal Nehru, 'Changing India', *Foreign Affairs*, 41, 3 (Apr. 1963), p. 463.

254. Ibid., pp. 458–9.

255. Jawaharlal Nehru, 'The Unity of India', *Foreign Affairs*, 16, 231 (1937), p. 241.

256. Steven Hoffman, *India and the China Crisis*, Berkeley: University of California Press, 1990, p. 165.

257. Deba Mohanty, *Arming the Indian Arsenal: Challenges and Policy Options*, New Delhi: Rupa, 2009, pp. 84–6.

258. Gopal, *Jawaharlal Nehru*, pp. 433–4.

5. 'SWUNG BACK'

1. Ramachandra Guha, *India after Gandhi*, New York: Harper Collins, 2007, pp. 88–9.

2. See Ghosh to Nehru, 2 Jan. 1963 and Nehru to Ghosh, 5 Jan. 1963, cited in Sudhir Ghosh, *Gandhi's Emissary*, London: Routledge, 2008, pp. 266–9. Also see Nehru Memorial Museum and Library [hereafter NMML], Nehru to TTK, 2 Dec. 1962, TTK Papers, correspondence with Nehru; NMML, Nehru to TTK, 23 Feb. 1963, TTK Papers, correspondence with Nehru.

3. H.R. Vohra, 'Interceptor Fighters from US Likely', *Times of India*, 30 Mar. 1963.

4. John F. Kennedy Presidential Library and Museum [hereafter JKLM], Galbraith to Robert Komer, 20 Feb. 1963, Komer Papers, India 1962–3.

5. Rusk to embassy in India, 25 Nov. 1962, *Foreign Relations of the United States* [hereafter *FRUS*], vol. 19, pp. 407–8.

6. State to India, 8 Dec. 1962, ibid., pp. 424–5.

7. Ghosh, *Gandhi's Emissary*, pp. 273–4.

8. John Kenneth Galbraith, *Ambassador's Journal: A Personal Account of the Kennedy Years*, Boston: Houghton Mifflin Company, 1969, p. 508.

9. B.G. Verghese, *First Draft: Witness to the Making of Modern India*, New Delhi: Tranquebar, 2010, p. 72; Meghnad Desai, *The Rediscovery of India*, London: Bloomsbury Academic, 2011, p. 338.

10. Katherine Frank, *Indira: The Life of Indira Nehru Gandhi*, London: Harper Perennial, 2001, p. 267.

11. Sarvepalli Gopal, *Jawaharlal Nehru: A Biography* (New Delhi: Oxford University Press, 2004), p. 447.

12. Note: the only exception to this can be found in Howard B. Schaffer, *The Limits of Influence: America's Role in Kashmir*, Washington: Brookings Institution Press, 2009, pp. 65–96.

13. Ghosh, *Gandhi's Emissary*, pp. 276–7.

14. Ibid., pp. 276–7.

15. B.K. Nehru, *Nice Guys Finish Second*, New Delhi: Viking, 1997, p. 456.

16. Note: the ceasefire line was delimited a few months following the actual call for a ceasefire. Srinath Raghavan, *War and Peace in Modern India*, New Delhi: Permanent Black, 2010, p. 146.

17. See Navnita Chadha Behera, *Demystifying Kashmir*, Washington: Brookings Institution Press, 2006, p. 13.

18. Note: the accession itself has been contested in the historiography of the conflict. See Raghavan, *War and Peace*, pp. 107–8; Victoria Schofield, *Kashmir in Conflict: India, Pakistan, and the Unfinished War*, London: I.B. Tauris, 2000, pp. 54–60.

19. Shuja Nawaz, *Pakistan: Its Army, and the Wars Within*, Oxford: Oxford University Press, 2008, pp. 67–8.

20. Schaffer, *The Limits of Influence*, p. 24; for a brief history see Dennis Kux, *The United States and Pakistan: 1947–2000*, Baltimore: Johns Hopkins University Press, 2001, pp. 27–39.

21. For a detailed note see Raghavan, *War and Peace*, pp. 146–8.

22. Schofield, *Kashmir in Conflict*, p. 71.

23. M.C. Chagla, *Roses in December: An Autobiography*, Mumbai: Bhartiya Vidya Bhavan, 2011, pp. 391–4.

24. Ian Talbot, *Pakistan: A Modern History*, London: Hurst, 2009, p. 139.

25. Cited by Bogra in Kux, *The United States and Pakistan*, p. 70.

26. NMML, Eisenhower to Nehru, 24 Feb. 1954, D.D. Eisenhower Papers, file no. 4.

27. 'Pakistan Asks US for Arms Aid', *Washington Post*, 23 Feb. 1954.

28. NMML, statement by President Eisenhower, White House, Washington, DC, 25 Feb. 1954, D.D. Eisenhower Papers, file no. 4.

29. Robert McMahon, 'United States Cold War Strategy in South Asia: Making a Military Commitment to Pakistan, 1947–1954', *The Journal of American History*, 75, 3 (Dec. 1988), p. 812.

30. 'Reds Burn Effigy of Mr. Dulles', *Times of India*, 21 May 1953.

31. Nehru to chief ministers, 15 Nov. 1953, in G. Parthasarthy (ed.), *Jawaharlal Nehru: Letters to Chief Ministers*, vol. 3, 1952–4, London: Jawaharlal Nehru Memorial Fund and Oxford University Press, 1987, p. 316.

32. McMahon, 'United States Cold War Strategy in South Asia', p. 812.

33. Raju Thomas, 'Security Relationships in Southern Asia: Differences in the Indian and American Perspectives', *Asian Survey*, 21, 7 (July 1981), p. 699.

34. NMML, Eisenhower to Nehru, 24 Feb. 1954, D.D. Eisenhower Papers, file no. 4.

35. Robert McMahon, *The Cold War on the Periphery: The United States, India, and Pakistan*, New York: Columbia University Press, 1994, pp. 139–50.

36. 'Memorandum of Informal US–UK Discussion in Connection with the Visit to London of the Honorable George C McGhee', 3 Apr. 1951, *FRUS*, vol. 5/part 2, p. 1689.

37. Nehru to Ali, 10 Nov. 1953, *Selected Works of Jawaharlal Nehru* [hereafter *SWJN*], vol. 24, p. 416.

38. Nehru to U Nu, 11 Nov. 1953, ibid., p. 421.

39. Nehru, 'Speech at the Inauguration of the Sixth Annual Session of the Trade Union Congress', Jalgaon, 3 Dec. 1953, ibid., p. 449.

40. Cited in 'US Military Aid to Pakistan', *The Hindu*, 24 Dec. 1953.

41. NMML, Eisenhower to Nehru, Washington, 25 Feb. 1954, D.D. Eisenhower Papers.

42. Nehru to chief ministers, 27 Jan. 1953, in Parthasarthy (ed.), *Letters*, pp. 236–7.

43. Schaffer, *The Limits of Influence*, pp. 62–3.

44. Ibid., p. 51.

45. See Vojtech Mastny, 'The Soviet Union's Partnership with India', *Journal of Cold War Studies*, 12, 3 (Summer 2010).

46. Michael O'Brien, *John F. Kennedy: A Biography*, New York: Thomas Dunne Books, 2003, pp. 233–4.

47. Schaffer, *The Limits of Influence*, pp. 69–71.

48. Cited in Ghosh, *Gandhi's Emissary*, p. 317.

49. Cited in Schaffer, *The Limits of Influence*, p. 69.

50. 'Paper Prepared by the Bureau of Near Eastern and South Asian Affairs', Washington, 10 Jan. 1962, *FRUS*, vol. 19, pp. 125–35. Also see: memorandum from Komer to Bundy, Washington, 12 Jan. 1962, ibid.

51. NMML, B.K. Nehru to M.J. Desai, 18 Jan. 1962, B.K. Nehru Papers, subject file no. 17.

52. Ibid.

53. NMML, Nehru to Kennedy, 27 Jan. 1962, ibid.

54. 'The Enemy of My Enemy', *The Globe*, 3 Jan. 1962.

55. National Archives, Kew Gardens, London [Hereafter NA], FO 371/164910, note, FO, London, 27 Feb. 1962.

56. Y.D. Gundevia, *Outside the Archives*, Hyderabad: Sangam Books, 1984, p. 261.

57. For a practitioner's perspective and a background, see Jagat. S. Mehta, 'Engaging with China', in Krishna V. Rajan (ed.), *The Ambassadors' Club*, New Delhi: Harper Collins, 2012, pp. 233–7.

58. State to the embassy in Pakistan, 16 Oct. 1962, *FRUS*, vol. 19, pp. 345–6.

59. Rusk to embassy in Pakistan, 27 Oct. 1962, ibid., p. 356.

60. NA, FO 371/164916, Delhi to CRO, 29 Oct. 1962.

61. NA, FO 371/164916, Karachi to CRO, 6 Nov. 1962, for a background see Kux, *The United States and Pakistan*, pp. 130–4.

62. NA, FO 371/164916, Karachi to CRO [second cable], 6 Nov. 1962.

63. NA, FO 371/164920, Nehru to Ayub Khan, 12 Nov. 1962.

64. State to embassy in Pakistan, 12 Nov. 1962, *FRUS*, vol. 19, p. 377, and State to embassy in Pakistan, Washington, 13 Nov. 1962, ibid., p. 379.

65. Galbraith to Kennedy, 13 Nov. 1962, ibid., p. 384.

66. NA, FO 371/164920, MoC between Saville Garner and M.C. Chagla, London, 19 Nov. 1962.

67. NA, FO 371/164920, Peshwar to CRO, 20 Nov. 1962.

68. NA, FO 371/164920, Karachi to CRO, 21 Nov. 1962.

69. NA, FO 371/164920, Delhi to CRO, 22 Nov. 1962.

70. Gundevia, *Outside the Archives*, p. 240.

71. According to Gundevia, see D.K. Palit, *War in the High Himalayas: The Indian Army in Crisis, 1962*, London: Hurst, 1991, p. 369.

72. Paul Gore-Booth, *With Great Truth and Respect*, London: Constable, 1974, p. 298.

73. Paul H. Nitze with Ann M. Smith and Steven L. Rearden, *From Hiroshima to Glasnost: At the Centre of Decision*, London: Weidenfeld and Nicolson, 1989, pp. 239–42.

74. 'Transcript of President's News Conference', *Washington Post*, 20 Nov. 1962.

75. Galbraith, *Ambassador's Journal*, p. 429.

76. JKLM, memorandum, 'Meeting with Prime Minister Nehru', 22 Nov. 1962, Hilsman Papers, folder 18.

77. Nitze, *From Hiroshima to Glasnost*, p. 242.

78. Gore-Booth, *With Great Truth and Respect*, p. 301, Neville Maxwell, *India's China War*, London: Jonathan Cape, 1970, pp. 434–6.

79. Note: Harriman met with Nehru on 22, 23, 25 and 28 Nov. Galbraith to Rusk, 30 Nov. 1962, *FRUS*, vol. 19, pp. 414–17.

80. 'Harriman Confers with Nehru', *The Hindu*, 24 Nov. 1962.

81. Ibid.

82. Galbraith, *Ambassador's Journal*, p. 433.

83. NMML, TTK to Nehru, 26 Dec. 1962, correspondence with Nehru, TTK Papers.

84. NMML, TTK to Nehru, MoC with Harriman, Nitze, Kaysen and James Grant, 24 Nov. 1962, ibid.

85. Quoted in Gore-Booth, *With Great Truth and Respect*, pp. 301–2.

86. JKLM, 'Report of the Harriman Mission', undated, Komer Papers, India–Harriman correspondence, 22 Nov. 1962 to 30 Nov. 1962.

87. Galbraith, *Ambassador's Journal*, p. 438.

88. NMML, Nehru to TTK, 16 Dec. 1962, file no. 2, correspondence with Nehru, TTK Papers. Also see Jawaharlal Nehru, 'Changing India', *Foreign Affairs*, 41, 3 (Apr. 1963), p. 458.

89. NMML, Nehru to Prime Minister Menzies, 23 Mar. 1963, correspondence with Nehru, TTK Papers.

90. Romesh Thapar, 'A New Phase is Opening', *Economic Weekly*, 14/51 and 52 (22 Dec. 1962).

91. MoC, Nassau, 20 Dec. 1962, *FRUS*, vol. 19, p. 450.

92. National Security Action Memorandum no. 209, Washington, 10 Dec. 1962, ibid., p. 429.

93. MoC, Sino-Indian dispute, Nassau, 20 Dec. 1962, ibid., pp. 448–50.

94. NMML, TTK to Nehru, 24 Nov. 1962, correspondence with Nehru, TTK Papers. Also see memorandum of the Executive Committee of the National Security Council, Washington, 3 Dec. 1962, *FRUS*, vol. 19, p. 418.

95. Moc from Komer to Kennedy, 16 Dec. 1962, ibid., pp. 435–7.

96. State to Galbraith, 8 Dec. 1962, ibid., pp. 425–8.

97. Macmillan to Kennedy in State to Rusk, 13 Dec. 1962, ibid., pp. 431–2.

98. NMML, Sudhir Ghosh to Nehru, 1 Dec. 1962, enclosed in a letter from TTK to Nehru, 2 Dec. 1962, TTK Papers, correspondence with Nehru.

99. NMML, Pitambar Pant, 'Defence Needs and Economic Policy', Planning Commission, Appendix attached to a letter from TTK to Nehru, 24 Nov. 1962, TK Papers, correspondence with Nehru.

100. Ibid. [emphasis added].

101. NMML, TTK to Nehru, 26 Dec. 1962, correspondence with Nehru, TTK Papers.

102. Ibid.

103. JKLM, 'Report of the Harriman Mission', undated, Komer Papers, India–Harriman correspondence, 22 Nov. 1962 to 30 Nov. 1962.

104. *Lok Sabha Debates*, vol. 9/10, 20 Nov. 1962.

105. Nehru to chief ministers, 22 Dec. 1962, in Parthasarthy (ed.), *Letters*, vol. 3, pp. 540–7.

106. Cited in JKLM, 'Soviet Reaction to US Military Aid to India', 21 Nov. 1962, Hilsman Papers, folder 18.

107. Galbraith, *Ambassador's Journal*, pp. 376–403.

108. Deputy secretary of defence to the undersecretary of state (Chester Bowles), 12 June 1961, *FRUS*, vol. 19, pp. 57–8.

109. NMML, M.J. Desai to B.K. Nehru, 5 Aug. 1962, B.K. Nehru Papers, subject file no. 17.

110. Jagat Mehta, 'Engaging China', in Rajan (ed.), *The Ambassadors' Club*, p. 241.

111. Odd Arne Westad, *Restless Empire: China and the World Since 1750*, London: The Bodley Head, 2012, p. 343.

112. NMML, Nehru to B.K. Nehru, 8 Mar. 1963, TTK Papers, correspondence with Nehru.

113. T. N. Kaul, *My Years Through Raj to Swaraj*, Bombay: Vikas Publishing House, 1997, p. 117.

114. NMML, T.N. Kaul to Nehru, 30 Nov. 1962, verbatim of two-hour discussion with Khrushchev on 24 Nov. 1962, T N. Kaul Papers, three instalments, correspondence with Nehru.

115. NMML, Kaul to B.K. Nehru, 29 Nov. 1962, T.N. Kaul Papers, correspondence between Kaul and B.K. Nehru.

116. NMML, TTK to Nehru, 16 Dec. 1962, TTK Papers, correspondence with Nehru.

117. Henry Kissinger, *On China*, New York: Allen Lane, 2011, p. 193.

118. Gundevia, *Outside the Archives*, pp. 256–7.

119. Zulfikar Ali Bhutto, 'Address to National Assembly', 1 Dec. 1962, available at: http://www.bhutto.org/1957-1965_speech13.php

120. Gundevia, *Outside the Archives*, pp. 260–1.

121. For details see McMahon, *Cold War*, p. 296.

122. Gore-Booth, *With Great Truth and Respect*, p. 303.

123. Galbraith, *Ambassador's Journal*, p. 457.

124. Gundevia, *Outside the Archives*, pp. 262–3.

125. See for instance 'Pak, China, Agree on Kashmir Border', *Hindustan Times*, 27 Dec. 1962.

126. NA, FO 371/170637, FO to Her Majesty's Representatives, 31 Dec. 1962.

127. Schaffer, *Limits of Influence*, p. 83.

128. Gundevia, *Outside the Archives*, p. 264.

129. NA, FO 371/170637, FO to Her Majesty's Representatives, 31 Dec. 1962.

130. NA, FO 371/170637, Booth to CRO, 1 Jan. 1963.

131. NA, FO 371/170637, Karachi to CRO, 31 Dec. 1962.

132. NA, FO 371/170637, Delhi to CRO, 1 Jan. 1963.

133. Gundevia, *Outside the Archives*, p. 266.

134. Ibid.

135. State to Delhi, 4 Jan. 1963, *FRUS*, vol. 19, pp. 464–5.

136. 'Aid Only to Check Red Menace, Galbraith Says', *Hindustan Times*, 3 Jan. 1963.

137. JKLM, Hilsman to Rusk, 7 Dec. 1962, Hilsman Papers, folder 18.

138. NA, FO 371/170637, Delhi to CRO, 10 Jan. 1963.

139. Note: Nehru recognises this himself. See Nehru to chief ministers, 1 Jan. 1963, in Parthasarthy (ed.), *Letters*, vol. 3, p. 264.

140. 'JS Urges Postponement of Indo-Pak Talks', *Hindustan Times*, 7 Feb. 1963.

141. 'CR Calls for Unambiguous Foreign Policy', *Hindustan Times*, 7 Feb. 1963.

142. Galbraith, *Ambassador's Journal*, p. 463.

143. Note: according to Booth's record of conversations with Gundevia. See NA, FO 371/170637, Delhi to CRO, 14 Jan. 1963.

144. NA, FO 371/170637, Delhi to CRO, 10 Jan. 1963.

145. NA, FO 371/170637, Delhi to CRO, 14 Jan. 1963.

146. Gundevia, *Outside The Archives*, p. 268.

147. NA, FO 371/170637, Delhi to CRO, 17 Jan. 1963.

148. Kennedy to Macmillan, 21 Jan. 1963, *FRUS*, vol. 19, p. 479.

149. NA, FO 371/170636, Delhi to CRO, 19 Jan. 1963.

150. Ibid.

151. Gundevia, *Outside the Archives*, p. 273.

152. NA, FO 371/170636, Delhi to CRO, 22 Jan. 1963.

153. NA, FO 371/170636, FO to Certain of Her Majesty's Representatives, 31 Jan. 1963.

154. NA, FO 371/170637, Karachi to CRO, 25 Jan. 1963.

155. Komer to Kennedy, 26 Jan. 1963, *FRUS*, vol. 19, p. 486.

156. Schaffer, *The Limits of Influence*, p. 84.

157. Galbraith, *Ambassador's Journal*, p. 472.

158. Gore-Booth, *With Great Truth and Respect*, p. 303

159. Editor's note, *FRUS*, vol. 19, p. 491.

160. Ibid.

161. Gundevia, *Outside the Archives*, p. 276.

162. Kennedy to Macmillan, 21 Jan. 1963, *FRUS*, vol. 19, p. 479.

163. Kennedy to Nehru, 6 Feb. 1963, ibid., pp. 490–1.

164. Gundevia, *Outside the Archives*, p. 279.

165. 'Talks Heading Toward Deadlock', *Times of India*, 11 Feb. 1963.

166. 'Indo-Pak Differences Still Considerable', *Times of India*, 12 Feb. 1963.

167. Sitanshu Das, 'Sino-Pak Border Pact Signed', *Times of India*, 3 Mar. 1963.

168. NMML, Nehru to B.K. Nehru, 8 Mar. 1963, TTK Papers, correspondence with Nehru.

169. NA, FO 371/170638, CRO to Lahore, 12 Feb. 1963.

170. Galbraith, *Ambassador's Journal*, p. 486.

171. Gore-Booth, *With Great Truth and Respect*, p. 304.

172. Ibid.

173. Rusk to Kennedy, 31 Mar. 1963, *FRUS*, vol. 19, p. 530.

174. Rusk to Kennedy, 19 Apr. 1963, ibid., pp. 550–1.

175. Kennedy to Galbraith, 22 Mar. 1963, ibid., p. 524.

176. NA, FO 371/170637 Gore-Booth to CRO, 29 Mar. 1963, no. 983.

177. NA, FO 371/170638, Delhi to CRO, 4 Apr. 1963.

178. MoC between Kennedy, Rusk, McNamara, Harriman, Bundy, Talbot, Maxwell Taylor and others, Washington, 1 Apr. 1963, *FRUS*, vol. 19, pp. 535–6.

179. NA, FO 371/170637, Ormsby-Gore to Foreign Office, 2 Apr. 1963.

180. NA, FO 371/170637, Macmillan to Nehru, 6 Apr. 1963.

181. NA, FO 371/170637, Delhi to CRO, 4 Apr. 1963.

182. Gundevia, *Outside the Archives*, p. 290.

183. Ibid., pp. 292–3.

184. Rusk to Kennedy, 25 Apr. 1963, *FRUS*, vol. 19, p. 552.

185. Komer to Kennedy, 24 Apr. 1963, ibid., p. 554.

186. State to Karachi, 24 Apr. 1963, ibid., p. 556.

187. MoC of president's meeting with Rusk, McNamara, Bowles, Nitze, Bundy, Komer and others, Washington, 25 Apr. 1963, ibid., p. 563.

188. NMML, Gundevia to G. Parthasarthy, 6 May 1963, correspondence with Nehru, TTK Papers.

189. Gundevia, *Outside the Archives*, p. 294.
190. NA, FO 371/170637, Bundy to Zulueta (Macmillan's private secretary), 11 May 1963.
191. NA, FO 371/170638, record of conversation between the foreign secretary and the president of Pakistan, president's palace, 1 May 1963.
192. Gundevia, *Outside the Archives*, pp. 294–310.
193. NA, FO 371/170638, Peshawar to CRO, 1 June 1963.
194. For details see Gundevia, *Outside the Archives*, pp. 305–10.
195. NA, FO 371/170637, Kennedy to Macmillan, 23 May 1963.
196. NMML, Nehru to B.K. Nehru, 8 Mar. 1963, correspondence with Nehru, TTK Papers.
197. NA, FO 371/170637, CRO to Delhi, 8 July 1963.
198. State to Galbraith, 18 May 1963, *FRUS*, vol. 19, pp. 599–600.
199. State to embassy in India, 18 June 1963, ibid., pp. 612–13.
200. B. N. Mullick, *My Years With Nehru*, Bombay: Allied Publishers, 1973, p. 575.
201. Nehru, 'Changing India', p. 463.
202. Ghosh, *Gandhi's Emissary*, pp. 329–37.
203. Easwar Sagar, 'Neglect of Our Public Relations in US', *The Hindu*, 4 Dec. 1962.

6. 'DIAOYUTAI'

1. Usha Bhagat, *Indiraji: Through My Eyes*, New Delhi: Penguin, 2005, p. 200.
2. The National Archives, College Park, Maryland, [hereafter TNA], Gandhi to Nixon, 5 Dec. 1971, National Presidential Material Staff [hereafter NPMS], presidential correspondence (1969–74), box 755.
3. Bhagat, *Indiraji*, p. 201.
4. J.N. Dixit, *India–Pakistan in War and Peace*, London: Routledge, 2002, p. 209.
5. TNA, Manekshaw to Niazi, 15 Dec. 1971, NPMS/NSC files, Indo-Pak, 'Chronological Order of Events'.
6. Cited in Pranay Gupte, *Mother India: A Political Biography of Indira Gandhi*, New Delhi: Penguin, 2009, pp. 378–88.
7. Cited in Robert Dallek, *Partners in Power: Nixon and Kissinger*, New York: Harper Collins, 2007, p. 7.
8. Cited in Dallek, ibid., p. 336.
9. Ibid., pp. 5–8.
10. Ibid., pp. 6–7.
11. Margaret Macmillan, *The Week that Changed the World: Nixon and Mao*, New York: Random House, 2007, p. 11.
12. For a brief but eloquent note see Jonathan D. Spence, *The Search for Modern China*, London: W.W. Norton and Company, 1990, pp. 627–52.

13. Henry Kissinger, *On China*, New York: Allen Lane, 2011, pp. 236–9.

14. Odd Arne Westad, *Restless Empire: China and the World Since 1750*, London: The Bodley Head, 2012, p. 368, also see Dennis Kux, *The United States and Pakistan: 1947–2000*, Baltimore: Johns Hopkins University Press, 2001, pp. 181–4.

15. For a detailed account see Kissinger, *On China*, pp. 236–74.

16. According to Kissinger, see minutes of senior review group meeting, W, 19 Apr. 1971, *Foreign Relations of the United States* [hereafter *FRUS*], vol. 11, South Asia Crisis 1971, Washington: United States Government Printing Office, 2005, p. 83.

17. For background see Omkar Marwah, 'India's Military Intervention in East Pakistan, 1971–1972', *Modern Asian Studies*, 13, 4 (1979); Richard Sisson and Leo E. Rose, *War and Succession: Pakistan, India, and the Creation of Bangladesh*, Berkeley: University of California Press, 1990; Satish Kumar, 'The Evolution of India's Policy Towards Bangladesh in 1971', *Asian Survey*, 16, 6 (1975).

18. National Archives, Kew Gardens, London [Hereafter NA], PREM 15/445, HC in ND to CRO, 9 Aug. 1971.

19. For a cursory survey see Robert H. Donaldson, 'The Soviet Stake in Stability', *Asian Survey*, 12, 6 (1972).

20. Cited in Kux, *The United States and Pakistan*, pp. 179–80.

21. Note: Nixon's approach was well illustrated in a 1967 article in *Foreign Affairs*, see Macmillan, *Nixon and Mao*, p. 6.

22. Nehru Memorial Museum and Library [hereafter NMML], 'Foreign Secretary Speech at the Overseas Writers Guild International Club', 18 Oct. 1973, T.N. Kaul Papers, subject file 1.

23. Bhagat, *Indiraji*, p. 204.

24. Katherine Frank, *Indira: The Life of Indira Nehru Gandhi*, London: Harper Perennial, 2001, p. 334.

25. Nayantara Sahgal, *Indira Gandhi: Her Road to Power*, New York: Fredrick Ungar Publishing Co., 1982, p. 84.

26. Cited by P. Lal in Bhagat, *Indiraji*, p. 202.

27. K.P. Misra, 'Non-Alignment and Indira Gandhi's Contribution', in A.K. Damodaran and U.S. Bajpai (eds), *Indian Foreign Policy: The Indira Gandhi Years*, New Delhi: Sangam Books, 1990, p. 47.

28. See abbreviated transcript of Gandhi's interview with Michael Charlston of the BBC: Pupul Jayakar, *Indira Gandhi: A Biography*, New Delhi: Viking, 1992, p. 232.

29. A.K. Damodaran, 'Introduction', in Damodaran and Bajpai (eds), *Indian Foreign Policy*, p. xv.

30. V.P. Dutt, 'India and the Super-Powers', in Damodaran and Bajpai (eds), *Indian Foreign Policy*, p. 23.

31. For a background see Muhammad Ghulam Kabir, *Minority Politics in Bangladesh*, New Delhi: Vikas, 1980; D.R. Mankekar, *Pak Colonialism in East Bengal*, New Delhi: Samaiya Publications, 1971; A.M.A. Muhith, *Emergence of a Nation*, Dacca: Bangladesh Books International, 1978, pp. 219–326; Kalyan Chaudhuri, *Genocide in Bangladesh*, New Delhi: Orient Longman, 1972, pp. 154–217; Jyoti Sen Gupta, *History of Freedom Movement in Bangladesh 1947–1973*, New Delhi: Naya Prakash Books, 1974, pp. 281–499.

32. For a survey see Mohammed Ayoob and K. Subramanyam, *The Liberation War*, New Delhi: S. Chand & Co., 1972; John H. Gill, *An Atlas of the 1971 India–Pakistan War*, Washington, DC: National Defense University Press, 2004. For details on India's war aims see: P.N. Dhar, *Indira Gandhi, The 'Emergency' and Indian Democracy*, New Delhi: Oxford University Press, 2000, p. 181. For military history of the conduct of war see Omkar Marwah, 'India's Military Intervention in East Pakistan, 1971–1972', *Modern Asian Studies*, 13, 4 (1979); Richard Sisson and Leo E. Rose, *War and Succession: Pakistan, India, and the Creation of Bangladesh*, Berkeley: University of California Press, 1990, Chapters 10 and 11.

33. Sheikh Mujibur Rahman, *The Unfinished Memoirs*, New Delhi: Penguin, 2012, pp. 193–5.

34. Sisson and Rose, *War and Secession*, pp. 9–12. Also see Robert Jackson, *South Asia Crisis 1971: India, Pakistan and Bangladesh*, London: Chatto and Windus, 1975.

35. Rahman, *The Unfinished Memoirs*, p. 144.

36. Ian Talbot, *Pakistan: A Modern History*, London: Hurst, 2009, p. 126.

37. For a very brief history of the six-point plan see Owen Bennett Jones, *Pakistan: Eye of the Storm*, New Haven: Yale University Press, 2002, pp. 146–57.

38. Sisson and Rose, *War and Secession*, p. 23.

39. Ibid., p. 54.

40. Ramachandra Guha, *India after Gandhi*, New York: Harper Collins, 2007, p. 45.

41. For a table of results see Talbot, *Pakistan: A Modern History*, p. 200.

42. Sisson and Rose, *War and Secession*, pp. 2–3.

43. Ayoob and Subramanyam, *The Liberation War*, pp. 113–52.

44. Rahman, *The Unfinished Memoirs*, p. x.

45. TNA, 'Indo-Pakistan Crisis, Chronology of Events', NPMS, NSC Papers, South Asia, box no. 573.

46. Inder Malhotra, *Indira Gandhi: A Personal and Political Biography*, London: Hodder and Stoughton, 1989, p. 133.

47. Ayoob and Subramanyam, *The Liberation War*, pp. 151–3.

48. For a brief account see Dennis Kux, *India and the United States: Estranged Democracies, 1941–1991*, Washington, DC: National Defense University Press, 1992, pp. 288–90.

49. M.C. Chagla, *Roses in December: An Autobiography*, Mumbai: Bhartiya Vidya Bhavan, 2011, pp. 447–9.

50. Frank, *Indira*, p. 327.

51. Note: following the demise of Nehru on 27 May 1964, Lal Bahadur Shastri was appointed prime minister by the Congress party on 9 June 1964. In the brief period between Nehru's death and Shastri's appointment, Gulzarilal Nanda served as the prime minister.

52. For details on the succession battle see: Guha, *India After Gandhi*, pp. 434–40.

53. For electoral results see 'Statistical Report on General Elections, 1967', p. 75, available at: http://eci.nic.in/eci_main/statisticalreports/LS_1967/Vol_I_LS_67.pdf

54. Sisson and Rose, *War and Succession*, pp. 134–5.

55. TNA, 'Indo-Pakistan Crisis, Chronology of Events', NPMS, NSC Papers, South Asia, box no. 573.

56. TNA, William Splenger to Joseph Sisco, 19 Feb. 1971, RG 59, box no. 4.

57. Ibid.

58. Dhar, *Indira Gandhi*, p. 154.

59. The fact that the refugee problem began to cause serious concern in India has been well documented in Dhar, *Indira Gandhi*, pp. 152–7.

60. TNA, 'Chronology of US Advances for Relief', compiled on 16 Dec. 1971, NPMS/NSC Papers, South Asia, box no. 573.

61. Dhar, *Indira Gandhi*, p. 155.

62. Note: those attending the meeting included Defence Minister Jagjivan Ram, Agriculture Minister Fakhruddin Ali Ahmed, Finance Minister Y.B. Chavan and External Affairs Minister Sardar Swaran Singh.

63. For details on Gandhi's core advisors see Dhar, *Indira*, p. 160.

64. Pupul Jayakar, *Indira Gandhi: A Biography*, New Delhi: Viking 1992, p. 223.

65. Ibid. Note: Jayakar writes that the meeting took place on 25 Apr., but other sources claim that the meeting took place on 29 Apr. Triangulation of these accounts suggests that the meeting did indeed take place on the 29th. For other accounts of the 29 Apr. meeting see: 'When Sam Quoted Chapter and Verse to Mrs. Gandhi', *Rediff Special*, 10 May 1999; Frank, *Indira*, p. 333; Dixit, *India–Pakistan*, p. 182; Depinder Singh, *Field Marshal Sam Manekshaw: Soldiering with Dignity*, Dehradun: Natraj Publishers, 2002, pp. 128–9; Krishan Bhatia, *Indira: A Biography of Prime Minister Gandhi*, New York: Praeger, 1974, p. 243.

66. Dixit, *India–Pakistan*, p. 182.

67. Singh, *Field Marshall Sam Manekshaw*, pp. 128–9.

68. Cited in 'When Sam Quoted Chapter and Verse to Mrs. Gandhi'.

69. For similar accounts see Dixit, *India–Pakistan*, p. 182; Jaykar, *Indira Gandhi*, p. 223; Kux, *India and the United States*, p. 290.

70. Jaykar, *Indira Gandhi*, p. 223. Note: similar advice was given to Gandhi by General Aurora, the commander of the Indian Army in the Eastern front. See: Ela Sen, *Indira Gandhi: A Biography*, London: Peter Owen, 1973, p. 148.

71. Dixit, *India–Pakistan*, pp. 182–3.

72. Ibid., p. 182.

73. Bhatia, *Indira*, p. 244.

74. NA, FCO 95/478, P.H. Roberts to J.G. McMinnies (Information Research Department, FCO), New Delhi, 1 Dec. 1969.

75. NA, FCO 95/478, 'Soviet Propaganda in India', *The Current*, 1 Jan. 1969, attached in a note from O. Stephenson to the FCO, New Delhi, 31 Jan. 1969.

76. TNA, State to Van Hollen, 15 Jan. 1969, Washington, RG 59, 1966–75, box no. 9.

77. NMML, Secretary of State Rogers' talk with Prime Minister Gandhi, 6 June 1969, Washington, T.N. Kaul Papers, instalment I–III, subject file 19.

78. NMML, T.N. Kaul to MEA, 7 Apr. 1969, P.N. Haksar Papers, 3rd instalment, subject file 203.

79. Ram Guha, *India After Gandhi*, p. 456.

80. NMML, R. Bhandari to D. P. Dhar, undated, P.N. Haksar Papers, 3rd instalment, subject file 203.

81. Ibid.

82. Ibid.

83. NMML, T.N. Kaul to MEA, 7 Apr. 1969, P.N. Haksar Papers, 3rd instalment, subject file 203.

84. Ibid.

85. Note: for further details on India's refusal to sign a treaty between 1969 and 1970 see Sisson and Rose, *War and Succession*, pp. 197–8.

86. NA, FO 95/478, H.C. Byatt to Stanley Tomlinson, 27 Jan. 1971.

87. Note: this had been clearly conveyed to US Secretary of State William Rogers by Indira Gandhi during her visit to the US in October 1970. NMML, 'Rogers' Talk with the Prime Minister and Foreign Minister', New York, 24 Oct. 1970, T.N. Kaul Papers, subject file 19.

88. A brief note on India's deep-rooted mistrust of China and the East Pakistani crisis can be found in Ayoob and Subrahmanyam, *The Liberation*, pp. 187–93.

89. TNA, FO 95/478, H.C. Byatt (FCO) to W.K. Slatcher, 16 Feb. 1971.

90. NA, FO 95/478, W.K. Slatcher to H.C. Byatt, 22 Jan. 1971.

91. NA, FO 95/478, H.C. Byatt to W.K.L. Satcher, 16 Feb. 1971.

92. NA, FO 95/478G, S. Barass, office of chargé d'affaires, Peking, to L.V. Appleyard, Peking, 17 Feb. 1971.

93. TNA, Gandhi to Nixon, 13 May 1971, NPMS/NSC Files, South Asia, box 578.

94. TNA, Gandhi to Nixon, NSC Files, presidential correspondence 1969–74, box 755.

95. 'Minutes of the Senior Review Group Meeting, Chaired by Henry Kissinger', 19 Apr. 1971, *FRUS*, vol. 11, South Asia Crisis, 1971, Washington, DC: US Government Printing Office, p. 83.

96. Memorandum from Kissinger to Acting Secretary of State John Irwin, Washington, 7 May 1971, *FRUS*, vol. 11, p. 104.

97. Nixon to Yahya, 13 May 1971, ibid., p. 105.

98. Memorandum of conversation, Jha with Kissinger, Washington, 21 May 1971, ibid., pp. 129–30.

99. Kissinger to Nixon, 26 May 1971, ibid., p. 149.

100. Marvin Kalb and Barnard Kalb, *Kissinger*, Boston: Little Brown & Co., 1974, p. 243.

101. Memorandum from Alexander Haig to Nixon, Washington, 25 June 1971, *FRUS*, vol. 11, p. 196.

102. For details on arms supplied by the US to India and Pakistan see Robert G. Wersing, 'The Arms Race in South Asia: Implications for the United States', *Asian Survey*, 25, 3 (Mar. 1985), pp. 265–91.

103. TNA, Harold Saunders to Kissinger, 21 July 1971, NPMS/NSC Files, South Asia Congressional Files, Apr.–Nov. 1971 to South Asia Military Supply 27 Aug. to 22 Nov. 1971, box 574.

104. Editorial note of Nixon's meeting with Singh, Jha and Joseph Sisco, Washington, 16 June 1971, *FRUS*, vol. 11, p. 183.

105. NMML, MoC, Singh's visit to London, 20 June 1971, T.N. Kaul Papers, subject file 19. For details on Soviet arms supplies to Pakistan between 1968 and 1971 see Robert H. Donaldson, 'The Soviet Stake in Stability', *Asian Survey*, 12, 6 (June 1972), pp. 475–82.

106. NMML, talk between Kissinger and Singh, New Delhi, 7 July 1971, T.N. Kaul Papers, subject file 19.

107. TNA, Saunders and Hoskinson to Kissinger, 17 May 1971, NPMS/NSC Files, South Asia Congressional Apr.–Nov. 1971 to South Asia Military Supply 27 Aug. to 22 Nov. 1971.

108. Note: the fact that US arms were sent to Pakistan until June 1971 has been recorded by Jack Anderson. See Jack Anderson with George Clifford, *The Anderson Papers*, New York: Random House, 1973, pp. 208–28.

109. TNA, Elliot to Kissinger, 4 June 1971, NPMS/NSC Files, South Asia Congressional Apr.–Nov. 1971 to South Asia Military Supply 27 Aug. to 22 Nov. 1971.

110. MoC by Saunders, New Delhi, 6 July 1971, *FRUS*, vol. 11, p. 220.

111. Ayoob and Subrahmanyam, *The Liberation War*, p. 176.

112. MoC with Kissinger, P.N. Haksar, Gandhi, Saunders and Kenneth Keating, New Delhi, 7 July 1971, *FRUS*, vol. 11, p. 222

113. Editorial note, Kissinger's meeting with Jagjivan Ram, New Delhi, 7 July 1971, ibid., p. 232.

114. Ibid. Note: Jha's description of his talks with Kissinger on 17 July has also been confirmed by the then director of the CIA. See memorandum from the director of the CIA to Kissinger, Washington, 29 July 1971, ibid., p. 291.

115. For details see Kux, *India and the United States*, p. 295.

116. Dhar, *Indira Gandhi*, pp. 163–70.

117. Dixit, *India–Pakistan*, p. 184.

118. NA, FCO 95/478, L.P. Appleyard to H. Davies, 19 Aug. 1971.

119. NA, FO 95/478, J.A. Birch to Appleyard, 27 Aug. 1971.

120. NA, FCO 37/819, 'Swaran Singh's Statement in Parliament', New Delhi, 9 Aug. 1971.

121. NA, PREM 15/445, New Delhi to CRO, 9 Aug. 1971. A brief analysis of Article 9 of the treaty can be found in Rajan Menon, 'India and the Soviet Union: A New Stage in Relations?', *Asian Survey*, 18, 7 (July 1978), pp. 731–6.

122. MoC, Jha's meeting with Kissinger, Washington, 9 Aug. 1971, *FRUS*, vol. 11, p. 316.

123. MoC, Nixon with Kissinger, Sisco, Irwin, Saunders and others, Washington, 11 Aug. 1971, ibid., p. 325.

124. MoC between Jha and Kissinger, Washington, 9 Aug. 1971, ibid., p. 316.

125. Memorandum from Kissinger to Nixon, Washington, 24 Aug. 1971, ibid., p. 360.

126. Ibid., p. 362.

127. Ibid., p. 364.

128. Anderson, *Anderson Papers*, p. 228.

129. NA, FO 37/819, 'JIC Assessment of the Treaty Drafted in Consultation with the FCO', London, 11 Aug. 1971.

130. NA, FO 37/819 New Delhi to CRO, meeting with Kaul, 10 Aug. 1971.

131. Ibid.

132. NA, FCO 37/819, P.J.S. Male to Alec Douglas Home, 16 Aug. 1971.

133. NMML, prime minister talks with Gromyko, New Delhi, 10 Aug. 1971, T.N. Kaul Papers, subject file 19.

134. NMML, Bhandari to Dhar, P.N. Haksar Papers, 3rd instalment, subject file 203.

135. Ibid.

136. Note: according to T.N. Kaul, India, and not the Soviet Union, had decided when the opportune time would be to sign the treaty. JKLM, US embassy in New Delhi to State, New Delhi, 16 Aug. 1971.

137. For details on Soviet thinking with regard to the signing of the treaty see Donaldson, 'The Soviet Stake in Stability', pp. 483–5, also see P.R. Chari, 'Indo-Soviet Military Cooperation: A Review', *Asian Survey*, 19, 3 (Mar. 1979), pp. 230–44.

138. NA, FO 38/820, Appleyard to CRO, London, 17 Aug. 1971.

139. For differences in US and UK perspectives on India's motives see Max-Jean Zins, 'Cold War South Asia: A Look at the British Archives on India, 1947–1971', in Max Jean Zins and Giles Boquerrat (eds), *India in the Mirror of Foreign Diplomatic Archives*, New Delhi: Manohar and Centre de Sciences Humaines, 2004, pp. 102–7.

140. Memorandum of meeting, Kissinger and Dobrynin, Washington, 17 Aug. 1971, cited in F.S. Aijazuddin (ed.), *The White House and Pakistan: Secret Declassified Documents, 1969–1974*, Oxford: Oxford University Press, 2002, p. 272.

141. Memorandum from Kissinger to Nixon, 24 Aug. 1971, *FRUS*, vol. 11, p. 363.

142. For a brief account of the Soviet Union's inability to influence India see M.S. Rajan, 'Bangladesh & After', *Pacific Affairs*, 45, 2 (Summer 1972), pp. 193–8.

143. NA, FCO 37/820, F.S. Tomlinson to South Asia Department, London, 23 Aug. 1971.

144. Memorandum for the president's file, Washington, 29 Sep. 1971, *FRUS*, vol. 11, p. 425.

145. MoC between Kissinger and Jha, Washington, 8 Oct. 1971, ibid., pp. 453–5.

146. TNA, Indo-Pakistani crisis, NPMS/NSC Files Indo-Pak, South Asia 14 Dec. 1971 to 15 Dec. 1971 to SA 17 Dec. 1971 to 31 Dec. 1971, box 573.

147. NA, PREM 15/960, 'Record of Meeting between PM and Indira Gandhi at Chequers', 31 Oct. 1971.

148. NA, PREM 15/960, 'Additional Note on Indira Gandhi's Meeting with the Prime Minister at Chequers', 31 Oct. 1971.

149. Ibid.

150. Ibid.

151. Ibid. For further details on Gandhi's visit to Europe see Sen, *Indira Gandhi*, pp. 137–41.

152. Note: according to an assessment made by the US embassy in Islamabad, Pakistan was the first to undertake major movements of forces in mid-Sep. It deployed its 6th and 17th divisions to the border areas in the west. Indian reaction took place in early Oct. TNA, US embassy in Islamabad to State, Islamabad, 21 Oct. 1971, NPMS/NSC Indo-Pak, box no. 570.

153. TNA, 'South Asia, Pakistan Chronology', NPMS/NSC, box 578.

154. TNA, US embassy in Islamabad to State, Islamabad, 13 Oct. 1971, NPMS/NSC, Indo-Pak, box no. 570.

155. TNA, NPMS/NSC Files, 'South Asia, Pakistan Chronology', box 578.

156. Ibid.

157. TNA, NPMS/NSC Papers, Indo-Pak War, South Asia, 23 Nov. 1971 to 30 Nov. 1971 to SA 5 Dec. 1971 to 6 Dec. 1971, box 571.

158. Gandhi to Nixon, New Delhi, 5 Dec. 1971, *FRUS*, vol. 11, pp. 630–1.

159. For details on the debate surrounding the deployment of the Seventh Fleet see Kux, *India and the United States*, pp. 305–6 and Kalb and Kalb, *Kissinger*, p. 260.

160. For further details on the 'Tilt' as well as Kissinger's thinking behind the deployment of the Seventh Fleet see Christopher Van Hollen, 'The Tilt Policy Revisited: Nixon–Kissinger Geopolitics and South Asia', *Asian Survey*, 20, 4 (Apr. 1980), pp. 339–61.

161. NA, FCO 37/756, British policy in the subcontinent prepared by the SADFCO, London, 18 Dec. 1971.

162. NMML, record of luncheon meeting between Kissinger and the ambassador, Washington, 15 June 1971, T.N. Kaul Papers, subject file 1.

163. NMML, note by Jha, Washington, 16 Nov. 1972, P.N. Haksar Papers, 3rd instalment, subject file 235.

164. Ibid.

165. Note: details of India's nuclear programme and the 1974 tests are outlined in detail in Chapter 8.

166. NMML, 'Foreign Secretary Speech at the Overseas Writers Guild International Club', Washington, 18 Oct. 1973, T.N. Kaul Papers, subject file 1.

167. Ibid.

168. NMML, Kaul to foreign minister, Washington, 1 Dec. 1973, T.N. Kaul Papers, subject file 1.

169. Indira Gandhi, *India and Bangladesh: Selected Speeches and Statements*, New Delhi: Orient Longman, 1972, p. 40.

170. 'US Military Aid to Pakistan', *The Hindu*, 24 Dec. 1953.

7. 'NINDA'

1. Amit Baruah, 'No Troops for Iraq Without Explicit UN Mandate: India', *The Hindu*, 15 July 2003.

2. C. Raja Mohan, 'Indo-US Talks on Iraq Today', ibid., 16 June 2003.

3. 'No Troops for Iraq, Home Truths Loom', *Hindustan Times*, 15 July 2003.

4. *Lok Sabha Debates*, 33/21, 8 Apr. 2003, 12th Session.

5. 'War in Iraq Stall Parliament', *Hindustan Times*, 8 Apr. 2003.

6. Kota Neelima, 'Iraq Resolution Waits for Words', *Indian Express*, 8 Apr. 2003.

7. Ibid.

8. For instance see Teresita C. Schaffer, *India and the United States in the 21st Century: Reinventing Partnership*, New Delhi: India Research Press, 2010, p. 4; David Malone, *Does the Elephant Dance? Contemporary Indian Foreign Policy*, London: Oxford University Press, 2011, p. 153.

9. Thomas. P. Thornton, 'India Adrift: The Search for Moorings in a New World Order', *Asian Survey*, 32, 12 (Dec. 1992), p. 1067.

10. Ramesh Thakur, 'India in the World: Neither Rich, Powerful, Nor Principled', *Foreign Affairs* (July–Aug. 1997), p. 20.

11. Cited in Kuldip Nayar, *Beyond the Lines: An Autobiography*, New Delhi: Roli Books, 2012, p. 340.

12. Author's interview with Brajesh Misra, New Delhi, 11 Aug. 2007.

13. C. Raja Mohan, *Crossing the Rubicon: The Shaping of India's New Foreign Policy*, New Delhi: Viking, 2003, pp. 29–36.

14. Author's interview (via teleconference) with Donald Rumsfeld, 13 Nov. 2008.

15. Shashi Tharoor, *Pax Indica: India and the World of the 21st Century*, New Delhi: Allen Lane, 2012, p. 15.

16. See Malone, *Does the Elephant Dance?* pp. 164–78; Howard B. Schaffer, *The Limits of Influence: America's Role in Kashmir*, Washington: Brookings Institution Press, 2009, pp. 169–92; Stephen P. Cohen, *India: Emerging Power*, Washington, DC: Brookings Institution Press, 2002, pp. 268–98; Srinath Raghavan, 'A Coercive Triangle: India, Pakistan and the United States, and the Crisis of 2001–2002', *Defence Studies*, 9, 2 (June 2009); Robert M. Hathaway, 'The US–India Courtship: From Clinton to Bush', in Sumit Ganguly (ed.), *India as an Emerging Power*, London: Frank Cass, 2003, pp. 6–31; Ian Talbot, *Pakistan: A Modern History*, London: Hurst, 2009, pp. 335–7; Dennis Kux, *The United States and Pakistan: 1947–2000*, Baltimore: Johns Hopkins University Press, 2001, pp. 324–48; Jasjit Singh (ed.), *The Road Ahead: Indo-US Strategic Dialogue*, New Delhi: Lancer International and IDSA, 1994; Shekhar Gupta, 'India Redefines its Role', *Adelphi Paper*, 293, Oxford: Oxford University Press and IISS, 1995.

17. Taylor Branch, *The Clinton Tapes, Conversations with a President: 1993–2001*, New York: Simon and Schuster, 2009, p. 247.

18. Cited in Gaby Wood, 'The Clinton Tapes by Taylor Branch', *The Guardian*, 11 Oct. 2009.

19. Branch, *The Clinton Tapes*, p. 560.

20. Michael Takiff, *A Complicated Man: The Life of Bill Clinton as Told by those who Know Him*, London and New Haven: Yale University Press, 2010, p. 1.

21. Hillary Rodham Clinton, *Living History*, London: Headline, 2003, p. 276.

22. Author's interview with General Joseph Ralston, Washington, 18 Sep. 2008.

23. Raja Mohan, *Crossing the Rubicon*, pp. 5–6.

24. I.K. Gujral, *Matters of Discretion*, New Delhi: Kay House, 2011, pp. 370–3.

25. Cited in Jaswant Singh, *A Call to Honour: In Service of Emergent India*, New Delhi: Rupa & Co., 2006, p. 122. Also see Strobe Talbott, *Engaging India: Diplomacy, Democracy and the Bomb*, Washington, DC: Brookings Institution Press, 2006, p. 37.

26. Author's interview with Bruce Riedel, Washington, 28 Aug. 2008.

27. Ibid.

28. Hathaway, 'The US–India Courtship', p. 7.
29. Singh, *Call to Honour*, p. 121.
30. Branch, *The Clinton Tapes*, p. 248.
31. Talbott, *Engaging India*, p. 2.
32. Ibid., p. 58.
33. Note: the text of the letter can be found in Singh, *Call to Honour*, p. 136.
34. Talbott, *Engaging India*, pp. 53–5.
35. Branch, *The Clinton Tapes*, p. 248.
36. Author's interview with General Ralston, 18 Sep. 2008.
37. Author's interview with Bruce Riedel, 28 Aug. 2008.
38. Talbott, *Engaging India*, p. 5.
39. For details see Singh, *Call to Honour*, pp. 298–319 and Talbott, *Engaging India*, pp. 74–231.
40. Talbott, *Engaging India*, p. 5.
41. Author's interview with Jaswant Singh, 16 July 2007.
42. For a variation in views see General V.P. Malik, *Kargil: From Surprise to Victory*, New Delhi: Harper Collins, 2006 and General Pervez Musharraf, *In the Line of Fire*, Islamabad: Free Press, 2006.
43. For an eloquent and substantive analysis based on primary source research see P.R. Chari, Pervez Iqbal Cheema and Stephen P. Cohen, *Four Crises and a Peace Process*, Washington: Brookings Institution Press, 2007, Chapter 5.
44. Author's interview with Bruce Riedel, 28 Aug. 2008.
45. Author's interview with Walter Andersen, 1 Oct. 2008.
46. Bill Clinton, *My Life*, New York: Arrow Books, 2005, p. 866.
47. Author's interview with Stephen Cohen, 11 Sep. 2008.
48. Author's interview with Brajesh Misra, 11 Aug. 2007.
49. John Harris, *The Survivor*, New York: Random House, 2005, p. 411.
50. Author's interview with Bruce Riedel, 28 Aug. 2008.
51. Branch, *The Clinton Tapes*, p. 561.
52. For details see Talbot, *Pakistan*, pp. 375–8.
53. Author's interview with Bruce Riedel, 28 Aug. 2008.
54. Talbott, *Engaging India*, p. 169.
55. Cited in Sidney Blumenthal, *The Clinton Wars*, New York: Farrar, Straus and Giroux, 2003, p. 45.
56. Cited in Talbott, *Engaging India*, p. 203.
57. Speech of Prime Minister Atal Bihari Vajpayee at the Asia Society, New York, 28 Sep. 1998. Available at: http://www.indianembassy.org/special/cabinet/Primeminister/pm(asiasociety).htm
58. Author's interview with Stephen Cohen, 11 Sep. 2008.
59. Author's interview with Bruce Riedel, 28 Aug. 2008.
60. Author's interview with Lalit Mansingh, Aug. 2007.

61. Author's interview with George Fernandes, 3 Aug. 2007.

62. Frank Bruni, *Ambling into History: An Unlikely Odyssey of George. W. Bush*, New York: Perennial, 2003, p. 3.

63. George W. Bush, *Decision Points*, New York: Virgin Books, 2010, pp. 82–3.

64. Author's interview with Walter Andersen, 1 Oct. 2008.

65. Condoleezza Rice, 'Promoting the National Interest', *Foreign Affairs*, 79, 1 (2000), pp. 55–7.

66. Condoleezza Rice, *No Higher Honour: A Memoir of My Years in Washington*, London: Simon & Schuster, 2011, p. xiv.

67. Bush, *Decision Points*, p. 214.

68. Author's interview with Walter Andersen, 1 Oct. 2008.

69. Author's interview with Donald Rumsfeld (teleconference), 13 Nov. 2008.

70. Author's interview with Douglas Feith, 10 Oct. 2008.

71. Bob Woodward, *State of Denial: Bush at War, Part III*, New York: Simon & Schuster, 2006, p. 240.

72. Author's interview with State Department official [name undisclosed], Sep. 2008.

73. Cited in Rajiv Chandrasekaran, *Imperial Life in the Emerald City: Inside Baghdad's Green Zone*, London: Bloomsbury, 2008, p. 212.

74. Ibid., p. 212.

75. Author's interview with Mullah Abdul Salaam Zaeef, 11 Feb. 2011.

76. Author's interview with Donald Rumsfeld (via teleconference), 13 Nov. 2008.

77. Raja Mohan, *Crossing the Rubicon*, p. xi.

78. Author's interview with Enders Wimbush, 22 Sep. 2008, also see S. Enders Wimbush, *Strategic India*, Washington: Smith Richardson Foundation, 2007, available at: http://www.hudson.org/files/publications/StrategicIndia-Final-Wimbush.pdf

79. Musharraf, *In the Line of Fire*, p. 202.

80. Author's interview with Hilary Synnott, 1 Apr. 2010.

81. Schaffer, *Limits of Influence*, p. 171

82. Singh, *Call to Honour*, p. 338.

83. Cited in 'Wait Watchers Club', *Outlook Magazine*, 43, 5, 10 Feb. 2003.

84. Author's interview with Kanwal Sibal, 24 Mar. 2010.

85. Chidanand Rajghatta, 'Iraq Conflict Brings India to Centre-Stage', *Times of India*, 10 Feb. 2003.

86. Amitabh Srivastava, 'I Refused to Help Bush: Vajpayee', *Hindustan Times*, 28 Mar. 2003.

87. Mahendra Ved, 'India Not to Back War, Says PM', *Times of India*, 26 Feb. 2003.

88. Ibid.

89. Praful Bidwai, 'Not In Our Name', *Hindustan Times*, 25 Feb. 2003.

90. Mani Shankar Aiyer, 12th Lok Sabha Session, 31/3, 19 Feb. 2003, p. 418.

91. Jaswant Singh, ibid., 19 Feb. 2003, p. 466.

92. Note: the text of the resolution can be found at http://www.un.org/Depts/unmovic/documents/1441.pdf

93. 'US Must Win UN Backing, Says PM', *Times of India*, 13 Mar. 2003.

94. Chidanand Rajghatta, 'Iraq Conflict Brings India to Centre Stage', *Times of India*, 10 Feb. 2003.

95. 'PM For Middle Path Approach To Iraq', *The Hindu*, 11 Mar. 2003.

96. Atul Aneja, 'India Pulls Out Diplomatic Staff', *The Hindu*, 18 Mar. 2003.

97. 'Most Indians Oppose War On Iraq, Survey', *Times of India*, 4 Feb. 2003.

98. Aditya Sinha, 'Delhiites against Iraq War', *Times of India*, 23 Feb. 2003.

99. J.N. Dixit, 'Arms and the Man', *Hindustan Times*, 13 Feb. 2003.

100. Author's interview with Brajesh Mishra, New Delhi, 11 Aug. 2007.

101. Author's interview with State Department official [name undisclosed], Washington, Sep. 2008.

102. 'PM Rejects Deadline, MEA Cautious', *Times of India*, 19 Mar. 2003.

103. 'Attack Lacks Justification: India', *Times of India*, 21 Mar. 2003.

104. Amit Baruah, 'Unjustified, Says India', *The Hindu*, 21 Mar. 2003.

105. Aunohita Mojumdar, 'India Won't Jeopardise Relations with US over Iraq', *Times of India*, 23 Mar. 2003.

106. V. Sudarshan, 'Age of Consent', *Outlook Magazine*, 43, 12, 31 Mar. 2003.

107. 'Centre Refuses to "Condemn" US Act', *Times of India*, 23 Mar. 2003.

108. Author's interview with Bruce Riedel, Washington, 28 Aug. 2008.

109. Author's interview with Marc Grossman, Washington, 3 Oct. 2008.

110. C. Raja Mohan, 'India and the Iraq War', *The Hindu*, 27 Mar. 2003.

111. C. Raja Mohan, 'Is the United Nations Relevant?' *The Hindu*, 19 Mar. 2003.

112. Mohan, 'India and the Iraq War'.

113. Satish Nambiar, 'Iraq: Behind the Smokescreen',' *Indian Express*, 8 Apr. 2003.

114. P.S. Jha, 'India Should Say "No"', *Outlook Magazine*, 43, 24, 15 June 2003.

115. Mani Shankar Aiyer, 'Baghdad Can Backfire', *Indian Express*, 1 Apr. 2003.

116. Praful Bidwai, 'Machinehead', *Hindustan Times*, 22 Mar. 2003.

117. Author's interview with George Fernandes, New Delhi, 3 Aug. 2007.

118. 'Samata Party Slams Govt. Stand on Iraq', *The Hindu*, 3 Apr. 2003.

119. V. Sudarshan, 'Neither and/or Nor', *Outlook Magazine*, 17 Apr. 2003.

120. Saba Naqvi Bhaumik, 'War on Iraq', *Outlook Magazine*, 43, 14, 14 Apr. 2003.

121. Author's interview with Lalit Mansingh, Aug. 2007.

122. Priya Ranjan Dasmunshi, 12th Lok Sabha Session, 32/20, 7 Apr. 2003, p. 4.

123. G.M. Banatwalla, ibid., 7 Apr. 2003, p. 4.

124. Congress Working Committee Resolution, ibid., 7 Apr. 2003, p. 8.

125. Somnath Chatterjee, ibid., 7 Apr. 2003, p. 18.

126. Iraq resolution, ibid., 7 Apr. 2003, p. 310.

127. Jaipal Reddy, ibid., 7 Apr. 2003, p. 311.

128. Aditya Sinha, 'Pak a Fit Case for Attack without UN Support', *Hindustan Times*, 6 Apr. 2003.

129. Note: this is based on a survey of House debates. *Lok Sabha Debates*, 12th session, 33:22, 9 Apr.; 33:23, 10 Apr.; 33:27, 24 Apr.; 34:31, 30 Apr.; 33:25, 22 Apr.; 33:28, 25 Apr.; 33:29, 28 Apr.; 34:36, 8 May; 34:37.

130. Rice, *No Higher Honour*, p. 239.

131. Rajnish Sharma, 'Ties with US: India to Take Middle Path', *Hindustan Times*, 20 Apr. 2003.

132. Robert D. Blackwill, 'A Case for War', *Indian Express*, 9 Apr. 2003.

133. Rice, *No Higher Honour*, p. 4.

134. Robert D. Blackwill, 'Defence of an Invasion', *Hindustan Times*, 6 Mar. 2003.

135. Author's interview with State Department official [name undisclosed], Sep. 2008.

136. These include: Robert D. Blackwill, 'It's Baghdad's Call', *Hindustan Times*, 6 Mar. 2003, Robert D. Blackwill, 'Disarm, Don't Defy', *Times of India*, 12 Feb. 2003.

137. Author's interview with State Department official [name undisclosed], Sep. 2008.

138. Woodward, *State of Denial*, p. 7.

139. Author's interview with State Department official [name undisclosed], Sep. 2008.

140. Jyoti Malhotra, 'US Ambassador Blackwill Pays for his Pro-India Line', *Indian Express*, 22 Apr. 2003.

141. Robert D. Blackwill, 'A Passage from India', *Indian Express*, 22 Apr. 2003.

142. Jyoti Malhotra, 'Govt Wants to Send Envoy Back to Iraq Soon', *Indian Express*, 9 Apr. 2003.

143. Jyoti Malhotra, 'India Readies to Greet New Order in Iraq without Saddam', *Indian Express*, 10 Apr. 2003.

144. Author's interview with Brajesh Mishra, 11 Aug. 2007.

145. 'India Inc Eyes Share in Iraq Reconstruction', *Indian Express*, 11 Apr. 2003.

146. Charubala Annuncio and Sandeep Singh, 'In Search of the Iraqi Pipeline', *Outlook Magazine*, 43, 22, 9 June 2003.

147. J.N. Dixit, 'Let's Get Practical Now', *Hindustan Times*, 16 Apr. 2003.

148. 'Troops to Iraq are Still Stuck', *Indian Express*, 27 May 2003.

149. 'Rafeeuddin Ahmed Named Special Advisor by Secretary General', 7 Apr. 2003, available at: http://www.unis.unvienna.org/unis/pressrels/2003/sga835. html

150. 'UN Security Council Resolution 1483', 22 May 2003, available at: http:// daccessdds.un.org/doc/UNDOC/GEN/N03/368/53/PDF/N0336853.pdf? OpenElement

151. Author's interview with George Fernandes, 3 Aug. 2007.

152. V. Sudarshan, 'Keeping America's Peace', *Outlook Magazine*, 43, 21, 2 June 2003.

153. C. Raja Mohan, 'India's Opportunity in Iraq', *The Hindu*, 2 May 2003.

154. Shishir Gupta, 'US for Indian Troops in Kurd Zone', *Indian Express*, 4 June 2003.

155. Author's interview with Brajesh Misra, 11 Aug. 2007.

156. Author's interview with Jaswant Singh, 16 July 2007.

157. Author's interview with a senior Indian official, coded in this chapter as [A], 2010.

158. Author's interview with a very senior Indian military officer, Aug. 2007.

159. *Lok Sabha debates*, 13th Session, 35/2, 22 July 2003.

160. Author's interview with Claudio Lilienfeld, Washington, 24 Sep. 2008.

161. Pradeep Kaushal, 'India's Line to US: Pak First, then Iraq', *Indian Express*, 11 June 2003.

162. Ashish Kumar Sen, 'The Iron Handshake', *Outlook Magazine*, 43, 24, 15 June 2003.

163. Sridhar Krishnaswamy, 'Bush, Advani Discuss Issue of Troops for Iraq', *The Hindu*, 11 June 2003.

164. Author's interview with Claudio Lilienfeld, 24 Sep. 2008.

165. Author's interview with Douglas Feith, 10 Oct. 2008.

166. Author's interview with Claudio Lilienfeld, 24 Sep. 2008.

167. Author's interview with Walter Andersen, 1 Oct. 2008.

168. Sridhar Krishnaswami, 'No Pressure to Send Troops to Iraq, Says Advani', *The Hindu*, 12 June 2003.

169. Author's interview with Natwar Singh, 24 July 2007.

170. Author's interview (telephone) with Pamit Pal Chaudhuri, 23 June 2007.

171. Sridhar Krishnaswamy, 'Bush, Advani Discuss Issue of Troops for Iraq', *The Hindu*, 11 June 2003.

172. Douglas Martin, 'Peter Rodman, Foreign Affairs Expert, Dies at 64', *New York Times*, 5 Aug. 2008.

173. Author's interview (via teleconference) with Donald Rumsfeld, 13 Nov. 2008.

174. Author's interview with Daniel Markey, 11 Sep. 2008.

175. Author's interview with Bruce Riedel, 28 Aug. 2008.

176. Author's interview with State Department official [name undisclosed], Sep. 2008.

177. 'No Troops for Iraq without Consensus, PM Assures Sonia', *The Hindu*, 16 June 2003.

178. Author's interview with Natwar Singh, 24 July 2007.

179. Author's interview with George Fernandes, 3 Aug. 2007.

180. Jyothi Malhotra, 'Get us UN Nod, We'll be There: India', *Indian Express*, 17 June 2003.

181. C. Raja Mohan, 'Decision on Iraq Remains Open', *The Hindu*, 17 June 2003.

182. Author's interview with Gurmeet Kanwal, 2 Aug. 2007.

183. V. Sudarshan, 'Staying Home', *Outlook Magazine*, 43, 28, 21 July 2003.

184. Vishal Thapar, 'Army was all Dressed up to go to Iraq', *Hindustan Times*, 15 July 2003.

185. Author's interview with Enders Wimbush, 22 Sep. 2008.

186. V. Sudarshan, 'Keeping America's Peace', *Outlook Magazine*, 43, 21, 2 June 2003.

187. Pranab Dhal Samanta, 'Troops to Iraq: US Tries to Clear Path', *Indian Express*, 16 June 2003.

188. Jyoti Malhotra, 'Get us UN Nod, We'll be There: India', *Indian Express*, 17 June 2003.

189. 'Army Doctors Reach Iraq to Build Hospital', *Times of India*, 18 June 2003.

190. Author's interview with a senior Indian official in the NSC, 12 July 2007.

191. Author's interview with George Fernandes, 3 Aug. 2007.

192. 'Government Buying Time on Troop's Issue?', *Times of India*, 17 June 2003.

193. Author's interview with Marc Grossman, 3 Oct. 2008.

194. Author's interview with Claudio Lilienfeld, Washington, 24 Sep. 2008.

195. For a blow-by-blow account see Hilary Synnott, *Bad Days in Basra*, London: I.B. Tauris, 2008.

196. Author's interview with Jasjit Singh, 31 July 2007.

197. C. Raja Mohan, 'Indo-US Talks on Iraq Today', *The Hindu*, 16 June 2003.

198. Satish Nambiar, 'Why We Should Say Yes', *Outlook Magazine*, 7 July 2003.

199. Raja Menon, 'To Send or Not to Send? Not a Question', *Indian Express*, 18 June 2003.

200. Cited in Ashish Kumar Sen, 'The Iron Handshake', *Outlook Magazine*, 43, 24, 15 June 2003.

201. Cited in Seema Sirohi, 'This Could Be Us', *Outlook Magazine*, 43, 27, 14 July 2003.

202. Author's interview with Kanwal Sibal, 24 Mar. 2010.

203. Author's interview with Enders Wimbush, 22 Sep. 2003.

204. Author's interview with [A], 2010.

205. Author's interview with Kanwal Sibal, 24 Mar. 2010.

206. Author's interview with George Fernandes, 3 Aug. 2007.

207. 'No Troops for Iraq, Home Truths Loom', *Hindustan Times*, 15 July 2003.

208. Harish Khare, 'India Not to Send Troops to Iraq', *The Hindu*, 13 July 2003.

209. Author's interview with Brajesh Misra, 11 Aug. 2007.

210. Ibid.

211. Shivshankar Menon, 'Old Fashioned Patriot', *The Hindu*, 9 Oct. 2012.

212. Author's interview with Brajesh Misra, 11 Aug. 2007.

213. Author's interview with George Fernandes, 3 Aug. 2007.

214. Jyothi Malhotra, 'India Won't be a Lackey', *Indian Express*, 3 June 2003.
215. Manoj Joshi, 'India is Still Non-Aligned, Says PM', *Times of India*, 3 June 2003.
216. Author's interview with [A], 2010.
217. Author's interview with S.D. Muni, 31 July 2007.
218. Author's interview with Lalit Mansingh, New Delhi, Aug. 2007.
219. Author's interview with [A], 2010.
220. Harish Khare, 'India Not to Send Troops to Iraq', *The Hindu*, 13 July 2003.
221. Author's interview with Jaswant Singh, 16 July 2007.
222. Harish Khare, 'India Not to Send Troops to Iraq', *The Hindu*, 13 July 2003.
223. Jyoti Malhotra, 'Between Iraq and a Hard Place', *Indian Express*, 14 July 2003.
224. Author's interview with S.D. Muni, 31 July 2007.
225. Author's interview (via teleconference) with Donald Rumsfeld, 13 Nov. 2008.
226. Author's interview with Bruce Riedel, 28 Aug. 2008.
227. Author's interview with Lalit Mansingh, Aug. 2007.
228. Saurabh Shukla, 'Won't Send Troops so Face Bushfire', *Hindustan Times*, 17 July 2003.
229. Seema Sirohi, 'I Do, I Don't', *Outlook Magazine*, 43, 45, 17 Nov. 2003.
230. Author's interview with Kanwal Sibal, 24 Mar. 2010.
231. Author's interview with Douglas Feith, 10 Oct. 2008.
232. Author's interview with Daniel Markey, 11 Sep. 2008.
233. Author's interview (via teleconference) with Donald Rumsfeld, 13 Nov. 2008.
234. Author's interview with Claudio Lilienfeld, 24 Sep. 2008.
235. For details see: Lok Sabha Elections 2004, Election Commission of India, available at: http://eci.nic.in/eci_main/StatisticalReports/LS_2004/Vol_I_LS_2004.pdf
236. Cited in John Cherian, 'A Shaky Start', *Frontline Magazine*, 21, 13, 19 June–2 July 2004.
237. Rao Inderjit Singh, *Lok Sabha Debates*, 14/5, 29 Nov. 2005, p. 370.
238. Author's interview with Natwar Singh, 24 July 2007.

8. '4.30 A.M.'

1. Author's interview with Walter K. Andersen, 1 Oct. 2008.
2. 'President Welcomes Prime Minister Singh of India in Arrival Ceremony', Washington, 18 July 2005, available at: http://georgewbush-whitehouse.archives.gov/news/releases/2005/07/20050718.html
3. 'President, Prime Minister of India Discuss Freedom and Democracy', Washington, 18 July 2005, available at: http://georgewbush-whitehouse.archives.gov/news/releases/2005/07/20050718-1.html
4. C. Raja Mohan, *Impossible Allies: Nuclear India, United States, and the Global Order*, New Delhi: India Research Press, 2006, p. 4.

5. Author's interviews with three senior representatives from both India and the US, hereafter and collectively referred to as [B], their names, titles and the locations and dates of each interview have been kept anonymous as requested by the interviewees.

6. Author's interview with Walter Andersen, 1 Oct. 2008.

7. C. Raja Mohan, *Impossible Allies*, p. 4.

8. 'Joint Statement between President George W. Bush and Prime Minister Manmohan Singh', Washington, 18 July 2005, available at: http://georgewbush-whitehouse.archives.gov/news/releases/2005/07/20050718-6.html

9. Author's interview with Lalit Mansingh, Aug. 2007.

10. 'Joint Statement between President George W. Bush and Prime Minister Manmohan Singh'.

11. For an account see Condoleezza Rice, *No Higher Honour: A Memoir of My Years in Washington*, London: Simon & Schuster, 2011, pp. 438–9.

12. Author's interview with Shyam Saran, May 2012.

13. D.N. Ghosh, 'Question for the Left', *Times of India*, 16 Nov. 2007.

14. 'CPI (M): Don't See the Nuclear Deal in Isolation', *The Hindu*, 9 Sep. 2007.

15. 'Centre: Surrendered to US: Advani', *Asian Age*, 6 Dec. 2007.

16. Brahma Chellaney, 'Pro-Deal But Anti Deterrent', *Asian Age*, 5 Jan. 2008.

17. Note: the newspaper in question was the *Asian Age*. Author's interview with M.J. Akbar [editor-in-chief of the *Asian Age*], New Delhi, 8 Aug. 2007.

18. 'Secretary of State Condoleezza Rice and Indian Minister of External Affairs Pranab Muckherjee at the Signing of the US–India Civilian Nuclear Cooperation Agreement', Washington, 10 Oct. 2008, available at: http://2001-2009.state.gov/secretary/rm/2008/10/110916.htm

19. Adlai Stevenson, 'More Nuclear Nations? Nuclear Reactors: America Must Act', *Foreign Affairs* (Oct. 1974), online version available at: http://www.foreignaffairs.com/articles/24525/adlai-e-stevenson-iii/more-nuclear-nations-nuclear-reactors-america-must-act?page=show#

20. For a brief note on the NPT and India see Swapna Kona Nayudu, 'Indo-US Nuclear Deal and Non-Proliferation Debate', in P.R. Chari (ed.), *Indo-US Nuclear Deal: Seeking Synergy in Bilateralism*, London: Routledge, 2012, pp. 161–7.

21. 'Treaty on the Non-Proliferation of Nuclear Weapons', International Atomic Energy Agency, 22 Apr. 1970, p. 4, available at: http://www.iaea.org/Publications/Documents/Infcircs/Others/infcirc140.pdf, http://www.armscontrol.org/events/20060215_India_Transcript

23. Strobe Talbott, 'Dealing with the Bomb', *Foreign Affairs* (Mar./Apr. 1999), online version available at: http://www.foreignaffairs.com/articles/54802/strobe-talbott/dealing-with-the-bomb-in-south-asia?page=show

24. See: 'Member States of the IAEA', International Atomic Energy Agency, available at: http://www.iaea.org/About/Policy/MemberStates/

25. Rice, *No Higher Honour*, p. 437 [emphasis added].

26. For a brief but eloquent background see Stephen P. Cohen, *India: Emerging Power*, Washington, DC: Brookings Institution Press, 2002, pp. 157–71; David Malone, *Does the Elephant Dance? Contemporary Indian Foreign Policy*, London: Oxford University Press, 2011, pp. 159–60.

27. Jaswant Singh, 'Against Nuclear Apartheid', *Foreign Affairs* (Sep./Oct. 1998), online version available at: http://www.foreignaffairs.com/articles/54391/jaswant-singh/against-nuclear-apartheid?page=show

28. 'Treaty on the Non-Proliferation of Nuclear Weapons', International Atomic Energy Agency, 22 Apr. 1970, p. 2.

29. Deepa Ollapally and Raja Ramanna, 'US–India Tensions: Misperceptions on Nuclear-Proliferation', *Foreign Affairs* (Jan./Feb. 1995), online version available at: http://www.foreignaffairs.com/articles/50584/deepa-ollapally-and-raja-ramanna/us-india-tensions-misperceptions-on-nuclear-proliferation?page=show

30. Jaswant Singh, 'Against Nuclear Apartheid'.

31. Ollapally and Ramanna, 'US–India Tensions: Misperceptions on Nuclear-Proliferation'.

32. 'Statement of the Permanent Mission of India to the Conference on Disarmament', New York, 4 Apr. 2012, available at: http://www.un.org/disarmament/content/news/disarmament_commission_2012/statements/india.pdf

33. Teresita C. Schaffer, *India and the United States in the 21st Century: Reinventing Partnership*, New Delhi: India Research Press, 2010, p. 92

34. 'What are the Guidelines?' Nuclear Suppliers Group, available at: http://www.nuclearsuppliersgroup.org/Leng/02-guide.htm

35. 'Review Conference of the Parties to the Treaty of Non-Proliferation of Nuclear Weapons', New York, 13 May 2010, available at: http://www.nuclearsuppliersgroup.org/Leng/PDF/NSG-H-statement.pdf

36. Gerard C. Smith and George W. Rathjens, 'Reassessing Nuclear Non-Proliferation Policy', *Foreign Affairs* (Spring 1981), online version available at: http://www.foreignaffairs.com/articles/34874/gerard-c-smith-and-george-w-rathjens/reassessing-nuclear-nonproliferation-policy

37. Rice, *No Higher Honour*, p. 436.

38. Jaswant Singh, 'Against Nuclear Apartheid'.

39. Ashley J. Tellis, *India as a New Global Power: An Action Agenda for the United States*, Washington: Carnegie Endowment for International Peace, 2005, pp. 6–7.

40. See for instance 'People Behind the Deal', *Times of India*, 3 Mar. 2006; 'Those Who Made the Deal Happen', *Indian Express*, 4 Mar. 2006; 'All the PM's Men', *Hindustan Times*, 5 Mar. 2006.

41. Strobe Talbott, *Engaging India: Diplomacy, Democracy and the Bomb*, Washington, DC: Brookings Institution Press, 2006, p. 216.

42. Tellis, *India as a New Global Partner*, pp. 12–13.

43. James Mann, *Rise of the Vulcans: The History of Bush's War Cabinet*, New York: Penguin, 2004, p. x.

44. Rice, *No Higher Honour*, p. 436.

45. Author's interview with State Department official [name undisclosed], Sep. 2008.

46. Bob Woodward, *State of Denial: Bush at War, Part III*, New York: Simon & Schuster, 2006, p. 52.

47. Rice, *No Higher Honour*, p. 153.

48. Author's interview with [B].

49. For a brief review see Sumit Ganguly, 'Behind India's Bomb: The Politics and Strategy of Nuclear Deterrence', *Foreign Affairs* (Sep./Oct. 2001).

50. Ashley Tellis, 'The United States and South Asia', prepared testimony for the House Committee on International Relations, Washington, 14 June 2005, available at: http://www.carnegieendowment.org/publications/index.cfm?fa=view&id=17070&prog=zgp&proj=zsa

51. R. Nicholas Burns, 'America's Strategic Opportunity with India', *Foreign Affairs* (Nov./Dec. 2007), online version available at: http://www.foreignaffairs.com/articles/63016/r-nicholas-burns/americas-strategic-opportunity-with-india?page=show#

52. Tellis, *India as a New Global Partner*.

53. Donald Rumsfeld, *Known and Unknown: A Memoir*, New York: Sentinel, 2011, p. 398.

54. Author's interview with Donald Rumsfeld (via teleconference), 13 Nov. 2008.

55. Author's interview with Douglas Feith, 10 Oct. 2008.

56. Rice, *No Higher Honour*, p. 437.

57. Author's interview with Douglas Feith, 10 Oct. 2008.

58. Cited in Glenn Kessler, *The Confidante: Condoleezza Rice and the Creation of the Bush Legacy*, New York: St. Martin's Press, 2007, pp. 49–52.

59. For a brief note on personalities see Harsh V. Pant, *The US–India Nuclear Pact: Policy, Process, and Great Power Politics*, New Delhi: Oxford University Press, 2011, pp. 65–73.

60. For a review see Ashley Tellis, 'The Merits of De-Hyphenation: Explaining IS success in Engaging India and Pakistan', *The Washington Quarterly*, 31, 4 (Autumn 2008).

61. R. Nicholas Burns, 'America's Strategic Opportunity with India'.

62. C. Raja Mohan, 'India and the Balance of Power', *Foreign Affairs*, 85, 17 (2006), p. 27.

63. Robert Blackwill, 'The India Imperative: A Conversation with Robert Blackwill', *National Interest* (Summer 2005), p. 11.

64. R. Nicholas Burns, 'America's Strategic Opportunity with India'.

65. Author's interview with Brajesh Mishra, 11 Aug. 2007.

66. Meghnad Desai, *The Rediscovery of India*, London: Bloomsbury Academic, 2011, p. 421.

67. See Andy Hillers interview with Bush in Nov. 1999. Cited in Ivo H. Daalder and James Lindsay, *America Unbound: The Bush Revolution in Foreign Policy*, Hoboken, NJ: John Wiley, 2005, p. 18.

68. For details of the 2004 meeting see 'The India–EU Strategic Partnership: A Joint Action Plan', available at: http://commerce.nic.in/trade/India_EU_jap.pdf

69. For details see Joint Statement, 'The Fifth India–EU Summit', The Hague, 8 Nov. 2004, p. 6, available at: http://www.consilium.europa.eu/ueDocs/cms_Data/docs/pressData/en/er/82635.pdf

70. Author's interview with Shyam Saran, London, 18 Apr. 2012.

71. Pant, *US–India Nuclear Pact*, pp. 65–6.

72. For a list of attendees see 'US–India Agenda', Udaipur, 14–18 Jan. 2002, available at: http://www.aspeninstitute.org/policy-work/aspen-strategy-group/programs-topic/us-india-agenda

73. Author's transcripts, roundtable with Ashley Tellis, London, 2 May 2012.

74. For details see C. Raja Mohan, *Impossible Allies: Nuclear India, United States, and the Global Order*, New Delhi: India Research Press, 2006, pp. 22–6.

75. Author's interview with Shyam Saran, 18 Apr. 2012.

76. Eric Gonsalves, 'Tarapur: Lessons from the First Episode in the Indo-US Nuclear Engagement', in Chari (ed.), *Indo-US Nuclear Deal*, pp. 19–32.

77. Mohan, *Impossible Allies*, p. 57.

78. Author's interview with Natwar Singh, 24 July 2007.

79. For details of Rice's itinerary see 'Travels of Secretary of State Condoleezza Rice', US State Department, available at http://history.state.gov/departmenthistory/travels/secretary/rice-condoleezza

80. Author's interview with Shyam Saran, London, 18 Apr. 2012.

81. Kessler, *The Confidante*, pp. 54–5.

82. See 'Remarks with India Foreign Minister Natwar Singh', New Delhi, 16 Mar. 2005, available at: http://2001-2009.state.gov/secretary/rm/2005/43490.htm

83. Kessler, *The Confidante*, pp. 54–5.

84. Mohan, *Impossible Allies*, pp. 58–9.

85. Author's interview with [B].

86. For a pithy note see Raymond E. Vickery Jr, *The Eagle and the Elephant: Strategic Aspects of US–India Economic Engagement*, Washington: Woodrow Wilson Press, 2010, pp. 55–9.

87. 'United States–India Joint Statement on Next Steps on Strategic Partnership', Washington, 17 Sep. 2004, available at: http://2001-2009.state.gov/r/pa/prs/ps/2004/36290.htm

88. 'Remarks with India Foreign Minister Natwar Singh', New Delhi, 16 Mar. 2005.

89. Author's interview with [B].

90. See note by Sheel Kant Sharma (Indian resident representative to the IAEA) to Mohammad ElBaradei, Vienna, 17 June 2005, available at: http://www.iaea.org/Publications/Documents/Infcircs/2005/infcirc647.pdf

91. For a note see: 'UN Security Council Resolution 1540,' 2004, available at: http://www.un.org/en/sc/1540/

92. Shyam Saran, 'India–US Civil-Nuclear Cooperation: Political Background and Strategic Significance', undated, author's copy.

93. Cited in Kessler, *The Confidante*, p. 55.

94. Author's interview with Daniel Markey, 11 Sep. 2008.

95. For a brief note see Pant, *The US–India Nuclear Pact*, p. 71.

96. Author's interview with [B].

97. Author's transcripts, roundtable with Ashley Tellis, London, 2 May 2012.

98. Marcus Mabry, *Condoleezza Rice: Naked Ambition*, London: Gibson Square, 2007, p. 266.

99. Author's interview with [B].

100. Kessler, *The Confidante*, p. 55.

101. Author's interview with Shyam Saran, 18 Apr. 2012.

102. 'Remarks with Indian Minister of External Affairs Natwar Singh Following Meeting', Washington, 14 Apr. 2005, available at: http://2001-2009.state.gov/secretary/rm/2005/44662.htm

103. Mohan, *Impossible Allies*, pp. 131–3.

104. For details on the team see: 'Announcement by MEA Official Spokesperson on the Visit of External Affairs Minister K. Natwar Singh to US, 8 April 2005', available at: http://www.indianembassy.org/prdetail1114/%09-announcement-by-mea-official-spokesperson-on-the-visit-of-external-affairs-minister-k.-natwar-singh-to-u.s.-

105. Author's interview with [B].

106. Author's interview with Natwar Singh, 24 July 2007.

107. Kessler, *The Confidante*, p. 58.

108. Author's interview with Shyam Saran, 18 Apr. 2012.

109. Rice, *No Higher Honour*, p. 439.

110. Mohan, *Impossible Allies*, pp. 153–7.

111. Author's interview with [B].

112. See 'Joint Statement between President George W. Bush and Prime Minister Manmohan Singh', Washington, 18 July 2005.

113. Mohan, *Impossible Allies*, pp. 153–7.

114. Author's interview with [B].

115. Kessler, *The Confidante*, p. 59.

116. 'Joint Statement between President George W. Bush and Prime Minister Manmohan Singh', Washington, 18 July 2005; author's interview with [B].

117. Ashley Tellis, 'Meeting at the CFR', New York, 13 Mar. 2006, transcript available at: http://www.carnegieendowment.org/files/cfrindianucleardeal.pdf

118. Author's interview with Shyam Saran, 18 Apr. 2012.

119. Author's interview with [B].

120. Jaswant Singh, 'Against Nuclear Apartheid', *Foreign Affairs* (Sep./Oct. 1998).

121. Kessler, *The Confidante*, p. 60.

122. Author's interview with State Department official [name undisclosed], Sep. 2008.

123. Ashley Tellis, 'A Bold Step Forward', *India Today International*, 12 Sep. 2005.

124. George W. Bush, *Decision Points*, New York: Virgin Books, 2010, p. xii.

125. Author's transcripts, roundtable with Ashley Tellis, London, 2 May 2012.

126. Kessler, *The Confidante*, p. 60.

127. Author's interview with State Department official [name undisclosed], Sep. 2008.

128. Rice, *No Higher Honour*, p. 440.

129. 'India–US Joint Statement on Indo-US Civil Nuclear Cooperation', New Delhi, 2 Mar. 2006, available at: http://164.100.119.21/?q=node/57

130. See 'Implementation of the India–United States Joint Statement of 18 July 18 2005: India's Separation Plan', available at: http://164.100.119.21/sites/default/files/press_sepplan.pdf

131. Cited in Elisabeth Bumiller and Somini Sengupta, 'Bush and India Reach Pact that Allows Nuclear Sales', *New York Times*, 3 Mar. 2006.

132. Ashley Tellis, 'Meeting at the CFR', New York, 13 Mar. 2006.

133. For a pithy note on the media and the deal see Vidya Shankar Aiyer, 'Prime Time Deal', in Chari (ed.), *Indo-US Nuclear Deal*, pp. 33–46.

134. Author's interview with [B].

135. Rice, *No Higher Honour*, p. 438.

136. Author's interview with Brajesh Mishra, 11 Aug. 2007.

137. For a brief note see Dhruva Jaishankar, 'Chronicle of a Deal Foretold: Washington's Perspective on Nuclear Agreement', in Chari (ed.), *Indo-US Nuclear Deal*, pp. 117–20.

138. Adam Clymer, 'Henry J. Hyde, a Power in the House of Representatives, Dies at 83', *New York Times*, 30 Nov. 2007.

139. 'Henry J. Hyde United States–India Peaceful Energy Cooperation Act of 2006', available at: http://www.gpo.gov/fdsys/pkg/BILLS-109hr5682enr/pdf/BILLS-109hr5682enr.pdf

140. Joe Holly, 'Henry J. Hyde, 83; Forceful GOP House Member', *Washington Post*, 30 Nov. 2007.

141. Author's interview with Shyam Saran, 18 Apr. 2012.

142. 'Remarks by President Bush in Signing of HR 5682—The US–India Peaceful Atomic Energy Cooperation Act', Washington, 18 Dec. 2006, available at: http://2001-2009.state.gov/p/sca/rls/2006/77928.htm

143. For the text see 'Atomic Energy Act of 1954', Aug. 1954, Section 128, vol. 1, pp. 1, 63, available at: http://science.energy.gov/~/media/bes/pdf/nureg_0980_v1_no7_june2005.pdf

144. Henry J. Hyde, 'United States–India Peaceful Energy Cooperation Act of 2006', Section 104, p. 4.

145. 'Atomic Energy Act of 1954', Aug. 1954, Section 123, vol. 1, pp. 1, 52.

146. For a brief note see Schaffer, *India and the United States in the 21st Century*, pp. 91–9 and Pant, *The US–India Nuclear Pact*, pp. 85–8.

147. For the text see 'Agreement for Cooperation [Between India and the US]' (title shortened), 1 Aug. 2007, available at: http://www.hindu.com/nic/123agreement.pdf

148. For a review see Fred McGoldrick, Harold Benglesdorf and Lawrence Scheiman, 'The US–India Deal: Taking Stock', Arms Control Association, 1 Oct. 2005, available at: http://www.armscontrol.org/act/2005_10/Oct-Cover

149. Michael Krepon, 'The US–India Nuclear Deal', The Stimson Center, 29 Mar. 2006, available at: http://www.stimson.org/pub.cfm?id=267

150. Bharat Karnad, 'Nuclear Test is a Must', *Asian Age*, 22 Feb. 2008.

151. Sharon Squassoni, 'Giving an Inch, Taking a Mile', *Washington Post*, 9 May 2007.

152. Sharon Squassoni, 'The India Nuclear Deal: The Top Rule Breaker Bends the Rules', *International Herald Tribune*, 16 Aug. 2007.

153. Seema Sirohi, 'Fusion Music', *Outlook Magazine*, 48, 32, 6 Aug. 2007.

154. For a short background see Pant, *The US–India Nuclear Pact*, pp. 70–3.

155. Neerja Chowdhury, 'The Importance of being Pranab Mukherjee Today', *Indian Express*, 10 Sep. 2007.

156. Cited in 'CPI (M): Don't See the Nuclear Deal in Isolation', *The Hindu*, 9 Sep. 2007.

157. Smita Gupta, 'The Hammers Fickle', *Outlook*, 47, 35, 27 Aug. 2007.

158. Smita Gupta, 'Even Lame Ducks Swim', *Outlook*, 47, 44, 29 Oct. 2007.

159. 'Don't Move an Inch Forward: Karat', *Indian Express*, 24 Sep. 2007.

160. 'Karat: It's Time for Congress to Choose', *The Hindu*, 9 Sep. 2007.

161. Venkat Parsa, 'Left in a Huddle on Changing Scene', *Asian Age*, 25 Sep. 2007.

162. Smita Gupta, 'Off on a Bicycle', *Outlook Magazine*, 48, 28, 14 July 2008.

163. 'Do a Rethink on Deal: CPI (M)', *The Hindu*, 5 Dec. 2007.

164. 'Congress, Left Refuse to Soften Position', *The Hindu*, 19 Aug. 2007.

165. Ramesh Ramachandran, 'Left, UPA Stick to their Stands', *Asian Age*, 20 Sep. 2007.

166. Hyde Act, p. 2.

167. Cited in '123 Agreement with US is Unacceptable to Us: Advani', *The Hindu*, 30 Nov. 2007.

168. Rupchand Pal, 'Nuclear Deal the Brainchild of BJP', *The Hindu*, 30 Nov. 2007.

169. 'Left, BJP Walk Out Over N Deal in RS', *Times of India*, 6 Dec. 2007.

170. 'Nuclear Deal Panel Finalised', *Times of India*, 5 Sep. 2007.

171. See Vinay Kumar, 'Crucial Left–UPA Panel Meeting on November 16', *The Hindu*, 14 Nov. 2007; Vinay Kumar, 'UPA–Left Committee to Meet Again to Finalise Findings', *The Hindu*, 26 June 2008.

172. Smita Gupta, 'Please, Mr. Karat', *Outlook Magazine*, 48, 26, 24–30 June 2008.

173. Vinay Kumar, 'Left Meet: Pranab Optimistic', *The Hindu*, 16 Mar. 2008.

174. Anita Saluja, 'SP Deal in Pocket, PM Set for G-8', *Indian Express*, 1 July 2008.

175. 'It is Nuclear Fundamentalism, Says SP', *The Hindu*, 26 Oct. 2007.

176. 'Govt. will Fall if Nuke Deal is Pursued,' *Indian Express*, 26 Oct. 2007.

177. Smita Gupta, 'The Hammers Fickle', *Outlook*, 47, 35, 27 Aug. 2007.

178. Cited in Smita Gupta, 'Off on a Bicycle', *Outlook Magazine*, 48, 28, 14 July 2008.

179. Cited in Smita Gupta, 'Half Life of an Ally', *Outlook Magazine*, 47, 36, 3 Sep. 2007.

180. Somnath Chatterjee, *Keeping the Faith: Memoirs of a Parliamentarian*, New Delhi: Harper Collins, 2010, pp. 200–1.

181. Seema Sirohi, 'What's There to Hyde Really?' *Outlook Magazine*, 47, 36, 3 Sep. 2007.

182. Smita Gupta, 'Blinkmanship', *Outlook Magazine*, 47, 37, 10 Sep. 2007.

183. 'David Mulford Meets Advani', *The Hindu*, 26 Oct. 2007.

184. Ramesh Ramachandran, 'BJP—N Deterrent Main Issue', *Asian Age*, 5 Dec. 2008.

185. 'Centre: Surrendered to US: Advani', *Asian Age*, 6 Dec. 2007.

186. Gargi Parsai, 'Sonia Gandhi Hits Out at BJP on Nuclear Deal', *The Hindu*, 7 Dec. 2007.

187. Chatterjee, *Keeping the Faith*, p. 160.

188. Editorial, 'Atomic Red Tape', *Times of India*, 19 Nov. 2007.

189. 'Talbott Questions BJP's Opposition to Nuclear Deal', *Indian Express*, 2 Mar. 2008.

190. 'Mulford Meets Jaswant, Sinha', *Asian Age*, 6 Nov. 2007.

191. Seema Mustafa, 'Govt. Woos BJP on Nuke Deal', *Asian Age*, 27 Nov. 2007.

192. 'Envoys Remark Land Govt. in Chicken Soup', *Times of India*, 22 Aug. 2007.

193. Smita Gupta, 'Half Life of an Ally', *Outlook Magazine*, 47, 36, 3 Sep. 2007.

194. Author's interview with [B].

195. Author's interview with Natwar Singh, New Delhi, 24 July 2007 and author's interview with Brajesh Misra, New Delhi, 11 Aug. 2007.

196. For details see 'Archive of General Elections 2009', Election Commission of India, available at: http://eci.nic.in/eci_main1/statistical_report.aspx

197. Author's interview with [B].

198. Author's interview with Brajesh Misra, 11 Aug. 2007.

199. Brahma Chellaney, 'Mortgaging Nuclear Crown Jewels', *Asian Age*, 17 Sep. 2007.

200. Author's interview with [B].

201. Ibid.

202. Bharat Karnad, 'A Permanent Nuclear Hobble', *Asian Age*, 14 Dec. 2007.

203. Ashley Tellis, 'A Bold Step Forward', *India Today International*, 12 Sep. 2005 [emphasis added].

204. Author's interview with [B].

205. For details see 'Implementation of the India–United States Joint Statement of 18 July 18 2005: India's Separation Plan'.

206. Anil Kakodkar quoted in Mohan, *Impossible Allies*, p. 228.

207. Author's interview with [B].

208. David Albright, Leonard Weiss and Daryl Kimball, 'US–India Nuclear Cooperation: A Critical Assessment', Arms Control Association, 15 Feb. 2006.

209. Michael Krepon, 'The US–India Nuclear Deal', The Stimson Center, 29 Mar. 2006, available at: http://www.stimson.org/pub.cfm?id=267

210. 'US–India Nuclear Deal Fails Non-Proliferation Test', Arms Control Association Press Release, 2 Mar. 2006, available at: http://www.armscontrol.org/pressroom/2006/20060302_India_Deal

211. Author's interview with [B].

212. See 'Implementation of the India–United States Joint Statement of July 18, 2005: India's Separation Plan'.

213. Author's interview with State Department official [name undisclosed], Sep. 2008.

214. Author's interview with [B].

215. 'Implementation of the India–United States Joint Statement of July 18, 2005: India's Separation Plan'.

216. Author's interview with [B].

217. Michael Krepon quoted in 'Meeting at the Council for Foreign Relations', New York, 13 Mar. 2006, available at: http://www.carnegieendowment.org/files/cfrindianucleardeal.pdf

218. Author's interview with [B].

219. Author's interview with Lisa Curtis, 7 Oct. 2008.

220. 'Seeing Through the Spin: "Critics" Rebut White House on the US–India Nuclear Cooperation Plan', Arms Control Association Press Release, 9 Mar. 2006, available at: http://www.armscontrol.org/pressroom/2006/20060309_India_Critics_Rebut_WH

221. Robert Joseph quoted in Wade Boese, 'US Puts Onus on India for Nuclear

Ties', Arms Control Association, 1 Dec. 2005, available at: http://www.armscontrol.org/act/2005_12/DEC-USIndia

222. Rice quoted in 'Congress Ponders Conditions for US–India Deal', Arms Control Association, 1 May 2006, available at: http://www.armscontrol.org/act/2006_05/CongressUSIndia

223. Shyam Saran quoted in 'Congress Ponders Conditions for US–India Deal'.

224. 'Meeting at the Council for Foreign Relations', New York, 13 Mar. 2006, available at: http://www.carnegieendowment.org/files/cfrindianucleardeal.pdf

225. Henry J. Hyde, 'United States–India Peaceful Energy Cooperation Act of 2006', pp. 3, 4–11. Also see Daryl Kimball and Fred McGoldrick, 'US–India Nuclear Agreement: A Bad Deal Gets Worse', Arms Control Association, 3 Aug. 2007, available at: http://www.armscontrol.org/act/2007_07-08/USIndia

226. Author's interview with [B].

227. Cited in Seema Sirohi, 'What's There to Hyde Really?' *Outlook* 47, 36, 3 Sep. 2007.

228. Ashish Kumar Sen, 'This Law is Your Law', *Outlook* 47, 43, 22 Oct. 2007.

229. Wade Boese, 'US–India N-Deal Advances', Arms Control Association, 31 Aug. 2007, available at: http://www.armscontrol.org/act/2007_09/USIndia

230. Author's interview with [B].

231. Text of the 123 agreement, 3 Aug. 2007, p. 13.

232. 'US–India Nuclear Agreement', US Department of State: Office of the Spokesman, 3 Aug. 2007.

233. Wade Boese, 'US–India N-Deal Advances'.

234. Author's interview with State Department official [name undisclosed], Sep. 2008.

235. Author's interview with Stephen Cohen, 11 Sep. 2008.

236. For the text see: http://dae.nic.in/sites/default/files/press_IaeaIndiaSGADrft.pdf

237. 'Kakodkar Outlines India's Stand at IAEA Meet', *The Hindu*, 20 Sep. 2007.

238. Mohamed ElBaradei, *The Age of Deception: Nuclear Diplomacy in Treacherous Times*, London: Bloomsbury, 2011, pp. 224–5.

239. Sandeep Dikshit, 'ElBaradei meets Manmohan', *The Hindu*, 12 Oct. 2007.

240. Arms Control Association Press Release, 30 July 2008, available at: http://www.armscontrol.org/node/3205

241. Siddharth Varadarajan, 'Perpetuity of Safeguards only with Perpetuity of Fuel Supply', *The Hindu*, 13 July 2008.

242. Siddharth Varadarajan, 'IAEA Board Approves India Safeguards Agreement', *The Hindu*, 2 Aug. 2008.

243. Wade Boese, 'NSG, Congress Approve Nuclear Trade with India', 6 Oct. 2008, available at: http://www.armscontrol.org/act/2008_10/NSGapprove

244. Pranab Dhal Samanta, 'India, France Ink Nuclear Deal, First After NSG Waiver', *Indian Express*, 1 Oct. 2008.

245. Sandeep Dikshit, 'Mega Uranium Deal with Russia', *The Hindu*, 6 Dec. 2008.

246. Siddharth Varadarajan, 'As NSG Members Mull New US Draft Fate of India Deal Hangs in Balance', *The Hindu*, 3 Sep. 2008.

247. Michael Krepon, 'Likely Consequences of the Nuclear Suppliers Group Decision', Stimson Center, 8 Sep. 2008, available at: http://www.stimson.org/pub.cfm?ID=673

248. Author's interview with [B].

249. Daryl Kimball, 'Averting a Non-Proliferation Disaster', Arms Control Association, 29 Aug. 2008, available at: http://www.armscontrol.org/act/2008_09/Focus

250. Michael Krepon, 'Likely Consequences of the Nuclear Suppliers Group Decision'.

251. Quoted by Inder Malhotra in K. Subramanyam, *Shedding Shibboleths: India's Evolving Strategic Outlook*, New Delhi: Wordsmith, 2005, p. vii.

252. Saba Naqvi, 'Fission "N" Fusion', *Outlook Magazine*, 48, 29, 21 July 2008.

253. For the text see: 'Rice and Mukherjee Signing Ceremony', Washington, 10 Oct. 2008, available at: http://2001-2009.state.gov/secretary/rm/2008/10/110916.htm

254. Siddharth Varadarajan, 'NSG all Set to Up-End India's Clean Waiver', *The Hindu*, 18 June 2011.

255. Siddharth Varadarajan, 'Turn the Nuclear Bill from Liability to Asset', *The Hindu*, 16 June 2010.

256. For details see Mohan, *Impossible Allies*, pp. 166–87; Pant, *The US–India Nuclear Pact*, pp. 82–5.

CONCLUSION

1. 'Can India Become a Great Power?' *The Economist*, 30 Mar. 2013.

2. Note: for a copy of the document as well as reactions to the same see 'Nonalignment 2.0: A Foreign and Strategic Policy for India in the Twenty-First Century', available at: http://www.cprindia.org/workingpapers/3844-nonalignment-20-foreign-and-strategic-policy-india-twenty-first-century

3. 'Can India Become a Great Power?'

4. An explanation of this point can be found in T.V. Paul, *The Tradition of Non-Use of Nuclear Weapons*, Stanford: Stanford University Press, 2009, pp. 2–3.

5. Harsh Pant, *The China Syndrome: Grappling with an Uneasy Relationship*, New Delhi: Harper Collins, 2010, pp. 121–2.

6. Popular accounts of this void can be found in Siddharth Varadarajan, 'It's Strategic Culture that Counts', *The Hindu*, 22 Jan. 2010; Amitabh Mattoo, 'Upgrading the Study of International Relations', *The Hindu*, 21 Apr. 2009.

7. Swarna Rajagopalan (ed.), *Security and South Asia: Ideas, Institutions, and*

Initiatives, London: Routledge, 2006; Rahul Sagar, 'State of Mind: What Kind of Power Will India Become?', *International Affairs*, 85, 4 (2009); and Kanti Bajpai, 'Indian Strategic Culture and the Problem of Pakistan', in Swarna Rajagopalan (ed.), *Security and South Asia*, New Delhi: Routledge, 2006.

8. George Tanham, 'Indian Strategic Culture', *The Washington Quarterly*, 15, 1 (Winter 1992) and George Tanham, *Indian Strategic Thought: An Interpretive Essay*, Santa Monica: RAND Corporation, 1992.

9. Stephen P. Cohen, 'Approaching India's Military and Security Policy, with a Detour through Disaster Studies', *India Review*, 7, 4 (2008) and Harsh V. Pant, 'The Trials of a Rising Power', *Livemint.com* and *The Wall Street Journal*, 29 Dec. 2009.

10. Jaswant Singh, *Call to Honour*, Delhi: Rupa & Co., 2006, p. 99. For a detailed analysis of the same see K. Subramanyam, *Shedding Shibboleths: India's Evolving Strategic Outlook*, Delhi: Wordsmith, 2005, p. 16.

11. For a detailed and excellent study on the structural state of the Indian MEA see Manjari Chatterjee Miller, 'India's Feeble Foreign Policy: A Would-Be Great Power Resists its own Rise', *Foreign Affairs* (May–June 2013), available at: http://www.foreignaffairs.com/articles/139098/manjari-chatterjee-miller/indias-feeble-foreign-policy?page=show

12. For examples of path-breaking and revisionist works on the history of Indian foreign policy see: Tanvi Madan, 'With an Eye to the East: The China Factor and the US–India Relationship, 1949–1979', doctoral thesis, University of Texas, Austin, 2012, and Pallavi Raghavan, 'The Finality of Partition: Bilateral Relations between India and Pakistan, 1947–1957', doctoral thesis, University of Cambridge, 2012.

13. Joe Klien, 'The Full Obama Interview', *Time Magazine*, 23 Oct. 2008.

14. For details see 'India's Stealth Lobbying against Holbrooke Brief', *Foreign Policy Magazine: The Cable*, 23 Jan. 2009, available at: http://thecable.foreignpolicy.com/posts/2009/01/23/india_s_stealth_lobbying_against_holbrooke. Also see: Siddharth Varadarajan, 'Promise and Pitfalls of Obama's South Asia Policy', *The Hindu*, 27 Jan. 2009.

15. Quoted in C. Raja Mohan, 'Barack Obama's Kashmir Thesis', *The Indian Express*, 3 Nov. 2008. Also see Barack Obama, 'Renewing American Leadership', *Foreign Affairs* (July/Aug. 2007) and 'The Struggle for Afghanistan', *Survival*, Special Issue, 51, 1 (Feb.–Mar. 2009).

16. Bruce Riedel, 'South Asia's Nuclear Decade', *Survival*, 50, 2 (Apr.–May 2008), p. 124.

17. 'India's Stealth Lobbying Against Holbrooke Brief'.

18. 'US President Barack Obama's Parliament Address', *The Hindu*, 8 Nov. 2010, available at: http://www.thehindu.com/news/national/article874394.ece

19. Barack Obama, *The Audacity of Hope: Thoughts on Reclaiming the American Dream*, New York: Crown Publishers, 2006, p. 322.

SELECT BIBLIOGRAPHY

Unpublished Primary Sources

<u>Manuscript Sources</u>

Nehru Memorial Museum and Library (NMML), New Delhi

B.N. Rao Papers
B.K. Nehru Papers
D.D. Eisenhower Papers
G.L. Mehta Papers
P.N. Haksar Papers
T.N. Kaul Papers
T.T. Krinamachari Papers
V.L. Pandit Papers
Y.D. Gundevia Papers
Oral History Interview with B.M. Kaul
Oral History Interview with Chester Bowles
Oral History Interview with the Dalai Lama
Oral History Interview with J.N. Chaudhuri
Oral History Interview with K.P.S. Menon
Oral History Interview with K.P.S. Menon
Oral History Interview with R.K. Nehru
Oral History Interview with Roy Butcher

Public Records Office, Kew, London

Foreign Office Papers

FO 371/76102
FO 371/170637
FO 371/170638
FO 371/105481

FO 371/105491
FO 371/164910
FO 371/164913
FO 371/164914
FO 371/164915
FO 371/164916
FO 371/164920
FO 371/164921
FO 37/819
FO 37/756
FO 38/820
FO 95/478

Dominions Office Papers

DO 35/2838
DO 35/2921
DO 133/70

Prime Minister's Office Papers

KV2/2512
KV2/2513
MI5 Papers
PREM 15/445
PREM 15/960

Liddell Hart Archives, King's College London

US National Security Files, 1946–50

John F. Kennedy Presidential Library and Museum, Boston

John F. Kennedy Papers
National Security Council Records, 1962–3
Roger Hilsman Papers

The National Archives, College Park, Maryland

Alexander Haig Papers
Ernest K. Lindley Papers
The Henry A. Kissinger Correspondence Files
National Presidential Material Staff, National Security Council Files, 1970–5
National Presidential Material Staff, National Security Council Files, Telephone
    Transcripts, 1970–5
Philip C. Jessup Papers

SELECT BIBLIOGRAPHY

Records of the Joint Chiefs of Staff, RG 218
Records of the Department of State, RG 59
Robert Komer Papers
The White House Special Files
See previous note—this is a continuation

The National Archives, Washington

Records of the Department of State, RG 59

The Library of Congress, Washington

Loy W. Henderson Papers

The National Security Archives, George Washington University, Washington

Russian and Eastern European Papers, 1962

Interviews

Ambassador Lalit Mansingh, New Delhi, 5 Aug. 2007
Ambassador Prof. S.D. Muni, New Delhi, 31 July 2007
Brajesh Misra, New Delhi, 11 Aug. 2008
Brigadier Gurmeet Kanwal, New Delhi, 2 Aug. 2007
Bruce Riedel, Washington, DC, 28 Aug. 2008
Claudio Lilienfeld, Washington, DC, 24 Sep. 2008
Daniel Markey, Washington, DC, 11 Sep. 2008
Donald Rumsfeld, Teleconference, 13 Nov. 2007
Douglas Feith, Washington, DC, 10 Oct. 2008
Enders Wimbush, Washington, DC, 22 Sep. 2008
General Joseph Ralston, Washington, DC, 18 Sep. 2008
George Fernandes, New Delhi, 3 Aug. 2008
Harinder Sekhon, New Delhi, 12 July 2007
Hilary Synnott, London, 1 Apr. 2010
Jasjit Singh, New Delhi, 31 July 2007
Kanwal SibaSingh, New Delhi, 16 July 2007
K. Natwar Singh, New Delhi, 24 July 2007
Lisa Curtis, Washington, DC, 7 Oct. 2008
Marc Grossman, Washington, 3 Oct. 2008
Mullah Abdul Salaam Zaeef, London, 11 Feb. 2011
Pamit Pal Chaudhuri, Teleconference, 23 June 2007
S.D. Muni, New Delhi, 31 July 2007
Stephen Cohen, Washington, DC, 11 Sep. 2008
Walter Anderson, Washington, DC, 1 Oct. 2008

SELECT BIBLIOGRAPHY

Undisclosed Interviews

Senior Indian official, coded as [A], 2010.
Senior Indian official in the NSC, New Delhi, 12 July 2007.
Three senior representatives from both India and the United States, coded as [B].
US State Department official, Washington, Sep. 2008.
Very senior Indian military officer, New Delhi, Aug. 2007.

Published Sources

Government Documents and Documentary Collections

Aijazuddin, F.S. (ed.), *The White House and Pakistan: Secret Declassified Documents, 1969–1974*, Oxford: Oxford University Press, 2002.
Das, Durga (ed.), *Sardar Patel's Correspondence*, vol. 2, Ahmedabad: Navajivan Publishing House, 1972.
Foreign Affairs Record, vol. 8, New Delhi: Government of India, 1962.
Foreign Relations of the United States, 1948, vol. 5, Part 1, Washington, DC: United States Government Printing Office, 1975.
———— 1950, vol. 5, Washington, DC: United States Government Printing Office, 1978.
———— 1951, vol. 6, Part 2, Washington, DC: United States Government and Printing Office, 1977.
———— 1955–7, vol. 8, Washington, DC: United States Government and Printing Office, 1987.
———— 1958–60, vol. 15, Washington, DC: United States Government and Printing Office, 1992.
———— 1961–3, vol. 19, Washington, DC: United States Government and Printing Office, 1996.
———— 1969–76, vol. 11, Washington, DC: United States Government and Printing Office, 2008.
Gandhi, Sajit (ed.), *The Tilt: The US & the South Asian Crisis of 1971*, Washington: National Security Archives Electronic Briefing Book 79, 2002.
Gandhi, Sonia (ed.), *Two Alone Together: Letters Between Indira and Jawaharlal Nehru 1940–46*, London: Hodder and Stoughton, 1992.
Gopal, Sarvepalli (ed.), *Selected Works of Jawaharlal Nehru*, 1st Series, 15 vols, New Delhi: Orient Longman, 1972–82.
Gopal, Sarvepalli, Ravinder Kumar, H.Y. Sharada Prasad, A.K. Damodaran, Mishural Hasan, Mridula Mukherjee and Aditya Mukherjee (eds), *Selected Works of Jawaharlal Nehru*, 2nd Series, 44 vols to date, 2011–
Loewenheim, Francis, Harold D. Langley and Manfred Jonas (eds), *Roosevelt and Churchill: Their Secret Wartime Correspondence*, London: Barrie and Jenkins, 1975.

SELECT BIBLIOGRAPHY

Lok Sabha Debates, 1962: 9/1 to 9/10, New Delhi: Government of India Press, 1962.

Lok Sabha Debates, 2003: 31/3 to 35/9, New Delhi: Government of India Press, 2003.

Papers of Harry S. Truman, President Secretary's Files, *Documentary History of the Truman Presidency Volume 1 and 2: Planning for the Postwar World*, Washington, DC: University Publications of America, 1995.

Parthasarthy, G. (ed.), *Jawaharlal Nehru: Letters to Chief Ministers*, vol. 1, 1947, London: Jawaharlal Nehru Memorial Fund and Oxford University Press, 1985.

——— (ed.), *Jawaharlal Nehru: Letters to Chief Ministers*, vol. 2, 1950–2, London: Jawaharlal Nehru Memorial Fund and Oxford University Press, 1986.

——— (ed.), *Jawaharlal Nehru: Letters to Chief Ministers*, vol. 3, 1952–4, London: Jawaharlal Nehru Memorial Fund and Oxford University Press, 1987.

——— (ed.), *Jawaharlal Nehru: Letters to Chief Ministers*, vol. 4, 1954–7, London: Jawaharlal Nehru Memorial Fund and Oxford University Press, 1988.

——— (ed.), *Jawaharlal Nehru: Letters to Chief Ministers*, vol. 5, 1958–64, London: Jawaharlal Nehru Memorial Fund and Oxford University Press, 1989.

Sinha, P.B., and A.A. Athale, *History of the Conflict with China, 1962*, India: Ministry of Defence, 1992.

Newspapers and Periodicals

The Asian Age, New Delhi
Business Standard, New Delhi
The Guardian
The Hindu, Chennai
The Hindustan Times, New Delhi
India Today, New Delhi
The Indian Express, Mumbai
New York Times
The New Yorker
Outlook, New Delhi
Time Magazine
Times (London)
The Times of India, Mumbai
Washington Post
Outlook, New Delhi

SELECT BIBLIOGRAPHY

Books

Anderson, Jack, with George Clifford, *The Anderson Papers*, New York: Random House, 1973.

Appadorai, A. (ed.), *Select Documents on India's Foreign Policy and Relations*, vol. 1, Oxford: Oxford University Press, 1982.

Ayoob, Mohammed, and K. Subramanyam, *The Liberation War*, New Delhi: S. Chand & Co., 1972.

Basrur, Rajesh, *Minimum Deterrence and India's Nuclear Security*, Stanford: Stanford University Press, 2006.

Basu, Aparna, *G.L. Mehta: A Many Splendoured Man*, New Delhi: Concept Publishing, 2001.

Behera, Navnita, *Demystifying Kashmir*, Washington: Brookings Institution Press, 2006.

Berger, Thomas, *Cultures of Anti-Militarism: National Security in Germany and Japan*, Baltimore: Johns Hopkins University Press, 1998.

Bhatia, Krishan, *Indira: A Biography of Prime Minister Gandhi*, New York: Praeger, 1974.

Bose, Sumantra, *The Challenge in Kashmir: Democracy, Self-Determination and a Just Peace*, New Delhi: Sage, 1997.

Bowles, Chester, *Promises to Keep: My Years in Public Life, 1941–1969*, New York: Harper and Row, 1971.

Branch, Taylor, *The Clinton Tapes, Conversations with a President: 1993–2001*, New York: Simon and Schuster, 2009.

Brandon, Henry, *The Retreat of American Power*, New York: Double and Company, 1973.

Brands, H.W., *Inside the Cold War: Loy Henderson and the Rise of the American Empire 1918–61*, New York: Oxford University Press, 1991.

Brendon, Diers, *Ike: His Life and Times*, New York: Harper and Row Publishers, 1986.

Brown, Judith, *Nehru: A Political Life*, New Delhi: Oxford University Press, 2003.

Brown, Norman, *The United States and India and Pakistan*, Boston: Harvard University Press, 1963.

Bush, George W., *Decision Points*, New York: Virgin Books, 2010.

Chadhuri, Kalyan, *Genocide in Bangladesh*, New Delhi: Orient Longman, 1972.

Chagla, M.C., *Roses in December: An Autobiography*, 12th edn, Mumbai: Bhartiya Vidya Bhavan, 2011.

Clinton, Bill, *My Life*, New York: Arrow Books, 2005.

Clinton, Hillary Rodham, *Living History*, London: Headline, 2003.

Cohen, Stephen P., *Emerging India*, Washington, DC: Brookings Institution Press, 2001.

Cohen, Warren I., *Dean Rusk*, Totowa, NJ: Cooper Square, 1980.

Coker, Christopher, *The Future of War: The Re-Enchantment of War in the Twenty-First Century*, London: Blackwell, 2004.

———— *Waging War Without Warriors? The Changing Culture of Military Conflict*, London: Lynne Rienner, 2002.

———— *Humane Warfare*, London: Routledge, 2001.

———— *Waging War Without Warriors? The Changing Culture of Military Conflict*, London: Lynne Rienner, 2002.

Croft, Stuart, *Culture, Crisis, and America's War on Terror*, Cambridge: Cambridge University Press, 2007.

Dallek, Robert, *John F. Kennedy: An Unfinished Life, 1917–1963*, New York: Allen Lane, 2003.

———— *Partners in Power: Nixon and Kissinger*, New York: Harper Collins, 2007.

Dalvi, John P., *Himalayan Blunder*, Dehra Dun: Nataraj Publishers, 1969.

Damodaran, A.K, and U.S. Bajpai (eds), *Indian Foreign Policy: The Indira Gandhi Years*, New Delhi: Sangam Books, 1990.

Dayal, Shiv, *India's Role in the Korean Question*, New Delhi: S. Chand & Co., 1959.

Desai, Meghnad, *The Rediscovery of India*, London: Bloomsbury Academic, 2011.

Dhar, P.N., *Indira Gandhi, the 'Emergency' and Indian Democracy*, New Delhi: Oxford University Press, 2000.

Dixit, J.N., *India–Pakistan in War & Peace*, London: Routledge, 2002.

———— *India's Foreign Policy 1947–2003*, New Delhi: Picus Books, 2003.

———— *Liberation & Beyond*, New Delhi: Konark Publishers, 1999.

Donald, Dipace (ed.), *John F. Kennedy and the New Frontier*, New York: Hill and Wang, 1966.

Dutt, Subimal, *With Nehru in the Foreign Office*, New Delhi: Minerva Associates, 1977.

Dutta, Krishna, and Andrew Robinson, *Selected Letters of Rabindranath Tagore*, Cambridge: Cambridge University Press, 1997.

Elliot, John, Bernard Imhalsy and Simon Denyer (eds), *Fifty Years of Reporting South Asia*, New Delhi: Penguin, 2009.

Farrell, Theo, *The Norms of War: Cultural Beliefs and Modern Conflict*, London: Lynne Rienner, 2005.

Fisk, Robert, *In Time of War: Ireland, Ulster and the Price of Neutrality, 1939–45*, Dublin: Gill & Macmillan, 1983.

Frank, Katherine, *Indira: The Life of Indira Nehru Gandhi*, New Delhi: Harper Collins, 2001.

Freedman, Russell, *Eleanor Roosevelt: A Life of Discovery*, New York: Clarion Books, 1993.

SELECT BIBLIOGRAPHY

Galbraith, John Kenneth, *Ambassador's Journal: A Personal Account of the Kennedy Years*, London: Hamish Hamilton, 1969.

Gandhi, Indira, *India and Bangladesh: Selected Speeches and Statements*, New Delhi: Orient Longman, 1972.

Gandhi, Rajmohan, *Mohandas: A True Story of a Man, his People and an Empire*, London: Penguin, 2006.

———— *Rajaji: A Life*, Penguin: New Delhi, 1997.

Ganguly, Sumit (ed.), *India as an Emerging Power*, London: Frank Cass, 2003.

———— *Conflict Unending*, New Delhi: Oxford University Press, 2002.

Ganguly, Sumit, Brian Shoup and Andrew Scobell (eds), *US–India Strategic Cooperation into the 21st Century: More Than Words*, London: Routledge, 2006.

Garver, John W., *Protracted Contest: Sino-Indian Rivalry in the Twentieth Century*, Seattle: University of Washington Press, 2001.

Ghosh, Sudhir, *Gandhi's Emissary*, London: Cresset Press, 1967.

Gill, John H., *An Atlas of the 1971 India–Pakistan War*, Washington, DC: National Defense University Press, 2004.

Gopal, Sarvepalli, *Jawaharlal Nehru: A Biography*, vol. 1, 1889–1947, London: Cape, 1975.

———— *Jawaharlal Nehru: A Biography*, vol. 2, 1947–56, London: Cape, 1979.

———— *Jawaharlal Nehru: A Biography*, vol. 3, 1956–64, London: Cape, 1984.

Gore-Booth, Paul, *With Great Truth and Respect*, London: Constable, 1974.

Gosnell, Harold, *Truman's Crisis: A Political Biography of Harry S. Truman*, London: Greenwood Press, 1980.

Gould, Harold A., *The South Asia Story*, London: Sage, 2010.

Gray, Colin, *Modern Strategy*, London: Oxford University Press, 1999.

———— *Strategic Studies: A Critical Assessment*, London: Aldwych Press, 1982.

Guha, Ramachandra, *India After Gandhi*, New York: Harper Collins, 2007.

Gujral, I.K., *Matters of Discretion*, New Delhi: Kay House, 2011.

Gupta, Jyoti Sen, *History of Freedom Movement in Bangladesh 1947–1973*, New Delhi: Naya Prakash Books, 1974.

Gupta, Shekar, 'India Redefines its Role', *Adelphi Paper*, 293, Oxford: Oxford University Press and IISS, 1995.

Gupte, Pranay, *Mother India: A Political Biography of Indira Gandhi*, New Delhi: Penguin, 2009.

Herman, Arthur, *Gandhi and Churchill*, London: Hutchinson, 2008.

Hewitt, Vernon, *Political Mobilisation and Democracy in India: States of Emergency*, London: Routledge, 2008.

———— *The New International Politics of South Asia*, Manchester: Manchester University Press, 1997.

———— *Reclaiming the Past? The Search for Political & Cultural Unity in Contemporary Jammu & Kashmir*, London: Portland Books, 1995.

Hoffman, Steven, *India and the China Crisis*, Berkeley: University of California Press, 1990.

Hopf, Ted, *Social Construction of International Politics: Identities and Foreign Policies, Moscow, 1955 and 1999*, Ithaca: Cornell University Press, 2002.

Isaacson, Walter, *Kissinger: A Biography*, New York: Simon and Schuster, 1992.

Jacobsen, Carl G. (ed.), *Strategic Power—USA/USSR*, New York: Macmillan, 1990.

Jaffrelot, Christophe (ed.), *India since 1950*, New Delhi: Yatra Books, 2011.

Jaykar, Pupul, *Indira Gandhi: A Biography*, New Delhi: Viking, 1992.

Jian, Chen, *China's Road to the Korean War: The Making of the Sino-American Confrontation*, New York: Columbia University Press, 1994.

Johnston, Alastair Iain, *Cultural Realism: Strategic Culture and Grand Strategy in Chinese History*, Princeton, NJ: Princeton University Press, 1995.

Jones, Owen Bennett, *Pakistan: Eye of the Storm*, New Haven: Yale University Press, 2002.

Kalb, Marvin, and Barnard Kalb, *Kissinger*, Boston: Little Brown & Co., 1974.

Kapur, Paul, *Dangerous Deterrent: Nuclear Weapons Proliferation and Conflict in South Asia*, Stanford: Stanford University Press, 2008.

Karnad, Bharat, *Nuclear Weapons and Indian Security: The Realist Foundations of Strategy*, London: Macmillan, 2002.

Katzenstein, Peter, *Cultural Norms and National Security: Police and Military in Postwar Japan*, Ithaca: Cornell University Press, 1996.

——— (ed.), *The Culture of National Security: Norms and Identity in World Politics*, New York: Columbia University Press, 1996.

Kaul, B.N., *The Untold Story*, New Delhi: Allied Publishers, 1967.

Kaul, T.N., *My Years through Raj to Swaraj*, New Delhi: Vikas Publishing House, 1996.

Kavic, Lorne J., *India's Quest for Security*, Berkeley: University of California Press, 1967.

Kennedy, Andrew B., *The International Ambitions of Mao and Nehru*, Cambridge: Cambridge University Press, 2012.

Kenton, Clymer, *Quest for Freedom: The United States and India's Independence*, New York: Columbia University Press, 1995.

Khan, Sultan, *Memories and Reflections of a Pakistani Diplomat*, London: The London Centre for Pakistani Studies, 1997.

Khera, S.S., *India's Defence Problem*, New Delhi: Orient-Longman, 1968.

Khilnani, Sunil, *Idea of India*, New Delhi: Penguin, 1997.

Kier, Elizabeth, *Imagining War: French and British Military Doctrine Between the Wars*, Princeton, NJ: Princeton University Press, 1997.

Kissinger, Henry, *On China*, New York: Allen Lane, 2011.

Krieg, P. Joan (ed.), *Dwight D. Eisenhower*, New York: Greenwood Press, 1987.

Kux, Dennis, *The United States and Pakistan 1947–2000: Disenchanted Allies*, Baltimore: John Hopkins University Press, 2000.

———— *India and the United States: Estranged Democracies 1941–1991*, Washington, DC: National Defense University Press, 1992.

Lall, John, *Aksaichin and the Sino-Indian Conflict*, New Delhi: Allied Publishers, 1989.

Lamb, Alastair, *The China–India Border*, Oxford: Oxford University Press, 1964.

Legro, Jeffery W., *Rethinking the World: Great Power Strategies and International Order*, Ithaca: Cornell University Press, 2005.

———— *Cooperation under Fire: Anglo-German Restraint during World War II*, Ithaca: Cornell University Press, 1995.

Levantrosser, William (ed.), *Harry S. Truman: The Man from Independence*, New York: Greenwood Press, 1986.

Lieven, Anatol, *Pakistan: A Hard Country*, London: Allen Lane, 2011.

Lindley, Ernest (ed.), *The Winds of Freedom*, Boston: Beacon Press, 1963.

Little, Richard, and Mark Wikham-Jones (eds), *New Labour's Foreign Policy: A New Moral Crusade?*, Manchester: Manchester University Press, 2000.

Loeffler, C. Jane, *The Architecture of American Diplomacy: Building America's Embassies*, 2nd edn, New York: Princeton Architectural Press, 2010.

Macmillan, Margaret, *The Week that Changed the World: Nixon and Mao*, New York: Random House, 2007.

Malhotra, Inder, *Indira Gandhi: A Personal & Political Biography*, London: Hodder & Stoughton, 1989.

Malone, David, *Does the Elephant Dance? Contemporary Indian Foreign Policy*, London: Oxford University Press, 2011.

Mankekar, D.R., *Pak Colonialism in East Bengal*, New Delhi: Samaiya Publications, 1971.

———— *The Guilty Men of 1962*, Bombay: Tulsi Shah Enterprises, 1968.

Maxwell, Neville, *India's China War*, London: Jonathan Cape, 1970.

McMahon, Robert, *The Cold War on the Periphery: The United States, India, and Pakistan*, New York: Columbia University Press, 1994.

McNay, John T. (ed.), *The Memoirs of Ambassador Henry F. Grady: From the Great War to the Cold War*, Columbia: University of Missouri Press, 2009.

Merrill, Dennis, *Bread and the Ballot: The United States and India's Economic Development, 1947–1963*, Chapel Hill: University of North Carolina Press, 1990.

Meyer, Christoph, *The Quest for a European Strategic Culture: A Comprehensive Study of Strategic Norms and Ideas on the European Union*, London: Palgrave, 2007.

Mohan, Raja C., *Impossible Allies: Nuclear India, the United States, and the Global Order*, New Delhi: India Research Press, 2006.

———— *Crossing the Rubicon: The Shaping of India's New Foreign Policy*, New Delhi: Penguin Viking, 2003.

Mohanty, Deba, *Arming the Indian Arsenal: Challenges and Policy Options*, New Delhi: Rupa, 2009.

Mosley, Leonard, *Dulles: A Biography of Eleanor, Allen, and John Foster Dulles*, London: Hodder and Stoughton, 1978.

Muhith, A.M.A., *Emergence of a Nation*, Dacca: Bangladesh Books International, 1978.

Narayanan, K.R., *In the Name of the People*, New Delhi: Penguin, 2011.

Nawaz, Shuja, *Pakistan: its Army, and the Wars Within*, Oxford: Oxford University Press, 2008.

Nayar, Kuldip, *Beyond the Lines: An Autobiography*, New Delhi: Roli Books, 2012.

Nehru, B.K., *Nice Guys Finish Second*, New Delhi: Viking, 1997.

Nehru, Jawaharlal, *Glimpses of World History*, New Delhi: Jawaharlal Nehru Memorial Fund, Oxford University Press, 1982.

———— *Discovery of India*, Calcutta: Signet Press, 1956.

Nehru, Jawaharlal, Arnold Toynbee and Earl C.R. Attlee, *India and the World*, New Delhi: Sagar Publication, 1962.

Nitze, Paul with Ann M. Smith and Steven L. Rearden, *From Hiroshima to Glasnost: At the Centre of Decision*, London: Weidenfeld and Nicolson, 1989.

O'Brien, Michael, *John F. Kennedy: A Biography*, New York: Thomas Dunne Books, 2003.

Palit, D.K., *War in the High Himalayas: The Indian Army in Crisis, 1962*, London: Hurst, 1991.

Pande, D.C., *India's Foreign Policy as an Exercise in Non-Alignment*, Nainital: Gyanodaya Prakashan, 1988.

Pandit, Vijayalakshmi, *The Scope of Happiness*, London: Weidenfeld and Nicolson, 1979.

Pant, Harsh V., *The US–India Nuclear Pact: Policy, Process, and Great Power Politics*, New Delhi: Oxford University Press, 2011.

Raghavan, Srinath, *War and Peace in Modern India*, New Delhi: Permanent Black, 2010.

Rahman, Mujibur Sheikh, *The Unfinished Memoirs*, New Delhi: Penguin, 2012.

Rajagopalan, Swarna, *Security and South Asia: Ideas, Institutions, and Initiatives*, New Delhi: Routledge, 2006.

Rajan, Krishna V. (ed.), *The Ambassadors' Club*, New Delhi: Harper Collins, 2012.

Reddy, Ramakrishna, *India's Policy in the United Nations*, Rutherford, NJ:- Fairleigh Dickinson University Press, 1968.

Rice, Condoleezza, *No Higher Honour: A Memoir of My Years in Washington*, London: Simon & Schuster, 2011.

Roosevelt, Eleanor, *India and the Awakening East*, London: Hutchinson, 1954.

Rosen, Stephen P., *Societies and Military Power: India and its Armies*, Ithaca: Cornell University Press, 1996.

Rusk, Dean, *As I Saw It: A Secretary of State's Memoirs*, London: I.B. Tauris, 1990.

Sahgal, Nayantara, *Civilising a Savage World*, New Delhi: Penguin, 2010.

———— *Indira Gandhi: Her Road to Power*, New York: Fredrick Ungar Publishing Co., 1982.

Schofield, Victoria, *Kashmir in Conflict: India, Pakistan, and the Unfinished War*, London: I.B. Tauris, 2000.

Sekhon, Harinder, *India and the United States: Breakthroughs, Prospects and Challenges Ahead*, New Delhi: ORF-Macmillan Press, 2008.

Sen, Ela, *Indira Gandhi: A Biography*, London: Peter Owen, 1973.

Schaffer, Howard, *The Limits of Influence: America's Role in Kashmir*, Washington: Brookings Institution Press, 2009.

———— *Chester Bowles: New Dealer in the Cold War*, Cambridge, MA: Harvard University Press, 1993.

Schaffer, Teresita C., *India and the United States in the 21st Century: Reinventing Partnership*, New Delhi: India Research Press, 2010.

Singh, Anita Inder, *The Limits of British Influence: South Asia and the Anglo-American Relationship 1947–56*, New York: St. Martin's Press, 1993.

Singh, Depinder, *Field Marshal Sam Manekshaw: Soldiering with Dignity*, Dehradun: Natraj Publishers, 2002.

Singh, Jasjit (ed.), *Nuclear India*, New Delhi: Knowledge World and IDSA, 2006.

———— (ed.), *The Road Ahead: Indo-US Strategic Dialogue*, New Delhi: Lancer International & Institute of Defence Studies and Analyses, 1994.

Singh, Jaswant, *Call to Honour*, New Delhi: Rupa & Co., 2006.

———— *Defending India*, London: Macmillan Press, 1999.

Sinha, Atish, and Madhup Mohta (eds), *Indian Foreign Policy: Challenges and Opportunities*, New Delhi: Academic Foundation, 2007.

Sisson, Richard, and Leo E. Rose, *War & Succession: Pakistan, India, and the Creation of Bangladesh*, Berkeley: University of California Press, 1990.

Snyder, Jack, *The Soviet Strategic Culture: Implications for Limited Nuclear Operations*, Santa Monica: RAND, 1977.

Sokolski, Henry (ed.), *Gauging US–India Strategic Cooperation*, Washington, DC: Strategic Studies Institute, US Army War College, 2007.

Sorenson, Theodore, *Kennedy*, London: Hodder and Stoughton, 1965.

Spalding, Elizabeth E., *The First Cold Warrior: Harry Truman, Containment, and the Remaking of Liberal Internationalism*, Lexington: University Press of Kentucky, 2006.

Spence, Jonathan D., *The Search for Modern China*, London: W.W. Norton and Company, 1990.

Steinmo, Sven, Kathleen Thelen and Frank Longstreth, *Structuring Politics: Historical Institutionalism in Comparative Analysis*, Cambridge: Cambridge University Press, 1992.

Stoeva, Preslava, 'Norm Development and Knowledge Creation in the World System—Protecting People, Intellectual Property and the Environment', Unpublished PhD thesis, University of Exeter, UK, Jan. 2005.

Strassen, Harold, and Marshal Houts, *Eisenhower: Turning the World towards Peace*, St. Paul: Magnus Publishing, 1990.

Subramanyam, K., *Shedding Shibboleths: India's Evolving Strategic Outlook*, New Delhi: Wordsmith, 2005.

Takiff, Michael, *A Complicated Man: The Life of Bill Clinton As Told By Those Who Know Him*, London and New Haven: Yale University Press, 2010.

Talbot, Ian, *Pakistan: A Modern History*, London: Hurst, 2009.

Talbott, Strobe, *Engaging India: Diplomacy, Democracy and the Bomb*, Washington, DC: Brookings Institution Press, 2006.

Tanham, George, *Indian Strategic Thought: An Interpretive Essay*, Santa Monica: RAND, 1992.

Tellis, Ashley, *India as a New Global Power: An Action Agenda for the United States*, Washington, DC: Carnegie Endowment for International Peace, 2005.

Thakurta, Paranjoy Guha and Shankar Raghuraman, *Divided We Stand: India in a Time of Coalitions*, New Delhi: Sage, 2001.

Tharoor, Shashi, *Pax Indica: India and the World of the 21st Century*, New Delhi: Allen Lane, 2012.

——— *Nehru: The Invention of India*, New York: Arcade Publishing, 2003.

——— *Reasons of State: Political Development & India's Foreign Policy under Indira Gandhi, 1966–1977*, New Delhi: Vikas, 1982.

Verghese, B.G., *First Draft: Witness to the Making of Modern India*, New Delhi: Tranquebar, 2010.

Waltz, Kenneth, *Theory of International Politics*, New York: McGraw-Hill Publishing, 1979.

Wersing, Robert, *India, Pakistan and the Kashmir Dispute: On Regional Conflict & its Resolution*, London: Macmillan, 1994.

Westad, Arne Odd, *Restless Empire: China and the World since 1750*, London: The Bodley Head, 2012.

——— *The Global Cold War*, Cambridge: Cambridge University Press, 2007.

Wolpert, Stanley, *Gandhi's Passion: The Life and Legacy of Mahatma Gandhi*, New York: Oxford University Press, 2001.

Zelikow, Philip, and Ernest May (eds), *The Presidential Recordings, John*

F. Kennedy: The Great Crisis, Volume 3, New York: W.W. Norton & Company, 2001.

Zins, Max Jean, and Giles Boquerrat, *India in the Mirror of Foreign Diplomatic Archives*, New Delhi: Manohar and Centre de Sciences Humaines, 2004.

Articles

Axelrod, Robert, 'An Evolutionary Approach', *The American Political Science Review*, 80, 4 (Dec. 1986).

Basrur, Rajesh, 'Nuclear Weapons and Indian Strategic Culture', *Journal of Peace Research*, 38, 2 (2001).

Berger, Thomas, 'From Sword to Chrysanthemum: Japan's Culture of Anti-Militarism', *International Security*, 17, 4 (Spring 1999).

Betts, Richard K., 'Is Strategy an Illusion?' *International Security*, 25, 2 (Autumn 2000).

Brodkin, E.I., 'United States Aid to India and Pakistan: Attitude of the Fifties', *International Affairs*, 43, 4 (Oct. 1967).

Cain, Anthony C., 'Iran's Strategic Culture and Weapons of Mass Destruction: Implications for US Policy', *Air War College, Maxwell Paper*, 26 (Apr. 2002).

Carter, Ashton, 'America's New Strategic Partner?' *Foreign Affairs*, 85, 4 (July–Aug. 2006).

Chari, P.R., 'Indo-Soviet Military Cooperation: A Review', *Asian Survey*, 19, 3 (Mar. 1979).

Cornish, Paul, and Geoffrey Edwards, 'Beyond the EU/NATO Dichotomy: The Beginnings of a European Strategic Culture', *International Affairs*, 77, 3 (2001).

Crabb, Cecil, 'American Diplomatic Tactics and Neutralism', *Political Science Quarterly*, 78, 3 (1963).

Dalgaard-Nielsen, Anja, 'The Test of Strategic Culture: Germany, Pacifism and Pre-Emptive Strikes', *Security Dialogue*, 36, 3 (Sep. 2005).

Desch, Michael, 'Culture Clash: Assessing the Importance of Ideas in Security Studies', *International Security*, 23, 1 (Summer 1998).

Deva, Yashwant, 'Indo-US Relations and India's Security Interests', *Strategic Analysis* (Aug. 1994).

Donaldson, Robert H., 'The Soviet Stake in Stability', *Asian Survey*, 12, 6 (1972).

Duffield, John, Theo Farrell, Richard Price and Michael C. Descsh, 'Isms and Schisms: Culturalism Versus Realism in Security Studies', *International Security*, 24, 1 (Summer 1999).

Farrell, Theo, 'Strategic Culture and American Empire', *SAIS Review of International Studies*, 25, 2 (Summer–Fall 2005).

——— 'World Culture and American Power', *Security Studies*, 14, 3 (Spring 2005).

———— 'Constructivist Security Studies: Portrait of a Research Programme', *International Studies Review*, 4, 1 (Spring 2002).

———— 'Memory, Imagination, and War', *History*, 87 (Jan. 2002).

Finnemore, Martha, and Kathryn Sikkink, 'International Norm Dynamic and Political Change', *International Organization*, 52, 4 (Autumn 1998).

Gentry, John, 'Norms & Military Power: NATO's War Against Yugoslavia', *Security Studies*, 15, 2 (Apr.–June 2006).

Gray, Colin, 'Strategic Culture as a Context: The First Generation of Theory Strikes Back', *Review of International Studies*, 25 (1999).

———— 'Comparative Strategic Culture', *Parameters* (Winter 1984).

———— 'National Style in Strategy: The American Example', *International Security*, 6, 2 (Autumn 1981)

Heiselberg, Stine, 'Pacifism or Activism: Towards a Common Strategic Culture within the European Security and Defence Policy?' *Danish Institute of International Studies*, IIS Working Paper 2 (2003/4).

Hewitt, Vernon, 'Containing Shiva? India, Non Proliferation & the Comprehensive Test Ban Treaty', *Contemporary South Asia*, 9 (2000).

———— 'Kashmir: The Unanswered Question', *History Today*, 47, 9 (Sep. 1997).

Hollen, Christopher Van, 'The Tilt Policy Revisited: Nixon–Kissinger Geopolitics and South Asia', *Asian Survey*, 20, 4 (Apr. 1980).

Hopf, Ted, 'The Promise of Constructivism in International Relations Theory', *International Security*, 23, 1 (Summer 1998).

House, Malcolm, 'India: Non-Committed and Non-Aligned', *The Western Political Quarterly*, 13, 1 (Mar. 1960).

Jian, Chen, 'The Sino-Soviet Alliance and China's Entry into the Korean War', *Cold War History Project*, Working Paper 1.

———— 'The Tibetan Rebellion of 1959 and China's Changing Relations with India and the Soviet Union', *Journal of Cold War Studies*, 8, 3 (Summer 2006).

Johnston, Alistair, 'Strategic Cultures Revisited', *Review of International Studies*, 25 (1999).

———— 'Thinking About Strategic Culture', *International Security*, 19, 4 (Spring 1995).

Jun, Niu, '1962: The Eve of the Left Turn in China's Foreign Policy', *Cold War History International Project*, Working Paper 48, Woodrow Wilson International Center for Scholars, 2005.

Kapur, Paul, and Sumit Ganguly, 'The Transformation of U.S.–India Relations: An Explanation for the Rapprochement and Prospects for the Future', *Asian Survey*, 47, 4 (July–Aug. 2007).

Keenleyside, T.A., 'Prelude to Power: The Meaning of Non-Alliance before Independence', *Pacific Affairs*, 53, 3 (Autumn 1980).

349

SELECT BIBLIOGRAPHY

Khilnani, Sunil, 'Looking for Indira Gandhi', *Seminar*, 540 (Aug. 2004).

———— 'The Idea of India', *Prospect Magazine*, 21 (July 1997).

Kumar, Satish, 'The Evolution of India's Policy towards Bangladesh in 1971', *Asian Survey*, 16, 6 (1975).

Lantis, Jeffrey, 'The Moral Imperative of Force: The Evolution of German Strategic Culture in Kosovo', *Comparative Strategy*, 21, 1 (2002).

———— 'Strategic Culture and National Security Policy', *International Studies Review*, 4, 3 (2002).

Legro, Jeffery, 'Which Norms Matter? Revisiting the "Failure" of Internationalism', *International Organization*, 51, 1 (Winter 1997).

———— 'Military Culture and Inadvertent Escalation in World War II', *International Security*, 18, 4 (Spring 1994).

Legro, Jeffery, and Andrew Moravcsik, 'Is Anyone Still a Realist?', *International Security*, 24, 2 (Autumn 1999).

Lerski, George J., 'The Pakistan–American alliance: A Re-Evaluation of the Past Decade', *Asian Survey*, 8, 4 (May 1968).

Levi, Werner, 'Indian Neutralism Reconsidered', *Pacific Affairs*, 37, 2 (Summer 1964).

Mahapatra, Chintamani, 'Looking at Indo-US Relations in a Changing World', *Strategic Analysis* (July 1991).

Markey, Daniel, 'Developing India's Foreign Policy Software', *Asia Policy*, 8 (July 2009).

———— 'From AFPAK to PAKAF: A Response to the New US Strategy in South Asia', *Council for Foreign Relations Policy Options Paper* (Apr. 2009).

Martinsen, Martin, 'Forging a Strategic Culture: Putting Policy into the ESDP', *Oxford Journal on Good Governance*, 1, 1 (2004).

Marwah, Omkar, 'India's Military Intervention in East Pakistan, 1971–1972', *Modern Asian Studies*, 13, 4 (1979).

Matlary, Janne Haaland, 'When Soft power Turns Hard: Is an EU Strategic Culture Possible?' *Security Dialogue*, 37, 1 (2006).

McMahon, Robert, 'United States Cold War Strategy in South Asia: Making a Military Commitment to Pakistan, 1947–1954', *The Journal of American History*, 75, 3 (Dec. 1988).

McGarr, Paul. M., '"India's Rasputin?" V.K. Krishna Menon and Anglo-American Misperceptions of Indian Foreign Policy Making, 1947–64', *Diplomacy & Statecraft*, 22, 2 (2011).

Mearsheimer, John J., 'The False Promise of International Institutions', *International Security*, 19, 3 (Winter 1994–5).

Menon, Rajan, 'India and the Soviet Union: A New Stage in Relations?' *Asian Survey*, 18, 7 (July 1978).

Merrill, Dennis, 'Indo-American Relations, 1947–50: A Missed Opportunity in Asia', *Diplomatic History*, 11 (1987).

Meyer, Christoph O., 'Theorising European Strategic Culture: Between Convergence and the Persistence of National Diversity', Centre for European Policy Studies, Working Document, 204 (June 2004).

Miller, Manjari Chatterjee, 'Recollecting Empire: "Victimhood" and the 1962 Sino-Indian War', *Asian Security*, 5, 3 (2009).

Mohan, Raja C., 'India and the Balance of Power', *Foreign Affairs*, 85, 4 (July–Aug. 2006).

Mukhopadhyay, Alok Rashmi, 'David Miliband's Visit to India', *IDSA Strategic Comments* (20 Jan. 2009).

Nehru, Jawaharlal, 'Changing India', *Foreign Affairs* (Apr. 1963).

Noorani, A.G., 'Balance of Power in South Asia', *Frontline*, 22, 8 (Apr. 2005).

Onuf, Nicholas, 'The New Culture of Security Studies', *Mershon International Studies Review*, 42 (1998).

Poore, Stuart, 'What is the Context? A Reply to the Gray–Johnston Debate on Strategic Culture', *Review of International Studies*, 29 (2003).

Raghavan, Srinath, 'Sino-Indian Border Dispute, 1948–1960, A Reappraisal', *Economic & Political Weekly* (Sep. 2006).

Rajan, M.S., 'Bangladesh & After', *Pacific Affairs*, 45, 2 (Summer 1972).

Rasmussen, Mikkel Vedby, 'A New Kind of War: Strategic Culture and the War on Terrorism', Danish Institute for International Studies, IIS Working Paper (2002/3).

Riedel, Bruce, 'South Asia's Nuclear Decade', *Survival*, 50, 2 (Apr.–May 2008).

Rosen, Stephen P., 'Military Effectiveness: Why Society Matters', *International Security*, 19, 4 (1995).

Scalpino, Robert, 'Neutralism in Asia', *The American Political Science Review*, 48, 1 (Mar. 1954).

Schroeder, Paul W., 'History and International Relations Theory: Not Use or Abuse, But Fit or Misfit', *International Security*, 22, 1 (Summer 1997).

Scobell, Andrew, 'China and Strategic Culture', Strategic Studies Institute, US Army War College (May 2002).

Sharma, Chattar Singh, 'Panchsheela and After: Sino-India Relations in the Context of the Tibetan Insurrection', *Asian Survey*, 21, 3 (May 1962).

Shean, Vincent, 'The Case for India', *Foreign Affairs*, 30 (1951–2).

Swidler, Ann, 'Culture in Action: Symbols and Strategies', *American Sociological Review*, 51, 2 (Apr. 1986).

Tanham, George, 'Indian Strategic Culture', *The Washington Quarterly*, 15, 1 (Winter 1992).

Telhami, Shibley, 'Kenneth Waltz, Neo-Realism and Foreign Policy', *Security Studies*, 11, 3 (2002).

Thakur, Ramesh, 'India in the World: Neither Rich, Powerful, Nor Principled', *Foreign Affairs* (July–Aug. 1997).

351

Thapar, Romesh, 'NEFA and All That', *Economic Weekly*, 14, 42 (20 Oct. 1962).

———— 'Handling the Chinese', *Economic Weekly*, 14, 41 (13 Oct. 1962).

Thomas, Raju, 'Security Relationships in Southern Asia: Differences in the Indian and American Perspectives', *Asian Survey*, 21, 7 (July 1981).

Thornton, Thomas P., 'India Adrift: The Search for Moorings in a New World Order', *Asian Survey*, 32, 12 (Dec. 1992).

Venkataramani, M.S., 'An Elusive Military Relationship', *Frontline*, 16, 7, 16, 8 and 16, 9 (9 Apr., 23 Apr. and 7 May 1999).

Walt, Stephen, 'Testing Theories of Alliance Formation: The Case of South West Asia', *International Organization*, 42, 2 (Spring 1998).

Wendt, Alexander, 'Anarchy is What States Make of It: The Social Construction of Power Politics', *International Organization*, 46, 2 (Spring 1992).

Wersing, Robert G., 'The Arms Race in South Asia: Implications for the United States', *Asian Survey*, 25, 3 (Mar. 1985).

Internet Sources

Albright, David, Leonard Weiss and Daryl Kimball, 'US–India Nuclear Cooperation: A Critical Assessment', Arms Control Association, 15 Feb. 2006 (http://www.armscontrol.org/events/20060215_India_Transcript).

Boese, Wade, 'NSG, Congress Approve Nuclear Trade with India', Arms Control Association, 6 Oct. 2008 (http://www.armscontrol.org/act/2008_10/NSGapprove).

———— 'Bush Promises India Nuclear Cooperation', Arms Control Association, 5 Sep. 2005 (http://www.armscontrol.org/act/2005_09/USIndia9-05).

———— 'US–India N-Deal Advances', Arms Control Association, 31 Aug. 2007 (http://www.armscontrol.org/act/2007_09/USIndia).

———— 'US Puts Onus on India for Nuclear Ties', Arms Control Association, 1 Dec. 2005 (http://www.armscontrol.org/act/2005_12/DEC-USIndia).

Bunn, George, and John P. Rhinelander, 'NPT Withdrawal: Time for Security Council to Step In', Arms Control Association, May 2005 (http://www.armscontrol.org/act/2005_05/Bunn_Rhinelander).

Enders, Wimbush S., 'Strategic India', Report prepared for the Smith Richardson Foundation, Washington, 2007 (http://www.hudson.org/files/publications/StrategicIndia-Final-Wimbush.pdf).

Kimball, Daryl, 'Averting a Non-Proliferation Disaster', Arms Control Association, 29 Aug. 2008 (http://www.armscontrol.org/act/2008_09/Focus).

———— 'India's Choice, Congress' Responsibility', Arms Control Association, 1 Jan. 2006 (http://www.armscontrol.org/act/2006_01-02/focus).

Kimball, Daryl, and Joe Cirincione, 'A Non-Proliferation Disaster', Arms Control Association, 11 Dec. 2006 (http://www.armscontrol.org/pressroom/2006/20061211_Nonproliferation_Disaster).

Kimball, Daryl, and Fred McGoldrick, 'US–India Nuclear Agreement: A Bad Deal Gets Worse', Arms Control Association, 3 Aug. 2007 (http://www.armscontrol.org/act/2007_07-08/USIndia).

Krepon, Michael, 'US–India Nuclear Deal Now Done, Reckoning to Come Later', Stimson Center, 1 Oct. 2008 (http://www.stimson.org/pub.cfm?ID=683).

———— 'Likely Consequences of the Nuclear Suppliers Group Decision', Stimson Center, 8 Sep. 2008 (http://www.stimson.org/pub.cfm?ID=673).

———— 'The US–India Nuclear Deal', The Stimson Center, 29 Mar. 2006 (http://www.stimson.org/pub.cfm?id=267).

———— 'Meeting at the Council for Foreign Relations', New York, 13 Mar. 2006 (http://www.carnegieendowment.org/files/cfrindianucleardeal.pdf).

McGoldrick, Fred, Harold Benglesdorf and Lawrence Scheinman, 'The US–India Deal: Taking Stock', Arms Control Association, 1 Oct. 2005 (http://www.armscontrol.org/act/2005_10/Oct-Cover).

McKinzie, Richard D., 'Second Oral History Interview with Loy W. Henderson', Washington, DC, 5 July 1973, Harry S. Truman Library and Museum (http://www.trumanlibrary.org/oralhist/hendrson.htm#transcript).

Tellis, Ashley, 'The US–India Global Partnership: Legislative Options', Prepared Testimony to the House Committee on International Relations, 11 May 2006 (http://www.carnegieendowment.org/files/ashleyjtellissrfctestimony.pdf).

Trachenberg, Marc, David Rosenberg and Stephen Van Evara, 'Interview with Carl Kaysen', (http://www.sscnet.ucla.edu/polisci/faculty/trachtenberg/cv/Kaysen%28MIT%29.pdf).

INDEX

INDEX

INDEX

INDEX

INDEX

INDEX

INDEX